P9-DFW-754

Maverick Marine

Maverick Marine

GENERAL SMEDLEY D. BUTLER
AND THE CONTRADICTIONS OF
AMERICAN MILITARY HISTORY

Hans Schmidt

THE UNIVERSITY PRESS OF KENTUCKY

Publication of this volume was made possible in part by a grant from the National Endowment for the Humanities.

Copyright © 1987 by The University Press of Kentucky

Scholarly publisher for the Commonwealth,
serving Bellarmine College, Berea College, Centre
College of Kentucky, Eastern Kentucky University,
The Filson Club Historical Society, Georgetown College,
Kentucky Historical Society, Kentucky State University,
Morehead State University, Murray State University,
Northern Kentucky University, Transylvania University,
University of Kentucky, University of Louisville,
and Western Kentucky University.
All rights reserved

Editorial and Sales Offices: The University Press of Kentucky
663 South Limestone Street, Lexington, Kentucky 40508-4008

Frontispiece: Smedley D. Butler during marine maneuvers in
Gettysburg, Pennsylvania, 1921. Courtesy of Thomas R. Butler.

02 01 00 99 98   5 4 3 2 1

Library of Congress Catalolging-in-Publication Data

Schmidt, Hans, 1938-
   Maverick Marine
      Bibliography: p.
      Includes index.
      1. Butler, Smedley D. (Smedley Darlington), 1881-1940.
   2. Generals—United States—Biography. 3. United States.
   Marine Corps—Biography. I. Title.
   VE25.B88S36   1987   359.9'6'0924 [B]   87-1990
   ISBN 0-8131-1619-9 (cloth)
   ISBN 0-8131-0957-4 (paper)

This book is printed on acid-free recycled paper meeting
the requirements of the American National Standard
for Permanence of Paper for Printed Library Materials.

∞ ✿

Manufactured in the United States of America

For Joan, Julie, and Jenny

I spent 33 years and 4 months in active service as a member of our country's most agile military force—the Marine Corps. I served in all commissioned ranks from second lieutenant to Major General. And during that period I spent most of my time being a high-class muscle man for Big Business, for Wall Street and for the bankers. In short, I was a racketeer for capitalism. I suspected I was just part of a racket all the time. Now I am sure of it. Like all members of the military profession I never had an original thought until I left the service.

—Smedley D. Butler (1935)

Contents

Acknowledgments ix

1 Introduction 1

2 The Boy Officer: Cuba, the Philippines 6

3 The Teenage Hero: China 14

4 Knight Errant: Honduras, Panama, the Philippines 27

5 The American Kitchener: Nicaragua 38

6 The Spy: Panama, Mexico 58

7 The Haitian General 74

8 General Duckboard: France 96

9 The Barnett Putsch: Marine Corps Politics 110

10 Pep and Pride: Quantico 129

11 Smashing Crime and Vice: Philadelphia 144

12 Devil Dog and Demon Rum: San Diego 161

13 The Marines Who Wouldn't Fight: China 173

14 To Hell with the Admirals: Washington 202

15 Renegade Marine: America in the 1930s 215

16 Epilogue 247

Notes 252

Selected Bibliography 281

Index 285

Illustrations follow page 214

Acknowledgments

Help has been received from a variety of sources. I thank Professors Lloyd C. Gardner, John Sherwig, L.K. Young, and Lee Ngok for academic support that gave me elbow room to dally extra years over this interesting and enjoyable project. Financial aid came from the State University of New York Research Foundation and the Inter-University Seminar for Armed Forces and Society.

The University of Zambia History Seminar suffered through crude early chapter drafts; my warm regards to colleagues and friends for their forbearance.

General Butler's children, the late Edith Butler Wehle and Smedley D. Butler, Jr., his surviving son Thomas R. Butler, and his granddaughters Edith Wehle and Philippa C. Chill, gave me an impression of an estimable family and an appreciation of Smedley Butler's humanity and personal endowments. Tom Butler patiently responded to my many letters, answered innumerable queries, and opened the Butler home and family papers to me with enthusiasm, curiosity, and commitment to historical scholarship. The extensive Butler Papers in Newtown Square, Pennsylvania, together with films, audio recordings, and myriad interesting memorabilia, were an inspiration. It is hoped that they will be suitably preserved.

Scholars who have read stages of the manuscript and offered many useful criticisms include Graham A. Cosmas, Benis M. Frank, Adam Horvath, Leonard Rayner, Jack Shulimson, and John Stabler. Other readers remain anonymous, but I hope will recognize their much appreciated contributions in the end result. My thanks also to Donald F. Bittner, Char Miller, Pennie Ojeda, Jeff Safford, Jerry and Sharon Slater, Andelina Tang, Robert H. Van Meter, and Richard Varbero for information, help, advice, and encouragement.

For examples of historical scholarship and academic commitment that I found particularly inspiring, kudos to Professors Richard Drinnon and the late Warren I. Susman.

I am grateful to the following individuals and archives for permission to use manuscripts and interviews: Columbia University Oral History Research Office for the Admiral Harold C. Train Reminiscences (Copyright

1975, Trustees of Columbia University), and the Lawrence Dennis Oral History memoirs. The late Professor Woodbridge Bingham for permission to cite the manuscript of his biography of his father, Senator Hiram Bingham. Maj. Gen. Robert Blake and Lt. Gen. Merwin H. Silverthorn for their interviews in the U.S. Marine Corps Oral History Collection. Mrs. Julian C. Smith for her late husband's (Lt. Gen. Smith) interview, and Mrs. Louis E. Woods for her late husband's (Lt. Gen. Woods) interview.

David Mandel, Charles E. Meilachowitz, Ben Singer, and Lowell Thomas provided helpful recollections.

For permission to use photographs, I thank Thomas R. Butler, the Library of Congress, and the U.S. National Archives.

My thanks to the following institutions and archivists for research guidance and access to materials: American Jewish Archives in Cincinnati; the U.S. Department of Justice for Federal Bureau of Investigation materials; the French Foreign Ministry Archives; the German Foreign Office Archives in Bonn; the Herbert Hoover Presidential Library; the Hong Kong University Library; the Hoover Institute for War, Peace and Revolution; the Lawrence, Massachusetts, Public Library; the Library of Congress; the U.S. Marine Corps Historical Center in Washington Navy Yard, particularly Chief Curator Charles Anthony Wood (remembering fondly the old days in bldg. 154) and archivist J. Michael Miller; the Marine Corps Oral History Collection and its director, Benis M. Frank; the U.S. National Archives, particularly Dr. Timothy K. Nenninger for finding Butler's 1914 Mexico invasion plan; the New York Public Library; the Public Record Office in London; the Franklin D. Roosevelt Presidential Library; and Yale University Library.

1 Introduction

Smedley D. Butler, impetuous, politically enterprising, a celebrated combat hero, campaigned in American military expeditions from 1898 onward—in Cuba, the Philippines, China, Honduras, Panama, Nicaragua, Mexico, Haiti, France, and finally China again in the late 1920s. The "stormy petrel" of the Marine Corps, especially in his willful flouting of bureaucracy, he evoked the warrior style of courageous manly defiance. He promoted a new Marine Corps mystique emphasizing physical stridency and egalitarian anti-intellectualism, at odds with the current trend to elitist, bookish professionalism in the officer corps. Winner of two Congressional Medals of Honor and other battlefield distinctions, Butler was an authentic archetypal hero whose exploits were lionized in the popular press and fictionalized in pulp adventure stories. He wrote or co-authored many imperialist genre potboilers himself. As a public spokesman on military and police affairs and then as a perennial attraction on the national lecture circuit, he remained closely in touch with popular military mores, always maintaining his credibility as a patriotic warrior hero whose courage, physical command presence, and vernacular coarseness epitomized the popular ideal of a soldiers' general.

Outspoken and irrepressible, Butler eventually ran afoul of the official military establishment. After publicly denouncing marine-rigged elections in Central America, he was passed over for the Marine Corps commandancy despite being the ranking major general. In 1931 President Herbert Hoover ordered him court-martialed, but a public uproar forced the government to drop charges. Retiring shortly thereafter, he fired a parting salvo at swivel-chair admirals dominating the naval bureaucracy, and then supported a succession of veterans', working-class, and left-wing causes in which he always took the part of the enlisted ranks. As a populist firebrand, he exposed the 1934 Wall Street "fascist plot" to enlist veterans in an attempt to topple the government. His set topics on the public lecture circuit, "Thirty Years in the Marines" and "Fighting Crime and Vice," increasingly gave way to antiwar and anti-imperialist themes. He became a major speaker for the League Against War and Fascism and the most prominent leader of the veterans' antiwar movement.

Butler's recantation was bold, sweeping, and insistent: "I spent 33 years and 4 months in active service . . . and during that period I spent most of my time being a high-class muscle man for Big Business, for Wall Street and the bankers. In short, I was a racketeer for capitalism." He had "helped in the raping of half a dozen central American republics for the benefit of Wall Street."[1] He stressed the analogy between overseas imperialism and domestic criminal gangsterism in his 1935 book *War Is a Racket*. Throughout, he remained a patriotic, red-blooded marine, denouncing "Wall Street flag wavers" while at the same time urging "an iron clad defense a rat couldn't crawl through," and boosting domestic law-and-order causes such as gangbusting by the Federal Bureau of Investigation.[2] Here was an anti-imperialist plea that connected popular patriotic military sentiment with the then nationally ascendant isolationist politics of neutrality. As interventionists used the cant of liberal internationalism to justify militaristic internationalism, Butler raised the alarm. Only a great mystification, he desperately warned, could popularize the revival of expeditionary militarism.

Butler's moral pilgrimage reflected his personal experience of vast changes in American military practices and mores. During his lifetime the U.S. Marine Corps, originally an auxilliary arm of the navy, grew to become an important expeditionary force around the world. From traditional duties policing navy yards and manning the fighting tops of sailing ships, the marines developed into colonial light infantry capable of achieving American aims in a succession of mostly small wars that punctuated U.S. emergence as a great world power.

Meanwhile American popular military traditions, rooted mythically in frontier warfare and Civil War epics, discorded with changing national purposes. In the 1910s and 1920s past glories of conquest were rekindled in several colonial punitive campaigns, but with increasing embarrassment offset by official apologies emphasizing liberalism, self-determination, and peace. U.S. foreign policy, now intent upon international commercialism, sought accommodation rather than violent confrontation with nationalist anticolonial movements. The military itself was becoming more cloistered, with managerial professionalism eclipsing adventure and heroism.

This derangement of military mores pertained to both shifting international strategies and a perceived crisis in domestic society, each of which inspired innovative military intervention. Internationally, there was a progression from nineteenth-century frontier and colonial tactics, characterized by relief expeditions, punitive raids, gunboat diplomacy, violent pacification, and outright American military government, to more mediatory intervention involving nonbelligerent peacekeeping troops, transitory police actions, unobtrusive military advisers, sponsorship of elite native armies, covert use of force, and carefully modulated relationships with client governments.

The new, sophisticated military expediencies required by American foreign policy of the 1920s and 1930s bore scant relation to traditional military lore, nor, for that matter, did governing interests of corporate capitalism and international power politics. Martial ardor descended from the frontier had to do with righteous enforcement of a white settler civilization on presumed American territory, epitomized by the rescue of white women and babies from menacing nonwhite savages. With the decline of jingo imperialism and with the disillusionment after the Great War, popular military sentiment was left increasingly at odds with current official and professional trends. Instead, popular sentiment tended to unofficial expression, even anti-official, as when huge, militant veterans' organizations backed the anti-imperialist, antiwar movement of the 1930s, under such banners as "Take the Dollar Signs Out of the Battle Flags." [3]

Domestically, militarization was an important coercive strategy during the culmination of progressive-era urban reform in the 1920s. Big-city corruption had been consistently, for three decades, a particular obsession. Now the signal achievement of national prohibition set the stage for a crowning effort, and city police were in the spotlight as primary enforcers, themselves tainted and vulnerable in a maw of bootlegging, syndicated vice, and ward-level politics. Reformers pressed for militarization of city police, and military commanders were co-opted to introduce military organization, discipline, and regalia.

More drastic proposals called for state and national paramilitary police forces, apolitical and rigorously professional, to join in an escalating "war" against metropolitan and nationally syndicated crime. Pertinent models were the European *Staatspolizei*, the Canadian Mounties, and especially the American colonial constabularies that had pacified and "cleaned up" conquered protectorates. But all this was offensive to American traditions of local autonomy, and was overly Prussianized and contrary to the frontier ideal of vigilante self-reliance. Indeed, gangsters rather than police were often celebrated as public heroes during the ensuing crime wars. Nevertheless, militarization attained considerable momentum, if only to prove largely disappointing, unwanted, and irrelevant.

How to explore these interesting antagonisms? What were successive American military expeditions like, and how did they relate to popular military sentiment? How did the military adjust to changing tactical and political requirements, shifting from punitive campaigns to rigging elections, then to diplomatic peacekeeping missions? What were the corresponding changes in careerist incentives and constraints within the military, and in perceptions of military professionalism? How did the military feel about its new roles, now often serving blatantly commercial ends seemingly at odds with warrior integrity? As colonial empire building fell into disrepute, how were overseas expeditions represented to the American public? How did the iconography of military intervention change, and what kinds of intervention had popular appeal?

With budgets drastically slashed and the armed forces competing for survival during the antimilitarist 1920s and 1930s, how did military publicists attempt to generate popular support? In which aspects of military life was the public interested? What was the potential for domestic military intervention, to what ends and against what obstacles? Why, during the world depression of the 1930s, did American veterans mobilize fitfully leftward, against militarism and imperialism, in marked contrast to vanguard rightist and Fascist veterans' movements elsewhere? To what kind of leadership, in a decade noted for demagoguery and vehement popular politics, did the veterans respond? How could radical left- and right-wing tendencies be fused into a compelling package? In all this, what became of popular American military traditions?

Smedley Butler's career significantly intercepts and lends substance to all these questions. His overseas exploits encompassed the Banana Wars, several memorable relief and punitive expeditions, colonial military occupations, manipulation of native politicians, and a brigade-level diplomatic intervention—from the jingoism of the Cuban war and the pillage and slaughter of the Boxer Expedition in 1900 to mediatory peacekeeping in the 1920s. Having built his reputation as an intrepid bushwhacker in colonial small wars, he also came to terms with bureaucratic trends in modern warfare. These he impetuously confronted as commander of the main embarkation camp in France through which a million men were rudely processed during World War I. And in making the transition from personal warrior-style leadership of small units to the hierarchic distancing that went with general-officer rank, he adapted his famous command presence to attain a guileless theatricality. This later blossomed into a knack for publicity in the civilian mass media.

On the domestic scene, Butler was renowned during the 1920s for keeping the Marine Corps in the public eye and for taking charge of Philadelphia's city police during a notable push for militarization. His battles with demon rum, military and civilian, culminated in the infamous "cocktail-court-martial." The marines did well in congressional budget battles largely because Smedley mounted highly successful publicity campaigns, working closely with his father, Congressman Thomas S. Butler, then chairman of the House Naval Affairs Committee. In some of the boldest peacetime military intrusions ever into domestic American life, Smedley launched annual marine expeditionary maneuvers from Quantico into surrounding states, featuring football games, barnstorm flying, and on-site Civil War battle reenactments. In sports, the Quantico Marines insinuated themselves into college football. With Butler as impresario, the Quantico circus was a uniquely ambitious and appealing, although shortlived, military extravaganza. So too were his attempts at militarizing civilian police, although ubiquitous paramilitary terminology and trappings survive as Draconian metaphors in American law enforcement down to the present.

2 The Boy Officer

CUBA, THE PHILIPPINES

Smedley Darlington Butler, swept up in enthusiasm for the Cuban war, volunteered for the Marine Corps in the spring of 1898. At sixteen he was two years underage and callow for an officer recruit. His way was eased by family political connections firmly rooted in the history of Chester County, Pennsylvania, where his ancestors included three prominent Quaker families, the Smedleys, Darlingtons, and Butlers. The Butlers traced their American origins to Noble Butler, who landed in William Penn's colony about 1710. Over the years, the families attained substantial means, prestige, and influence in local affairs as successful farmers, lawyers, and politicians. Smedley's two grandfathers, presidents of the two principal banks in West Chester, were both active in politics. Samuel Butler had been state treasuer of Pennsylvania, and Congressman Smedley Darlington served two terms in Washington representing the same district that was subsequently taken over by his son-in-law. Smedley's father, Thomas S. Butler, a lawyer, served briefly as a judge and then sat in Congress continuously from 1896 to 1928 representing Chester and Delaware counties.

Smedley, the eldest of three sons, was born a blue baby in West Chester on 30 July 1881. As a child, he had a nurse and wore fauntleroy suits. His Hicksite Quaker mother, Maud Darlington Butler, saw to it that he attended Friends meeting twice a week. From Friends Graded High School in West Chester, he went on to nearby Haverford School, the elite secondary school for sons of upper-class Quaker families in and around Philadelphia. Haverford has been credited with fielding the first all native-born American cricket club. The Butler family spoke the plain Quaker language of "Thee" and "Thy"; so did Smedley's father as a congressman in Washington. Smedley was schooled in pacifist doctrine, perused the Bible (he eventually told his son he had read it seven times through), and paid Quaker meeting dues, mostly in absentia, all his life.[1] But family commitment to Quaker ways was offset by a maverick streak. Grandfather Samuel Butler, the precursor "Fighting Quaker," was expelled from Orthodox Meeting during the Civil War. In 1898 Smedley's mother blocked his expulsion by threatening to create a new branch of the Society. His father, also a "Fighting Quaker," was well known for staunch sponsorship of the navy and marines during a tenure lasting three decades on the House Naval Affairs Committee. He often spiced his conversation with what he called "an honest damn" and encouraged his son to do likewise.

At Haverford Smedley was an indifferent student but a keen athlete. Although scrawny (as an adult he was 5 feet 9 inches, about 140 pounds, and somewhat stooped in posture), he was captain of the Haverford baseball team and quarterback of the football team. Had he not joined the marines, he almost certainly would have finished Haverford and gone on to college. Both his brothers—Samuel, who was three years younger, and Horace, twelve—went to college, and years later Smedley's father gave him $4,000 in compensation for having missed out.[2]

After enlisting, Smedley reported to the old Marine Barracks behind the commandant's house at "Eighth and Eye" in Washington, where training consisted of three weeks' parade ground drill plus lectures on military regulations, with heavy emphasis on blind obedience and rote learning. The more subtle aspects of military leadership were left to experience in the field and to the innate courage, honor, and intelligence that presumably distinguished officers from enlisted ranks. Butler and other officer recruits drilled alongside privates and were instructed by a sergeant major, who rose in deference to their rank when they recited their lessons. Mastery of spit-and-polish was spurred by exciting news from the front lines, where a detachment of 700 marines, accompanied by war correspondent Stephen Crane, had landed at Guantánamo, routed the local Spanish forces, and established the first American camp on Cuban soil.

In early July 1898, Smedley and two other fledgling second lieutenants were standing off the Cuban coast in an army transport when they had their first glimpse of war, sighting the burned hulks of Spanish cruisers wrecked on the beach after their disastrous attempt to outrun a U.S. squadron. Trudging up into the dusty hills in search of Guantánamo battalion headquarters, the three boot lieutenants kept their heavy black-braid-trimmed uniforms tightly buttoned despite the tropical heat, only to find their commanding officer to be, as Butler later recalled, a "dirty little man" amongst a group of "unkempt men sitting on packing boxes."[3]

Here was the antediluvian Marine Corps that had survived at skeletal strength after the Civil War, serving as shipboard guards and landing parties, and issuing forth from navy yard barracks for occasional riot duty in America's troubled East Coast industrial cities. Marines landed in dozens of gunboat diplomacy interventions during the 1870s, 1880s and 1890s—in Argentina, China, Hawaii, Korea, Nicaragua, Samoa, and so on. The commander at Guantánamo, Lieutenant Colonel Robert W. Huntington, was a veteran of the First Battle of Bull Run and in 1898 sported a full white beard. The second-in-command, Henry Clay Cochrane, had been in President Lincoln's personal guard at Gettysburg and had at long last been promoted to major in the spring of 1898. Huntington and Cochrane were two of the most senior officers in the Corps. But presently the Corps would expand phenomenally. Smedley Butler's company commander at Guantánamo was sixty-one-year-old Captain Mancil C. Goodrell; Smedley would be breveted captain before his nineteenth birthday.

For Smedley, apprenticeship to these veterans meant kindly patronization that intensified the pressure to attain martial standards of courage and command presence. His youth and his father's political credentials had been duly noted by the battalion hierarchy. Major Cochrane, who kept a meticulous diary, recorded on 10 July the arrival of three young second lieutenants sent from headquarters, with the annotation: "Lieut. B. brought letter from his father Thos. S. Butler, *MC*, Ho Naval Comm 6th Dist. Pa." (Member of Congress, House Naval Affairs Committee, Sixth District, Pennsylvania). Two days later Cochrane replied to the honorable congressman, beginning a polite relationship that lasted through the summer and early fall of 1898, so long as Smedley continued to serve under him. When Smedley was sick, Cochrane brought him cookies, noting that the boy "enjoyed them very much, is only 18 years old." (It was in fact the day before his seventeenth birthday.) Such attention no doubt accentuated the humiliations he suffered at Guantánamo. Years later as a battalion commander at Veracruz, Butler relived his boyhood initiation: "Two young 2nd Lieutenants joined the Battalion yesterday," he wrote his wife, "nice looking boys and pretty well scared—not of the enemy but of their own seniors. They remind me of my own self 16 years ago when I reported for duty in Cuba and I shall certainly see that these boys are not as much teased as I was."[4]

And there was no opportunity at Guantánamo for him to prove himself under fire. The marines and allied Cuban *insurrectos* had already cleared out the local Spanish detachment and set up camp on the slopes overlooking Guantánamo Bay. Occasional sniper fire and recently emptied sardine cans brought in by Cuban scouts indicated continuing Spanish presence near American lines, but there were no skirmishes. Smedley learned military bearing from Captain Goodrell, who took him along on nightly inspections. As the two walked across open fields between marine outposts, Goodrell strode ahead, indifferent to danger. When they were fired at by a sniper, Butler sprawled on the ground. Goodrell looked down contemptuously and demanded, "What in hell is the matter?" Smedley earnestly mastered the unflinching style.[5]

On 9 August, the Guantánamo battalion steamed two hundred miles west along the coast in a transport under escort of the cruiser *Newark* to bombard and capture the garrisoned city of Manzanillo. After a night exchanging fire with shore batteries, as the marines made final preparations for what looked likely to be a bloody landing, daybreak brought news that an armistice had been declared by the United States and Spain. To Smedley, this had special meaning; it was the thirteenth, his lucky number. The war was over.

The battalion arrived home in Portsmouth, New Hampshire, to a heroes' welcome including parades and a great clambake hosted by local citizens. Colonel Commandant Charles Heywood and Congressman and Mrs. Butler, who had come up together from Washington, added luster to social functions at the Hotel Kearsage. Clearly, young Smedley was politically well connected. But the reunion with his parents in the social presence of his superiors must have caused him anguish. Cochrane recorded in his diary, "Young Butler at bkfst unmindful of his ma. Wife [Cochrane's] amused." In his endpage diary notes on officers met in 1898, Cochrane described George Reid, who had gone through officer school and arrived at Guantánamo with Butler, as "happy and bright," while Smedley is down as "quiet and respectful."[6]

The battalion was then dispersed. This had been the largest Marine Corps expedition to date, pieced together out of levies from all marine units on the East Coast and hastily assembled for embarkation at Brooklyn Navy Yard. The battalion, 650 men out of the total Marine Corps strength of 2,000, had proved that the Corps could mount an infantry strike force for overseas duty on the shortest notice, substantiating claims to a new mission at a time when traditional marine combat roles, such as manning the tops of sailing ships, had become obsolete. While actual participation in the war was marginal compared to the army and navy, exhaustive press coverage had made Guantánamo a celebrated epic. And the marines did manage to get there first and without much fuss, which contrasted favorably with nearly catastrophic bungling by army mobilization and logistics. As the United States ventured upon a prolonged series of overseas interventions, the marines would henceforth vie for large-scale expeditionary assignments far exceeding their previous duties as an appendage of the navy. Smedley Butler, entering the Corps at this turning point, could look forward to an interesting and busy career.

During his few days' leave, West Chester shared in the glory through the timely homecoming of its most prominent fighting son. Butler then reported as junior marine officer to the armored cruiser *New York* berthed at Brooklyn Navy Yard. Four months aboard ship, including a cruise to the Caribbean, introduced him to the panache, ceremony, and technological sophistication of the modern steel navy. By the time he was detached in February 1899 and ordered home to be mustered out of service, he had, in eight months as a marine, tasted both the excitement of camp life ashore under wartime conditions and a glamorous tour of sea duty.

Back home in West Chester he refused, despite family pressure, to go back to school. Several main themes of his career had already been predicted. Having quit school in favor of a military initiation into manhood, he picked up the warrior cult of physical masculinity and a corresponding anti-intellectualism. And while he owed his elevation as a precocious boy officer to upper middle-class prerogatives, class traits of gentility and education had proved an embarrassment in the field. By identifying with the warriors, Butler set himself apart from better-educated peers and aligned instead with uneducated, roughneck tendencies within the marines. This anomaly would become acute when he reached the upper echelons of the officer corps.[7] Except for the Cuban-Philippine war volunteers, the Marine Corps was taking junior officer entrants from among U.S. Naval Academy graduates.

Belligerently and defensively, Butler came to pride himself on having learned his trade in the field, and to despise highbrow trends in military professionalism. This had strong social-class implications, insofar as the enlisted ranks remained a repository for the old-guard warrior ethos, while the officer corps assimilated new middle-class masculine ideals, such as "the male as master of rational knowledge."[8] Butler, despite upper middle-class prerogatives and ongoing social ties, committed himself to what were becoming increasingly lower-class military mores—roughneck values descended from the frontier which survived in popular culture, in contrast to elitist officer professionalism with its growing emphasis on educational credentials and mastery of esoteric doctrine. Whatever early inclinations he may have had were now, at age seventeen, confirmed by his unwillingness to resume formal education.

When Congress authorized a threefold increase of the Corps, reflecting its proven usefulness and a new demand for expeditionary troops in the Philippines, temporary officers from the Cuban war were given preference. Smedley came in second among thirty-two officer veterans who took the qualifying examination.[9] In April 1899 he accepted a first lieutenant's commission and was ordered to the Philippines.

Filipino resistance to American invasion was developing into a determined guerrilla war. Filipino *insurrectos*, like their Cuban counterparts, had been fighting to overthrow Spanish colonialism long before the arrival of the Americans. As in Cuba, white Americans fraternized with the Spanish enemy and viewed native comrades in arms with contempt, referring to them as "niggers" and "gugus." As in Cuba, when the Spanish were defeated the United States opted for ongoing control, in this case to be established in a formal colonial regime. The *insurrectos* renewed their struggle accordingly.

Butler and a battalion of marines went by special train across the United States and embarked at San Francisco for the 7,000-mile trip to the Philippines. After a month at sea, their ramshackle transport finally anchored in Manila Bay in sight of the walls of the Spanish City and the protruding masts of Spanish warships sunk by Commodore George Dewey's Asiatic Squadron. They set up camp at the old Cavité naval base on the tip of a narrow peninsula ten miles south across the bay from Manila. Following colonial usage, Butler and other officers each had a locally hired "China boy" whose chief occupation, according to Smedley, was to serve whiskey. Garrison duty at Cavité blended tedium and enervation in the tropical heat with occasional forays against nearby Filipino forces and lively night life in Manila. At one point Smedley was temporarily demoted from company command after a drunken escapade in his quarters. Manila, he recalled, "was gay in those days and jazzed up with plenty of drinking."[10]

American units had begun to attack surrounding hostile Filipino forces, but the marines at Cavité were at first shielded from action by an army unit further down the peninsula. Butler, seeking intervention from on high, complained in a letter to his mother and asked that "Papa to go to the President . . . and request that I be ordered for duty with one of the army Regiments up at the front." This would mean being temporarily detached from the Marine Corps, but it was a "disgrace" to be so near the fighting and not take part, and "if you have any ambition for me to make a name for myself please have this done." Smedley's unit soon went into action as the campaign intensified, obviating this jejune maneuver. At other times he scrupulously disavowed patronage, declaring soon thereafter that he would "never use any influence I may have to get a station or away from another"—this when faced with the bleak prospect of a stint on Guam.[11]

The one substantial operation in Butler's year at Cavité led to his first serious confrontation with deadly enemy fire. Early on a Sunday morning in October 1899, 300 marines left Cavité equipped with Lee rifles, canteens, ponchos, and a day's rations. Their progress along the neck of the peninsula was covered from the bay by the gunboat *Petrel*, which laid a barrage along the shore to clear the way ahead of two advancing marine columns. Because of narrow roads and restricting swamps, the marines had to march single or double file and the lines became correspondingly distended and disorganized. Companies separated and men of different units intermingled. There was firing without orders and trouble getting the firing to stop. The objective, coordinated with army units attacking from the mainland side, was to take the town of Noveleta at the base of the Cavité peninsula, an important anchor point in General Emilio Aguinaldo's perimeter around Manila. The captain of Butler's company was made battalion commander, leaving Smedley in command of the lead company of his column although he was quite junior in rank and untried in action.

Coming around a bend in the road, Butler's company was greeted by heavy fire from Filipino trenches ahead and to either side. After a moment of panic, he took charge and competently directed several volleys of rifle fire, then participated in a pursuit across mud flats and rice paddies as the marines drove the *insurrectos* ahead of them. The first two men in Butler's company, including his top sergeant, were wounded in the initial encounter. Butler was judged by his regimental commander, Lieutenant Colonel George

F. Elliott, to have done well, in contrast to another junior officer who had become overexcited and was reported unfit to lead troops in combat. By noon the marines converged with army units and took Noveleta as the Filipinos broke in direct confrontation with superior firepower and tactical discipline. After an hour's rest during which Elliott assembled the battalion under a great mango tree to sing "America," the marines burned houses and huts along the road where they had been ambushed and trekked back to the base at Cavité. They had suffered one dead and ten wounded, plus fifty cases of temporary prostration in the oppressive tropical heat.[12]

Thereafter, garrison duty at Cavité reverted to routine, except for occasional brief sallies to relieve harassed American outposts. In a blatant act of consecration to the marine cult and to manhood attained, Smedley had himself tattooed from throat to waist with a Marine Corps globe-and-anchor insignia. And at this time he attached himself to a short, stocky Virginian with an imperious military bearing and large mustache who would in many ways become his alter ego, Major Littleton W.T. (Waller Tazewell) Waller. Waller was the same age as Smedley's father. Butler revered him thirty years later as "the greatest soldier I have ever known. . . . He had a magnificent face and carriage. On a horse he was impressive. He always took off his hat with a flourish. I can see him, straight as a ruler, his head thrown back, his enormous nose outlined against the sky, as he saluted the flag. Waller may have liked to talk about himself, but he had plenty to talk about."[13] At the turn of the century in China and the Philippines, Waller was in his prime as a celebrated field commander. His career, dating back to the Egyptian intervention in 1882, would intertwine with Butler's in China, Panama, Mexico, and Haiti.

Butler's first two campaigns in Cuba and the Philippines marked the serious intrusion of U.S. military power into regions hitherto only sporadically contested by gunboat diplomacy. Naval bases at Guantánamo Bay in Cuba and Subig Bay in the Philippines laid the strategic foundations for the whole series of military expeditions in the Caribbean area, Central America, and the Far East that would provide the main opportunities of Butler's career. Most immediately, the large number of troops on hand to suppress the Philippine rebellion, including two-thirds of the U.S. Army, enabled the United States to launch its first major expedition to the Asian mainland.

In the spring of 1900, Major Waller received orders posting him to Guam, a remote island 3,300 miles west of Hawaii that had recently been taken from Spain and was now designated a U.S. naval station. It was considered a highly undesirable post, yet when Waller was permitted to select five officers and chose Butler among them, Smedley willingly agreed. As the Guam contingent was preparing to embark in June, an urgent message ordered that a company of marines be dispatched to China where antiforeign violence had escalated dangerously. Already packed, the Guam contingent sailed immediately. The marine commander at Cavité first designated Company A under Butler, but sensing "the need of a Field Officer there" obtained authorization to send an entire battalion under Waller. At sea on the hospital ship *Solace*, Smedley wrote his mother, "it is needless to say that I am the happiest man alive and that for the last few days my feet have not touched the ground at all. I solemnly promise that I will never cry about bad luck again as long as I live." *Solace* soon joined other foreign transports and warships standing off Taku Bar, staging area for the relief of Tientsin and Peking.[14]

3 The Teenage Hero

CHINA

The international fleet disgorging troops at Taku Bar was an extraordinary spectacle. The Great Powers strained their military resources in common effort, while elsewhere they vied with each other in quest of empire, their rival imperialisms fired by jingoistic nationalism. Allied intervention in China contrasted strangely with the contemporary crises in Venezuela, the Upper Nile, the Philippines, Manchuria, Panama, and the Balkans. These same armies, now joined in tenuous alliance to share death, glory, hardship, and loot on the plains of North China, would fourteen years later direct their full fury against each other.

Two days before Butler's arrival, the allies had sent in shallow draft gunboats to reduce and capture the Chinese forts at Taku. The Chinese responded by starting systematic bombardment of the foreign settlement inland at Tientsin, and on 20 June 1900, as Butler went ashore at Taku, Boxers attacked the foreign diplomatic legations in Peking. This marked the beginning of the famous fifty-five-day siege. The Boxers, or Society of Righteous and Harmonious Fists, were irregular peasant soldiers spearheading a violent uprising against foreign encroachment. They had been joined, after unsuccessful attempts at repression, by Imperial Chinese government armies that were put into the field by the alien Manchu Dynasty. The Manchus survived precariously by cunning and duplicity, menaced both by internal rebellion and by the foreign powers, appeasing each with measured capitulations.

Advance notice of the uprising had been signaled by killings of foreign missionaries and Chinese Christian converts. Although some missionaries had remained to face death alongside the converts, most had withdrawn to the relative safety of Peking and Tientsin where, along with a few businessmen retreating from the interior, they formed burgeoning refugee populations that strained foreign settlement resources on the eve of the sieges. In January 1900 the American consul in Tientsin reported a total of 301 Americans, including women and children, in his North China district.[1]

Butler's battalion was part of the first attempt to break through to the beleaguered foreign settlement at Tientsin. All was haste and improvisation. The marines were ferried ashore across Taku Bar on a passing German freighter commandeered by the German admiral. At Tongku, terminus of the Peking-Tientsin railway, they activated a train of flatcars with the help of firemen from the veteran gunboat USS *Monocacy*, a side-wheeler that had been a China Station fixture since the 1860s. The marines advanced inland, repairing torn up track and telegraph lines along the right of way which ran parallel to the Pei (Hai) River. The river would presently be filled with corpses floating down from Tientsin.

Sixteen miles from Tongku, still twelve miles from Tientsin, the marines caught up with a regiment of Russian infantry accompanied by Cossack outriders. The combined force of 131 marines and 400 Russians bivouaced that night at the point where the railway could no longer be repaired, then decided to press forward rather than await reinforcements. There were an estimated 50,000 regular Chinese troops supported by modern Krupp artillery besieging the foreign quarter at Tientsin.

The advance early next morning, with the marines following the Russians, proceeded without opposition until seven o'clock when it was stopped by frontal and flanking fire from several thousand Chinese. A Boxer unit attacked across the open fields "waving their swords and banners frantically," but they were cut down and broken at about 500 yards. As heavy fire continued unabated, the badly mauled Russians fell back, leaving the marines as rearguard in a desperate four-hour ordeal. During the retreat, Butler and five others struggling to evacuate a wounded comrade were isolated even farther behind the organized rear guard and had a particularly difficult trek. For this, four enlisted men received Congressional Medals of Honor, while Butler—officers not being eligible for CMHs—was praised in Major Waller's official dispatch for having distinguished himself by "saving a wounded man at the risk of his own life under a very severe fire." [2]

Butler, in his autobiography, *Old Gimlet Eye* (1931), alluded to the leatherneck fighting spirit that sustained them during the retreat: "An old corporal who marched with us was shot on the inside of the leg. He limped along for fifteen miles without complaining or mentioning his wound. The old Marine gave the rest of us an invaluable object lesson. Another old Marine, a sergeant, was walking beside me. Crack! A stream of blood trickled down his face. The sergeant pulled his hat down over the wound and walked right on." Stoicism, epic in inspiration and here nearly caricatured to suit the popular military-adventure market for which Butler wrote, was central to the warrior ideal. Officers were expected to take the lead: "Thanks be to God," one of them later remarked, "I was enabled to set a good example of courage and of indifference to shot and shell, which I think may have encouraged my men." [3]

Very conspicuous as a teenage company commander, Smedley was not to be outdone in heedless bravery, as he proved in these weeks of death-defying heroism. Leatherneck élan entailed honor-bound yet fickle personal loyalty, rigorous manliness, and a competitiveness in which comrades rivaled each other in feats of bravado. Fear in battle could actuate intense self-doubt or shame, and dread of public disgrace for cowardice, so that in the end physical fear might perversely energize acts of desperate bravery. Butler in retrospect described a "natural desire to hide one's own weakness, combined with the certainty that the others are equally frightened, [which] gives courage to the group and spurs on some men to heroic deeds." Hero worship was another enveloping persuasion in the marines and other Victorian military subcultures that impelled Smedley forward as a teenage daredevil. He remembered being greatly impressed by the "strikingly attractive," gallant, and fashionable British naval officer David Beatty, whom he saw outside Tientsin several days later prancing about on a white horse and dangerously exposing himself to enemy fire, his theatrical posture enhanced by a wounded arm in sling and a hat tilted affectedly at a rakish angle.[4] Less convincing simulations abounded, the more so as the allied contingents surpassed each other in martial swagger and ostentatious gallantry.

The marines, with four dead and nine wounded, and the Russians returned exhausted to the base camp, where they were joined by reinforcements and a trainload of supplies. Next day the regrouped column, now totaling 2,000, including British, Japanese, Germans, and Italians, moved up again to the railhead, and on 23 June an advance guard led by the marines pushed ahead against slight resistance to reach the besieged foreign settlement. The Chinese withdrew their main force and artillery inside the Walled "Native" City a mile further upstream on the Pei.

Hardly a single building in the foreign concession—a miniature Western-style city—was left unscathed after a week of shelling. Had the Chinese organized a mass attack, they surely could have overrun the thinly manned barricades and slaughtered the garrison and civilian refugees, a specter reminiscent of the Tientsin Massacre of 1870. Marines, approaching on the twenty-third, could hear heavy guns being fired at the concession, while on the inside the defenders were given renewed hope that relief was finally on the way. Herbert Hoover, a civilian engineer, recalled the moment in his memoirs: "How we strained our ears! . . . We saw them coming over the plain. They were American Marines and Welch Fusiliers. I do not remember a more satisfying musical performance than the bugles of the American Marines entering the settlement playing 'There'll Be a Hot Time in the Old Town Tonight.'" Grimy and tattered after hiking and fighting for five days, the marines unfurled their flags and marched up the settlement's main street to a reception by cheering crowds that Butler remembered in middle age as the most thrilling he ever experienced.[5]

There was still the main task of eliminating Chinese forces inside the Walled City, prerequisite to the eventual dispatch of a relief column to the besieged legations in Peking. During three weeks of preparation for the assault, Butler and his company manned barricades beyond a rickety pontoon bridge that ran from the foreign settlement. At one point Butler and eighty marines joined a battalion under a British colonel in an unsuccessful attempt to capture a particularly annoying enemy gun that had been moved to one of the villages across the Pei. Following hand-to-hand combat, a platoon of the British Weihaiwei regiment was unable to extricate when ordered to retreat. Butler, according to Waller's report, deployed his marines, advanced quickly, and opened fire by volleys, which allowed the British-Chinese regiment to retreat safely: "He then fell back by sections in fine order and without casualty. I have before mentioned the fine qualities of Mr. Butler, his control of men, courage and excellent example in his own person of all the qualities most admirable in a soldier."[6]

At 3 A.M. on 13 July, one thousand American troops marched out of the international settlement under the command of marine Colonel Robert L. Meade, who had arrived the day before with reinforcements from Cavité and who now briefly took over from Waller as senior officer in the 350-man marine contingent. Meade also assumed nominal overall command of the Ninth U.S. Infantry, since he outranked the army colonel, who was killed soon afterward in any case. The entire operation was commanded by the most senior officer, a British general, although fully half the troops involved were Russian. This was the beginning of a badly confused command structure, freighted with petty jealousies, that added a strong element of absurdity to all subsequent operations. The often-slighted French General H. Frey described the battle of the thirteenth as a case in which the endurance and great valor of the troops contrasted starkly "with the absolute lack of unity among the high command."[7]

The marines had problems of their own. Meade was nearly crippled with rheumatism that caused him to go into battle with his hands and feet heavily bandaged, and he had a drinking problem. He was sent home under escort two weeks later, "very lame in hands and feet," according to Waller's official report. But his eventual replacement, Colonel Henry Clay Cochrane, recorded in his diary several months later: "Long call from Major Waller who told of Col. Meade bgdk [being drunk?] and offensive to Lt. Butler and others at mess table in Cavite, dk in Tientsin & suspdg him [Waller] from comd [command] after Tientsin fight a/c of remk. abt. Lt. Leonard, his wounded adjt." At about the same time Cochrane wrote his wife, "Think I told you that Meade was sent home [sketch of bottle and glass]. Same old story and the wonder is how long it lasts." Meade's regression, as remembered by another officer, caused "great upheaval" in the marine organization.[8]

Marching in two extended columns, the allies approached the Walled City and divided according to assigned sectors, with the Russians attacking from the north while the British, Japanese, Germans, French, and Americans launched a loosely coordinated assault from the south. The defenses were awesome. The rectangular Wallèd City, its forty-foot-high stone battlements commanding the plain below, was additionally protected to the south by an outer network of canals and a twelve-foot-high mud barrier built partly at the behest of erstwhile European military advisers. Between the mud and the stone walls lay a thousand yards of cemeteries, rice paddies, and swamps intersected by irrigation ditches, completely flat except for such cover as could be found behind grave mounds and dikes and in the ditches. Herbert Hoover, who knew the area from recreational horseback riding, accompanied the marines as "a sort of guide" for their part in the attack and was "completely scared, especially when some of the Marines next to me were hit" as they came under sharp fire.[9] The Chinese had partially flooded the plain in anticipation of the attack. Inside the Walled City were many thousand Chinese troops and about sixty artillery pieces manned by skilled gunners.

The marines and other allied units assembled outside the southern perimeter about 5 A.M., while allied artillery began an all-day duel with the Chinese guns on the city wall. At 5:45 a British lyddite shell auspiciously and spectacularly detonated the main Chinese magazine in the city, sending, according to Lieutenant Henry L. Leonard, a "column of smoke and men going up a thousand or more feet in the air, and the shock being plainly felt a mile and a half away." At 6:30 the marines, including Butler's A Company, joined the Welch Fusiliers at the extreme left of the allied formation in a bold frontal assault up and over the mud wall, proceeding as best they could in a skirmishing line, advancing by rushes across the fire-swept plain until stopped about 800 yards short of the stone wall. They remained pinned down in this position from 8 A.M. until they could retreat under cover of darkness at 8 P.M., exposed to fire described by Colonel Meade as "fearfully accurate as the casualty list will evidence and I thank God for the mounds and dykes . . . the enemy had so well covered our position that their shots struck the crests of the trenches and threw dirt in our faces—many being hit." Marines, along with British bluejackets, were particularly good targets in their blue shirts, standing out in contrast to khaki elsewhere down the line. In addition to heavy artillery and rifle fire, Chinese assault troops twice sallied forth on the run from the South Gate and almost outflanked the marines, threatening to cut them off short of ammunition in a fight in which, as Meade noted, "no prisoners were taken on either side." The 180 rounds per man that the marines started out with was fast being expended. Elsewhere on the line soldiers and sailors of the various nationalities were similarly bogged down in waist-deep ditches, huddling for cover behind grave mounds, trapped by withering fire from the wall.[10]

The marines at the far end of the line suffered all day in the blazing summer heat while mired in water that was much too filthy to drink. Even when digging into relatively solid ground, they hit water at two to three feet. Moving about meant making a break for it, slipping and stumbling from one grave mound or rice paddy dike to the next.[11]

Butler's part in this torment did not last long. Shortly after the initial advance was stopped and pinned down, he ventured forth to help one of the wounded and was shot in the back of his right leg. The bullet hit halfway between hip and knee, and came out the front without hitting bone. He managed to drag himself back to an improvised line of trenches, but was unable to get all the way back to the safety of the mud wall and was left lying in an exposed position. Meade saw him and told his adjutant, Lieutenant Leonard, that Butler ought to be removed from the field as Chinese on the flank might imminently drive the marines from their forward position. When Meade then expressly refused to order anyone to rescue Butler because it was too dangerous, Leonard gallantly volunteered and, with the help of two enlisted men, brought Smedley in safely over the mud wall.[12]

From here Butler joined another officer, also wounded in the leg, for what Smedley described in a letter home as "a pretty tough walk" back to the hospital in the foreign settlement. The two leaned on each other in an unassisted shuffle that took several hours, during which Smedley's wound continued to bleed. He spent the rest of the battle helping attend other more seriously wounded until he himself was treated in the evening. Back on the field, Leonard was gravely wounded. One of two enlisted men who carried him out later described conditions: "The bullets came like hail. I had the heel shot from my shoe and a hole through my hat, which I did not know about until we had crossed the outer wall. We started about 11 A.M. and did not cross the wall until 4 P.M., and that was the hardest five hours I think I ever spent."[13]

Withdrawal began at nightfall. Survivors were ordered to sleep on their arms so as to be ready for renewed attack in the morning. Shortly before daybreak a Japanese unit crept up and succeeded in blowing the South Gate clear out of its arch. A Japanese assault through the breach followed by Russian entry from the north broke the back of the defense. Chinese troops abandoned their positions and were hunted down in the streets. Allied casualties for the whole engagement totaled 716 killed and wounded, of whom 354 were Japanese. Americans came next with 25 dead and 98 wounded. The American consul estimated 15,000 Chinese were killed or wounded.[14]

The ensuing occupation and plundering of the Walled City was grotesque, excessive even for a colonial punitive campaign. Scandalous misbehavior by allied troops, amply reported in the world press, belied the motif of civilization versus savagery in which the expedition had been righteously cast, particularly the racial aspect inasmuch as Japanese troops were conspicuously well-disciplined throughout. Marine Corporal James Bevan remembered "old men, women and little children were lying in every conceivable position . . . Chinese were running in every direction. Many were brought down like rabbits on the run." Lieutenant Frederick M. Wise, who in his memoirs devoted a lurid chapter to "The Sacking of Tientsin," wrote that he "never saw such looting," and described his company's quarters as having resembled "a wealthy Chinese lady's private apartment as the men sat around off duty comparing trophies." [15]

Butler, in the hospital, missed the early frenzied days and only rejoined his company toward the end of the month; by then, orders against looting had been effectively enforced. The wound in his leg, a bullet hole about a half inch in diameter at point of entry, healed so that after ten days he was able to walk around, and a week and a half he later set out gamely on the long trek to Peking.

While recuperating, Smedley basked in praise and was breveted for gallantry to captain, attaining this rank while in the hospital a few days before his nineteenth birthday. The British commanding general, in a panegyric addressed to the U.S. command, wrote: "Among many instances of personal bravery in the action I propose especially to bring to notice in despatches the conduct of 1st Lieutenant Smedley D. Butler . . . in bringing in a wounded man from the front under heavy and accurate fire." Recognition from the British, who enjoyed great prestige as imperialists, was sweet. Butler wrote home, "The General is reported to have said that I will receive the Victoria Cross, but don't breathe that as I am afraid it is a rumor [it was] and I am not going to blow my own horn." [16]

In fact, awards and promotions were so liberally distributed during the campaign that General A.S. Daggett, who as colonel had commanded the Fourteenth U.S. Infantry, raised the issue in his memoir *America in the China Relief Expedition* (1903): "When one examines the long lists of recommendations for brevets and medals of honor, he feels that the value of these honors has been so cheapened as to have no significance . . . skill in framing descriptive phrases was exhausted in attempts to make ordinary good conduct appear heroic." Tokens of heroism were essential to Victorian military conceit. Marines in the Boxer campaign, topped by Meade who was breveted to brigadier general, accounted for eight officer brevets and thirteen enlisted Congressional Medals of Honor.[17] Butler's bravery was amply demonstrated and widely attested to, his efficiency as a combat leader clearly established; on the other hand, he was very young for a captain.

Having won promotion, Smedley found himself barred by an eye defect which turned up in the required physical examination. With an increasingly sure touch he reached for the political strings, writing his mother, "If the Admiral [Asiatic Station] does not see fit to waive my defect, I shall have to ask father to help me out once more." And in the next sentence he mentioned rumors that America might declare war on Turkey, in which case he wanted a major's or lieutenant colonel's commission in any ensuing volunteer army.[18] Clearly, he was acquiring confidence and an eye for the main chance.

There was no war with Turkey, and the admiral waived his physical defect upon appeal by Major Waller, who at this point was intently cultivating his young subaltern. Smedley, describing Waller as "a very fine officer," wrote home: "While I was in the hospital, wounded, he came two or three times a day to see me, and sent me choice things to eat. He treats me like a son, and has taken a place in my affections second only among the old officers to Captain Haines [his battalion commander at Cavité]." But three weeks later in Peking, Butler referred to Waller's kindnesses with circumspection: "He showed numerous attentions, and on several occasions he even embarrassed me by them." This wariness apparently had to do with Waller's pending brevet to lieutenant colonel. Smedley pondered, "Now, although Major Waller has his peculiarities, he is a good officer and soldier, and has few equals in the service," but he was "a man that I do not care much for personally, being too much impressed by his own worth." On balance, he concluded that if "Father would put in a good word for him here and there, it would help his cause considerably." Meanwhile, Waller wrote Congressman Butler telling of Smedley's wound, and received in reply the grateful assurance that "when my services are needed by you to aid in the promotion of your ambitions . . . simply point the way that I may not go blindly, nor fall short of the object desired." [19]

For a teenager maturing precociously in violent and grueling surroundings, this remarkable relationship with his commanding officer as both benefactor and beneficiary fostered an early sophistication in the intricacies of power, trust, and vulnerability that were the makings of military politics. Apart from the formal command structure of deference and rank, senior officers often co-opted promising juniors who in turn attached themselves to the professional and political fortunes of their patrons. Butler and Waller were both chancy in the respective roles, Butler with his perhaps ephemeral big-time civilian political connections, and Waller with his cantankerousness and prima donna knack for alienating people.[20] As it shortly developed, Waller's star was permanently dimmed by a nasty court-martial in the Philippines. That Smedley remained a true friend for the next quarter century through thick and thin testifies to his loyalty, affection, and tolerance. As with reckless bravery on the battlefield, this involved a paradox of self-denial and ambition. Convincing instances of self-sacrifice authenticated honor and altruism, both fundamental to the officer code. And Waller and Butler no doubt came genuinely to admire each other's pugnacious style.

Returning to his company at the end of July, Butler joined in the march to Peking ninety miles further inland. The legations had now been under siege for six weeks, cut off from the outside world. On 16 July, the London *Daily Mail* published sensational news that the defenders had been overrun and massacred to the last man, woman, and child. But in the following weeks fragmentary messages reported their tenuous survival even as several world capitals went into mourning. Spurred by the distinct possibility that further delay might beget disaster—with censure for those responsible (witness the recent disgrace of those who arrived several days too late to save General Gordon at Khartoum)—while timely rescue would mean glory and laurels particularly for those in the vanguard, the allies in Tientsin set out on what became a footrace across the plain to Peking.

By this time some 25,000 foreign troops were assembled in Tientsin, 2,000 of whom were Americans—500 marines plus two U.S. infantry regiments. Several of the powers were old hands at mounting colonial expeditions, using subject peoples from elsewhere in their empires to fight the Chinese. Most of the French contingent were Tonkinese brought up from Indochina, while the British were largely Indians troops in turbans who had their own special foods served by bearers wearing loincloths. White troops included French marine infantry in blue and white hats, British sailors, and Welch Fusiliers. All this helped make the Boxer campaign the great military spectacle of the age, the premier armies of the world showing their best and worst features. The Americans were noted for their larger physiques and "free and easy ideas on the subject of discipline," particularly the "casual manner in which a private addressed an officer" which, according to a British officer of the Indian Army, "astonished and shocked their Continental critics." General Frey concurred, adding that American units alarmed their neighbors by random firing at all times, near and far from the enemy, as they shot pigs and chickens and otherwise roisted about.[21]

In a letter dated 4 August, the day the long columns set out from Tientsin, Butler wrote his mother not to worry, "Remember if I am killed I gave my life for women and children, just as dear to some poor devil as thee and [his seven-year-old brother Horace] are to me." This gallant gesture, trite but true to the romantic formula of rescuing the innocent from menacing natives, also reflected real uncertainty as to the dangers lying ahead. The march across the almost treeless plain, covered with wheat fields in midsummer growth, was an ordeal for all concerned whether directly involved in skirmishing with Boxers or not. The heat and dust were terrible as thousands of men and horses churned up huge clouds of choking dust under a relentless sun. Some men died of sunstroke and many dropped out along the roadside, so that as many as half the marines would be missing at sundown and then come straggling into camp during the night. Horses were abandoned, and shoes, underwear, ponchos, and blankets lay strewn all along the line of march as men discarded everything but essentials. Once an entire marine company, prostrated by heat in a wheat field, failed to move forward in an assault on a village. Perversely, it rained at night making it "sort of nasty," as Smedley wrote home, for those (including himself) who had no shelter. His leg gave him constant pain, and he once nearly succumbed but managed to "worry through" by clinging to the horse of a mounted officer.[22]

These hardships corresponded insensibly to what was becoming a ruthless campaign. According to the colonial formula, nonwhite savages who menaced white women and children were to be taught a lesson. No matter that this was China, and that foreign presence had come to be hated with good reason. A U.S. Army general who passed along the line of march afterward described a wasteland: "The villages had been burned and looted by the allied columns, the people had fled from their homes . . . the sedgy banks of the Peiho were reeking with the stench from the floating bodies of dead Chinamen."[23]

Throughout the march the marines had been relegated to the rear of the column, reflecting the current army domination of U.S. command politics. They covered the last twelve miles to Peking in a night march intended to catch them up before the city walls in time for the first assault. Marching through mud and rain, during which they got lost, they joined the battle at noon. As they came under fire from the outer city wall near the Tungchow gate, Butler was shot in the chest and knocked unconscious. The bullet, Corporal Bevan remembered, "must have been partly spent or it would have killed him." It flattened the second brass button on his uniform blouse, the button in turn gouging out a piece of Latin America from the globe-and-anchor tattoo on his chest. Smedley wrote home, "The shock was terrible and for about a half an hour I could hardly breathe." At first it was thought he had been shot in the heart, but when he began gasping for breath it was seen that he had escaped with a large and very painful bruise plus internal hemorrhaging that caused him to cough up blood for days afterward. He rejoined his company which was meanwhile fighting its way through the outer Chinese City to the inner wall of the Tartar City. The marines spent a rainy night just outside the legation quarter. Butler rolled up in his blanket on the ground with his chest "aching abominably."[24]

British Sikhs won the honor of being first to reach the legation quarter, by crawling through a grill in a drainage canal. During the following days the marines were welcomed and thanked by European survivors of the siege who came out from the legations. According to Bevan, "There was a lot of hand-shaking and though we were filthy with mud, grime, and sweat of our ten days on the march some of us were soundly kissed by the women of the party much to our embarrassment." Smedley wrote his mother that "all the hardships were forgotten when we gazed on the women and children we had saved." Among the 400 foreign civilians, about half had been women and children. Sixty-four foreigners had been killed, including one American child and seven marines from the legation guard. The defenders had been subjected to deprivations, heat, crowded conditions, and terror that, capping the dramatic story of their presumed massacre and subsequent rescue, made this the world-renowned saga of the day.[25] The Imperial Court fled Peking at dawn on 15 August. Butler's company, positioned on the Tartar Wall in the upper floors of the great Chien gate, maintained a brisk rifle fire in support of the final allied assault on government troops holding out in the Imperial Palace. Then, having taken the city, the allies sacked it.

The marines, moving to an assigned occupation zone in the western part of the Tartar City, joined in wide-open pillaging that animated not only the military but also foreign diplomats and even missionaries. Corporal Bevan remembered going out on "foraging expeditions by squads." Lieutenant Wise, billeted along with Butler in the Palace of the Eighth Prince, described the officers' quarters: "piles of loot were growing bigger and bigger. More Chinese trunks and chests were added to each officer's room." Butler's attitude, stated somewhat defensively in retrospect thirty years later, was that the "Peking rabble" had first pickings and left "contents of whole shops spilled out on the streets. It took stronger wills than we possessed not to be tempted by brocades and furs lying in the gutters."[26]

For all the exotic surroundings and stories of fabulous booty, Butler's impressions were bleak: "Peking is a dirty slop hole as far as I can see. The Imperial City is a little better than the rest, and before the trouble, I imagine it was very handsome, but now, or at least up to the last week or so, dead Chinamen adorn the highways with their swollen persons." The marines busied themselves cleaning up the city, establishing street patrols, filling in open sewers in front of their quarters, and foraging for food. With the mass exodus of Chinese and ongoing military operations, the local marketing system broke down, and foraging by allied armies numbering 30,000 quickly stripped the surrounding countryside. The marines went back on navy rations. In public places they were harried by beggars. "We would toss a few coins with a hole in the middle," Bevan recalled, "and they would scramble for them like dogs. Small Chinese boys followed us, turning handsprings and cartwheels, never stopping until we threw them a few coins." Patrols daily shot dogs roaming in packs in the streets. Smedley's letters home reflected the general stringency: "Do not imagine that we are having luxurious fare by any means, but our men forage quite successfully, and keep us supplied with a small variety of green vegetables."[27]

These grim surroundings and the letdown after of a strenuous campaign were conducive to prodigious drinking. Alcohol abuse was habitual among marines and interesting in Butler's case because of his later fame as a militant prohibitionist. A remarkable unsigned narrative entitled "Butler's Bawl," purported to have been written by a participant and found in the personal papers of Marine Commandant Ben H. Fuller (1930-34), describes a night of drunken revelry in the Palace of the Eighth Prince. The setting was a party for senior officers hosted by Major Waller. Junior officers, separate in their adjacent quarters, were drinking and smashing a collection of Buddhas which had to be dispensed with because of antilooting orders. Instead of precious stones or pearls, they found only wisps of hair and trifles. As the whiskey took hold, Butler began singing "Sailing Down the Coast of High Barbaree," audible "high above the turmoil of the senior party." He continued obsessively into the morning hours, ultimately fixing on a single hoarse refrain while his drinking partners lay "comotose on or under the table." At dawn he was still at it, having been joined occasionally by emissaries sent to quiet him, and, ending finally with "a triumphant glance at the unreceptive figures around him, [he] raised his voice in one last yelp of exultation . . . then with a smile on his rugged features he fell into slumber, his Wellington nose flattened on the table."[28] A cameo true to the marines and the circumstances.

The occupation lasted into October, when the powers began negotiating with the Imperial Court for indemnity and new concessions. A highlight was the ceremonial violation of the Forbidden City, inner sanctum of Imperial mystique, for which Butler was chosen among the officers representing his regiment. The military pageantry, with martial music and marching contingents from eight nations, made a great spectacle, but otherwise the occupation produced little in the way of grandeur or edification. Fights broke out between allied troops, leading to stricter segregation by zones and fears of serious trouble on the part of the commanders. Allied punitive sorties extended the pillaging and slaughter into the outskirts, with the U.S. commander, General Adna R. Chaffee, reporting that "it is safe to say that where one real Boxer has been killed since the capture of Peking, fifty harmless coolies or laborers on farms, including not a few women and children, have been slain." Colonel Cochrane, arriving in mid-September, found the marines "generally demoralized" and "behaving badly," with instances of rape, sodomy, and looting, and the brig full.[29]

The marines pulled out in early October, marching in cold and rain and then riding in railway freight cars for the final leg down to the coast at Tongku. The trip afforded them a last look at the North China countryside, still desolate two months after the grim allied march to Peking. Tientsin, garrisoned by allied troops, was being reconstructed by local draft labor working under allied supervision. Plans for renovation included leveling the walls of what had been the Walled City, making it much less picturesque but also less of a military obstacle for the future, a factor that would concern Butler when he returned in the 1920s. The city was to remain a garrison town for international troops until the late 1930s according to terms of the Boxer Protocol presently under negotiation.

At Tongku, two companies of marines including Butler's boarded the flagship *Brooklyn* for an excursion cruise, reward for the hardships and successes of the campaign, via Yokohama, Nagasaki, and Shanghai to Manila.

Smedley, coming down with typhoid two days out, missed the tourist treats and instead spent the cruise aboard ship reliving his China experience in feverish hallucinations. While in the throes of delirium, he had visions of his own death in which he and two fellow officers approached the River Styx in the underworld. The two friends boarded a boat while Smedley was left behind; they meanwhile succumbed to fever while Smedley survived. Years later he told his children that he felt he had actually experienced death and never feared it afterward. He retained a feeling for extrasensory perception. In fact, it seems he had a close call; he weighed only ninety pounds on arrival in Manila.[30]

Apart from personal scrapes with death, the campaign left many lasting impressions. In China, Butler learned the rudiments of a style of handling men that ultimately would combine old-guard physical presence with an audacious egalitarianism. This was still incipient, but he was beginning to appreciate the interdependent relationship between officers and men, seniors and subordinates. In *Old Gimlet Eye* he recalls "an easy and friendly relationship [that] prevailed between officers and enlisted men on the march. We were sharing the same hardships." Two days out of Tientsin, a thirty-year veteran with enough savvy to have filled his knapsack with bread and cheese before setting out, shared these with him and continued to in the following days. In the same vein, he remembered Captain Goodrell's advice to carry even a single enlisted man's canteen, and the entire company would move no matter how exhausted, although on the Tientsin-Peking trek it was Butler who was being helped. Elsewhere in the column, Corporal Bevan helped his company commander prepare a nightly fire and meal, and was "always well rewarded with a stiff drink from his bottle, which helped a lot." Butler claimed never to have forgotten the lessons: "The old fellows took care of us youngsters and taught us the tricks of the trade. The men got drunk every pay day and caused me endless trouble, but when I was dead tired, they carried my pack, and they shared with me the food they managed to steal. I've always had a deep affection for the veterans who brought me up."[31]

His various impressions were, of course, to a great extent subsumed in the color and action of the campaign. In China, more than in Cuba or the Philippines, Butler had taken part in the great military spectacle of the day. The pageantry, drama, fabled setting, and global repercussions made this the most widely discussed of the contemporary colonial expeditions. Veterans could hold up their heads in military circles not only for having participated in famous exploits, but for having seen the armies and navies of the world concentrated in battle array. Thirty years later Butler wrote a friend, "Indeed I haven't forgotten those times; I was just a boy at the time, and still consider the Boxer campaign as the most interesting period of my life."[32]

4 Knight Errant

HONDURAS, PANAMA, THE PHILIPPINES

Wasted from his bout with typhoid during the three-week cruise from Taku to Manila on the *Brooklyn*, Butler spent a month in the sweltering naval hospital at Cavité and was finally sent home in late November 1900. His parents made the long train trip across the country to meet him in San Francisco. The subsequent homecoming in West Chester, where local newspapers had been avidly reporting his adventures, was celebrated by a public reception sponsored by the local Grand Army of the Republic. A few days later the town of West Chester hosted another reception, graced by the secretary of the navy and the commandant of the Marine Corps, plus the Marine Band which was brought up from Washington for the occasion. After three months of home leave, Smedley was assigned to the Marine Barracks in the Philadelphia Navy Yard. This gave him a year more near home before setting out again on expeditionary duty, and a chance to make new acquaintances in the Philadelphia area, where the marines had their historic roots and many social connections.

In the fall of 1902 Butler, in command of a company of marines, joined the newly organized advanced-base force battalion on the transport *Prairie* for training maneuvers in the Caribbean. The advanced-base idea had been spawned with the Cuban, Philippine, and Chinese operations, and it was henceforth an integral part of military planning by the General Board of the Navy to cope with projected requirements of an overseas island empire. Part of the Marine Corps was to be trained, equipped, and permanently ready on short notice to capture and defend strategic overseas bases. Apart from these grand designs for future wars against big-power imperialist rivals, the advanced-base capability gave the United States a ready instrument for military intervention into weaker nations in the Caribbean and Central America, which became exercise grounds, simulated and real, for several generations of advanced-base outfits.

The varied potential of the advanced-base format was demonstrated by events in the Caribbean in 1902. Against a background of impending American takeover in Panama and Anglo-German naval blockade of Venezuela, involving putative German designs on the island of Margarita, the United States established a permanent Caribbean squadron, transferred the island of Culebra off Puerto Rico to the Navy Department, and mobilized the fleet, concentrating all its capital ships at Culebra for advanced-base maneuvers. The maneuvers were both a pointed display of American power and a trial run in its use.[1] To the marines in this first advanced-base exercise, it was both the beginning of coordinated large-scale amphibious operations with the navy and a prelude to President Theodore Roosevelt's "big-stick" diplomacy. When the fleet dispersed the day after Washington received conciliatory Anglo-German submissions regarding Venezuela, the marines remained at Culebra, on call for new trouble spots.

Collaboration between the marines and navy was, as often, problematic. The basic task was to take the small, desolate island of Culebra and fortify it as an advanced base. The navy was in command so that, in Butler's version, the marines were given most of the hard work and very little of the credit. In one episode they were assigned to dig a canal, backbreaking labor such as was seldom done by whites in the tropics. This misery culminated in an outbreak of Chagres fever, Butler being carried out on his cot to a hospital in one of the few remaining ships. According to *Old Gimlet Eye*, the situation did not long go unnoticed in Washington: "A Marine officer on one of the ships wrote to my father . . . [who] raised hell with the Navy Department. By the time I recovered, the Admiral had a message from the secretary of the navy, who directed that no more Americans should be worked on the canal." Predictably, this reprieve did not end the affair for Smedley. As soon as he was off the sick list, he was assigned again to the canal, this time in charge of a native work force. When the job was almost completed he had a second attack of fever, going down with a temperature of 104 degrees. The marines (and presumably the local hired labor) received "not one word of praise" in speeches at the naval ceremony opening the canal. Butler concluded, "I have never forgotten that. My lack of affection for the Navy dates from my Culebra experience."[2]

In mid-March 1903, the marines and several ships of the new squadron were dispatched from Culebra 1,500 miles westward across the Caribbean to Honduras, where a revolution was threatening U.S. interests. A routine exercise in gunboat diplomacy, this was also the beginning of three decades of escalating U.S. military intervention in the Central American republics that became known in North American jargon as the Banana Wars.

Butler later satirized the 1903 Honduran intervention in a 1931 magazine article entitled "Opera-Bouffe Revolts: What Usually Happens When the Marines Have Landed."[3] His sarcasm, both in contemporary letters home and in later reminiscences, reflected a prevalent superciliousness in American attitudes regarding neighbors south of the border. An excerpt from popular military-adventure literature, Richard Harding Davis's stereotyped 1897 novel *Soldiers of Fortune*, illustrates the tendency, with a North American adventurer hectoring a Latin general:

Try to break that concession, try it. It was made by one Government to a body of honest, decent business men, with a Government of their own back of them, and if you interfere with our conceded rights to work those mines, I'll have a man-of-war down here with white paint on her hull, and she'll blow you and your little republic back up there into the mountains. Now you can go. . . . [Mendoza, the general, retreats to his horse. Clay, the adventurer, draws his pistol.] I'm not going to hurt you; I'm only going to frighten you a little. . . . [Clay shoots out a lantern inside a nearby house with three shots and twirls the revolver around his middle finger.] I'm sorry I had to make a gallery play of that sort, but it was the only way to make that sort of man understand.[4]

U.S. policy was informed by the same mentality. Military interventions in the following decades frequently lacked substantive military objectives and were characterized by campaigns undertaken largely for presumed psychological effect—or as vindications of U.S. power when political mastery proved otherwise elusive.

Butler, in "Opera-Bouffe Revolts," described Honduran generals ("every twentieth person one met was a general") as wearing "uniforms that would put to shame the drum major of a leading college band." These lesser breeds were seen to be absurdly aping their Anglo-Saxon betters—who had by this time divested themselves somewhat from Napoleonic and Victorian military plumage which was giving way to egalitarian trends and functional considerations such as camouflage. Smedley, for one, keenly indulged in flashy uniforms when he got the chance. The "opera-bouffe" stereotype said as much about smug U.S. pretentions as it did about Latin backwardness and insecurity.[5]

Butler and several hundred marines arrived off Puerto Cortés in the converted banana boat *Panther*, "prepared," as he wrote home, "to land and shoot everybody and anything that was breaking the peace." But instead of offering action and adventure, Puerto Cortés proved to be a torpid backwater with little indication of vigorous activity, revolutionary or otherwise.[6]

The completion of the Panama Railway in 1855 diverted ocean traffic to the Pacific Coast, which was nearer to the capital cities in the highlands, leaving the Caribbean ports desolate and neglected, cut off by the hot, humid, unhealthy tropical lowlands from the bulk of the population, which lived in the mountainous interior. In 1903, Puerto Cortés and the several other ports along the Mosquito Coast of northern Honduras were little more than clusters of wooden and corrugated iron shacks along the beach, interspersed with a few two-story homes and warehouses. This desultory interlude, however, was coming to an end with the arrival in the 1890s and thereafter of American capitalists who started plantations, railways, and steamship lines connecting to urban markets in the United States. By the mid-1920s, the Caribbean ports were entrepots for the great United and Standard Fruit empires, establishing Honduras as the world's leading banana exporter and transforming the Mosquito Coast into an appendage of North American capitalism, complete with a substantial population of imported black West Indian laborers.

The 1903 Honduran revolution involved a struggle for the presidency between a Liberal president whose term was expiring, his protégé J.A. Arias who, having failed to win a three-way popular election, was installed directly by a rump congress, and Conservative aspirant Manuel Bonilla who won the popular vote. The latter then took to the field in rebellion rather than acquiesce in the established government's coup. As the Bonillista cause gained momentum in February, alarmed foreign residents pressed their diplomatic representatives for military intervention, the "protection of lives and property" to which whites in the tropics were entitled according to current renderings of international law. In La Ceiba, twenty-eight purported U.S. citizens signed a petition stating they were menaced by a "reign of terror" in which "hundreds of rifle shots were promiscuously fired by lawless and half drunken bands throughout the city some of which bullets penetrated the wooden houses occupied by American citizens."[7]

British, Spanish, and Mexican consuls called for warships, and their nationals joined with the American colony in abusing U.S. consuls for failing to react with sufficient urgency. In asserting its regional hegemony, the United States blocked military intervention by other powers. It therefore took upon itself "the exercise of an international police power," publicly proclaimed the following year as the Roosevelt Corollary to the Monroe Doctrine. In the present test case, the arrival of American warships and marines preempted a threatened alternative British action. Opposing the pressures for intervention, the senior American consul on the coast reported that there was little real danger to foreigners and "no reason why Honduras should be subjected to indignity." And in Washington there was skepticism regarding exaggerated appeals made by American citizens overseas seeking maximum military and diplomatic support for their often dubious commercial undertakings. But a show of force always seemed to enhance American prestige and to have a general quieting effect. As the consul at Utila put it, "the respect which this people have for the American Navy is sometimes ludicrous—always wholesome."[8]

Arriving at Puerto Cortés on 21 March, Butler and the marines in the *Panther*, plus marine detachments from the supporting warships of the Caribbean squadron, stood by while arrangements were made for peaceful surrender by the Arias (government) forces to about 1,500 Bonilla troops. The *Panther* then steamed eastward along the coast, where government garrisons were also capitulating to the Bonillistas. A one-day stopover at La

Ceiba was enough to ascertain that the revolution was proceeding calmly despite earlier reports of insurgents shooting up the town, so the *Panther* moved fifty miles further down the coast to Trujillo, arriving to the sound of gunshots from a fifty-five hour battle in which Bonillistas held the town and regulars the fort. A detachment of marines went ashore and marched to the American consulate, where Butler, in "Opera-Bouffe," claims to have found the consul, a Honduran national, hiding between the floor beams wrapped in an American flag. As the marines passed through the town, both the government and rebel forces apparently ceased firing in an impromptu truce. When they had departed with the consul the battle resumed until the final collapse of the government side.[9]

By the time the *Panther* returned to La Ceiba, the Bonillistas had taken complete control. Butler went ashore to look around, and wrote home that the town had about eighty white people among its population of 4,000— twenty-eight of whom presumably signed the aforementioned petition claiming protection as U.S. citizens. Smedley described the whites as "a pretty poor lot, most of them having left their country for their country's good, I imagine." The rebel army was "very similar to that of the government and even more ridiculous." The marines were to stand offshore on call to mount a rescue expedition into the interior, so Smedley was "anxiously waiting for a nigger to throw a stone. The weather is beastly hot, temperature about 110, they say this is the hell hole of the earth and I believe it." The vice-consul at La Ceiba reported that the *Panther's* presence had "greatly redounded to the prestige of the United States" and "made the local authorities keenly alive to their obligations and responsibilities."[10]

The *Panther* returned to Puerto Cortés for a final three weeks' offshore picket duty. After five days, Butler came to the conclusion that "the trouble seems to be all over around here and in fact there never was any reason for our presence." Despite his eagerness to attend an uncle's wedding, he added, "I won't ask Father to help me get home because I have brought enough trouble his way and would rather have him help my friends." His judgment regarding the pointlessness of U.S. military involvement was attested to by the absence of damage to foreign interests, the relative tranquility of the revolution itself, and the marginal nature of the intervention, which was mainly an offshore naval watch. On the other hand, the commanding officer of H.M.S. *Alert*, which spent four days showing the British flag along the Honduran coast in mid-April, advised the Admiralty that the lack of damage and violence was attributable to the "excellent effect produced by the presence of the American Squadron."[11]

At any rate a pivotal step, however pedestrian, had been taken in establishing exclusive American hegemony based on unobstructed military reach. The use of force, actual or abeyant, purposeful and seemingly uncomplicated, henceforth became the primary instrument of U.S. policy in the area, notwithstanding attempts to substitute "dollars for bullets," as will be seen. In Honduras, Bonilla retained the presidency until 1907, and took over again in 1911 with the support of the United Fruit Company. The development of the Mosquito Coast by United Fruit and Vacarro Brothers, subsequently Standard Fruit, progressed apace.

After leaving Honduras in April 1903, Butler returned home for six months' standby duty attached to receiving ships at the Philadelphia Navy Yard. In November he joined an expeditionary battalion for service in Panama, where a week earlier the new Republic of Panama had declared its independence from Colombia and, within a fortnight, granted the United States sovereignty over the ten-mile-wide strip that became the Canal Zone.

The marines' part in this operation was to midwife the revolution by maintaining order in the streets and by interdicting Colombian troops sent to put down the insurgents. Then, with the coup effectively executed, it remained for the United States to build up sufficient military presence to thwart an expected large-scale Colombian counterattack. Butler's battalion arrived in mid-December and went into camp at Bas Obispo. Several weeks later another two battalions arrived from Philadelphia along with Brigadier General Commandant George F. Elliott and his staff, a rare concentration of the Corps' strength and prominent personalities. Building camps, hiking, drilling, and map making proceeded under what was felt to be a serious threat of Colombian invasion. Butler, who left in early March after Colombian defiance had waned, took part in general camp routine as a company commander and in at least one major reconnaissance into the interior.

Returning home, he took advantage of fifteen months at the Philadelphia Navy Yard to court and marry beautiful, socially prominent Ethel Conway Peters. "Bunny," as Smedley called her in private and in the many affectionate letters he wrote her from foreign duty stations over the years, was the daughter of a patrician family influential in Philadelphia since the eighteenth century. A resolute and self-possessed woman in her own right, she loyally stood by him through the erratic convulsions of what would be a stormy career. Their engagement was celebrated in the local press as a storybook romance joining gallant young hero and society belle. One paper ran a full double-page spread with pictures of the attractive couple set against a background of flags under the banner, "Cupid Marks Time for a Yankee Boy Hero in Three Wars," and the subheadings "Uncle Sam's Youngest War Captain, Whom Bullets Couldn't Kill, Now Pierced Through and Through by Love's Little Dart . . . Like a Story from Kipling . . . A Baseball Hero, Too." Ethel was presented as granddaughter of the late Samuel M. Felton, president of the Philadelphia, Wilmington and Baltimore Railroad and grand-niece of a president of Harvard University. The *Philadelphia Evening Bulletin* announced the event in a two-column front-page story. They were married in June at the family summer home in Bay Head on the New Jersey seashore, with Lieutenant Colonel Waller as best man. The couple took a leisurely honeymoon trip via Europe, India, and Singapore to Smedley's new duty station, reporting at Cavité, Philippine Islands, in mid-October 1905.[12]

From Cavité Naval Station Captain and Mrs. Butler were sent fifty miles northwest to the Olongapo Navy Yard on Subig Bay at the base of the Bataan Peninsula, the projected new American strongpoint where marines had begun advanced-base exercises the previous year. This work continued, with building of base facilities, field maneuvers, and eventually installation of twenty portable six-inch guns plus others of lesser caliber. The urgency of the issue was heightened by the 1906-1907 Japanese-American war scare which pinpointed the Philippines as dangerously vulnerable. At the time of Butler's tour, from 1905 to 1907, Olongapo was designated the concentration point for Pacific advanced-base materials and the focal point for the anticipated showdown with Japan.

Until now Olongapo had been a double row of nipa thatched houses plus a few Spanish buildings strung along the beach, fringed with palm trees and sheltered from seasonal typhoons by a ring of high mountains. But it was pleasant enough for a young married couple surrounded by junior-officer cronies from previous campaigns, including several other newlyweds. Fritz Wise, who recalled having run through eleven cases of whiskey in a single month's entertainment when stationed at Cavité in 1904, transferred to Olongapo and found it a "petticoat post" run by motherly Mrs. Joseph H. Pendleton, wife of the commanding officer. Garrison duty, with its ample homelife and rounds of dinner parties, was invigorated by a monthly regimen of cross-country marching into the interior, where Butler would lead his company through rough terrain, impeded by rain squalls and typhoons, covering upward of twenty miles a day on weeklong excursions.[13]

A year after their arrival, Ethel gave birth to the first of three Butler children, a daughter named Ethel Peters after her mother but thereafter nicknamed "Snooks" after the tallest member of the Second Regiment, she having been immediately adopted as the smallest. The "crowd" got drunk to celebrate the event, and a few weeks later the Butlers gave a big Thanksgiving dinner for the enlisted men with baby Snooks as guest of honor.

Butler's tour at Olongapo ended on an uncertain note when he was sent home after being surveyed by a medical board which came to the conclusion, as narrated in *Old Gimlet Eye*, that he "had displayed evidence of a nervous breakdown." The actions that prompted this judgment were clearly aberrant when set against peacetime standards of cautious restraint expected of military professionals, who were well-advised not to run afoul of regulations and to "cover your ass" if things went wrong. On the other hand his behavior, again as narrated in *Old Gimlet Eye*, was not very different from the style and flair that would win him combat laurels in Nicaragua and Haiti a few years later.

He had been sent with fifty men to the far shore of Subig Bay to place guns in the mountains for defense against the Japanese naval threat. It was a "miserable existence"; heavy rains inundated tents pitched on steep slopes and there was a very restricted diet of hardtack, coffee, and canned beef. With rations running out and no resupply in the offing, Butler personally set out across the bay for Olongapo in a native outrigger accompanied by two enlisted men. They apparently were nearly drowned in a sudden storm which swept away the sail and paddles, but somehow made it to Olongapo where Butler obtained permission from the commandant of the navy yard, who "had swallowed considerable cheer to fortify him against the weather," to "do anything you want. Take anything you want." Butler loaded a tug with provisions and headed back across the bay, only to find the dock at his camp washed away by the storm. He then tore off the wooden falsework from the tug to build rafts onto which were lashed beef, vegetables, and other provisions; these were thrown overboard and drifted close enough so that the men ashore, forming human chains, could pull them in.[14]

Butler's service record indicates that he was detached from Olongapo in August 1907 and ordered home, having spent three weeks in the hospital at Cavité for an unspecified illness in late June and early July. According to a quasi-autobiographical 1931 newspaper account, he had undergone extensive tests which failed to explain loss of weight and "mental and physical lethargy." Back in the States he reported in person to the commandant following which he was assigned to temporary recruiting duty in Philadelphia, and in January 1908 he was granted nine months' sick leave, with no diagnosis mentioned. According to *Old Gimlet Eye*, he had come down with recurrent Chagres fever, originally contracted in Culebra, that caused him to run a temperature every day for several months after returning home. The navy medical board recommended high altitude and light employment based on suspicion of tuberculosis.[15]

Through a family friend, he landed a job as manager of a coal mine near Firecreek, West Virginia. Early every morning he took a dinner pail and went down to the mine, leaving his wife and baby alone for the day with two bulldogs in their mountain cabin. He fired the mine superintendent for drunkenness—facing a drawn pistol during the confrontation—and had recourse on several other occasions to marine methods in dealing with the miners, who were mostly "Hungarians and Slavs." And he was badly bloodied and bruised when thrown from a runaway coal car. Attempts at sociability with the lesser ranks that passed for egalitarianism in rigidly stratified military society did not work here; when the Butlers threw a Fourth of July celebration complete with cake, sandwiches, lemonade, and expensive fire-

works, none of the miners showed up. Smedley, learning from the experience, acknowledged that "they had an idea they were being patronized."
After giving serious consideration to a "tip top offer" to stay on at the mine,
he went to Washington for medical examination in September, passed, had
the unexpired portion of his sick leave canceled, and was duly reinstated in
the Corps. The marines were in his blood. The following month he was
promoted to major. He spent the next year on recruiting duty in Philadelphia
and at the navy yard.[16]

Throughout these years of Butler's itinerant postings to experimental
advanced-base exercises, tentative expeditions, provisional brigades and uncertain outposts, the Marine Corps had been an object of controversy in
Washington. Since the 1890s, the Corps's enemies in the political-military
hierarchy, especially strong in the navy, had sought to restrict or relegate its
functions, while powerful patrons, mainly in Congress, provided counter-
vailing support. Congressman Thomas S. Butler was in the forefront of this
perennial struggle, amply encouraged by his son Smedley.

The dispute came to a head in the fall of 1908 when Roosevelt took a
firm stand by severing the marines' principal link with the navy; they were
removed from thirteen major warships by presidential order. While they
were left with various other duties, such as garrisoning naval stations and
expeditionary service, the intent seemed clear. A few weeks after announcing the move Roosevelt wrote the army chief of staff, Leonard Wood, "I think
the Marines should be incorporated in the Army." As light infantry serving
in the army, the marines' jealously guarded integrity would have been nearly
obliterated. Roosevelt elaborated in private to Captain Archie Butt, his military attaché, blaming the marines for their own downfall: "They have augmented themselves such importance and their influence, has given them
such an abnormal position for the size of their corps that they have simply
invited their own destruction. I do not hesitate to say that they should be
absorbed into the army and no vestige of their organization should be allowed to remain. They cannot get along with the navy, and as a separate
command with the army the condition would be intolerable."[17]

Roosevelt's plans, however, ran afoul of such congressional opposition
that he was forced to equivocate, arguing during the final showdown in late
February 1909 that removal from the ships was intended to free the marines
for more important expeditionary duty, "services of value which they have
repeatedly rendered during the past decade," as they had in Panama. This
point had already been made by Admiral Dewey, who favored concentrating
marines so they could be embarked on "ships especially fitted to carry expeditionary forces and advanced base material." Had such a force been
available with him at Manila Bay, there would have been no Philippine In-
surrection.[18]

On 3 March during the final hours of Roosevelt's administration, Congress passed the 1910 Naval Appropriations Act with a rider that no funds be expended unless marines were returned to the warships. Congressman Butler, acting chairman of the Naval Affairs Committee during the Marine Corps hearings, played a key role in formulating the "Butler rider" and marshaling marine political supporters. Incoming President Taft, previously Roosevelt's secretary of war and like-minded regarding the marines, complained to Butt a few months later, "I am getting tired of having the orders of the Navy Department curtailed by Marine Corps officers lobbying at the Capitol, and the next time I hear of any such influence being used to check the government in its plans for this corps, one gentleman will find himself in the Philippines and another at Guantanamo." Butt was instructed to get the message to the two colonels involved, after which he wrote his sister-in-law that he knew what Taft meant: "He referred to the influence which the Marine Corps has built up in Washington by admitting sons of every Congressman who happens to have a boy who has failed at everything else." This applied most pointedly to Major Smedley Butler.[19]

But clearly there were limits on the Butlers' political influence even as both father and son gained in seniority and wiliness over the years. An early setback indicating the capriciousness of Washington politics, was their failure in backing Colonel Waller for the commandancy in 1910. Smedley, suspicious of a prolonged interregnum during which no appointment was made, wrote his father from Panama that it was "the entering wedge, by which the Navy Department intends to take over the whole management of our affairs, especially the spending of our money." He urged his father to push for Waller, who would no doubt have been a strong commandant representing the fighting Corps as against marine staff officers, Washington politicos, and the Navy Department.[20]

Waller appeared to have the job in hand when he was recommended by the secretary of the navy and approved by President Taft, but was then shunted aside in favor of Colonel William P. Biddle, who had strong personal connections in, ironically for the Butlers, Pennsylvania Republican politics. Taft, according to Archie Butt, "says he feels as if he were held up on the public road and relieved of his purse and watch. He had intended to name Major [sic] Waller, and this in spite of the fact that Waller had once been court martialled for shooting a few of the little Brown Brothers in the Philippines without a trial of any kind. But Waller is the idol of the corps and certainly the only man in the entire body who has any fitness for the position at the present time." Senator Boies Penrose had interceded emphatically on behalf of Biddle, scion of the proper Philadelphia Biddles, and Taft, not to mention the Butlers, was in no position to resist. Butt, commenting on "that which grips the President's conscience in the matter," narrated the episode as follows: "Penrose is a gentleman by birth, but a guttersnipe by instinct. He owns Pennsylvania, and every member from that state in the House and every office holder back in the state is an abject tool to him in politics. For instance, Representative Butler of the House, who has a son in the Marine Corps and who is Waller's greatest friend, withdrew his endorsement on a whisper from Penrose. Butler had actually fought for Waller and told the President that unless Waller was appointed his son would resign from the service. Penrose went to him and said: 'See here, I want you to withdraw from this Marine fight at once,' and Butler fell from it as if he had fallen from a ladder." Penrose went to Taft and told him bluntly that it was Biddle or else no support for the administration's legislative program. Taft "said he never saw a man more vulgar in his demand," but capitulated even in the face of Biddle's "unfitness."[21]

This was Waller's best chance for the commandancy, and failure cast a pall over the remaining years of his career. For Smedley, it was a demonstration of the fickleness of Washington politics. Soon he would experience fortuitous successes and failures in his own right. Meanwhile, mature, well-married, professionally experienced, he was nicely fixed to play a leading role as a field-grade officer in the series of Central American and Caribbean interventions that were now the marines' special preserve.

5 The American Kitchener

NICARAGUA

In November 1909 Butler took command of the Panama battalion, which shipped out from Philadelphia for the Canal Zone, crossing over immediately to Balboa on the Pacific side to board the transport *Buffalo*. The strategic function of the mobile Panama battalion, which Butler commanded until the opening of the canal in 1914, was to be ready on alert for expeditionary duty up either coast of Central America.

This entailed three successive missions to Nicaragua—Smedley dubbed them the "Punic Wars"[1]—which greatly furthered his experience in colonial warfare and international politics. As a young field-grade officer with irrepressible zeal and warrior instincts, he was the ideal commander for colonial small wars where adept light infantry operations could be the critical factor in discouraging resistance and efficiently consolidating American domination.

In the first venture, the *Buffalo* lay off Corinto on the Pacific coast of Nicaragua in early 1910 threatening intervention, while an incipient Conservative rebellion against the anti-American Liberal government fizzled across the country on the Caribbean coast. Corinto, Smedley recalled, was "the hottest place this side of hell . . . one thousand of us packed like sardines in our little transport." Three months of this were hard to take. Even after just a few weeks, he wrote his wife: "This is a d——d fool expedition anyhow, I would really like to know what Father's friend [Secretary of State] Philander Knox is trying to do. We have done absolutely nothing here but lie peacefully at anchor off the most sleepily peaceful country I have ever seen."[2]

While most of the marines were encamped on a nearby island in the Gulf of Fonseca, Butler's only stint ashore was a brief reconnaissance along the narrow-gauge, woodburning railroad connecting Corinto with Granada and the capital, Managua, in the interior. Two marine junior officers off the *Buffalo* submitted an intelligence report for this trip, describing detachments of barefoot infantry posted at stations along the line, some with old-fashioned rifles but others with good equipment. Recruits, marching under guard and often bound together with hands tied behind their backs, were being brought in from the countryside in what appeared to be a general mobilization.[3]

When it became apparent in March 1910 that the government had successfully contained the revolution at the Conservative stronghold in Bluefields on the Caribbean coast, the *Buffalo* returned to Panama, disgorging the marines, who went into camp first at Las Cascadas and then at Bas Obispo. In May, Smedley was joined by Ethel, their son Smedley, Jr., who had been born the previous year at Philadelphia Navy Yard, and three-year-old Snooks. Before the month was out the battalion was ordered on a few hours' notice to embark for Bluefields, where the Conservatives were surrounded and menaced with terminal defeat by a large government army. The regulars threatened to storm the town despite the commander of U.S. naval forces in the harbor having declared it a sanctuary. Mrs. Butler returned from a shopping trip to Panama City to find that Smedley had already left.

The crisis at Bluefields marked the abandonment of U.S. efforts to revamp Nicaraguan politics through peripheral gunboat diplomacy and sponsorship of regional anti-Zelaya diplomatic alignments. José Santos Zelaya was one of the more durable of the Liberal dictators who dominated Central American politics, broadly representing technological modernization, accelerated economic development, secularization, and the ambitions of an emerging commercial bourgeoisie. His sixteen-year rule, while marked by political repression and corruption, coincided with a significant start in coffee and banana production for export. But, as a belligerent nationalist, he abrasively monitored foreign business activities, canceled concessions, and was deliberately offensive in dealing with British and American representatives. His small-scale imperialistic incursions into neighboring states disrupted grander American attempts to consolidate the region as a U.S. sphere of influence.

The American military interventions of 1909-12 were decisive in toppling Zelaya and the Liberals. Anti-Zelaya revolutionaries began military operations on the Caribbean coast in October 1909 when General Juan J. Estrada turned coat. Given the remoteness of the region from population centers on the Pacific slope, plus antagonisms between Zelaya and foreign banana companies, the east coast was seething with pro-American, anti-Zelayista intrigues. Assistant Secretary of State F.M. Huntington Wilson noted that "the respectable American element doing business in Eastern Nicaragua, where, by the way, ninety per cent of foreign interests are American, seem unanimous in their approval of the [anti-Zelaya] attitude of this Government." Estrada, in a 1912 interview, said American commercial interests contributed $1 million to the 1909 revolt.[4]

The State Department was intent on getting rid of Zelaya, and it clearly foreboded military intervention with numerous expressions of official contempt. Secretary of State Knox, breaking diplomatic relations in late 1909, proclaimed Zelaya "a blot upon the history of Nicaragua," and President Taft publicly referred to him as a "medieval despot." Behind the scenes, Assistant Secretary Wilson, who had purview over Latin American affairs, characterized Zelaya as "an unspeakable carrion who mulcted his people of a huge fortune during his sixteen years of outrageous despotism which he rounded off with the brutal murder of two American citizens." [5] This pious rhetoric might well have been kept on file for reference to future U.S. client dictators.

Zelaya's downfall in late 1909 and the ensuing reduction of Nicaragua to an American protectorate were precipitated by his dogged, and in the circumstances provocative, financial independence. This ran hard against the incoming Taft administration's self-styled dollar diplomacy, whereby financial control was to replace military intervention as the primary mechanism of U.S. regional hegemony. By scrupulously paying Nicaragua's foreign debt, Zelaya not only avoided the snares of American fiscal arbitration but established solid enough credit to float a £1,250,000 loan with a European syndicate in the spring of 1909, despite strenuous State Department efforts to quash the undertaking. [6]

These intolerable disputes explain the bizarre American seizure of what was taken to be the last straw—the "brutal murder" of two American soldiers of fortune who were captured by government forces while serving in the field as commissioned officers in a rebel army. This was an extraordinary pretense, even in an age of extraterritorial rights for citizens of the Great Powers. The American mercenaries were duly shot, while a French colleague was spared in what seemed yet another pointed insult against the United States. Huntington Wilson wanted to seize Corinto in retaliation, but given the dubious legal grounds the United States finally opted for a break in diplomatic relations accompanied by official expression of support for the revolution.

Zelaya resigned in mid-December 1909 and left the country in order to forestall American intervention. The Zelayista Congress unanimously elected protégé José Madriz as the new president. Madriz, controlling the majority Liberal party and the government, proceeded to trounce Estrada and the Conservatives in the field while Butler and the marines lay menacingly off Corinto during the early months of 1910. By May, Madriz was on the verge of complete victory, with Estrada and the Conservatives reduced to last-ditch defensive positions under the guns of American warships at Bluefields. But the United States was undeterred.

It was at this point that the American consul in Bluefields cabled for marines from Panama to reinforce a hundred sailors sent ashore earlier in the month. Madriz forces, estimated at several thousand, were poised to attack the 400 revolutionists in the city. The consul calculated that continued frustration of the attack by U.S. interdiction would ultimately weaken the government side, camping out precariously in the forest as they were, far from their supply bases and increasingly insecure now that the rainy season was starting.[7]

Butler and 200 Panama marines landed on 31 May and cleared positions on the outskirts of the city from which both factions, in keeping with the U.S. pretext of neutrality, "could be held in check and American interests protected." By mid-June the company of sailors had been withdrawn, and Butler was left in command of a protracted marine occupation of Bluefields, connected by a field wireless set with three U.S. warships at anchor offshore. Butler, lampooning the mock neutrality in *Old Gimlet Eye*, said that he told government commanders they were free to attack, but only without firearms lest they accidentally hit American citizens, while the rebels were permitted to keep their guns. When government generals complained that this was unfair, Smedley replied suavely, "There is no danger of the defenders killing American citizens, because they will be shooting outwards, but your soldiers will be firing toward us."[8]

The marines moved directly into a Sunday School loaned for barracks by the Moravian Mission. Since the possibility of attack was virtually eliminated by their presence, they turned their attention to cleaning up the town—by now a routine facet of U.S. military occupations in the tropics. Yankee fastidiousness no doubt also reflected a general disdain for the surroundings. "Conditions are improved," Butler reported, "considering the vile state previously existing." Prisoners from the government army, working under guards furnished by the rebels, dug six miles of street ditching for drainage to the bay plus additional short feeder ditches "to empty pools of stagnant water, drain yards, out houses, marshes, etc."[9]

The command drilled regularly, avoided trouble with inhabitants, and prepared maps for the Bureau of Naval Intelligence. Marines rounded up and deported fifty foreign mercenaries, "beach-combers" and "tramps" according to Butler, originally hired through a New Orleans soldier of fortune to bolster the revolutionary army but now superfluous. A naval intelligence report referred to this "so-called Foreign Legion" as "renegade [sic] Americans," mostly "mercenaries [who] did no fighting whatever" and were "forcibly deported for the good of the country." So much for U.S. indignation at the aforementioned deaths of two of their colleagues![10]

Butler spent three months in Bluefields languishing in what he referred to as "the dull apathy of a third rate Central American port." The marine occupation broke the back of the government cause. It is unclear why, but the inability of the Madriz government to reestablish its authority in the face of determined U.S. interference apparently undermined it to the extent that the Liberal cause collapsed. Butler, in 1935, wrote facetiously that the Madristas "gave up in disgust" and retired from Bluefields to the town of Rama twenty-five miles inland. The rebels in Bluefields would have been content to stay where they were "and start levying taxes at once," except for State Department prodding: "Finally the revolutionists were convinced that they should attack Rama and defeat the government forces. We sent an American beachcomber on ahead to Rama to be sure there would be another American life to protect and then re-enacted the farce at Bluefields. . . . We forbade shooting by the government forces and they finally melted away, convinced of the hopelessness of opposing the revolutionists backed by the marines. The revolution ended then and there." [11]

In any case, Conservatives around the country asserted themselves, and their military forces succeeded in finally routing the Liberals. U.S. consuls reported a corresponding wave of strong anti-American resentment around the country, as in Managua where people roamed the streets shouting "death to the Yankees." The Madristas, with popular support estimated by the ranking British diplomat as 70 percent Liberal in tendency, became more emphatically identified with nationalism while the Conservatives, in attaining power, were reviled as handmaidens of Yankee imperialism. [12]

As Estrada entered the capital he received detailed U.S. demands including indemnities for the two mercenaries' deaths. A State Department envoy mediated the Conservatives' internecine disputes and organized a rump constitutional convention, Liberals excluded, which elected Estrada president. An American financial adviser assisted the new government in preparing for an American loan and customs receivership.

These arrangements proved ephemeral. U.S. intervention, having succeeded in overthrowing Zelayism and destabilizing the existing order, unraveled in the fecklessness of client-state politics. Arcane maneuvers were punctuated by the spectacular explosion of the government fort at La Loma overlooking Managua in which the garrison of sixty-five was lost, causing intense excitement and heightening the political confusion. In spite of dubious political underpinnings, the United States proceeded with dollar diplomacy schemes. Wall Street banks put up a loan secured by a lien on the government's National Railroad, and they financed a debt-refunding project secured by the customs receiverhip under supervision of an American nominated by the bankers and approved by the State Department. A new National Bank was organized under American auspices along with a Mixed Claims Commission of two Americans and one Nicaraguan. These measures left the United States not only in substantial control but committed to maintaining a client regime in Managua. But would dollars suffice as substitutes for bullets?

Increasing American control was paralleled by disintegration of the Conservative political coalition. President Estrada yielded to Vice President Adolfo Díaz who, amid accusations that he was selling out the country to the Americans, was set upon by Minister of War Louis Mena.[13] By mid-1912 Mena, supported by the Liberals, was in open revolt. President Díaz, described in a State Department memorandum as having a "slight following except from personal friends and a small minority who are pro-American in their ideas" in a country that was "overwhelmingly Liberal," now asked for U.S. troops to prop up his isolated regime. Anti-American demonstrations greeted Secretary of State Knox during a goodwill visit to Managua. Knox, "in view of the specific request of the Nicaraguan Government and of the seemingly possible danger of resultant anarchy," proposed sending Butler's Panama battalion to salvage the fragile satellite state.[14]

Smedley sailed with his battalion in the *Justin*, "a horrible little collier with no space down below so that the 350 of us will have to live on the iron deck in the rain." They had cleared camp at Bas Obispo, packed sixty days' equipment and supplies in railway cars for the trip to Balboa, and were on board ship ready to sail in a little over forty-eight hours. At sea Butler wrote home whimsically, "Well here we are again on our way to Corinto. I had hoped, when I left that 'hole' on March 16, 1910, never to see it again."[15] In fact, the upcoming campaign was to afford him full scope for his energy and talents, a wide-open command scenario unique even in the relatively tumultuous mode of emergency colonial relief expeditions. And the United States was no longer pulling its punches; this was to be a thorough campaign.

Even as the *Justin* was steaming up from Panama, the fortunes of the Díaz government were deteriorating perilously. A detachment of a hundred sailors from the *Annapolis* went ashore as an emergency legation guard on 4 August, so U.S. Minister George T. Weitzel was reasonably safe. But on the sixth, cable and rail connections between Managua and the sea were cut. The American corporation that held the lien on the railroad complained to the State Department that revolutionaries had seized its property, and also that Mena had commandeered several company steamships for military operations on Lake Nicaragua. The officer in charge on the *Annapolis* predicted alarmingly that, without the railroad, the route to the capital would be "impassable except for a very large and well equipped army."[16]

Tension mounted when the rebels attacked Managua with artillery bombardments and frontal infantry assaults, beginning on the eleventh as Butler's relief force was putting to sea at Balboa. Minister Weitzel's reports to Washington were heavily laced with moral outrage: the shelling had been done "wantonly and barbarously," Zelayistas were "pillaging and robbing without pretense of giving receipts," had "seized and tortured prominent merchants," and were sustained by "financial support from some secret source"—an allusion to suspected German or Japanese involvement. In a newspaper article several months later justifying "'Dollar Diplomacy' The Policy of Realities," Assistant Secretary Huntington Wilson stated that

American citizens "were exposed to violence in the very capital at the hands of what were no better than the Chinese 'Boxers.'" In the event, one American was slightly wounded. The siege terminated abruptly with the arrival of Butler's relief column on the fifteenth.[17]

Smedley and his 350 marines disembarked at Corinto and proceeded directly to Managua at night on the 75-mile railway, unobstructed through rebel territory, and reached the capital at 10 in the morning. In the following days Butler moved out of buildings provided in the city by American residents and erected Camp Weitzel on a school site near the Loma. The route to Corinto was now definitely cut as the revolutionary army drew away from Managua and concentrated at León, the former Spanish colonial capital and longtime Liberal stronghold, and at other points along the railway.

With Corinto itself threatened by an uprising, additional troops had to be landed from the *Justin* and *Annapolis* to bolster a paramilitary force of civilians from the American colony. At the same time twenty-five American and other foreign women and children were taken aboard *Justin* for safety. American forces went ashore at Bluefields to put out incendiary fires. On the seventeenth, a government army of about 500 was surrounded and massacred in the main square at León. These several developments fixed the broad outlines of the coming campaign. The mobile Panama battalion had proved adequate for holding the fort at Managua, albeit the client government's army was badly cut up in the process, but a durable solution on peremptory American terms required more thoroughgoing intervention. On the twenty-first, the Navy Department ordered the *California*, flagship of the Pacific Fleet, to Corinto "with all possible despatch," there to land forces and then steam south to Panama to pick up 750 additional marines being sent down forthwith from the advanced-base force at Philadelphia.[18]

In the following days it seemed that even these measures might be inadequate, and Weitzel, supported by Huntington Wilson, who was acting secretary of state, urged that rather than wait for marines, the army garrison at Panama be sent up immediately to land on the beach at Panaloya and attack inland. President Taft, observing that the situation was "analogous to the Boxer trouble in China" and fearing that Butler's marines might be "surrounded by a lawless band of cutthroats and overwhelmed by numbers," ordered the Tenth Infantry to Corinto but was subsequently dissuaded by Secretary of War Henry L. Stimson and by last-minute optimistic reports from the field. Stimson objected to bringing in the army, replying to Taft's order, "Most strongly urge advisability of sending marines [to] Nicaragua instead of troops [army], even at greater expense and delay. Greatly fear international aspect [that would be] caused by appearance of troops."[19] The marines, identified with transient gunboat diplomacy, might evade the stigma of outright invasion and conquest that would attach to regular infantry. While the army forthrightly garrisoned colonial regimes in Panama, Hawaii, Alaska, the Philippines and Puerto Rico, and its Fifteenth Infantry was similarly entrenched at Tientsin, the marines were establishing their preeminence as colonial infantry for surgical interventions where the United States preferred, for reasons of flexibility and limited liability, to emphasize a degree of continuity in local sovereignty.

For this, Butler's style and methods were deemed most appropriate. He now took charge of the capital's security, including control of the client government's soldiers. These he described as "poor little fellows they are scared to death." He wrote his wife, "this morning I practically took command of the Government Army of about 4,000 men and have been issuing instructions to Chamorra [government commanding general] all day—this move of mine must not become public for I really have no authority for such a course but it is the only way for this Government to win and the State Department, I surmise, is anxious that it should continue in power." [20]

The clamor for reinforcements was dramatized when the senior American officer in Managua, Commander Warren Terhune of the *Annapolis*, left by rail with a party of forty sailors and ten marines in an attempt to run the gauntlet and return to his ship at Corinto, testing the rebel envelopment of Managua in the process. The train, "flying Old Glory," according to an indignant cable forwarded to the State Department by Wall Street bankers from their representative in Managua, was "appropriated by rebels" at León. Terhune had met with a "very hostile demonstration" and, as reported by Weitzel, "was not allowed to pass, and the Captain considering himself threatened and menaced by superior armed force under General Baca abandoned the train and marched on foot back towards the Capital arriving here at five this morning." Hardly a bravura performance such as was needed to reassert American primacy. It had rained heavily throughout the episode, adding to the bedraggled appearance of the returning column. Terhune had not fought, had suffered no casualties, and reputedly lost his personal belongings. He was henceforth derisively nicknamed "General Walkemback" by the troops. Butler was disdainful and cavalierly demanded a chance to redress the humiliation. He wrote home, "If the Old Senior Officer Present [Terhune] and the Minister would only let me move I could open the railroad and the whole thing would be over in no time." [21]

Terhune approved a second attempt, in which Butler was to lead an advance escort of eighty marines and forty bluejackets. This was his first dangerous assignment as a field-grade officer. His letter to Ethel on the eve of departure betrayed a rare and vaguely hysterical streak of bombast: "I am going to Corinto this time or 'bust.' . . . it is not like Marines to sit still and especially as the idea prevails *very strongly* that Marines are not soldiers and will not fight. I can't stand any slur on Our Corps, Dearest, and I will wipe it off or quit." He added queasily that "if anything *should* happen to me bring my Blessed Son up with the idea firmly planted in his head that his Dadda was not a coward—whatever else he was (I mean hot tempered and profane at times) also my Precious Nooksie." [22]

Leaving Managua at midnight, the train worked its way slowly toward León, stopping often so that the men could repair torn-up tracks and crib over damaged culverts, putting to good use field training Butler had given them in Panama. The revolutionists had evidently been emboldened to confront the Americans, since the right of way had been passable during the Terhune fiasco a week before. Outside León, a rebel detachment demanded that the train return to the capital, but Butler bluffed his way through. Alexander A. Vandegrift, at the time a young lieutenant, retold the story in his memoirs "as an example of the flair for showmanship and desire for fun that were so characteristic of Smedley Butler": "With a fat rebel general looking on, two husky Marines cranked up a generator of a spark-gap radio that possibly would carry ten miles [Corinto was about twenty miles]. Standing with feet apart and hands on hips, Butler dictated to an operator who sent a great shower of sparks and odd noises. After thirty minutes Butler nodded imperceptibly to the men, who repeated the performance with the operator taking down [Admiral] Southerland's 'message.' Frowning in concentration Butler read this and then told the general he was sorry but orders were to carry on. So impressed was the poor man that he took his force and disappeared." [23]

Further down the line, they encountered the main rebel force manning a barricade of stones across the tracks. With the opposing forces facing each other across a trestle, Butler, as narrated in *Old Gimlet Eye*, stood up to a pistol-brandishing rebel general by simply disarming him with dime-novel audacity: "I couldn't retreat and lose face. If I signaled to the Marines to shoot, there would be a frightful slaughter. I had to act quickly. I made a grab for the General's gun and had the luck to tear it out of his hand. A bit theatrical [sic] I emptied the cartridges out of the barrel. His army burst out laughing. They could appreciate a joke, even when it was on them. I made the General ride with us as a hostage and the train proceeded across the bridge." [24]

Passing through León, the party was met by hostile crowds, but pushed on without violence after a show of calculated nonchalance. From León to Corinto, there were sixteen breaks in the tracks and several damaged bridges plus reports of mines that caused Butler to post Lieutenant Vandegrift at the front of the train as lookout. Vandegrift, subsequently commanding general at Guadalcanal and a commandant of the Marine Corps during World War II, was given his nickname "Sunny Jim" by Butler for having come through this episode with "a kind of grin" fixed to his face. [25]

The marines, safely in front of Corinto with Terhune sitting humbly in the rear of the train, were able to savor their triumph while waiting for naval working parties to ignominiously relay the last section of track which they had torn up as precaution against rebel attack. From Corinto Butler wrote his wife, "I am ashamed of my weakness in writing such rot to thee as I did before leaving Managua but everybody was sure, after the 'Captain's Retreat From Moscow' as it is called, that we would have trouble."[26]

Reinforced by several hundred sailors from the *California*, Butler set out immediately on the return trip to Managua in order to consolidate American control of the railroad. The rebels had in the meantime been busy dismantling the right of way, so the journey again involved repairing blown up track and bridges. At León there was another confrontation with the rebel army during which Ensign Harold C. Train vividly recalled "sitting on the flat car with my company and staring into the muzzle of a machine gun aimed at us." Again Butler gave short shrift to rebel threats and brazenly pushed on without incident. A few days later he wrote his wife, "My passages through Leon, coming and going, were, I think, the best jobs I have ever pulled off. The slightest slip or sign of weakness on my part would have meant a slaughter for, all agree, that my show of verve or bluff was what made the expeditions absolutely bloodless."[27]

Having left guards of 125 sailors at Chinandega, 300 at León, and squads of twenty at important bridges, Butler and seventy-five marines reentered Managua with a flourish on 22 September, crashing through the night past government outposts when the train's brakes failed. Smedley wrote home that he had "had exactly 17 hours sleep, was up every second of 5 nights and have lost 10 pounds," but that the "week I spent opening the railroad was the hardiest I have put in since the China troubles of 1900, I enjoyed it more thoroughly than any like period of activity since the Boxer campaign. . . . this is the most exciting experience American troops have had since China and I have apparently been the main 'guy.'" Within a few days, the consul at Corinto reported, "backbone of Liberal uprising appears broken by opening railroad." At León, Ensign Train was able to go into town unarmed and buy medicine for his men at a drugstore, and received a steer as a gesture of appeasement from the local revolutionary commander.[28]

Nevertheless, Minister Weitzel still pressed for infantry, and the buildup of marine reinforcements continued. Colonel Joseph H. Pendleton, Smedley's former commander at Olongapo, arrived with a force of about 1,150 that henceforth subsumed Butler's Panama battalion. But Smedley, although quite junior in rank, remained the sparkplug of forthcoming operations, having clearly established his preeminence in the tactics of colonial warfare—bold, imperious leadership of small units so as to bluff the natives into submission, thereby avoiding the escalating costs, perils, and embitterments attendant to massive violence.

Immediately upon Pendleton's arrival in Managua, Butler was sent to Corinto for a conference with Admiral William H.H. Southerland, commander in chief, Pacific Fleet, and henceforth senior officer in Nicaragua, to discuss plans for clearing the railway which at this point was still open only to Managua and only to American troops. Southerland, on instructions from Washington, issued orders defining the situation as "analogous to that of the Boxer uprising in China," with the military mission restricted to reopening communications, conventional protection of American life and property, and enforcement of "the rules of civilized warfare." No distinctions were made between rebel and government forces. Of course it was "obvious from the outset," as British diplomat H. Cavendish-Venables put it, that the American presence retrieved the status quo, personified by client-President Díaz. The posture of neutrality signified restraint in order to limit the extent of direct American intervention.[29]

Returning from the conference with Southerland, Butler rode a night train to Managua, waking up at 5:30 A.M. after three hours' sleep with a temperature of 104 degrees. His next assignment, opening the railway to the southern terminus at Granada, was delayed four days while he partially recuperated from recurrent malaria, which he described in a letter to his wife as "exhaustion fever . . . . I was pretty sick the first day, was so stiff I could hardly roll over in bed." The mission focused on the rebel stronghold at Masaya, midway between Managua and Granada on the railway, where a large government force had the rebels strongly invested on a fortified hill. Colonel Pendleton intended to send Butler and his battalion through to Granada, "even though in doing so it may be necessary to appear to be interfering in their fight."[30] Rebel General Benjamin F. Zeledón's position, encompassing the Barranca and Cayotepe hill athwart the railway at Masaya, had the reputation of being impregnable.

Butler, his Panama battalion, and one company of sailors pulled out of Managua on the morning of 15 September, heading south to confront Zeledón and the remaining rebel concentration under General Mena at Granada. His orders from Pendleton were to deliver a carload of food and Red Cross supplies to "the suffering people of Granada," while avoiding "any appearance of an alliance" with either side, with the additional nuance that "in taking these supplies to Granada it must not appear that this is the object of the expedition but that we are exercising our rights under orders." It was hoped Smedley would fox his way through. A few hours later the encounter opened with artillery fire from Cayotepe, three shots falling near the approaching train, which bore a prominently displayed U.S. flag. Butler backed up two thousand yards and sent a message to Zeledón declaring a "neutral attitude" and intentions to open the railroad and proceed through to Granada with Red Cross supplies, also threatening to attack if no reply was received. The marines and sailors bivouaced in and around the train and waited four days while Zeledón evasively deflected *pourparlers*, playing upon the apparent American reluctance to join the issue in a fire fight.[31]

On Zeledón's insistence, Colonel Pendleton and Admiral Southerland came forward to engage in what Butler referred to as "hot air" discussions with the "Spigs," giving Smedley, still feverish, a chance to drop out for two days' rest back in a hospital in Managua. Among other things, Zeledón claimed that American pretensions to ownership of the railroad were in fact "a violent seizure of property" inasmuch as "we Nicaraguans hold [it] to be National property," an arguable point since transfer of the railroad had been part of recent financial capitulations made by the Díaz cat's-paw regime to American bankers. The exchange of demands and protests culminated in the ultimatum that Zeledón surrender his positions threatening the railroad by 6 A.M. on the nineteenth or be driven out. At 4:15, with Butler back in command, the marines and sailors moved up in battle order with a battery of automatic guns to a position threatening the rebel trenches. Promptly at 6 A.M. Zeledón gave in, and by evening Butler's battalion was reloaded onto the train, ready to push on with what the rebels promised would be an unobstructed journey to Granada.[32]

Going up the grade through the rebel lines the light, narrow-gauge locomotives lost their traction on rails smeared with soap and milkweed so that the troops had to get off and pull the whole train up the hill. The engines were in the middle separated by boxcars, preceded and followed by a number of flatcars carrying troops and machine guns. Butler rode into the darkened rebel town of Masaya sitting on the lead flatcar next to the train's only light, a lookout lantern for switches and obstructions. Out of the darkness, as Smedley wrote a few days later, came a rider on horseback: "When he was about 10 yards away he pulled his revolver and fired right at me, probably at the lantern sitting by my side . . . . The ball missed me and hit a poor Corporal sitting beside and a little to the rear of me." This was apparently the cue for the ambush that followed, a brisk exchange of rifle and machine gun fire between the darkened town and the darkened train in which four American enlisted men were wounded. Butler subsequently reported having learned that sixty-eight rebels were killed and sixty wounded. The train proceeded through the town and stopped on the far side in front of government lines where the track had been torn up. The admiral commented, "Butler has his own Panama marines and is fully equal to the occasion. Expect soon to close the military side of this situation."[33]

A purported message from Zeledón to Mena, intercepted the following day by government forces and passed on to Weitzel in Managua, revealed a treacherous plan whereby Zeledón had intended to lure Butler into Masaya for the ambush and would now attack from the rear. Weitzel, waxing strong for a punitive scourge, cabled an elaborate report to Washington and noted with inferable dismay that he had shown the purported message to the admiral, "but he attaches no importance to it."[34] At this point the tactical military priorities of the intervention remained firmly fixed on limiting violence.

Butler approached Granada by rail the morning after the Masaya ambush. Progress was slow as breaks in the line had to be laboriously repaired, and the battalion halted at San Blas, four miles out, to relay a long section of torn-up track. Smedley opened negotiations with General Mena by demanding surrender of the railroad and other American property, warning that "the firing of even a single shot at us will mean an attack by this entire force, big guns and automatics." The railroad would be opened whether Mena consented or not. On the other hand, he emphasized that his purpose was to protect American lives and property: "My orders direct me to be strictly neutral, so should you consent to the free and unobstructed entry of trains into Granada, I shall not interfere with you to any greater extent than is necessary for the proper protection of my command." Later he sent a copy of Admiral Southerland's current campaign orders reiterating "absolute neutrality" of American forces and denial of the railroad to either side. In conclusion he also suggested, by negative inference, the possibility of American protection should Mena cooperate: in the event the Americans were forced to attack, "should you or any of your forces, fall into their [government] hands I shall be unable to assist or protect you." [35]

Mena, seriously ill and beset by military reverses, was in no position to resist. Butler concocted a martial demonstration featuring himself glaring down at Mena's representatives with feverish bloodshot eyes from an elevated camp chair. Nevertheless Mena hedged on several points. So, early on the morning of 22 September, Butler's 424-man battalion advanced on the town in battle array supported by three-inch field pieces and nine machine guns. At 5 A.M., still a mile from the city, a delegation came out bearing Mena's signed agreement to all the American demands. Marines and sailors repaired the last section of track into the railroad station, encamped nearby, and took over the American-owned steamers on Lake Nicaragua that were in port. All was quiet the remainder of the day and through the night. American officers went into the central part of the city without interference. This marked the completion of what had until this time been Butler's assigned mission, to open the railway and secure American property.

The final days had been particularly frantic. He wrote Ethel, "For a week I had had nothing to eat but quinine and limeade so I had not much strength." Racked with malaria, sallow with bloodshot eyes, Smedley had, as Vandegrift put it, "not only held on but carried on . . . he impressed not by words but by action. He was a fighter in the fullest sense of the word." Ensign (later Admiral) Train reminisced, "I can say without equivocation that he's the only man I've ever known well who was without any fear whatsoever." His feverish, assiduous leadership during the week's run to Granada earned him the most enduring of his many nicknames; his men began calling him "Old Gimlet Eye." Now he experienced the inevitable letdown. "I am so sick of it all," he wrote his wife, "am not strong I guess but all this rotten wrangling and bluffing makes me so tired." [36]

In fact, there was more duplicity than Butler, with his soldier's code of honor and combat-oriented directness, had naively thought. Less than twenty-four hours after entering Granada unopposed on the pretext of American neutrality, which he had personally guaranteed, he was forced to renege: "The situation has become very much involved over an order from the Admiral, received at 3.00 this morning, virtually changing our status from neutral to partisanship with the Government forces. This goes back on all the things I have told the rebels and I am therefore to be made scapegoat after I have done all the hard work."[37] American policy had shifted decisively, and indeed conveniently in terms of tactical timing, to the punitive emphasis long advocated behind the scenes in the State Department by Minister Weitzel and Acting Secretary Huntington Wilson.

The turnabout for Butler involved orders received on the morning of 23 September to stop 400 rebel troops who had been on the march for two weeks from León to join Mena. Smedley dutifully complied with the spirit of the new policy, though not without cost to his personal sense of honor: "The Leon people had already come in and of course could not be kept out. . . . I concluded that the most practicable way of preventing any movement of rebel troops in or out of the town was to shut them all up in their Barracks with our guards around them. . . . I hated my job like the Devil after writing to Mena two days before that I was entirely neutral, but orders are orders and of course I had to do it."[38]

Butler prepared an ultimatum, signed by Colonel Pendleton, who arrived at noon. Mena along with his 750 soldiers were, as Admiral Southerland found them when he arrived in the evening of the twenty-fourth, "practically barricaded in the three principal strategic positions in the town, i.e.— the three big churches [actually two churches and a hospital]—from which he had command of the principal streets." Mena later said that, despite Butler's having surrounded each site with a company, a large number of his soldiers got away in the night to join Zeledón at Masaya. The rebels were required to place all their artillery and machine guns in front of the churches for inspection as proof of good faith, which they did.[39]

Butler went to see Mena that night at the old San Francisco church, a large, thick-walled building with massive towers that contained most of the rebel rifles and ammunition. After passing through the cordon of marines, he was escorted by Mena's son, "who was a General of course," into the darkened sanctuary, which he described as "weird, the great emptiness of the Cathedral lighted only by ordinary American lanterns suspended from long ropes to the dome." He found Mena on a canvas cot, "the heart and soul of the Rebellion, groaning and moaning with Bright's Disease. He had been sick on his back since August 6th, just after the show started. . . . He remembered me being in Bluefields, but was too sick to talk much." Smedley then told him "the whole sad story" and asked for unconditional surrender. If Mena would "throw himself upon the mercy of the Admiral, I felt sure the Admiral would take care of him and remove him from the country, sending him to Panama on a warship. Mena pondered for a little while but finally consented." [40]

For Butler, there was one more trauma when the admiral received orders, reflecting the new punitive turn, to arrest and hand over to the client government all captured rebels: "I must admit that I just broke down at the thought that I should, a second time be required to break my word to Mena—but the Admiral patted me on the shoulder and said he would stick by me, that he had given his word to take Mena out and that he would cable Washington that the message had been received one hour and forty minutes too late." [41]

While Red Cross supplies were distributed to the beleaguered civilian population, Pendleton and Southerland left Granada taking along Mena, his son, and a body servant. The latter three were sent on to Corinto and thence on a warship to Panama where Mena, unable to walk, was admitted to the hospital at Ancón. Butler was left in command with orders to take charge of Granada and restore the original government officials to their posts. A few days later he was ordered to dispatch 300 Leonese Menistas out of the city after dark, each with a pass and perhaps, as Southerland suggested, "a little hard bread to start on" for the long walk back to León. [42]

The main rebel force was thus disposed of and the revolution's leader removed from the country, all done with relatively little violence thanks to the U.S. policy of restrained intimidation plus deceit, neatly executed through Butler's tactics of wrangle and bluff. There remained the last rebel stronghold at the Barranca, where Zeledón with about eight hundred men was still holding out, surrounded by over three thousand government troops. Southerland reported that, from past experience, he had "every reason to believe that the Government forces will remain inactive and simply follow at our heels to reap the fruits of our work." Indeed, because of government fecklessness, the marines had to repair and operate the railroad themselves, for which Southerland requested two additional battalions. [43]

Huntington Wilson, whose role has been elucidated in detail by historian Richard D. Challener as decidedly "more militaristic than the military," had throughout the campaign urged upon a reluctant President Taft a policy of vigorous repression so that "the moral effect upon the whole revolution-ridden region of Central America and the Caribbean should be greatest." In a sense, this was Butler's field tactics of bluff and intimidation writ large. But Wilson's punitive emphasis required salutary carnage which, combined with scornful U.S. rhetoric, would presumably humiliate, terrorize, and thereby obliterate all miscreants. American military on the ground in Nicaragua had previously avoided confrontation in the interests of minimizing antagonisms and building a conciliatory peace, more in keeping with the "dollars for bullets" option. In Wilson's approach the *latinos* were given scant credit for national pride or idealism, a brutish people best managed by brute force. Punitive war as an instrument of policy, rooted in contempt, was being introduced from the highest level of civilian politics at a critical point in the accelerating buildup of U.S. regional hegemony. Taft's acquiescence in the hard-line policy had triggered Butler's turnabout in Granada and now set the stage for the dubious Battle of Cayotepe.[44]

Pendleton, with 500 marines and sailors, approached from the north while Butler and 400 came up from Granada in the south. Zeledón was informed of the policy of the U.S. government that "no disturbers be permitted to occupy any position menacing the railroad," and of President Díaz's terms of surrender, which were similar to those offered Mena. Pendleton, on the eve of the battle, speculated that Zeledón would "take all the time that is allowed and then will probably crawl down." Instead Zeledón replied defiantly, referring to George Washington, Abraham Lincoln, and "the Great American Nation that prides itself on being the guiding spirit of the Democratic Republics of the American Continent." He would mount "the resistance that the case requires, and that the dignity of Nicaragua, which we represent, demands, and, afterwards, there will fall upon you, your chiefs, and the mighty nation to which you belong, the tremendous responsibility which history will set forth and the eternal reproach of having employed your arms against the weak, who have been fighting to reconquer the sacred privileges of the Fatherland."[45]

On 3 October, as Smedley wrote his wife several days later, "we were all up at daylight with or eyes fastened on the hills for white flags, everybody afraid they would appear and again cheat us out of a scrap." There were no white flags. Promptly at 8 A.M., deadline for surrender, Butler opened fire with three field guns joined by two more American guns firing from another sector in an attempt to raze rebel fortifications on both Barranca and Cayotepe. There was no answering fire from the rebels' two Krupp guns. Before dawn on the fourth, Butler and his battalion started up the southeast slope of Cayotepe while Pendleton closed in from the east. Government troops who were to have taken part in the assault "did not materialize," according to Pendleton's report, but formed about a mile and a half away near Masaya. The Americans closed the gaps in their attack formation and, shortly after 5 A.M., launched a "spirited assault" that overran the main rebel defensive position and planted an American flag on top of Cayotepe in thirty-seven minutes. Zeledón's forces were then driven from trenches and gun positions connecting along a ridge to the Barranca itself, where the marine company that had led the attack and suffered most of the casualties "was given the honor of placing the flag on the Barranca, and marched out to that duty with colors flying and bugles playing—cheers were plentiful." Pendleton estimated that the rebels lost about sixty killed, fifteen or twenty wounded. The rest escaped westward. The United States lost four marines dead and five marines and sailors wounded.[46]

The final bloodletting of the campaign took place three days later in León when sailors and marines marched into the city in accordance with prior surrender arrangements with the rebel commanders and received a volley from a band of reportedly drunken rebel soldiers. Three sailors were killed and two seriously wounded; an estimated fifty insurgents were killed in the return fusillade. Relating the news to his wife, Smedley commented, "It is terrible that we should be losing so many men fighting the battles of these d——d spigs—all because Brown Bros. [one of the New York banking houses] have some money down here."[47]

Resentment against the crass economic motives behind American military interventions was commonplace in the contemporary officer corps, which saw its high codes of honor being prostituted for commercial ends.[48] In Butler's case, skepticism regarding American motives and resentment at being shamed in deceitful subterfuges were offset by personal and professional achievements. As the campaign drew to a close, he wrote home that everyone was praising him, that he was considered "the whole show." Colonel Pendleton submitted an exceptionally laudatory report referring to initiative, courage, intelligence, efficiency, astute handling of men, and "personal conduct under fire . . . such as could only add to his well known record in the past in this respect." Weitzel singled him out first on the list of "special mention" stalwarts submitted to the State Department. At home, the *St. Louis Globe Democrat* ran a front-page 3 by 5-inch picture with the caption, "U.S. Marines Commander Narrowly Escapes Death in Nicaraguan Affray." At a large celebration dinner in Managua, he was hailed in a speech by an Englishman as the "Kitchener of Nicaragua." Along with the kudos went a fearsome reputation. He wrote home that an American told him "that she had understood I was a sort of walking Devil—that I was a regular fire eater—could just look at a Nicaraguan and scare him to death." In León, an antigovernment newspaper denounced "the blond pigs of Pennsylvania advancing on our garden of beauty." A decade later, an anti-imperialist American magazine, *The Nation*, reported Nicaraguan mothers still using the admonition, "Hush! Major Butler will get you," to frighten their children.[49]

Smedley's distaste for the intervention's political underpinnings was heightened when he was dismissed from command at Granada, in deference to returning Conservative officials. After Cayotepe he had again taken up administering the city and arranging transfer of power to the government party. But when he tried to redistribute captured war booty to rightful owners, the Conservative politicos "realized that I was in earnest and *honest* . . . [and] intended to search the *gang's* houses and seize their *loot*," and appealed to Southerland. The admiral promptly relieved Butler rather than alter concessions made to the client government. Smedley felt "terribly snubbed," but as consolation was given a medal and petition of gratitude for having justly restored order, signed by 216 Granadan women who in an annotation by a local physician were described as "of the best social position in the city." A company of marines was left behind to buttress the new political order.[50]

In a gesture toward revamping the country's military and police forces and stripping them of potential for rebellion against inherently unstable minority client governments, Butler promoted the creation of a Nicaraguan constabulary, to be developed under American auspices. "Tuesday," he wrote his wife, "I spent talking 'Mounted Constabulary' to the Bankers and other controlling interests in Managua. . . . This proposition all the decent people—to say nothing of the representatives of our investors—heartily endorse and approve of but the 'Government Crowd,'—that is the 'McNichol Gang'—are dead set against it as it spells the end of 'graft' and that is what the party in power lives on."[51] Colonial constabularies or "native police," such as the Khyber Rifles and German African *Schutztruppe*, were commonplace around the world, and the United States had itself recently created the Philippine Constabulary using U.S. Army officers and equipment.

These forces were designed to be impervious to local political factionalism, anchoring whatever government emerged in the flux of colonial and comprador politics. In practice such structural pacification often yielded durable military dictatorships. In Nicaragua, a marine-sponsored Guardia Naçional obliterated revolutionary "banditry" in the early 1930s and served as a unitary power base upon which its commander, Anastasio Somoza, built the client dictatorship that survived for more than four decades, throughout which there would be little concern over stigmas of brutality, corruption, and greed for which the United States had belabored Zelaya. Butler himself, declining suggestions that he stay on for police work in a private capacity, would soon found the Gendarmerie d'Haiti.

A Nicaraguan constabulary scheme would have to await subsequent developments. Instead, Admiral Southerland ordered a mounted expedition into the interior for reconnaissance "and in order to show the flag and demonstrate the power of the United States Government." Butler, who went along as second in command to Colonel Pendleton, felt that the admiral was also anxious to "reassure a lot of Americans living up there." The trek entailed two weeks' hard riding through driving rains and across swollen streams. Outside Matagalpa in the central highlands the party was welcomed by seventy mounted Americans, other foreigners, and local officials, and escorted into town. Upon returning to Managua, Pendleton reported great success in impressing Nicaraguans that U.S. forces could be "depended upon to go anywhere, at any time," and that "the United States Government does not intend longer to tolerate Central American Revolutions, such as have been almost constant in this distressed country for more than twenty years."[52] On the latter point he ignored the sixteen-year *pax Zelayista*, which had been terminated by the U.S. destabilization, followed by violent pacification on American terms. American rhetoric henceforth emphasized the blessings of peace and stability under the new order.

To the familiar preoccupation with law and order characteristic of all imperial systems, the United States, model republic of the hemisphere, added a preoccupation with constitutionalism. This meant legitimization by nominally democratic processes, and Nicaraguan elections in November 1912 exemplified the ritual democracy supervised by American troops around the region during this period. While Butler was off showing the flag in the central highlands, the admiral prepared for elections along the occupied line of rail, including dispatch of "an expeditionary force" to outlying towns that were "extremely Liberal in politics." There were no disturbances, either to public order or to the affirmation of minority Conservative rule. Díaz was the only candidate for the presidency; Liberals did not participate. Years later as a major general, Butler created a stir by publicly referring to these elections: "The opposition candidates were declared bandits when it became necessary to elect our man to office. Our candidates always win. In one election nobody liked the fellow; . . . the district was canvassed, and 400 were found who would vote for the proper candidate. Notice of the opening of the polls was given five minutes beforehand, the 400 voters were assembled in a line and when they had voted, in about two hours, the polls were closed." His letters home in 1912 reflected the same sarcasm, but privately.[53]

Admiral Southerland pulled out his cruisers on 14 October, and Pendleton, Butler, and most of the marines shipped out a week later from Corinto in the troopship *Buffalo* bound for Panama. Colonel Pendleton, wanting to go back to Philadelphia, had a scare on receiving an inquiry about the extent of provisions he and Butler were carrying, sounding as if Panama would be a reprovisioning stopover for a new expedition. He wrote Southerland, probably without irony but wise to the ways of his trade, "I feared from the inquiry from Captain Halford regarding ammunition and clothing, that it might be another Cuban election."[54]

Whether the militarization of American regional policy was necessary or wise was disputed at the time, and, following the spate of military interventions characteristic of Woodrow Wilson's presidency, the trend was for several decades renounced as counterproductive and aberrant. British diplomats, assessing the 1912 Nicaraguan intervention from a comfortably detached and perhaps condescending point of view, were skeptical as to what the United States had accomplished. Godfrey Haggard in Guatemala noted that 3,000 U.S. troops were the largest number ever landed in a country not at war, and that this placed the Díaz government under virtual American protection, "guaranteeing it," for better or worse, against all opposition. Cavendish-Venables in Managua reported: "I do not think that even among the Conservative element the intervention has been popular. . . . It had lasted some ten weeks and cost over 2,000 lives. A barbarous and futile combat; it has established no principle, pacified none of the discordant political elements in the country, and has left Nicaragua morally and economically weakened." In London a Foreign Office official commented that while the United States had "no doubt scored a triumph . . . their act does not seem to have brought them any increase in popularity, and is indeed barely justifiable even in a Central American Republic."[55]

For Butler and the marines, the new emphasis on militarization meant plenty of action and scope for professional advancement. Depending on how positively the United States wished to assert its regional power, the marines remained the obvious choice for those interventions where restraint short of outright invasion and formal colonial occupation seemed prudent. They could easily upgrade from landing parties to punitive expeditions as need arose. And Smedley Butler was the conquering prodigy—in Nicaragua perhaps "the whole show"—among junior field-grade officers needed to lead small detachments in this multifaceted type of warfare.

6 The Spy
PANAMA, MEXICO

Returning to Panama in late November 1912, Butler put his battalion back into camp and then left on seven weeks' home leave to rejoin Ethel and the two children for Christmas at West Chester. The family sailed back to Panama in January, settling in at Camp Elliott for the last of a four-year stint, not counting time off for the three Nicaraguan interventions. There were no more expeditions, so the battalion resumed training and played its role as part of the Canal Zone garrison prior to the army takeover when the canal opened in 1914.

The canal had been building since Butler's first visit during the 1903 revolution. By 1912 there was a substantial American colony complete with American-style homes, churches, baseball, YMCA, band concerts, bowling, dances, bridge parties, fireworks on the Fourth of July, and at least one circus per year stopping off en route to Los Angeles. The canal works employed a racially segregated polyglot force of 50,000, about half of whom were black British West Indians. A large American military establishment of soldiers, sailors, and marines contended with the motley host of contract laborers for such seedy attractions as were offered by the red-light districts just outside the Zone in Colón and Panama City. These potential brawlers, mostly young, deracinated aliens in an expatriate no-man's land, confronted an increasingly hostile indigenous population.

The big smashup during Butler's era came in 1912 just before the third Nicaraguan expedition. Disturbances started after a sports competition between army and marines in Balboa and degenerated into what the *New York Times* called a "common riot." Brawling marines and soldiers hit the bars in the red-light district across the line in Panama City. Panamanian police lost control and clumsily fired, killing and wounding about a dozen Americans, and were in turn attacked by the mob. Butler arrived on the scene and, as he recalled in *Old Gimlet Eye*, tried to "hurl thunder" at the men, but with little effect as the troops were by now "drunken mad and vicious." Ultimately they were herded into the railroad station, which was cordoned off until trains could clear them out to the camps.[1]

By contrast Camp Elliott, on a hill at the end of the gigantic Culebra Cut fifteen miles inland from Panama City, was remote from the honky-tonks and ugly tensions of the port cities, a secluded monastic enclave dedicated to marine virtues. Butler, a meticulous dresser for proper occasions, which for him included barracks routine, required formality despite the oppressive climate. This was a showcase post for the Marine Corps, often visited by top U.S. politicians on inspection junkets. When not off on expeditions, the 400 men in the battalion trained at useful skills: rifle shooting, hiking, making bridges out of trees and lashings, railway roadwork, and the like. Discipline was strict, with morning reports in 1910 indicating a special problem with drunks, a dozen or so every day out of 700 then in camp. Julian C. Smith, who served as a lieutenant in one of "Butler's two famous Panama battalions" later observed, "If you got by without getting court-martialled, you were lucky . . . . I won't say it was a particularly happy command, but we had a very efficient command. Butler was a hard worker."[2]

Camp Elliott was a frequent stopover, more so as the canal neared completion, for politicians who came down to view the great engineering wonder of the day. President Taft dropped by for lunch, chatted about Pennsylvania politics while reviewing the troops, and held Snooks and Smedley, Jr., on what there was of his lap. Representative Thomas S. Butler passed through with a congressional delegation, paying due attention to his son's efforts and to his new grandson, Thomas Richard Butler, born in the Zone. In late 1913, Secretary of War Lindley M. Garrison came accompanied by Colonel George W. Goethals. Smedley wrote exultantly to his father that Goethals "always likes to show us off" and that "the men fairly out-drilled themselves." During a tour of camp facilities, Garrison was "dumbfounded" and "much pleased" at seeing all the work done by the marines themselves—no need for local labor or civilian technicians.[3]

On returning to the States, Garrison mentioned Smedley to Secretary of the Navy Josephus Daniels, a progressive Democrat intent upon introducing education and wholesome living into the naval services. Daniels, in his memoirs, asserted that "the whole value of schools was first impressed upon me" by Garrison's observations, which had Butler and other officers teaching Spanish to marines.[4] The story is suspect in that Butler was always useless at foreign languages despite years of exposure. The education program in Panama, like his subsequent involvement in Daniels' marine schools program, was mainly vocational. At any rate, this was an early indication of kindred spirits, foreshadowing future collaboration.

At the same time, true to the warrior instinct for perseverance in the field, Butler was relentlessly hostile to war colleges and professional schools. Neither the starch and polish at Camp Elliott nor his lifelong fascination with spiffy military regalia implied giving any quarter to highbrow pretensions within the Corps. Nor did his scrupulous deference to the bourgeois proprieties of the civilian political world. Indeed, excellence in the proprieties was a corrective to any suggestion of lowbrow vulgarity that might otherwise attach to the warrior cult. Lieutenant Smith recalled that in Panama "Butler always referred to me as a high brow because I had this little extra education"—this for having studied artillery at Advanced Base School. "He had hardly a high school education himself. He always threw up this business of going to school. He didn't believe in it. He said people were trying to make the Marine Corps high brow, and he wanted to be roughneck. He asked me which I would prefer, I said, 'I don't care. I can be either one of them.'"[5] Not Butler; his articulateness in correspondence and considerable executive abilities were essentially self-taught.

In early 1914, seven months before the canal opened, Butler's marines were withdrawn from Panama and dispersed to warships patroling off the Gulf Coast of Mexico. Smedley was ordered to report as battleship squadron marine officer. He was extremely distressed both at leaving Panama and at his new orders, and complained heatedly in a long letter home to his mother: "Bunny and I stop every few minutes to look around at our beautiful Camp and *home* [double underlined], and I tell thee it is almost more than we can bear . . . . to have the Marines, who took this place withdrawn *entirely* before the ships go through is terribly hard. I only hope something terrible will happen to our enemies in the Navy Department."[6]

As for losing his own independent command and being ordered to the fleet, he intended to apply for orders home "as soon as I find there is nothing doing in Mexico." He had "spent the best four years of my life here and the happiest and most successful," and now would "have to go back to a subordinate position under some old fool." The only command independent of the navy was the Washington Barracks, and he could not get that unless Colonel Waller was appointed commandant. Alternatively, Colonel Goethals had offered to take him along on his next civilian job, possibly the police commissionership of New York City, in which case Smedley would be deputy commissioner. He concluded bleakly, "Ah Mother we are both so unhappy we can hardly bear it." In communicating his "keen disappointment" to Daniels, he referred to the opportunity Camp Elliott had afforded "to make useful citizens as well as first class Marines," and noted that the educational programs the secretary had admired were now "necessarily cut short."[7]

Smedley's sense of professional well-being was presently dealt another blow. Although first in seniority, Waller was passed over in favor of Colonel George Barnett, a somewhat lackluster functionary with an unblemished record and almost no combat experience who, as the first Naval Academy graduate to attain the commandancy, embodied the new trend to bookish professionalism. Following Waller's eclipse by Biddle in 1911, this second depreciation boded ill for the old-guard fighting corps. Waller, a southern Democrat, had run afoul of Senator Penrose and the Republican Taft administration in the earlier episode. Now he had the endorsement of thirty-one senators, not to mention Congressman Butler. But he was shot down by the Democratic and southern-cast Wilson administration in the person of North Carolinian Josephus Daniels, who objected, on moral and political grounds, to Waller's record of atrocities in the Philippines. Although acquitted by court-martial, Waller "was of the old-type officer and, like most of them, believed the Filipinos were an inferior people." Daniels preferred the young and talented Lieutenant Colonel John A. Lejeune, a southerner and academy graduate, but Lejeune was unacceptably low in rank and in the end Daniels opted for Barnett as a feasible compromise.[8] Smedley Butler was left without strong inside connections in the upper reaches of the Corps hierarchy, except insofar as his friend Lejeune was subsequently appointed assistant commandant.

Butler and his battalion left Panama in January 1914 to join battleships of the Caribbean Squadron stationed off Veracruz on prolonged naval watch. Simultaneously, an Advanced Base Brigade was mobilized under Lejeune for exercises with the fleet at Culebra, the largest field demonstration of advanced-base tactics to date and the first since Olongapo. As with the 1903 Culebra exercises, the massing of naval and expeditionary strength in the Caribbean supported current strategic initiatives, focusing on the revolution in Mexico. Army troops had been massed on the Mexican border and warships carrying marines had been picketed along the Gulf Coast for more than a year already. An additional troopship and marine regiment were kept on call at Guantánamo.

The Mexican intervention up to this point had been an overblown exercise in gunboat diplomacy, with a battleship division in lieu of erstwhile gunboats, presumably indicating greater American resolve commensurate to the larger scale of U.S. interests ashore. As in Panama, Honduras, and Nicaragua, a revolution was in progress which the United States wished to constrain and manipulate, but here the country was unmanageably large and disorganized, the violence more widespread and deeply rooted in mass discontent, and rival machinations by other great powers compromised U.S. regional primacy. And, perversely, the extent of American investments ($1 billion) and prospects (oil) was much greater. How an awesome offshore naval demonstration and saber rattling at the border would influence chaotic events hundreds of miles in the interior was never clear from the outset, and, for want of a more cogent rationale, American policy was inaptly characterized by President Woodrow Wilson as "watchful waiting."

President Woodrow Wilson was a progressive Democrat, rhetorically critical of big business and sympathetic to victims of oppression. But in practice he readily adopted established procedures for dealing with weak satellite states. Indeed Woodrow Wilsonian moral uplift on a regional scale came to bear a striking resemblance to Huntington Wilson's moral purgation of Nicaragua. American strategic and economic interests remained paramount throughout. Military intervention was the common denominator.

In January 1914, British Ambassador Sir Cecil Spring-Rice had a talk with his old friend U.S. Army Chief of Staff Leonard Wood, in which the Mexican scenario was placed squarely within the past and future continuum of colonial-style military interventions. Observing that Wilson would not recognize the current military strongman, General Victoriano Huerta, Wood said (as paraphrased by Spring-Rice):

> There was now no alternative, as no one of the Constitutionalists [Huerta's rivals] was strong enough or respectable enough to deserve recognition. The necessary—the absolutely necessary—result was some form of intervention. General Wood did not regard the task of pacification as very difficult. The immense majority of the Mexican people were wholly indifferent to politics. With regular pay it would be possible to organize the *rurales* into a good police force. He had done the same in Cuba. As to the initial difficulties (those of a more decidedly military character) he thought very little of them. He did not think that the loss on the American side would exceed 2,000 or 3,000 men. The subsequent operations should, he thought, be entrusted to a native gendarmerie with American inspectors. . . . [Wood] did not believe for a moment that the Administration had now, or ever had had, a deliberate plan in Mexico. . . . Order must in the end be established, and in default of annexation, (to which the objections were, in his opinion, insuperable) he thought the end might be secured by an American-controlled native gendarmerie.[9]

This prescription almost exactly fits the Wilsonian intervention in Haiti the following year, in which Butler and Waller would play leading roles, and it indicates the practical options for asserting American power in Mexico.

On assuming office in 1913, Wilson had withheld diplomatic recognition from General Huerta and was therefore ironically stuck with pro-Huerta diplomats who had abetted Huerta's counterrevolutionary coup in the famous Pact of the [U.S.] Embassy. Sending a new ambassador would itself be tantamount to recognition. The embassy in Mexico City was therefore circumvented by sending special diplomatic agents who gathered information and made contacts pursuant to Wilson's anti-Huerta policy. Wilson's premier special agent, John Lind, former progressive governor of Minnesota, was inexperienced in diplomacy and represented a fresh point of view that might lead to a breakthrough in what was fast becoming an inextricable tangle of violence and intrigue.

In late 1913, after two months in Mexico, Lind reported the outlines of a future policy to his good friend Secretary of State William Jennings Bryan: trade with Mexico was "worth more to United States than the trade of South America for next fifty years." Therefore, it was "of vital importance that we secure confidence and good will of part of Mexican people if we cannot of the whole. . . . sooner or later we will be compelled to come in to assist at least in the establishment of order and it would in my judgment be most desirable if we could come with the friendship and good will of the most efficient portion of the people. Coming under such circumstances it would be a bloodless campaign." [10] Presumably Lind and his superiors were looking to collaborate with a "progressive" segment of the Mexican bourgeoisie that would forgo nationalism in favor of reciprocal benefits under American patronage. A Mexican counterpart to Nicaragua's Adolfo Díaz would have been ideal.

It was a patently neocolonial and, under the circumstances, inoperable scheme that showed very little sensitivity to the dynamic forces of revolutionary nationalism in Mexico. Little wonder that Lind soon preferred military methods. Unable to achieve any diplomatic leverage, he observed imperiously that "Mexicans respect power and nothing else," and presently recommended that "a demonstration of power justly, efficiently and generously exercised is the most effective argument we can make." [11]

Pressure on the United States intensified as escalating revolutionary violence threatened not only Huerta but, contingently, British and American oil interests in Tampico and the large foreign colony in Mexico City. Foreign nationals demanded protection, and the various powers dispatched warships to both coasts. Any joint intervention, such as the Boxer campaign, would seriously weaken U.S. regional ascendancy, particularly as the British strongly favored Huerta. Moreover, the British admiral offshore outranked American Admiral Frank Friday Fletcher and would therefore be entitled to command any international expedition, while the ranking officer in Mexico City, who would by rights command the international force of legation garrisons, was the German minister, Admiral Paul von Hintze. [12]

So, by early March 1914 Lind, in close consultation with Admiral Fletcher, was coordinating plans for an immediate, unilateral American military thrust: "Every day of Huerta's further continuance [is] a distinct and serious menace, not only to the future welfare of Mexico, but to our own relations with the nations interested in Mexico. . . . If there is no decided change by the fifteenth I believe he should be eliminated within forty-eight hours after that date. It can be done and our preparations at this end are so complete that I believe it can be accomplished without the military loss of an American [life]." Preparations, bearing strong resemblance to the reliefs of Peking in 1900 and Managua in 1912, were entrusted to Major Smedley Butler. Upon hearing that Butler might be superseded in command, presumably by someone senior in rank corresponding to large numbers of troops, Lind cabled Bryan that this would be "most unfortunate." Smedley was a "discreet and efficient, experienced military man" and "in absolute accord" with Admiral Fletcher.[13]

On 1 March, Fletcher and Butler went ashore at Veracruz, where they met the American superintendent of the Inter-Oceanic Railway and surreptitiously rode in his private car up the line seventy-five miles to Jalapa and back. This, Butler wrote his wife, "was arranged that I might have a chance to talk over an expedition I was planning." He was to go alone as a spy into the interior and then draw up a comprehensive invasion plan: "I want to stay so badly now [his orders home were being rescinded] for Dearest I have the most spectacular job in my hands that any American in my day has been entrusted with."[14]

In reporting Butler's mission to Washington, Fletcher noted that the gunnery officer of the HMS *Suffolk* had already been in Mexico City for several weeks, staying at the British legation. Fletcher and Lind had also been anxiously keeping track of a buildup of machine guns, ammunition, and troops in foreign legations which, as Lind put it, "in effect places the Huerta Government, so far as the Powers are concerned, in the same class with China and the semi-civilized countries of the East." The British fully appreciated the Boxer analogy and U.S. sensitivities.[15] The planned marine expedition, preempting military action by the other powers, was to consist of one or more units of one thousand men to advance on Mexico City with the cooperation of railroad authorities. Fighting with Mexican armies was "not contemplated," as there might be "an upheaval in Mexico City where the organized forces of both contestants have become demoralized. In such a state of confusion it is believed to be practicable to put through a force of one thousand Marines before being opposed by any organized force." To this end the admiral was utilizing "the valuable experience and knowledge of Major Butler."[16]

Butler set out by train on his spy mission, stopping at Puebla, the major city and military concentration on the route to Mexico City. Here he reconnoitered with a railroad official, visiting tourist sites and making military observations while posing as a former Canal Zone employee representing "some capital looking for a place to lose itself." Puebla, he wrote Ethel a week later, was "a pretty good town, quite civilized and up to date," with "some rather decent looking people." The train to Mexico City was a "wonderful ride" up over 9,000-foot mountains and then down into the Valley of Mexico. On his first night in the capital, he "could not sleep at all, due to the rare air and the incessant working of my brain."[17]

His arrival at the U.S. embassy was melodramatically recorded by Edith O'Shaughnessy in the published version of her letters home, *A Diplomat's Wife in Mexico* (1916): "As I was reading last night, waiting for dinner to be served, a visitant, rather than a visitor, appeared in my drawing room *incognito*—a simple 'Mr. Johnson,' eager, intrepid, dynamic, efficient, unshaven!" Posing as a railroad official, and thereby exploiting the Huerta government's solicitude toward American business interests, Butler spent three days visiting the several federal garrisons in the city accompanied by the chief railroad detective. They were ostensibly searching for a missing railroad employee who was thought to have been drafted. As Lind reported with relish, "they did not find him but they located every gun in the possession of the Mexican army in the city and noted its size and state of efficiency." Additionally, the railroad lines were checked and "absolutely correct maps obtained. No detail has been omitted." [18]

Butler returned to Veracruz on 7 March with up-to-date information to support his invasion plan. Several days later he wrote proudly to his wife that his efforts "were characterized by the Admiral as *brilliant* and so enthused Governor Lind that he cabled my resultant scheme to the President and recommended it as a solution. . . . It is enough to say, Darling, that if the President approves Mr. Lind's recommendations and I can get away with it, I will make good to thee my promise, when we were engaged, to be a great soldier." The spying adventure had been "simply great—especially the different disguises as to object, I assumed." [19]

As against the above account based on contemporary sources, Butler's subsequent autobiographical, fictionalized versions follow the same basic story line, and were interwoven with fragments lifted from his own contemporary letters home. Most flamboyant and elaborate was the boys'-story potboiler *Walter Garvin in Mexico* (238 pages, 1927), written by Brigadier General Smedley Butler and his aide, First Lieutenant Arthur J. Burks. It projects the entire escapade squarely in the genre of popular pulp military-adventure literature, replete with warrior manliness, homoeroticism, fair play, patriotism, righteous vengeance, and native protagonists either despicably cunning or hopelessly naive. And indeed the actual spy mission and intended expedition were remarkably felicitous to the same formula. This was conceived as an old-fashioned colonial exploit, plunging into the "heart of darkness" to rescue beleaguered white civilians while boldly mastering native recalcitrance.

But as a how-to-do-it recipe, the relief expedition formula was an anachronism which the realities of Mexico in 1914 would not allow. Official sponsorship was still there; concepts of U.S. regional hegemony remained to a great extent rooted in the mentality of the Indian Wars. But the spy mission and projected invasion were irrelevant, a fantasy that envisaged military action along the lines of the Boxer expedition. Faced with international complications and seemingly open-ended possibilities for unproductive military ensnarement, the scheme failed to provide enough leverage and was ultimately shelved. Some form of mediatory intervention, rather than violent coercion, was called for. Colonial warfare still went down well as a commercial enterprise for the boys' adventure market in the 1920s, and even down to the present, but the real world was changing.

On returning from the spy mission Butler shifted quarters to the flagship, where he lived apart from his battalion. Invasion plans were finalized the next day. The minimum objective of rescuing imperiled foreign nationals, necessary to preempt multilateral foreign intervention, was now eclipsed by a strong emphasis on securing unilateral American political control. Lind's recommendation to Washington, prepared in conference with Butler and Admiral Fletcher, proposed the capture of Huerta, who would then "be held in safety until such time as he could be turned over to the proper domestic authority." Since there was, in the self-serving American view, no lawful government in Mexico nor anyone who could legally succeed to the presidency, an American military government would take over "for the time being." There was a "lawfully elected Mexican Congress . . . which would be brought together if deemed prudent." Lind was not in touch with the Constitutionalists, erstwhile recipients of American overtures who were now descending on Mexico City from the north, and therefore he had formulated no further plans. But it could be inferred that seizure of the capital was expected at long last to enhance the bargaining power of the United States. The marines on hand in Veracruz were sufficient for the expedition, no formal orders were needed, only President Wilson's authorization. Lind expected to "arrive in Mexico City shortly before daylight unheralded and [Butler] expects to possess the city before noon." A few days later, with disarming innocence, Lind added that "the temporary taking of Mexico City" to stop Huerta and give the Mexicans a chance to "resume orderly government, should not be regarded as intervention in the offensive sense it seems to me."[20]

Thus Lind, cardinal emissary of Wilsonian moral diplomacy in this first test case involving satellite states, opted for the jackboots of war as his only concrete plan for interjecting U.S. power and influence into the Mexican arena. An explanation for his narrowly military orientation was suggested by the French chargé in Mexico City, who reported to Paris that Lind was spending all his time at Veracruz on an American warship where "the portholes of his cabin afforded him a very limited view of the Mexican question." But the fact that Lind ensconced himself with the fleet indicated the conceptual and practical limitations of American policy, rather than military influence as such. Butler's selection for the key role was itself evidence of Lind's intent, and the resulting invasion plan was quite consistent with Smedley's well-known scope of expertise.[21]

There had been a whole series of Mexico City invasion schemes that predated the Lind project. The General Board of the Navy had developed Mexican war plans beginning in 1909. Butler began drafting plans imme-

diately upon arrival in his capacity as squadron marine officer, the first of
which, dated 24 February, called for the deployment of the Panama battalion
as a provisional regiment expanding to 1,000 men. This became the basis
for the Lind plan. Indeed, all the plans bore strong similarity not only to
China 1900 and Nicaragua 1912, but to previous Mexican expeditions
(Cortés, Scott, Maximilian) inasmuch as the basic military problem was getting from Veracruz via the historic invasion route to Mexico City in the interior. The novelty of Butler's plan was its heavy reliance on the railroad, its
commando speed and daring dependent on conspiratorial support from resident American civilians—a colonial fifth column—and finally the rather
eccentric touch (perhaps Lind's contribution, as it is not in the plan proper)
whereby the president of Mexico was to be in effect kidnapped. When the
U.S. military attaché in Mexico City eventually forwarded the plan for future study at the Army War College, he added a notation describing it as
"the spectacular 'wild goose chase plans' prepared by U.S.M.C." [22]

The plan called for close collaboration with the American railroad superintendent, who would arrange with the expatriate—probably American—superintendent of telegraphs and telephones to cut wires and tracks
at designated places on the Inter-Oceanic and Mexican railroads. Expatriate
yard masters would make up trains after dark, marines coming ashore would
push the cars and handcouple them. The terminal superintendent at Mexico City would clear the belt line and secure switches. Marines would cut
all communications around Veracruz and continue to do so as the pilot train
proceeded up the line. The trains were to reach Mexico City, a distance of
260 miles, having achieved surprise, in twenty-two hours. Troops would
disperse and capture military strongpoints and the radio station. The operation called for 1,000 men, rations and medical supplies for sixty days, and
six field guns, all to be carried in four trains. The pilot train, as in Nicaragua,
would be preceded by a flatcar, then the engine and a boxcar with tools and
materials for repairing torn-up track. In advance of arrival all switches in
Mexico City were to be spiked, locked, and "guarded by trusted Americans." Information on 9,615 foreign nationals, including 1,000 Americans,
was appended to facilitate rescuing the foreign colony. [23]

Lind pressed for approval of the plan throughout the remainder of
March, boosting it as the best way to eliminate Huerta, to prevent "international complications," and to "save the people of Mexico from tyranny
and ourselves from humiliation." Why humiliation, if not to suggest that
American prerogatives were being compromised? He acknowledged that the
expedition would be a "hazardous undertaking." [24]

The decision faced by Wilson and Bryan in Washington was not so
much whether to intervene, but to what extent and under what pretext.
Timing was ultimately determined by the pressure of events, and on 9 April
1914 the brief detention of a small American naval landing party by Huer-

tista authorities at Tampico was seized by the United States as an insult to the American flag and cause for war. On 21 April marines and sailors went ashore at Veracruz, rather than Tampico, to intercept an arms shipment arriving for Huerta on a German steamer.

Butler had been sent up the coast with one of his companies as part of a general fleet concentration off Tampico following the insult of 9 April. The awkward last-minute switch of the landing site to Veracruz sent him and his marines steaming at flank speed southward into the night on the scout cruiser *Chester*. Landings at Veracruz had begun on the morning of the twenty-first, deploying sailors and a regiment of marines that had arrived in early March just after Butler got back from Mexico City. The *Chester*, cleared for action with all her lights screened and marines lined along the deck ready to fire their rifles, steamed directly into the darkened inner harbor at Veracruz just after midnight on the twenty-second, permitting Butler with one company of marines and one of sailors to land immediately. It was a quiet night. Smedley reported to Lieutenant Colonel Wendell C. Neville in the railroad terminal yards at 3:30 A.M.[25]

The *New York Times* for 21 April carried front page headlines: "MA-RINES READY TO SEIZE ROAD TO MEXICO CITY—PICKED FORCE FROM PANAMA TO CAPTURE VERA CRUZ LINE WHEN OPERATIONS BEGIN—MAY DASH TO CAPITAL—MAJOR SMEDLEY D. BUTLER'S MEN SELECTED TO RESCUE AMERICANS IF THEY ARE IN PERIL," dateline Washington, 20 April. Secretary of War Garrison was quoted as saying that Butler's Panama marines, "one of the finest bodies of soldiery he had ever seen," would push sixteen miles inland to capture bridges. The story continued: "Elaborate plans drawn for Mexico City operations contemplate a quick dash to or toward the City of Mexico to rescue Americans and other foreigners in the event of expected riots and the overthrow of Huerta, with consequent disorganization of his army." It was not known whether the original plans, drawn up when chaos was feared in the capital, were still in effect. Butler's Panama battalion, trained "with remarkable farsightedness in the operation of railroad locomotives and trains," would "constitute the pioneers of any quick advance on the Mexican capital. Major Smedley D. Butler, an officer of large experience, commands this contingent, which is now aboard ships at Tampico." A story on page 2 told of Thomas S. Butler opposing "as unnecessary" President Wilson's joint congressional resolution saying the use of force was justified. The *Times*' lead Mexico photographs on the twenty-second featured pictures of warships, Admiral Fletcher, and Butler "in command of the marines."

As it turned out, Butler's role was not so spectacular at all. Neville was in command of the regiment that made the initial landing and was superseded somewhat abashedly as brigade commander by Lejeune, who thrashed his way ashore later in the morning of the twenty-second after having jumped prematurely from his boat and plummeted into the water short of the customhouse seawall, heavily weighted with pistol, haversack, binoculars, and ammunition belt. The initial landings had been unopposed. American troops seized the customhouse, cable station, and railroad terminal with little difficulty, but not before Mexicans had made off with most of the locomotives and rolling stock. Street fighting broke out only after the marines and sailors had captured the key points, and lasted several days, involving mostly sniping by Mexicans and random firing by Americans, particularly the sailors. Marine Captain Fritz Wise, previously encountered in China and the Philippines, remarked: "If ever an outfit shot up a town, they did Vera Cruz. I heard a lot of shooting there, but never a shot I knew to be Mexican. . . . We learned that most of the American casualties were due to wild shooting by our own people." Butler wrote home that the sailors "were terribly mixed up, wretchedly led and frightfully excited." [26]

On the twenty-second, the intervention was consolidated systematically and with few casualties by house-to-house clearing of snipers. "Much time was lost," Neville reported, "in beating in the doors as in many instances the inhabitants were too scared to open." Butler's battalion moved south through the railroad yards and cleared avenues Netzahualcoyotl and Jiménez to Lerdo Street, during which one marine was wounded slightly in the cheek. In the following days Smedley established his battalion headquarters at the railway terminal, whence he would be well-placed for the Mexico City strike if authorized. His men slept in the roundhouse and the officers in boxcars. They dug trenches and did outpost duty in the sand hills west and along the road north of the city. By the twenty-sixth, 5,800 sailors and marines had landed and pacification was complete. American forces had suffered seventeen dead and sixty-three wounded, mostly sailors, while a U.S. naval surgeon tallied 126 Mexican dead and 195 wounded, the latter figures too low by perhaps half. Most of the Mexican casualties were civilians because army units had withdrawn into the interior after the first skirmishes.[27]

But there was no push up the railway into the interior. Secretary of War Garrison, supported by oil companies, railroad interests, and the American colony, urged the immediate capture of Mexico City that would have activated the Butler-Lind marine strike, but he was opposed in the cabinet by Bryan and Daniels. After a war conference on 24 April, President Wilson, taken aback by unexpected Mexican resistance and bloodshed, canceled plans for further invasion and trimmed the expedition to a prolonged seizure of Veracruz coupled with international mediation.[28] In May and June, the U.S. Army general commanding the occupation persisted in recommending an expedition up the line of rail to Mexico City, to involve 7,000 soldiers and marines who would have to "cut loose from base and could not be heard from after leaving." By this time there were new difficulties, with bridges and long stretches of track destroyed.[29] The recommendations were ignored. Subsequently, a deep-strike punitive expedition was authorized, but this was for a different purpose; cavalry under General John J. Pershing pursued Pancho Villa and clashed with Constitutionalist forces in northern Mexico in 1916-17. That campaign was partly successful in driving Villa from the U.S. border and breaking up his followers, but otherwise demonstrated the inherent difficulties facing a large force even with a limited and specific mission.

The strike to Mexico City would have been, in contrast, much more daring and fortuitous, possibly leaving the United States in occupancy of the capital and communications center of the country but, unlike Nicaragua in 1912, unable to effectively extend its authority beyond. Colonial small-war tactics were simply inadequate to the problems at hand. Mexico was too big, amorphous, and politically recalcitrant to be invaded and effectively occupied even by an enormous military undertaking, which would, in any event, have strained current American military capabilities, General Wood's aforementioned optimism to the contrary. And there was increasing wariness in Washington about getting bogged down in a major war in Mexico that would limit American options elsewhere, particularly after August 1914 when the Great War started in Europe. There was suspicion of German intrigues aimed at tying down U.S. forces in Mexico.[30]

The intervention at Veracruz incited strong anti-American reactions around the country as expected, but there was little personal violence against foreigners. Plans had been perfected in Mexico City to operate thirty automobiles and run trains to transport the entire American colony to Veracruz, an exodus that probably would have required military escort drawing upon some variant of the Butler-Lind plan, but only about 100 Americans had come down on the train by 23 April. In Mexico City, rioting mobs broke windows at the American Club and Sanborn's Drugstore, Fiske's Curiosity Shop was sacked, the placard was torn off the American embassy gate, a group of irate women marched through the city repeatedly trampling an American flag, and a statue of George Washington was toppled. There was rioting in Mazatlán, the consulate at Monterrey was invaded and its flags burned, and there were major disturbances at Tampico, forcing American and other foreign nationals to flee to German and British warships. In Veracruz, the city was quiet by the twenty-third, the trams were running again, and three American ships' bands came ashore to give concerts.[31]

The buildup of U.S. forces continued; six more battleships joined the already large assemblage of warships in the roadstead, and on 27 April Army General Frederick Funston arrived with a 3,000-man infantry brigade. The decision to land infantry emphasized the stern intent of the coming full-blown military occupation and suggested an imminent expedition into the interior. Anticipating the army takeover, Lejeune gave orders to convert one of the marine battalions into a "mobile, mule-drawn force" so that the marines could accompany the army on any overland trek.[32] Funston assumed command of the Military Government of Vera Cruz. Sailors and ship's marines were returned to the fleet, and the marine advance base brigade was temporarily detached from the navy to become part of the army of occupation under army discipline and regulations.

Veracruz, a city of 40,000 people with substantial commercial houses, banks, hotels, plazas, and narrow cobblestone streets, as well as extensive squatter encampments for the poor, was Mexico's major port. Control of the customhouse not only interdicted Huerta's supplies of arms from overseas but also cut off the government in Mexico City from its major source of revenue. The occupation was to persist until Huerta fell from power, and thereafter until U.S. forces could be extricated in political negotiations with whatever revolutionary protagonists Washington could deal with. It was to be a long, hot, boring, mosquito-infested summer.

Edith O'Shaughnessy, expelled along with her husband, the American chargé, when Huerta broke diplomatic relations the day after the invasion, found Butler in his headquarters—a freight car—at the railroad terminal when passing through Veracruz a week later. She described the encounter in her book: "A few disconsolate mules and horses were browsing in the dry, sandy grass near by; they had been taken against payment. 'In the good old days in Nicaragua it was otherwise. You *took* what you *needed*. This government running things is too pious and honest to suit me,' was his disgruntled observation when I asked if the steeds belonged to him."[33]

Butler and the marines settled down to occupation routine. A British officer touring marine quarters was "struck by the really astonishing cleanliness of the men, both off and on duty." On the other hand, a naval officer wrote home that the soldiers and marines seemed apathetic, and were "drinking a lot and generally going to pot." There was no fighting. And with a large expeditionary army poised too long waiting for what might have been a daring campaign, the situation was conducive to braggadocio, a mood fueled by sixty-odd increasingly desperate war correspondents. These journalists, including the premier American adventure writers of the day—Richard Harding Davis, Frederick Palmer, Jack London—whetted the appetites of the American public back home with racist-imperialist teasers. For instance, London's vignette "Mexico's Army and Ours" in *Collier's* magazine: "The peon soldier is not a coward. Stupid he well is, just as he is illy trained and sillily officered; but he is too much a fatalist as well as a savage to be grossly afraid of death."[34]

One of these reporters, after a month gone by without action, came up with the story of Butler's spy mission, reportedly told by a first-class seaman on the battleship *Utah*. The published version, datelined New York, 23 May, appeared under the headline "Major Of Marines Invades Mexico Alone; Smedley Butler Maps Route to Capital; Latest Adventure Is Fully In Keeping With Whole 'Dime Novel' Career Of Youthful Warrior." The story continued in the familiar overblown epic style, complete with tinsel allusions to the prestige of high command: "Kipling's heroes 'have nothing on' one Smedley Darlington Butler, youthful major in command of all the marines at Vera Cruz, and who directed the taking of that city by our troops. Heroism is an everyday sort of occurrence with Butler." Details had Butler going to Mexico City "disguised as a Chinaman" to make maps needed for the expedition. Later, he was seized by Huerta's police just before returning to ship, but without the incriminating maps. The rest of the piece consisted of filler rehashing "the life story of Major Butler [which] reads like that of some hero of boy literature." [35]

The reality of the occupation bore little resemblance to any pulp adventure story. But boredom and discomfort aside, this was a vintage campaign for Marine Corps command cadres. Colonel Waller, doyen of the old guard, soon arrived to supersede Lejeune as brigade commander. Lejeune and Neville would dominate the command hierarchy during the coming Great War and as successive commandants in the 1920s. Butler, the "stormy petrel" of the Corps (as Admiral Dewey always called him), would be in the thick of military-civilian politics as heir apparent and finally as ranking major general *manqué*.[36] Of the next generation, Butler's protégé Vandegrift would be one of the Corps's top leaders in World War II. This group, all of them friends, were here united in the field for the last time. Tainted, according to Butler's warrior criteria, was John H. Russell, who would be the State Department's candidate for the commandancy in the early 1930s.

A curious feature of the Veracruz intervention was that although there was little fighting and very few casualties related to enemy action, there were more Congressional Medals of Honor awarded, fifty-five in all, than in any other engagement before or since. Thirty-seven went to officers, nine of these to marines. (Congress passed a law in 1915 authorizing CMHs for officers on the same basis as for enlisted ranks, making Veracruz the first campaign thereafter in which officers were eligible.) In contrast to some officers who avidly sought the medal, notably army Major Douglas MacArthur, Butler refused his in a letter to Secretary of the Navy Daniels, stating that he had done nothing to deserve it. To his mother, he wrote that the medal was for "*Heroism,*" and "to have it thrown around broad cast" was "unutterably foul." He could not stand having his sons "proudly display this wretched medal, or rather wretchedly awarded, some time and have a bystander smile or wink—when they, my Boys, had always been under the impression that their father had honestly deserved all he left them. . . . I *do not intend that any man for political reasons shall make a joke of it or insert, without my consent, the element of fraud into it.*" The impression had "rather gotten around" that he was spurning the medal "for theatrical effect," but he was deadly earnest and wanted "Father to see that they" took the medal back. He referred to the formal presentation in 1916 as a "farce" that made him "party to a vile perversion of our Sacred Decoration." After persistent appeals, he was ordered by Daniels to keep it.[37]

The occupation dragged on through the summer of 1914 without any decisive breakthrough for American policy. Huerta was toppled and fled the country, but this did not resolve either the perplexities of Wilsonian intervention or the trauma of the Mexican Revolution. Venustiano Carranza, chief of the Constitutionalists, eventually became somewhat conciliatory, and the United States finally pulled its troops out in November. Butler had meanwhile departed on home leave at the end of September. It would be a number of years before successor regimes in both the United States and Mexico finally achieved a stable relationship based upon accommodation between American capitalists and a new Mexican elite.

But the Veracruz intervention left a baleful legacy, which would have been exacerbated had the Butler-Lind expedition been attempted. Facing an embarrassingly hostile reception in 1933, U.S. Ambassador Josephus Daniels, who formed a personal link between Wilsonian interventionism and the subsequent Good Neighbor Policy, consoled President Franklin D. Roosevelt, who had been assistant secretary of the navy in 1914: "I do not think any of us apprehended that the people of Veracruz would regard it as an attempt to invade their territory, or in any way resembling the action taken when naval vessels entered Veracruz in 1846-47." [38] In fact, Veracruz in 1914 came to symbolize Yankee imperialism, perhaps more than any other single episode.

7 The Haitian General

Upon returning to the United States in October 1914, Butler was assigned to the advanced-base force, then undergoing a general upgrading in firepower and technological sophistication in Philadelphia. With Smedley close to home, the Marine Corps became correspondingly more visible in West Chester. In November, Congressman Butler requested a hundred marines, plus band, to take part in a naval parade; publicity connecting with Smedley's renown as a war hero and the prestige of the naval services was apparently appreciated on all sides. The following June, Smedley came out to West Chester with his brigade for a three-day encampment.[1] Then hometown shore duty was cut short by a new overseas expedition. After frustrations in Mexico, U.S. policy was reverting to straightforward colonial tactics.

On 28 July 1915, 330 marines and sailors from the armored cruiser *Washington* landed at Port-au-Prince, capital of Haiti, in an operation that had been hanging fire during previous months of missed opportunities. Marine reinforcements from Guantánamo and Philadelphia quickly built up the force to 2,000. Butler sailed from Philadelphia on 10 August in command of a battalion aboard the battleship *Tennessee*, and disembarked at Cap Haitien. The marines were virtually taking over the country.

The advanced-base regiment landing at Cap Haitien, commanded by Colonel Eli K. Cole, was elaborately equipped with what Smedley referred to as an "avalanche" of 400 tons of materiel, representing "some misconception of what is actually required for Marines in the field." Cole was apparently executing current advanced-base doctrine for capturing and fortifying beachheads, representing the marines' big-war capabilities. But in practice, advanced-base units were mainly deployed during these years in colonial small wars, fighting poorly trained peasants. This anomaly fueled an ongoing dispute within the officer corps between those concerned with technological upgrading and sophisticated big-war concepts, and accomplished bushwhackers like Butler who continued to excel in the field. Butler now wrote his wife that Cole, a graduate of the Army War College, was "trying to make a big thing of this with the hope that it will make him a General Officer but I can't see how he can—these poor wretched people don't want any trouble."[2]

The ensuing guerrilla war against Haitian "bandits"—known as *cacos*, "or bad niggers as we would call them at home", according to Smedley— provided plenty of scope for a Butler-style commando campaign. Although still only a major, he again loomed larger than higher ranking officers by virtue of his boldness, efficiency, and reputation. Colonel Waller, his old mentor, whom Smedley now characterized as "more than ever my ideal of a soldier," arrived to assume overall command in Haiti. Waller had great confidence in Butler as against grave doubts regarding Colonel Cole. These sentiments Waller freely expressed in a series of letters to Assistant Commandant Lejeune in Washington, an "unofficial" line of communication that had been arranged by Commandant Barnett. Lejeune showed Barnett all the letters and Waller knew it. A week after landing at Cap Haitien, Waller wrote that Cole was "very nervous." When Cole asked for reinforcements, Waller took men away from him. Instead of pressing into the interior, Cole was staying in Cap Haitien under the guns of American warships, giving the *cacos* time to organize. After a month, Waller complained that if his orders were not carried out, he would ask that Cole and other "timid individuals be removed to the United States. . . . Hesitation at this time with these people means bloodshed. Positive firmness means that they will give up." [3]

Butler of course sided with Waller in what they saw as a clear choice between their warrior prowess and bravery, and Cole's educated professional effeteness. Smedley wrote his father:

I had sat up here for five weeks watching the War Lords [Cole and the navy] endeavoring to defeat an ignorant, treacherous crowd of niggers by 'constructive' warfare, that is by writing a letter to their chiefs every few hours saying that such or such was the case and then going to the club to celebrate . . . . Now this sort of warfare will pass and gain you much credit and high marks in a million dollar war college . . . . Colonel Waller has never been to a War College and does not, therefore, grasp the full scope of such warfare, is of the old fashioned school that believes the way to end a row with a savage monkey is to first go into the region or territory occupied by that monkey and find out how savage he is. If the monkey attacks you, return the compliment but only to a degree necessary to impress him with the danger he runs by repeating his attacks. This beats letter writing to death and leaves you, perhaps minus some member of your body, but in full possession of your self-respect. [4]

As Waller's trusted protégé dating back to the Boxer expedition, Butler eclipsed Cole despite the formal chain of command. His aggressive patrols, often under detached orders directly from Waller, provided the main thrust of the campaign in the north.

By mid-September, *cacos* had turned in several thousand rifles in response to a bribery campaign paid out of Haitian government funds, disbursed under U.S. auspices. Silver bullets were backed by threat of lethal ones, and several *caco* armies held out, either for more money or in patriotic resistance to American invasion. Consistent with Secretary of the Navy Daniels's singular insistence on avoiding firefights, Waller and several Haitian intermediaries went north to negotiate. After an inconclusive conference with over a hundred *caco* chiefs, Waller invited them to come along for the ride when he opened the railroad from Cap Haitien fourteen miles inland to Grand Rivière. The *caco* leaders, referred to by Butler as "shaved apes, absolutely no intelligence whatsoever, just plain low nigger,"[5] refused, claiming they held the countryside around Cap Haitien and would stop any train, and that the tracks were torn up. Since Cole had been wary of the *cacos*, the train trip was crucial as a demonstration of Waller's methods for pacifying the north.

Waller, Cole, Butler, and three squads of marines set out with two flatcars in front, fortified with sandbags and machine guns, followed by the engine and a passenger-baggage car. Waller related facetiously to Lejeune that they "passed an outpost whose attitude was very threatening but we simply laughed at them and went on." When the front car derailed at an outpost of about 150 *cacos*, Waller sent four men into the bush about forty feet from the *cacos* who became "violently excited" and "broke and ran, being chased by their officers who endeavored to bring them back." Aside from a few more ties pulled out, the remainder of the trip was uneventful. Waller concluded that the road should have been opened three weeks earlier, "The timidity of the people up there had made the Cacos believe that we were afraid of them." The *cacos* were "inconceivably miserable" and incapable of offering serious resistance, "murderous chicken thieves" who were "of no earthly value as a soldier."[6]

This initial incursion, accomplished with masterful ease, marked the start of active patrolling into the interior. The following day Waller and Butler steamed south 120 miles by sea to the coastal town of Gonaives where the marine garrison had been sealed off from water and food supplies by hostile *cacos*. Butler advanced inland with a patrol of fifty marines and bluejackets. They were ambushed three times but suffered no casualties, and returned fire, killing seven *cacos* and wounding three. At the thatched-hut village of Poteau, they caught up with the main rebel force of several hundred under General Pierre Benoit Rameau. Rameau had proclaimed a rebellion, denouncing the Americans for "treading our soil as masters"— menacing the country with return to racial slavery, against which Haitians had guarded their independence since overthrowing the French in the 1790s. Butler accosted Rameau and pulled him off his horse, which, according to *Old Gimlet Eye*, "was more humiliating to him than defeat in battle." The supreme commander of the intervention, Admiral William B. Caperton, commented in his memoirs: "I could not but commend Butler's success and often wondered at his methods. Unarmed, in Nicaragua, three years previously, he had done the same thing, in even a more telling manner." [7]

The relatively bloodless success of these two ventures, which dispersed the *cacos*, penetrated their territory, and revealed them as weak, confirmed Waller's program of tactical patrols as a means of breaking resistance. As at Poteau, the marines were ordered never to shoot first but to respond if attacked, this in deference to Secretary Daniels's orders to refrain from offensive operations. Returning to Port-au-Prince, Waller conferred with the admiral; then he reported privately to Lejeune, "When I told Caperton the instructions I had given Butler he nearly had a [fit] but, when he learned of the success of the work he rejoiced and wired the Department that he had given Butler the instructions. Smedley is carrying out my instructions to the letter." [8]

Very likely Caperton, Daniels, Butler, everyone else at the command level, and Waller himself were acutely aware of Waller's record of atrocities in the analogous 1901 pacification of the Philippines, when "burn and kill" had been the orders of the day. The prime mover in restraining the present campaign was Secretary Daniels, a pacifist who was the conscience of the Wilson administration regarding militarism and colonial warfare. But enlightened colonialism, based on "indirect rule" as in certain British precedents in Africa, had little currency in Haiti given U.S. policymakers' racist contempt for the Black Republic.[9] And with overwhelming military superiority, there seemed little reason at this point to tolerate native institutions or consider turning them to advantage. In effect, Daniels was reduced to ordering a punitive campaign minus the punishment: thus the proviso that the marines should never fire first. In terms of reducing violence, Waller and Butler offered the best expertise for an efficient and therefore relatively bloodless victory.

Beginning on 25 September, patrols fanned out into the interior from Cap Haitien. Butler was back from Gonaives, having opened the railroad twenty miles to Ennery, and now took charge of a patrol to Plain du Nord. He encountered few *cacos*, collected a dozen rifles, and reported seeing almost no men in villages along the way. But the following day, despite orders to shoot only in self-defense, another patrol ran into a stiff firefight in which ten Americans were wounded and forty dead *cacos* were counted on the road afterward.

Waller, writing on his fifty-ninth birthday, bemoaned the bloodshed. He had "no desire to slaughter these people and almost all movements can be successfully made without fire," but found himself in a "curious" position. "We have taken the army from the Haitians leaving them [a new American-sponsored client government] nothing to protect themselves with but we are not allowed to take offensive action against the Cacos. . . . If we could fire first we would have them on the run." He also noted "a disposition here [Caperton] is to blame me for the firing but to take the credit for the result." [10]

On the twenty-ninth Waller reached a settlement with top *caco* generals whereby major rebel units sold their rifles and disbanded in return for amnesty and a chance to join a projected gendarmerie which would soon be formed under American auspices. There were also allusions to possible political patronage for leaders in the emerging client government, plus $6,600 in bribes. Waller returned to Port-au-Prince, leaving Butler in charge in the north as far as active operations were concerned. [11]

There remained mop-up operations against small bands of *cacos*, now stigmatized definitively as outlaw "bandits" subject to pursuit and extermination. Butler commanded a makeshift battalion under orders to clear the Dominican border and then the last mountain retreats in the interior. It was rough going, very rugged 5,000-foot mountains with poor trails, weak communications by radio, and unfavorable weather with the onset of the rains. There were also pleasant aspects; great coffee, the "sweetest and juiciest" oranges Lieutenant Adolph B. Miller had ever eaten, and a moderate climate which Waller described as "very comfortable now and far better than Veracruz at its best," with the coming winter likely to be "very fine," in a land he saw as "beautiful and rich, the gem of the Antilles—Only man is vile." Smedley wrote his father, "Oh the wildness of it all, the half clothed, vicious natives, the wonderful scenery and fine clean air, there is no country like it that I have ever seen." [12]

Butler ran patrols out of Fort Liberté to capture *caco* weapons, burn camps and villages, and wreck their often "very poor attempts at fortifications." The *cacos* themselves were elusive, knowing the country better than the marines and able to keep a step ahead. At Terrier Rouge, one of Butler's lieutenants captured 116 rifles. A few days later another turned up a three-inch Krupp field gun in good condition. Frequent skirmishes involved ineffective ambushes and return fusillades by the marines and sailors, sometimes with a Colt machine gun on wheels which was dragged along into the bush. The *cacos'* marksmanship was invariably poor, in part because of faulty rifles and mismatched ammunition. At times the mosquitoes were so bad that American hands and faces swelled and the men could not sleep. At night, the marines and sailors listened to hair-raising sounds of *cacos* nearby in the bush drumming "tom-toms," yelling, and blowing conch shells. Lieutenant Miller's capricious diary entry for 22 October, enroute to Le Trou, read: "As we forded the stream a great number of black Venuses were bathing in their birthday clothes. Our presence was a matter of indifference to them. Major Butler and a few squads of men reconnoited down to Carocol 6 miles away on the sea coast. They burned a Caco village."[13]

In mid-October Waller reported, "I have always said that we could go as far and about as fast as these people can and I am sure of it now. They go faster at first but they cannot stick it out." With the coastal areas pacified, Butler and his battalion now pressed on into the interior, following trails of discarded orange peels. Captain Chandler Campbell, commanding the southern of two columns and claiming proudly in a letter to his mother that he had "beaten Butler's column in every move and have captured all the forts," employed classic counterinsurgency tactics as noted in his company diary: "Through their women, I have tried to communicate to the Cacos the fact that, if in the future a single shot is fired by them, or if they blow any more conches, or otherwise create any disturbances, we would return and burn all their houses and completely destroy their crops."[14]

In *Old Gimlet Eye*, Butler stated that "a lot of north Haiti was burned before we got through."[15] But this is surely an exaggeration. Reports indicate selective burning as against a general plan of appealing to the rural population by offering protection from depredations by the *cacos* who, as their vernacular name meaning "bird of prey" implied, lived off the land.

Penetrating into the mountains meant hard marches and ever more desperate opposition as the *cacos* were driven back to their last bastions. After dark on 24 October near Bahon, Butler and a patrol of about forty men were ambushed from three sides by an estimated 400 *cacos* while crossing a river in a deep ravine. After fighting their way forward to a defensible position the marines stayed put for the night, surrounded by *cacos* who kept up a steady but inaccurate fire. At dawn, squads broke out in three directions and ran the *cacos* before them, killing eight for sure, probably more—Butler estimated seventy-five in *Old Gimlet Eye*. They then demolished nearby Fort Dipitié and burned surrounding houses. The column proceeded along the river through deserted countryside and villages, taking occasional sniper fire from the flanking hills but suffering no casualties. When rainstorms and flooding made further progress impossible, the patrol stayed a second night on the river banks. They trudged exhausted into La Vallière on the morning of the twenty-sixth, having covered forty miles on foot over rough trails in fifty-five hours without rest for either men or pack animals. Local officials at La Vallière, according to Miller's diary, "thought we were wonderful heroes to come though the Caco infested valley with only 40 men."[16]

One marine was subsequently awarded the Congressional Medal of Honor for heroism at the ambush site. (This was Sergeant Dan Daly, the only other marine besides Butler to win two CMHs.) The whole region, as Butler described it in his report, was "alive with hostile Cacos and many forts." With the target area now clearly defined, Butler returned to Fort Liberté to regroup his forces and consult with Waller, who came up from Port-au-Prince to help plan the final onslaught.[17]

In early November Butler and 700 marines and sailors went back up into the mountains to finish the job. They were to clear an area measuring thirty by twenty miles. Waller, posing as the reprobate master bushwhacker, commented, "I know that the experts of the brain trust will say that we are violating all the rules, but I am sure that if they were here they would not move out of the towns." As before, Butler and his men were repeatedly fired upon along the way, and at the temporary headquarters base at Le Trou they had to beat off a dawn attack from all directions by about 100 *cacos*. Fort Capois, a group of huts surrounded by a loose stone wall atop a 3,500-foot mountain, was taken with apparently heavy Haitian casualties judging from the bloodiness of the site afterward, but there were no wounded or corpses. Survivors from the estimated 150 defenders escaped in fog on a labyrinth of trails unknown to the Americans. In the days that followed, other forts and ramparts fell, now usually with token resistance or none at all, and were dynamited or burned along with nearby thatched-roof houses.[18]

This left the last, most remote, and most formidable *caco* redoubt at Fort Rivière, an old French edifice with thick walls about 100 feet square, ranging from fifteen to twenty-five feet high, 4,000 feet up on top of Montagne Noir. The fort had been taken once before by Captain Campbell but had been reoccupied. Campbell wrote his mother, "We don't expect much fighting as we have taken most of it out of these people, but we will have to give them a few more lessons before they will know enough to quit."[19]

On the seventeenth, according to efficiently executed plan, Campbell blew his whistle at 7:50 A.M., and advanced with his company in skirmish formation, Benet automatic rifles providing cover from the flanks. The fort had been surrounded by about 100 marines and sailors in three converging columns; every avenue of escape was closed. "Fire from the garrison," as Butler described it in his report, "was heavy, but inaccurate, and we had no casualties." The only entrance to the fort was a breach in the west wall large enough to admit only one man at a time. A sergeant, a private, and then Butler himself dashed into the breach, followed by the remainder of the Fifth Marine Company. "A melee," according to Butler's report, "then ensued inside the fort for about ten minutes, the Cacos fighting desperately with rifles, clubs, stones, etc. during which several jumped from the walls in an effort to escape, but were shot by the automatic guns."[20]

The entire battle lasted less than twenty minutes, fifty-one Haitians were killed, there were no prisoners, no survivors. Butler radioed Colonel Cole at 8:50 A.M. that "no operation could have been more successfully carried out. Professional efficiency of the officers and splendid grit of the men." Years later he commented: "The futile efforts of the natives to oppose trained white soldiers impressed me as tragic. As soon as they lost their heads, they picked up useless, aboriginal weapons. If they had only realized the advantage of their position, they could have shot us like rats as we crawled one by one, out of the drain." The only American casualty was a man who lost two teeth when hit in the face with a rock.[21]

The battle of Fort Rivière ended the campaign. Dead *cacos*, including a top general and three division chiefs, were searched and their bodies thrown into a large hole in the center of the fort. Two days later the fort itself was dynamited. About sixty "shacks" south of the fort were burned, as well as the district to the west. Columns of marines and sailors returning to the coast were greeted all along the route, according to Butler, "by natives who expressed their gratitude in no uncertain terms for our work in ridding them of the Caco terror which had hung over them for so many years," this perhaps reflecting a genuine appreciation for at least that aspect of imperial pacification.[22]

The *cacos* had presumably learned their lesson. Captain William P. Upshur, who served in the north throughout, wrote home two months later that "they have learned that the white man is on the job night and day—and that we go everywhere and are liable to arrive at anytime." Colonel Waller, discussing Haitian public sentiment midway through the following year, noted obliquely that residual effects of the punitive campaign were still evident: "You know how the nigger is. It takes very little to sway him either way. Of course, in the North they have a deadly fear of us but we have not had a real good whack at them elsewhere."[23]

Reaction to Fort Rivière in Washington was generally favorable. Secretary Daniels, whose pressure to moderate violence had been offset by supporting the overall policy of relentless coercion, belatedly ordered suspension of offensive action "in order to prevent further loss of life." But at cabinet meetings Daniels was the only pacifist left at this point, and colleagues sniggered at his scruples, mocking him as "Josephus the First, King of Haiti." The two enlisted men who went into the fort ahead of Butler, and Smedley himself, were awarded Congressional Medals of Honor specifically on the recommendation of Daniels's junior Navy Department colleague Franklin D. Roosevelt, currently assistant secretary in charge of the Marine Corps. Daniels presumably approved. On visiting Fort Rivière with Butler in 1917, Roosevelt hyperbolized the battle, writing in his travel diary that Smedley and eighteen comrades had killed over 200 *cacos*.[24]

In fact, the pacification of northern Haiti was methodically unexceptional as a colonial military exercise, and Waller and Butler could well be praised, as they indeed were, for minimizing casualties in accordance with both Daniels's restrictions and their own pride as competent professionals.[25] And militarization was fundamental to the Wilson administration's program in Haiti from the outset, as was the case elsewhere in the Caribbean, which was being garrisoned by U.S. troops to a greater extent than ever before or since. After the punitive campaign, intervention in Haiti evolved logically into a prolonged military occupation, in which Butler and Waller were chosen to play principal roles.

Military intervention in Haiti marked the culmination of U.S. policy dating back to 1910 when the State Department, as an aspect of dollar diplomacy, forced Haiti and its European creditors to accept American financial control. Wall Street financial interests took over the National Bank of Haiti and the National Railway. By 1914, both were managed by Roger L. Farnham, who was simultaneously vice president of National City Bank of New York and the National Bank of Haiti, president of the National Railway, and the Wilson administration's principal adviser on Haiti. In 1914 the State Department demanded a U.S. customs receivership—the Farnham Plan. Until now Haiti had scrupulously paid its foreign debt, thereby forestalling intervention, but Farnham was in a position to force the issue. In January 1915, the German minister at Port-au-Prince reported to Berlin that Farnham was "trying to completely ruin Haiti . . . and to thereby create such chaos that the American Government will have to occupy the country, so that he can then fish in muddy waters above all to receive high compensation for his outrageously shoddy railroad." Among other things, he was withholding a currency stabilization fund of 10 million francs of government money deposited in the National Bank, "thereby forcing the Haitian Government into destitution and promoting discontent and revolution." [26]

This "enemy" source was corroborated by a U.S. naval intelligence report which stated that the National Bank "refuses to pay money rightfully belonging to the Government," that it was the "chief contributor to the present financial stagnation of Haitian commerce," and "directly responsible for present political conditions [revolution] in Haiti." "Assistance of the State Department" had been "practically obtained to put a weaker but solvent country in the hands of a receiver." The report also included detailed allegations that Bank management was in several ways defrauding both the Haitian government and commercial depositors—in sum, a convincing critique by a naval officer of the predatory methods by which Wall Street and Washington were joined in subverting a foreign government. [27]

As pressure mounted, U.S. warships maintained a naval watch in Haitian waters, supported occasionally by troopships carrying marines. Intervention was narrowly averted in late 1914. In the spring of 1915, Secretary of State William Jennings Bryan recommended to President Wilson that the United States control Haiti through a "resident advisor" similar to the Dutch regime in Java and the British in India. [28] A bloody revolutionary debacle in late July presented the long-awaited opportunity for intervention.

The circumstances, in which the president of Haiti was publicly dismembered in the streets, seemed to confirm the worst white American racial prejudices and was taken to justify military action by the United States as self-appointed guardian of higher civilization.

The United States was unwilling to truck with local factions, preferring complete authority thinly veiled behind a facade of local retainers. Philippe Sudre Dartiguenave, a politician with no significant power base, was installed as client president with a marine bodyguard henceforth in constant attendance. Admiral Caperton recommended him to Washington as one who "realized that Haiti must agree to any terms demanded by the United States," which included complete financial control and settlement on American terms of differences between the Haitian government and the National Bank and Railway. Martial law was declared and remained in effect until 1929. After pacification of the north, the Wilson administration proceeded with militaristic resolve to install Colonel Waller and Butler as colonial satraps, precedent to the formal establishment of a marine general as resident high commissioner in the 1920s.[29]

The new client government acceded by treaty to U.S. control of almost all governmental functions. First priority went to the establishment of a peacekeeping force run by American officers, the Gendarmerie d'Haiti, which Butler started in December 1915, less than two weeks after the Battle of Fort Rivière. As with the occupation in general, the gendarmerie was not conceived of as a temporary expedient. Perhaps some variant of the familiar colonial strategy of divide and rule, recruiting martial tribesmen from remote, backward regions, might have sufficed. But this was intended to be an integrative national organization, transcending regional or ethnic-racial divisions, a politically neutral, loyal professional force, a bulwark of institutional authority and stability. The Haitian army and police were entirely displaced. Waller put it succinctly in testimony to the House Naval Affairs Committee in 1916: "We have taken arms from the people, and we have disarmed the leaders who led them in revolt, taken their positions from them, and given them no control over the people in any way . . . the power to organize the people has been removed."[30]

The Americans built the gendarmerie from scratch as a pervasive American network. For the marines, this was the pilot project for several Caribbean and Central American constabularies that would be molded in the leatherneck image, and the experiment was launched with enthusiasm, personal sacrifice, and hard work. Butler expressed interest in the top post, which he saw as a challenging and well-paying opportunity for independent command. It was similar to the mounted constabulary scheme he had proposed for Nicaragua in 1912. He was strongly recommended by Waller as someone who would "put a lot of ginger in the bunch," so as to create a "good, thorough, snappy corps of men." Almost immediately, racist references to "savage monkeys" disappeared from Smedley's letters, replaced by a new, albeit appallingly paternalistic, personal commitment and pride in his new outfit. Now it was "my little chocolate soldiers," and "my little black army . . . I am beginning to like the little fellows." He was determined to help Haiti to its feet, to do his "level best to make a real and happy nation out of this blood crazy Garden of Eden." [31]

Indicating commitment to building a self-sustaining Haitian force, Waller wanted to make Haitians company officers as soon as possible, calculating that their love of "form and ceremony" would serve as "a big incentive to them." But American racism effectively precluded this. Waller himself was almost instinctively wary of Smedley's black troopers, and once remarked, "you can never trust a nigger with a gun." His ancestral legacy included the massacre of Mrs. Levi Waller and ten white children at the Waller farm (they had eighteen slaves) in Southampton, Virginia, during the Nat Turner rebellion in 1831. With scant sense of delicacy in corresponding with his superiors in Washington, Waller wrote Lejeune: "I say this without any spirit of egotism, I know the nigger and how to handle him. The same quality is going to be needed in San Domingo as well as here." [32]

Butler took charge as commandant, assuming the rank of major general by commission from the Haitian government while simultaneously retaining his rank of major in the marines. This pattern was repeated down through the ranks. Most of the officers in the gendarmerie were marine enlisted men who enjoyed officer status, greater responsibilities, and much higher pay as inducements for volunteering. There was a good deal of fascination in this dual structure and sensitivity, marines being keen on "form and ceremony" in their own right. Waller, observing that Smedley was now a "Haitien General of Division" and would be independent in all matters except movement of troops, wisecracked to Lejeune, who as a Louisianian could appreciate down-home southern racial humor: "He asked me where he would sit if he came to my mess. I told him that if he came as a Major of Marines he would take his place according to rank and if as a Haitien General, he would feed in the pantry." [33]

Sportive racial slurs aside, the efficiency and morale of the new outfit required sympathy at the top, and both Waller and Lejeune gave strong support. Smedley, drumming up marine recruits, emphasized not only the extra rank and pay but also humanitarian aspects. "That man could talk the stripes off a zebra," Lieutenant Vandegrift recalled, "and here he nearly reduced us to tears—we faced an obvious challenge, a country that needed our help." In a letter published in the *Congressional Record*, Butler argued that Haiti was "well worth saving" despite the "shiftlessness of its population," and it was "a matter of Corps, as well as National, honor to assist the Haitians in getting on their feet." When he sent Lejeune a list of officers he wanted assigned to Haiti, he specified several to be omitted—one in particular was unfit "for many reasons, the chief being his brutal attitude towards these little black fellows." [34]

The gendarmerie made rapid progress and legally assumed police functions in February 1916. Morale was built upon benevolent paternalism, camaraderie, and marine élan. The chasm between white officers and black enlisted ranks, inherited from the marine model, served as a convenient pivot for racial segregation according to American norms. Meanwhile the Waller-Butler satrapy shook down amidst tough jurisdictional infighting with the navy and then with the Dartiguenave client government. The marines pressed hard for control over post, telegraph, and public works, amounting to a countrywide gendarmerie network that nailed down the occupation as a marine enterprise. In the end they had much of it their way, although naval engineers and surgeons and American civilian officials took over some key posts, notably in fiscal administration.

The infighting featured a head-on clash between Colonel Waller and Admiral Caperton, both domineering personalities and jealous of their prerogatives. Each undermined the other in his "unofficial" correspondence with Washington. Waller, commander of Marine Expeditionary Forces ashore, complained to Lejeune that the admiral was "insane" and that "instead of backing up men who are working for him, he knifes them when they do well." Butler referred to Caperton as "old simpleton." Meanwhile Caperton, senior U.S. officer in Haiti sitting in his battleship offshore, made a point of cultivating the local élite socially, and accused Waller of being "very vindictive" and using "intimidation" which made the occupation unpopular. The case against Waller is supported by a variety of sources, including the French minister, who described him as an "uncouth soldier who cared little about hiding his thoughts." But one wonders about Caperton's commitment to tactful bonhomie; his memoirs are filled with racist stereotypes, including scornful caricature of élite clothing—gold lace, "vivid robin's egg blue" coats, and "beautiful parrot green" waistcoats. [35]

Waller and Butler, left in charge with a thousand marines when Caperton departed in early 1916, were less inclined to niceties than the admiral and came to despise élite politicians for their craftiness. Being in charge of day-to-day affairs, they could hardly remain aloof, making gracious gestures. Waller knew that tact was important, and said he did "not wish to be outdone in formal politeness," cautioning Butler against using high-handed methods lest "more harm [be] done by such an act than can be remedied by months of work and labor." But the virulent racism revealed in Waller's correspondence surfaced often enough to justify his evil reputation. Smedley applauded Waller's pugnacity, writing a State Department officer in the fall of

1916 that "just this minute things are not particularly humiliating as the Colonel keeps these grasping niggers off our backs, but when he goes then will be some fun."[36]

Smedley was encouraged by his mentor's example to persist with the aggressiveness that had made him a top bushfighter, as he now turned to client-regime political skirmishes. Handwringing came later from those assigned to consolidate and mollify. For the moment U.S. policy, Daniels and Caperton included, emphasized the hard-driving military nature of the occupation. Why else would Waller and Butler, both well known as tough field commanders, have been given sweeping authority in the first place? And then, despite detailed revelations attendant to the Waller-Caperton feud and other sources, be sustained with ongoing support and praise?

Waller, with fondness, recognized Butler's impulsiveness as a factor in their joint stratagems, once observing to Lejeune that Smedley had blown a political mission in Washington because "he probably did all the talking and did not notice that no one was agreeing to his remarks." Smedley was in good form for his introduction to Dartiguenave at the close of the *caco* campaign in 1915:

> I took Butler to see the President a short while ago. After the usual compliments and some little chat I got up to go. Butler asked if he should say something. I told him that it would be proper for him to do so. Turning to the interpreter he said, in his inimitable manner and making that gesture of rubbing the back of his hand again and again across his nose,—'Here! You tell the President not to be worried by the Cacos. If the Cacos come we *shoot 'em*. If Cacos come BOOM!! Cacos all run.' By that time the President had recovered from the first 'SHOOT EM' and was laughing heartily. I nearly died with laughter and the beauty of the whole thing is Butler did not realize that he had said anything out of the way, I mean funny. Really, it was rich to see the gestures accompanying the address to the interpreter.[37]

While this style could be endearing, it was a far cry from the formal politeness by which the Haitian *élite* distanced itself from the masses. To be treated with coarse familiarity, particularly by a white foreigner, was insulting.

The French minister sent a similar character cameo to Paris, describing Butler as having "great military qualities" but now "made the mistake of mixing in politics. In fact, he has directed American politics. Naive, self-confident, excessively optimistic, speaking no French, he has been easily duped by the local politicians." He had manipulated an election but once the candidates were in office, all turned against the occupation. He predicted that the National Assembly would declare war against Germany by a big majority, as desired by the State Department: "The declaration of war having been unanimously rejected, the secretary of state finally opened his eyes to the incompetence of this impromptu diplomacy. Major Butler is here, because of his ineptness, a veritable menace." Subsequently the minister attributed the January 1917 election debacle to plans laid prior to his departure the previous November by Waller, who had hoped to "find support amongst the opposition in order to break up the Dartiguenave government." [38]

By 1917 the occupation was embroiled with both Dartiguenave and the elected National Assembly, each of which, while powerless, was able to keep up a steady harassment by sniping, tricking, and plotting. Waller and Butler, lacking finesse at arcane colonial comprador politics and quite intolerant of devious insubordination from Haitians, were enraged. In July 1916, as relations began to deteriorate seriously, Waller wrote Lejeune, "It is really a fact that they think we will remain here under the direction of the President of Haiti. Did you ever hear of anything so fantastic in your life." He also averred cryptically that "I suppose I am getting old and a little bit crusty but I notice that I have held out when the others have gone to pieces mentally." Smedley fumed that the client government, "a miserable lot of liars and thieves," had "lied to me two or three times, and I do not intend again to trust it or anybody in it." [39]

Butler was set for a fight to the finish, and wrote Lejeune that "as far as I am able, this country will be run as a piece of machinery, with no preference being shown any negro owing to a supposed superiority due to the infusement of white blood in his veins"—a reference to the predominantly mulatto *élite*. "There will be a dead-line drawn between me and the Haitiens, the same as there is in Egypt—between the British agents and the Egyptians." The rather desperate struggle that followed in late 1916 and 1917 coincided with a deterioration of social courtesy that culminated in Jim Crow racial segregation. Butler once called Dartiguenave a "damned liar" to his face, in front of cabinet officials. After a "socially objectionable" incident involving Butler in late 1917, the *élite* Cercle Bellevue club was closed to U.S. military and ordered off-limits by Butler. No marine was subsequently elected to the Cercle Bellevue until 1960. [40]

Élite resentment was articulated in the emergence of *négritude*, eventually a regional and pan-African movement that gained early momentum in reaction to the U.S. occupation. Many of its Haitian literary works dwell upon American racism. The arch-villain of Stephen Alexis's novel *Le nègre masqué* (1933) was Major Smedley Seaton, no doubt an allusion to the occupation's most renowned protagonist. In a bitter showdown preceding the Haitian hero's arrest by a squad of marines, Seaton accuses him, "Goddam! Son of a monkey, pariah, cannibal, I'll teach you to beslaver my race." In reply, the hero launches a diatribe against American arrogance: "You think, imbecile, that your domination over the weak will be eternal? Your power totters, undermined by silent and subterranean forces! . . . One morning, mechanical man, you will be annihilated under the debris of your skyscrapers, your factories. There is nothing, nothing to your civilization of scrap iron, of cement and linoleum!" The Haitian wins the white girl and dignity under extreme duress, while Smedley Seaton is exposed, offending decent moral sensibility to the same degree as his "flashy Cadillac" offends local decorum. (Butler's large touring car had been conspicuous at a time when Haiti was suffering wartime economic deprivation.)[41]

Waller and Butler interpreted their nasty entanglements in *élite* political intrigues as confirming their special affinity to the black peasant masses. Smedley divided the population into two classes when he explained Haiti to a U.S. Senate committee in 1921: "One class wears shoes and the other does not." The shoeless class were "the most kindly, generous, hospitable, pleasure-loving people" he had ever known. But "when the other 1 per cent that wears vici kid shoes with long pointed toes and celluloid collars, stirs them up and incites them with liquor and voodoo stuff, they are capable of the most horrible atrocities: they are cannibals." In their "natural state," the peasants were "the most docile, harmless people in the world." The shoe class he "took as a joke." Waller professed to be "intensely popular with the people," whom he likened to "the same race in our country in the South, except perhaps they work a little harder." They were "very docile." Trouble came from ungrateful scheming politicians who were being artificially kept in office under American protection, causing resentment against the otherwise popular marines.[42]

The extent of popular support for the marines was, of course, a matter of speculation. In May 1916 Admiral Caperton observed that "the people have so far been very quiet and sullen, ignoring us, you might say, which after all has prevented any unpleasantness."[43]

The dichotomy between a treacherous local elite and deferential, docile, even appreciative peasants was a characteristically "democratic" American rationale to explain native resistance to beneficent imperialism. Invoking the silent masses contrasted with a manifest inability to collaborate effectively with the local political class, even with those retainers who accepted American pay. Trouble with local compradors reflected both the special sensitivities of the Haitian *élite* and the imperiousness of the Americans. The deviousness by *élite* politicians that was so repulsive to Butler and Waller was a function of their weakness, quislings in particular, relative to the brute force of the conquerors. Their two-facedness was necessary to maintain some local credibility. An outright puppet, as Dartiguenave was indeed commonly held to be, was almost useless as an instrument of governance, except perhaps as a foil for diverting hatred from the Americans.

Waller and Butler, unskilled in the management of these affairs, were not inclined to be indulgent.

As for the peasants, Waller's and Butler's terms of affection—docile, happy, idle, irresponsible, kindly, shiftless, pleasure-loving, trustworthy—belie democratic allusions, for these were clearly the patronizing stereotype of the "good nigger" who knew how to keep his loyal, unthreatening place according to white racial norms imported from the United States. President William McKinley concocted the imperial prototype with his reference to Little Brown Brothers in the Philippines. "We were all imbued with the fact," as Butler kindly put it, "that we were trustees of a huge estate that belonged to minors." By contrast, educated *élite* politicians who contested American command prerogatives were resented according to American norms as "uppity niggers." Waller and Butler objected to special treatment for the *élite* on the basis of their "thin varnish of education and refinement," or "supposed superiority due to the infusement of white blood." [44] This was particularly galling because the *élite* considered its cultural attainments in the French tradition—Haiti the land of poets—to be far superior to those generally evidenced by the marines.

In January 1917 the Wilson administration dispatched Assistant Secretary of the Navy Franklin D. Roosevelt on a Caribbean inspection tour to further articulate, among other things, U.S. policies in Haiti. Although FDR was accompanied mainly by military aides, including Marine Commandant Barnett, the visit to Haiti also had diplomatic purposes. But even gracious gestures to the Haitian client government were heavily laden with military overtones, as described by Captain Upshur in a letter home: "The Atlantic Fleet of 'Fifty-seven sail' put into harbor, and you can well imagine that it was a wonderful sight. . . . when the president of Haiti passed through the fleet on the tender Yankton, every ship of war, in the great fleet, fired a national salute of 21 guns, and their thunder, not only 'shook the deep,' but the harbor was veiled in white powder smoke, which was pierced in every part by the vivid flashes of the guns." [45] Dartiguenave must have seemed both greater as an American client and smaller as president of Haiti.

In the days that followed, Roosevelt was hosted by the Butlers, repeated the same speech in French at various ceremonial functions, and attended a gendarmerie ball in the new, partly completed presidential palace, where Mrs. Butler received guests alongside Dartiguenave, who was a bachelor. At the ball American men danced with Haitian women but American women refused to dance with Haitian men, foreboding the advent of Jim Crow. Roosevelt himself was punctilious in observing protocol throughout. According to a possibly facetious anecdote told years later by his traveling companion George Marvin, Dartiguenave started to get into his official limousine ahead of FDR only to have Butler seize him by the collar and pull him back, but FDR stepped aside and insisted the president go first. [46]

In Port-au-Prince FDR met his cousin, marine Major H.L. "Harry" Roosevelt, Butler's quartermaster in the gendarmerie and henceforth FDR's leg man in pursuing private investment schemes in Haiti. Then FDR's party, dressed in marine khaki, set out on horseback accompanied by Butler, 150 marines, and 50 gendarmes on an excursion into the interior during which they visited "famous Fort Rivière," as FDR described it in his travel diary. Duly impressed, he certified the aforementioned Congressional Medals of Honor for Butler and two others. Next came the historic Citadel and Sans Souci palace of King Henry Christophe, which FDR thought had tourist potential; guests could "use Fort Rivière with its cool nights for living purposes." The trip resulted in sweeping kudos for Butler and the marines. FDR concurred "entirely" in an expanded role for the gendarmerie, and later recommended Smedley's achievements to the chief of insular police in Puerto Rico. Commandant Barnett sent profuse thanks, calling Butler's work "a big feather in the cap of the Marine Corps."[47]

Smedley, now promoted to lieutenant colonel, had connected with a new patron at the apex of Marine Corps politics in the person of FDR, and with a network of key figures in Haitian affairs. Accompanying FDR on the inspection tour had been John H. McIlhenny, chairman of the U.S. Civil Service Commission, soon to be appointed financial adviser to Haiti with complete control over client-government finances. After FDR's departure, his cousin Harry, on duty with the gendarmerie, surveyed investment possibilities—port development, sisal and sugar plantations, cattle, cotton, coffee, and the like—and reported his findings unofficially to FDR and McIlhenny. While nothing materialized from these purely private pursuits, FDR and McIlhenny were actively interested until the end of McIlhenny's tour as financial adviser in 1922, when FDR proposed setting up a Haitian-American import-export company. Also involved was McIlhenny's friend, the banker and Haiti mogul Roger L. Farnham.[48]

Butler and the marines were available for supporting roles. In early 1918, with McIlhenny as intermediary, Butler organized cargo handling by prisoners for freight that Farnham was importing into Saint Marc. Marine gendarmerie officers supervised the operation. Smedley had responded enthusiastically to Farnham, "We are all standing by ready to lend a hand wherever possible. We can handle this freight and in fact can put over nearly any other 'roughstuff' you may suggest." He cautioned that it would be unwise "to depend on us permanently for this work as conditions might change," but for the moment the marine brigade commander, Colonel John H. Russell, had given tacit approval. McIlhenny mentioned that he and FDR thought German influence, which dominated Haitian wholesale trade, "should not be tolerated for an instant longer than is necessary," to which Smedley replied by offering to help drive the Germans out—declaration of war by Haiti "would permit us to take most any step we saw fit towards the German holdings down here."[49] In turn, Butler worked the FDR-McIlhenny-Farnham connection in his desperate attempts to get to the frontlines in France after American intervention in the Great War.

Prospects for American investment required voiding the prohibition of alien land ownership, which had been Haiti's constitutional bulwark against foreign domination dating back to the overthrow of French slavery. Plantation agriculture remained the main attraction. A new American constitution, which FDR claimed to have drafted himself, remedied this, but under Haitian law it could be enacted only by the National Assembly.

The new constitution forced a climax in the confrontation with local political opponents, and termination of Haiti's electoral institutions. After the attempt to manipulate elections in January 1917, Butler tried to negotiate an accommodation with the National Assembly. By June that body was in open revolt, rejecting the U.S. draft constitution and in the midst of passing a defiant anti-American constitution. Cabinet ministers customarily delivered legislative dissolution decrees, but the task fell by default to Butler: "I walked into the assembly amid hisses and jeers, which had no effect, of course, and notified Mr. Vincent [the president of the Senate] that I had a communication from the President of the Republic." In the commotion that followed squads of gendarmes in attendance under a marine captain loaded their rifles, and Smedley had to stop proceedings and make them unload. After the decree was read, Butler grabbed it from Vincent's hand and was able to produce it in 1921 at U.S. Senate hearings to refute allegations that he had acted on his own authority. "It was a graphic story," Secretary Daniels wrote in his memoirs, "told inimitably, that Smedley related to friends when he returned home—how he got the President to sign the paper dissolving the National Assembly and how there came about a virtual shotgun adoption of the Constitution." Butler wrote McIlhenny that the Assembly "became so impudent that the Gendarmerie had to dissolve them, which dissolution was effected by genuinely Marine Corps methods."[50]

The gendarmerie efficiently administered the country, backed by the passive presence of a marine brigade of about 1,000 garrisoned at Port-au-Prince and Cap Haitien. FDR's journalist companion Marvin wrote that "the actual running of the Government comes pretty near being vested in General Butler and his young [gendarmerie] colonels and majors." Another American civilian observed that a marine in the gendarmerie was "clothed with practically unlimited power," sitting as district judge in all civil and criminal cases, collecting taxes, disbursing all national government funds, and even serving as "ex-officio director of the schools, inasmuch as he pays the teachers." Fritz Wise, who had been in command at Jérémie, remarked, "In Cuba we didn't have the absolute authority we had here." Vandegrift felt that "in a sense our task formed a civil counterpart to the work of Christian missionaries who were devoting their lives to these people."[51]

Butler ran the gendarmerie from Port-au-Prince. It was a demanding job and at times he despaired, as when he lost a political skirmish and wrote his father, "Instead of having practically the whole of Haiti to run, am simply the very subservient chief of a nigger police force." But by 1917, he had things pretty much under control and was taking pride in the achievements. In October, Congressman Butler forwarded to FDR a description of the gendarmerie from one of Smedley's letters, with the elder Butler's accompanying note, "It is a part of your personal administration and will in time to come, give you credit for the creation of another Republic, put it on its feet and start it on its high road to success." Smedley described his outfit as comprising 3,000 gendarmes, busy with 6,000 men working on the public road system (the corvée), 2,000 prisoners in 125 lockups, nineteen schoolhouses abuilding, the national telegraph and telephone systems, a coast guard that hauled paid freight, six plantations, agricultural experiment stations, prison shoe and clothing factories, repair shops, sales department—altogether nearly 14,000 men under his control.[52]

The most controversial operation during Butler's regime was the inauguration of a national road system featuring a 170-mile unpaved highway connecting Port-au-Prince with Cap Haitien. Roads, as was urgently appreciated by the marine command, were vital to effective military control. Despite the 1915 pacification, extensive patrolling continued, and in September 1916 Butler himself led a "flying column" on a two-week incursion across the border into the Dominican Republic in support of the Dominican intervention commanded by Colonel Pendleton.

Roads would also serve as transportation infrastructure for economic development. Since the client government lacked adequate funds, Butler adapted an 1864 Haitian corvée law by which peasants were required to work on local roads in lieu of paying road taxes. "They had the option," Butler later testified, "nobody had any money, so they reported for work." Nearly 9,000 men worked on the road. They were encouraged by little prize flags to hang on gateposts and weekly pep talks by Dartiguenave and cabinet ministers whom Smedley brought out to "impress upon them that they were doing this for their own country and not for the white man."[53]

The operation was similar to the corvée used by the British in the 1880s to dredge canals in Egypt. In Haiti under Butler, workers were given food or, as indicated on a cost sheet for November 1917, four cents gold per day. They were supposedly safeguarded from abuse, with care taken that nobody be forced to work outside his home district, and they were allowed to have what Butler called "voodoo dances," otherwise outlawed by the occupation. In January 1918 a presidential party of twenty-seven vehicles ceremoniously opened the road by driving to Cap Haitien with stops along the way for speeches and band performances. Butler received enthusiastic congratulations from FDR—"Well done. McIlhenny and [Livingston] Davis concur"—and from Farnham, who had notified the others.[54]

In acknowledging the congratulations, Butler wrote FDR that "it would not do to ask too many questions as to how we accomplished this work." To McIlhenny he suggested open-ended possibilities: "We have over 15,000 at work in the whole of Haiti, a goodly-sized body of intelligent voters for any project the United States may wish to put across. . . . just tell us what you want done and everybody from the President [Dartiguenave] down will shout for it."[55] He probably meant to curry favor by offering himself as loyally and discreetly available for any "roughstuff," as he had put it to Farnham, for which his superiors might not wish to issue explicit orders or officially know details and methods. But whatever the conspiratorial banter, the basic workings of the corvée as a forced labor system were public knowledge, and readily apparent in Butler's highly touted cost statistics in which food and cement were the major items.

Brutalization of the corvée eventually culminated in a major uprising. When Butler left Haiti in March 1918, the corvée was, as he later testified, "in full blast." Stories of abuse date from the subsequent period, but since systematic inquiries were delayed and then frustrated by marine coverups so flagrant they "stunned" Secretary Daniels, the issue remains obscure. From available evidence, it seems that Butler ran the corvée as a "square deal" and with a certain amount of panache. Certainly, the situation deteriorated alarmingly after his departure. Abuses included workers being roped together in gangs and kept under guard by gendarmes to prevent escape. A marine lieutenant colonel sent into the interior to investigate in early 1919 reported a "reign of terror" with "indiscriminate strong-arm work being pulled off," and Commandant Barnett ordered Colonel Russell to stop the "indiscriminate killing of natives." The Haitian peasants' contribution to the historical record was the rebellion itself, lasting from late 1918 until an ill-fated frontal assault on Port-au-Prince in early 1920.[56]

McIlhenny wrote FDR in May 1919 that Butler's successor, Colonel Alexander S. Williams, had "made an entire failure as Commander of the Gendarmerie," which was now "discredited in every section of the island and all of the good work of Butler has been lost." Butler was, indeed, generally regarded as being an efficient officer, and a marine later recalled how they had together perfected a laborers check-off system protecting against abuses. Daniels, in 1930, related the same sequence: Butler, "with consummate ability of understanding the sensibilities of people in all parts of the world," had started the corvée and it worked well; abuses came later as succeeding officers forced Haitians to work away from their homes.[57]

The benign view of Butler's role in founding the corvée is supported by an evident mellowing in his attitude toward Haiti after the bitter 1916-17 political infighting, although he remained hostile to the *élite* as a class. In 1920, when a close friend mailed him a newspaper photo of Dartiguenave with the notation "he is not a bad looking old coon," Smedley replied, referring to Dartiguenave as a "colored gentleman" who "really is a pretty good old fellow and we became quite devoted to him. Of course, he is as crooked as a 'dog's hind leg,' but he is so nice about it." In *Old Gimlet Eye*, the Haiti chapters are, to be sure, laced with 1930s Amos 'n Andy-style buffoonery, such as Smedley and Dartiguenave touring together with Smedley getting first chance at the bathwater and sleeping in bed while the president slept on the floor, but there is also the gracious compliment, however condescending, that Dartiguenave "had the unfailing dignity and the urbanity and education of a cultured white man." [58]

Butler was definitely more at ease after the arrival of Ethel and the three children in late 1916, except that the American declaration of war against Germany in 1917 set him passionately in pursuit of a chance to get to the front. Otherwise, he seemed to like Haiti, and in January 1918 wrote a friend that, "were it not for this awful [European] war, this duty would be very attractive." Life in Haiti, especially in Port-au-Prince where the Americans took over the best housing and established a flourishing American colony, had its attractions. Wartime economic depression hit the *élite* hard, while marines had their steady dollar salaries, augmented for many by gendarmerie "topping-up." Waller acquired a house he described as "delightful" and "really beautiful." Butler, who in 1916 grossed $7,256, paid $95 monthly for "a big comfortable house with wide verandas and a pleasant, shaded garden." The family slept under mosquito netting and made do with an outside two-holer toilet but had eight servants to bring up hot water for baths and look after other domestic chores. Butler imported a used Stutz 4-C touring car, named the "blue bird" in the Haitian press, which he proudly described as "one of the heaviest, lowest hung cars." Snooks and Smedley, Jr., attended a French school along with local children, although later an American school was established for white children. [59]

The Butlers left Haiti before Jim Crow segregation was fully institutionalized, but the transition took place while they were there and they went along with the crowd. Indeed, those few who resisted were ostracized. Mrs. Butler, one of the two or three leading ladies of the occupation, considered it offensive for white women to dance with white men while refusing Haitians, but she did not dance with Haitians either. She danced with neither, the solution apparently adopted en masse by white American ladies who went out into the garden during the aforementioned 1917 gendarmerie ball. On hearing from a Haitian friend that the woman a marine was about to marry was part Negro, Smedley passed on the information so that the marriage was quashed. In another instance, recalled in a letter to Lejeune, he "had to transfer [a marine] around Haiti to keep him from marrying a colored woman." But these were the American racial mores of the day. If anything, the Butlers were perhaps relatively liberal, and at least made an effort to be polite and gracious.[60]

In retrospect, Butler's role in the early days of the occupation was singled out as perniciously militaristic and offensively rude. B. Danache, Dartiguenave's cabinet secretary, ranked Butler first among Americans who had left behind "sombre memories" of insults and humiliation, a "monster" whose boorishness had been deeply resented. But interestingly, even Danache conceded Smedley's high reputation, among resident Americans, for verve and wit: "I watched him one day, at a distance, in a social gathering on the Champs de Mars . . . . He was surrounded by women and men who drank his words as if they fell from the lips of a demigod: all throats sang his praise, all grinned effusively in appreciation." Throughout his adult life Smedley was a vivacious and enthralling talker, the center of attention. Danache's charges of uncouthness must be partly understood from the perspective of *élite* social-class prete asions; he went on to characterize the marine officers as "not having been chosen from the cream of American society," while their wives, "gangsters in skirts," came from "one did not know what slum."[61] When confronted with insolence such as this, Butler would no doubt have been quite caustic.

Financial Adviser William W. Cumberland, who was the dominant American civilian official in the mid-1920s, said in his reminiscences that "some of the earlier authorities were in constant turmoil with the Haitians, usually on racial and personal grounds." He singled out Butler as a "misfit" and "a man with about as little tact as one could ever meet . . . all of us heaved a sigh of relief when he was sent to other duties . . . . For years some of us had the job of trying to heal up the scars which that gentleman left."[62] This was based on hearsay, but apparently reflected impressions of the previous era that Cumberland received in the State Department and on arrival in Haiti, and was the legacy he had to contend with in his own efforts, such as they were, at mollifying the Haitian *élite*. This evil reputation later contributed to Butler's being passed over at the last minute for the post of high commissioner to Haiti in 1922, as we shall see.

But, as has been argued, the occupation was conceived as a military exercise, imbued throughout with racist assumptions. Butler did the job in the spirit in which it was assigned, and both he and Waller went to great lengths to keep open channels of communication with superiors in Washington, receiving encouragement or tacit approval in reply. Handwringing came later from those assigned the task of conciliation. When it was subsequently considered politic to increase civilian participation in the occupation, Butler and Waller served as convenient scapegoats for renouncing the previous hard line.

8 General Duckboard

FRANCE

For almost a year after American intervention in the European War, Butler's numerous appeals to Marine Corps headquarters to get himself detached from Haiti and sent to the front came to naught. Ironically, his achievements as commandant of the Haitian gendarmerie proved to be an obstacle; he was said to be irreplaceable. Financial Adviser McIlhenny, banker Farnham, Assistant Secretary of the Navy Roosevelt, Marine Commandant Barnett, and the State Department all pointed to the importance of his work there, and at one point Roosevelt alluded to fears of unrest if Smedley was not on hand to keep the lid on, particularly now that extra troops for Haiti could no longer be spared. But friends in high places also sympathized, more so after completion of the corvée-built trunk road to the north. Farnham wrote that he "said and did at Washington all possible" to help Smedley get to France.[1]

Butler was desperate to get to the front. "I tell you both very frankly," he wrote his parents, "that I shall never show my face in West Chester again if I am not allowed to go to France." By October 1917 all his able-bodied male kinfolk had volunteered and were involved in the war. His younger brother Horace was a "real soldier," while he was only a "black tin one." Someday his grandchildren would be "subjected to the remark 'Where was *your* grandfather during the Big War?' and they will have to hide their heads in shame and either lie or say 'He was a policeman in the service of a foreign black Republic.'" He took off his colonial war medals and would "never wear them again unless I get into this 'show' as they represent play soldiering." He had "no use for any American who doesn't want to fight and use every endeavor to get into it."[2]

Most professional soldiers wanted to get to France for the usual inextricable mix of honorable and careerist motives. Butler's chances were especially problematic because of the political aspect. He felt that "the present gang" at headquarters would never let him go. Commandant Barnett's references to vitally important work in Haiti were "just an excuse on the part of Headquarters to put me off and get their friends abroad." Meanwhile Smedley's deputy in the gendarmerie, Major Alexander S. Williams, returned from Washington and told him that Barnett said privately "that I had used all the political pull possible to get this job and could stay here and enjoy it." Barnett no doubt resented Smedley's brazen political influence, including a 1916 lobbying trip to Washington on behalf of gendarmerie legislation and a pending Marine Corps personnel bill, for which Congressman Butler got Secretary of the Navy Daniels to override Admiral Caperton's refusal to grant Smedley special leave to make the trip.[3]

But there was a sense that in fairness to his ability and past achievements he should not be left out. At least not for mean political reasons—all this was part of an ongoing factional battle within the Marine Corps. Barnett and others were approached by members of the House Naval Affairs Committee on Smedley's behalf, and his father's political leverage, amounting to twenty years' seniority in Congress, could not be discounted.[4]

At this point Thomas S. Butler was the senior Republican on the Naval Affairs Committee, and on good terms with Secretary Daniels. He had played a key role in passing the Democratic administration's historic 1916 "navy second to none" building program; in fact, the *New York Times* ran the subheading "Move Started By Quaker." But he was reluctant to press Smedley's case, although well aware of claims he might make for military favors. In January 1918 he wrote Smedley that "thee and General [Leonard] Wood will be two of the soldiers well known to the American people who will be used before long, in the effort to show that the present Administration is promoting and pushing forward, friends of its Democratic allies." But no good would come of this. "I can bring it about, I believe, but I will not do it. I cannot assume the risk; it must come in a natural way, and then the responsibility will be that of the Government alone."[5]

Meanwhile, Smedley was actively beseeching his longtime friend and best contact at headquarters, Assistant Commandant John A. Lejeune, who throughout these years played an honest-broker role between Waller and Butler in the field and Commandant Barnett in Washington. Lejeune thereby apparently enhanced his standing with both factions, and gradually superseded the aging Waller as Smedley's mentor. He was also able to work the Butler connection in Congress for the benefit of the Corps, which Barnett could not do because of simmering mistrust. During the Wilson administration's 1916 military preparedness drive, Lejeune had written asking Smedley to "drop a line to your father" regarding appropriations for a new East Coast marine base in the Chesapeake Bay area, which was "the concentration point for the fleet in the event of war."[6] This soon materialized at Quantico, thirty miles south of Washington on the Potomac. Quantico was detached from the usual navy base connection and was sufficiently vast for artillery practice and field maneuvers. Marine recruits were to be given basic training at Parris Island, South Carolina, and Mare Island, California, and then sent to Quantico for advanced exercises before shipping out overseas.

After the declaration of war in April 1917, Lejeune left headquarters to organize an expeditionary brigade at Quantico, and promised to try and get Smedley command of one of the regiments.[7] This fell through, but within a year Smedley was ordered to Quantico, where he took over as base commander from Lejeune, who then left for France. Training at Quantico was meant to be realistic. French and Canadian officers with extensive battle experience served as advisers. Troops built trenches and dugouts representing Allied and German sides, with a barbed wire no-man's-land in between, and then attacked by sapping, artillery barrages, trench raids, and frontal assault. One trainee remarked, "What do you think? I am at Château-Thierry! . . . A whole section of the Virginia woodland has been taken over and blasted, dug, and mined by the miners and sappers of the Marine Corps until it is almost an exact replica of the country around Château-Thierry and Vimy Ridge." According to marine General Lester A. Dessez's reminiscences, Butler had a hill flattened to conform to the Château Thierry map, much to the distress of a French captain who insisted that the map should conform to the ground, and not vice versa.[8]

Recruits undergoing this training were a new breed to the marines, as wartime enthusiasm and the marine slogan "First in the Fight" brought in volunteers with higher educational standards and loftier social backgrounds. A colonel who commanded Quantico at the outset during the summer of 1917 had a regiment with 60 percent college men, with two-thirds of one company straight out of the University of Minnesota. Given Butler's long-standing preference for "roughneck" soldiering, and his fostering many a "comrade in illiteracy" against the growing pressures for educational qualifications, it is impressive to see him emerging in these relatively civilianized, middlebrow circumstances as an effective mass leader. Unlike many commanders who persisted in Draconian methods considered appropriate for the riffraff and immigrant recruits of the prewar era, Butler proved to be very much in tune with citizen-soldier military sentiment. After ten hours of drill and instruction during the day, he rallied the troops by personally leading nightly inspirational songfests. Captain Upshur wrote home, "You have never really heard 'Onward Christian Soldiers' sung before—never as it is sung here . . . it makes the tears run down your cheeks."[9]

But as Smedley watched Lejeune leaving for France, his own prospects were to be stuck at Quantico indefinitely: "I was at outs with Marine headquarters because I opposed elevating the Commandant of the Corps to the rank of lieutenant general so long as the soldiers were getting no extra reward for doing the heavy work in the trenches." He had written home urging his father to oppose the proposed legislation because "it promotes practically no one but Staff Officers who went into a Staff Department because they preferred an easy life and are now anxious to get the fruits of the Line's labors and sufferings." [10]

Congressman Butler helped defeat the so-called Barnett amendment, denouncing it on the floor of Congress as favoring "swivel chair officers" to the "disadvantage of the fighting men of the Marine Corps." In an extraordinary outburst that included allusions to Barnett's using his wife's prominent Washington social position for political advantage, he pointed to the gallery and exclaimed, "The place for fighting men is at the front, not here in the gallery!" Sitting in the gallery were Commandant and Mrs. Barnett and Barnett's Annapolis classmate and crony, General Charles H. Lauchheimer, who had been at odds with the Butlers dating back to the 1908-10 succession controversy. The elder Butler saw the promotions as tantamount to wartime peculation, characterizing them to FDR as the "selfishness of these men who are endeavoring to take care of themselves only." [11]

Getting Smedley to the front therefore required circumventing Barnett. He received direct orders from Secretary Daniels to take his Thirteenth Marine Regiment to France. "It was probable," recalled General Dessez, "the Commandant was not amused." Butler explained in *Old Gimlet Eye* that Josephus Daniels, Jr., "joined the regiment and literally dragged us overseas. . . . It would never do for the son of the Secretary of the Navy to stay in the United States. So it was not my military record but young Josephus Daniels that finally got me to France." [12]

Josephus, Jr., twenty-four years old, had come a long way since the American declaration of war a year earlier, when his father recorded in his diary: "He told me about a vicious article in the Greensboro News, saying none of my boys had enlisted—a vicious, dirty article that wounded him. . . . The dear boy's health did not permit him to study and he is not prepared for leadership in any military training & both of us are at sea as to what we ought to do. Marine Corps may be best." Later General Lejeune wrote Daniels that he had talked with Barnett about "the best thing to do for your boy," having in mind a post with the Marine Corps publicity bureau in New York, but this scheme failed to materialize. The ultimate solution apparently again involved Lejeune, who noted in his memoirs, "Frequently he [Secretary Daniels] sent callers to me with a card of introduction on which was written, 'Do for Mr. ———'s son what you did for Josephus.'" [13]

He joined the marines as a private and was attached to the supply depot in Philadelphia. "He isn't very strong," noted Secretary Daniels, who "feared he would not be able to stand it; & that sleeping in room with 30-40 men &c would go hard with him," but he took it all "bravely & cheerfully." In another entry, "JD Jr. said the worst thing about marine life was the cursing and swearing at men & the vulgar language. Must be ended." Barnett informed the secretary in Janaury 1918 that Josephus, Jr., had been recommended for second lieutenant. In July he applied to go to France in Colonel Butler's outfit and was transferred accordingly, but on a trip up from Quantico in August he told his father that "Headquarters will not let Butler go unless I [the secretary] see to it." [14]

At Quantico, Butler took Josephus under his wing and the Thirteenth Regiment became special. A few days before leaving for France, Smedley wrote Mrs. Addie Daniels to "tell you how your four thousand devoted children appreciate their 'Mother.'" The letter was gushy, but no doubt sincere and not out of keeping with the gallant, sentimental style of the times, particularly as men went off to a quite ghastly and lethal war: "The sweetness of your voice and your words last Friday night is still most distinctly present with me and I know with all the rest of 'Your Regiment' and will help us to do better the job which all Christians have in hand at this time. There is no force which operates more powerfully for good than the love of strong men for a good woman . . . . The pennants are being made and we shall always carry them with the tenderest thoughts of Our Mother." On the eve of departure, Secretary and Mrs. Daniels had dinner with the Butlers and then slept with Josephus, Jr., in the chaplain's quarters. [15]

The Thirteenth Regiment, with several months' advanced combat training, shipped out in mid-September 1918. "What a fine looking outfit they were," remembered Dessez, "as they passed in review with 4,000 men, fixed bayonets, and a really big band playing 'Onward Christian Soldiers.' It was a solemn moment not to be forgotten." And for once Smedley was able to indulge fully his talismanic fancy; he nicknamed the Thirteenth the "Hoodoo Regiment" (he had previously intended to name it after FDR) and obtained thirteen black cats as mascots. The outfit left Quantico on Friday the thirteenth in seven trains of thirteen cars each, with Butler sitting in seat thirteen in the parlor car. They sailed from Hoboken two days later. [16]

The crossing was not auspicious. Just at this point the 1918 influenza epidemic that killed a half million Americans hit with a vengeance. Butler himself was sick in bed but recovered before reaching France. There were twelve hundred cases in the regiment and over a hundred deaths. Looking down at the "white, drawn faces" in the lighter going ashore at Brest, Butler called out for everyone to sing, and as they broke out in "Sweet Adeline" crews from two transports nearby came to the rails and cheered. [17]

The debarkation camp three miles up the hill at Pontanezen Barracks offered scant refuge, being little more than a wretched sea of mud and pup tents. It rained almost constantly. Medical facilities were overwhelmed by the influx of sick and dying coming in off the transports, providing Brest, according to a recent scholarly study, with "a greater and more constantly replenished supply of fresh victims for influenza than at any other location in Europe." [18] Already racked by flu, Butler's men were now quarantined in the open fields with cases of spinal meningitis, sleeping in the pup tents they brought with them on their backs. Every evening he assembled them for singing, with himself as choral leader, in an attempt to keep up spirits.

After a miserable week, Butler, instead of being ordered to the front, was detached from the marines and given command of Camp Pontanezen. His "crack regiment," as he described it, was broken up to do manual labor and guard duty in rear zones as part of Services of Supply (S.O.S.). Butler lamented in his memoirs: "I always felt that the command at Brest was wished on me because it was a lemon. The camp had been a disgrace ever since the A.E.F. [American Expeditionary Forces] first landed at Brest, and when the influenza epidemic swept over France it became a pest trap. . . . When the people at home found out about conditions at Brest there was bound to be a national scandal." When Commandant Barnett passed through Pontanezen, Smedley wrote his wife, "He is a weak old woman and to blame for my failure to get to the front." Amid so many intrigues, there were grounds for suspicion on all sides. But in fact Barnett had been pressing hard for a full marine combat division in the A.E.F. and was thwarted by the army and General Pershing, who wished to limit marine and navy interference. Butler's fate and the dispersal of his regiment were consistent with an established preference to use marines as support troops and post marine officers to command army units. A.E.F. headquarters was also intent upon building up S.O.S. with high-quality personnel. Faltering logistics had assumed enormous importance with million-man armies, and were fraught with political ramifications should mismanagement peeve volunteer citizen-soldiers.[19]

Pontanezen Barracks, part of a French military complex that dated back to the seventeenth century, consisted of six large old stone buildings capable of housing 300 men each. A marine posted there in 1917 before the deluge described it as "sort of a quaint old place in the charming Brittany countryside."[20] The port of Brest, where the westernmost coast juts far out into the Atlantic, had for centuries been an important French naval base and was one of the few deep harbors available for large American transports. It had originally been intended to favor Bordeaux, 300 miles to the south. But better harbor facilities, a sheltered roadstead, and the desirability of condensing North Atlantic convoy lanes to protect against German submarines made Brest the premier A.E.F. debarkation port, despite its miserable climate with almost incessant rain.

Conditions in the fall of 1918 were appalling. According to the official army medical history, the site was assessed as "fairly satisfactory for about 10,000 men, provided certain improvements were made." Apart from the cold, wetness, and "deep and tenacious mud," deficiencies included "insufficient kitchens, . . . inadequate means of sterilizing mess kits, poor latrines, limited bathing and disinfecting facilities, limited means for washing hands, shortage of fuel, and an inadequate water supply, which was polluted." With no mess halls, troops ate out in the rain.[21]

Successive units coming off the ships complained bitterly about the squalor, and the camp did in fact become a public scandal back in the States, especially after the influenza deaths in the fall of 1918. There were 1,817 burials at Brest in September-November 1918, and another 3,500 deaths from November to February 1919. Most of these, however, were dead and dying coming in off the transports, and the mortality statistics must be measured against the heavy traffic—by February, 985,000 men had transited via Brest. The accusation in the House by a Missouri congressman that "our boys are dying like pigs from criminal carelessness of the War Department at Brest" was extravagant, but drastic action was, in fact, urgently needed.[22]

Butler took over just as the crest of the influenza epidemic was breaking. It was also the time of late autumn and early winter rains, the heaviest of the year, and of maximum pressure on camp facilities with ongoing debarkation augmented by mass embarkation following the November armistice. Several hours after he took command, the largest American transport, the *Leviathan*, came in with 10,000 men, 4,000 of whom had flu. In the absence of vehicles, Butler released his Thirteenth Regiment from quarantine and sent them down to the docks to fetch the sick on improvised stretchers: "For two days and nights my regiment went along the rows of desperately sick men, giving them hot soup and coffee and warm blankets wherever they happened to be lying. . . . I waded through acres of mud, running from group to group to speed the work and to encourage the invalids." Roaring bonfires were built. He set regimental bands to playing jazz, ragtime, and military marches in continuous shifts around the camp.[23]

His own energy and drive were crucial to the hard work and rapid improvements that followed. A decade later, an army officer wrote him recalling his battalion's arrival in a driving rain storm: "Your ears must have been ringing with our remarks of the camp and I can picture today you coming up to the fire and introducing yourself. I think, after 15 minutes conversation with you, we were sold on the camp and you, for after your departure, there was no more grumbling."[24] It was certainly a great situation for inspired leadership, and Butler rose to the occasion, drawing upon the self-confidence and audacity that had marked his earlier exploits in colonial small wars. Second Lieutenant Ray A. Robinson, who eventually served as his personal aide for twelve years, reminisced as a retired general: "I think he is the greatest leader of men we've ever had. He could take a unit ready to rebel, and in 15 minutes they were cheering and throwing their hats."[25]

Butler's career progressed apace. Most professionals were being rapidly promoted to fill senior posts in the expanded wartime military. Within a month of taking command at Pontanezen, Smedley was promoted to temporary brigadier general. At age thirty-seven, this made him the youngest general ever in marine history, and one of the youngest in the U.S. services at the time. However well-deserved in terms of past record and present responsibilities, the promotion may have been influenced by the Daniels axis. Josephus, Jr., wrote his mother: "Let me thank both you and Father for this a thousand and one times. The first thing that General Butler did was to make me one of his aides." He asked that Butler next be given command of a brigade and sent to the front. "It would only take a word from Father to do it—just as he made the Colonel a General. Now please work both of these matters for me at once and I will be your darling boy forever." In the following weeks he wrote how he and Butler were having "great times together since 'We' have been made a Brigadier General," and chidingly urged his father to speed up formal notification, "Get on the job 'old man'"—so that he could officially take up his new duties.[26] The war, however, was over on 11 November, so there was no more getting to the front, and inflated wartime temporary ranks were likely to depreciate.

At Brest, problems of efficiency and morale were compounded by a morass of army red tape; the system was experiencing obvious convulsions in expanding to million-man proportions. Butler, particularly when in warrior guise and roused to the attack, tended toward creative flexibility, not to say insubordination, and could be openly contemptuous of bureaucratic procedure. In the present circumstances he was supported by his army superiors, Generals Eli A. Helmick and James G. Harbord of S.O.S., in taking unorthodox measures to straighten out the extraordinary mess at Pontanezen.

The great turnabout, henceforth fastened upon as symbol of dauntless assiduity, was Butler's raid on the warehouses at Brest from which he had been unsuccessfully trying to requisition supplies from army quartermasters. The incident, which occurred shortly after the armistice, recalls his 1907 "nervous breakdown" in the Philippines:

> Piled in the warehouses were eighty thousand sections of duckboard [wooden slats], made to be laid on the bottom of trenches. I wanted them for sidewalks, so the men wouldn't have to wade through the eternal mud. I submitted request after request for the material . . . . Finally I got sick and tired of waiting. Helmick was away, so that I was temporarily in command of that section of France. One afternoon I marched down to the docks with seven thousand men and burst into the warehouses. As long as we were invading the sacred premises, I though we might as well make a clean sweep. We needed shovels, axes, picks and kettles as well as duckboards.[27]

Butler himself carried a duckboard back up the hill to camp, thereby shaming stragglers and grumblers. His empty Cadillac flying a general's star received the usual deferences while Smedley was up ahead trudging along with the troops. Thereafter, as Pontanezen prospered, he was known as General Duckboard. The fabled duckboard symbol, implying heroic defiance of army red tape, was painted on camp vehicles, duckboard rosettes decorated horses' bridles, a contest to name the camp newspaper resulted in *The Duckboard*, and A.E.F. supreme command authorized a white duckboard on maroon background as shoulder patch for the permanent garrison. "That duckboard story," Butler concluded, "built the camp." [28]

The armistice increased the press of troops as embarkation to the States began immediately, even as new troops continued to arrive. A year later Butler could refer back to "the battle of the mud" and "the dark days of last December" with a sense of heroic nostalgia, but at the time the situation was grim. And it was just at this point that political pressure from back home was greatest. [29]

The War Department tried to avert public censure by sponsoring its own investigation, and sent the popular author of mystery novels, Mary Roberts Rinehart, to Brest as a "troubleshooter." She came prepared, as she put it, "to send a blistering report to Washington. . . . Scandal had broken loose back home, brought by returning soldiers, and the War Department found itself facing a Senatorial investigation . . . men were dying like flies in all the camps." For three days she toured Pontanezen in high rubber boots and raincoat, looked into tents, stood on line with tin cup and plate of food, and talked with the men. Morale was "excellent" despite squalid surroundings. And, corroborating the duckboard saga, she came away with high praise for Butler, "that dynamo of energy, courage and sheer ability" who "was no red tape man . . . he had raided the wharf at Brest of the duckboards no longer needed for the trenches, [and] carried the first one himself up that four-mile hill to camp." He was giving out double rations of food, serving hot soup all day, and issuing six blankets to each man, all "in defiance of regulations." Her radio report to the secretary of war supported Smedley's urgent appeal for tent flooring, stoves to heat tents and barracks, a delousing plant, and laundry machinery, all of which were soon forthcoming. The report, according to Butler, "went a long way toward stopping the abuse that had been heaped on us." [30]

In the early months of 1919 Pontanezen developed prodigiously to reach its maximum size and efficiency. Rinehart felt things "had improved incredibly" by the time she returned in January. [31] At its greatest size, the camp extended onto surrounding farmland from the original 90 to about 1,000 acres. As Pontanezen became an awesome monument to the bureaucratic rationalization of military life, Butler acquired competency in the new scheme of things and ameliorated some of the more inhuman aspects with his sense of showmanship. Of course the duckboard saga ultimately became a promotional hype, a heroic fantasy, intended to make more palatable the

very regimentation it purported to deny, even as Pontanezen came to epito-
mize regimentation with a vengeance. Modern war, logistical bottlenecks in
particular, required cooperation and discipline, not heroism. But in a pinch,
it was men and morale that won through, as symbolized by the duckboard.
Indeed, *morale*, the psychology of moving mass armies, was just being introduced into American military argot as learned from the French.

Compared even to the enormous British bases at Boulogne, Havre, and
Rouen, Pontanezen became the embarkation camp *par excellence*, with the
most highly organized techniques and procedures. Relative to the other
American ports, 117,000 troops shipped out of Brest in March 1919, as
against 37,000 from Saint-Nazaire, 29,000 from Bordeaux, and 9,700 from
Marseilles.[32] Built up to an average of 20,000 permanent garrison plus
60,000 transients, Pontanezen occasionally exceeded 100,000, depending
on ship movements. It was necessary to have on hand a large reserve ready
to embark on short notice when the big ships came in. Speed and efficiency
were the watchwords, to keep the ships moving and maximize flow.

Pontanezen eventually had 1,100 buildings, 55 miles of plank roads and
sidewalks, 60 miles of duckboards, and 15 miles of narrow-gauge railway.
Daily food consumption averaged 72 steers, 12,000 pounds of bacon,
45,000 loaves of bread, 4,000 pounds of coffee. In one day 2,674 pounds of
candy were dispensed. In one month, three million packs of cigarettes were
sold and another million issued through the mess. Musical bands made the
rounds of sixteen huge kitchens, each capable of feeding 5,000.[33]

Whatever pride might be taken in awesome statistics, there was also a
new scale of human dignity, or lack thereof. Little play here for the warrior
ideal—except in the realm of duckboard public-relations fantasies. Troops
often ate standing up, which was found to take only eight minutes while
sitting took twenty. Units heading home were processed in groups of 480
through a delousing plant where, according to the army medical history:
"The men stripped to their undershirts and stood on the benches, two rows
facing each other. The medical inspector then passed between each two
rows examining for venereal disease and vermin, thus making it unnecessary
for the inspector to stoop. The men then stepped down from the benches
and pulled their undershirts over their heads and the inspector passed along
a second time examining for skin diseases, scabies, and body lice."[34] All this
would no doubt have confirmed M. Sinclair of *Le nègre masqué* in his loathing
for "mechanical men" and American linoleum civilization.

Even after material deficiencies had been corrected, Pontanezen had
the reputation of being a nightmare, and Butler was subject to criticisms as
a "martinet ruler."[35] A transient black unit, the 369th Infantry, which had
been under fire for 191 days at the front, had a bad time going through
Pontanezen in January 1919. Some of the troopers shouted "Who won the
war?" at Butler's military police and were severely harassed in return. One

of the officers recalled that during their three-week stay, "no day passed (and but a few hours) during which we failed to get some notice of petty fault-finding coupled with a threat of disciplinary action against the entire organization by placing its name at the bottom of the list for embarkation." A 369th soldier's diary read: "Deloused and detailed night and day and it seems as if we at last had struck something worse than the Germans and many were taken sick as a result of the conditions under which we were compelled to live and work. The word 'attention' comes into its own at this camp, being very strictly enforced by the front-dodging M.P.'s [military police], the pampered pets of the war." [36]

Whites had similar experiences. William L. Langer, subsequently a noted historian, wrote a unit history in which he described his outfit's transit through Brest, also in January 1919: "We began to get night details, the first one at Brest unloading timber from a large freighter. It was a beastly night and we had to wait an exceptionally long time for trucks that were to take us down. As I think back on those hours of misery—useless misery and discomfort—I realize to the full my inability to adequately picture what we and thousands of others of the 'brave and victorious American boys' suffered at the hands of the Service of Supply authorities." Langer's group, "despite the most rigid regulations," built fires out of duckboards, around which they huddled at night for warmth against the gusting wind and rain.[37] So much for the duckboard cult.

Butler's egalitarian touch probably made all this go down somewhat more easily. His prestige as a two-time Congressional Medal of Honor winner helped mitigate the S.O.S. stigma, and the occasional human touch was evident. At least everyone might know that the problems were recognized. There were the duckboard symbols everywhere, and the legend was perpetuated in the camp newspaper with its "Splashes O' Mud" joke column and first-rate cartoons. The spirit and slogan of "putting 'em away with a smile," billeting large numbers of incoming troops in all weather and at all times of day and night, emanated from Butler's office. "Beaucoup Seconds and Home Tout Sweet" hung over all the mess hall entrances. Troops were gorged with food of increasing variety and quality. The kitchen serving the best food in a given week flew a banner the next. Langer conceded that the food was "fairly good," but not the standing on "interminable" lines waiting in the cold rain, nor the standard of courtesy in the kitchens, "where a lot of marine recruits, lately arrived from overseas, glorying in their bit of authority, raged and raved till they made one's fists itch." [38]

Through all the confusion, frustration, and herculean effort that characterized the ordeal of Camp de Mud, Butler was sustained by very congenial relationships with his staff. Most of the garrison was army. About a third were blacks serving as stevedores, messmen, and laborers; indeed, S.O.S. had been given its euphemistic title to suppress the stigma associated with "labor battalions." Smedley's two marine aides, Josephus Daniels, Jr., and Ray A. "Torchy" Robinson, were especially close. "I loved Torchy and Joe like sons," he wrote in *Old Gimlet Eye*, and they reciprocated in kind. Other close cronies were army Colonels Morris M. "The Marshall" Keck and Louis "Dutch" Sherer. Judging from subsequent letters there was a good deal of convivial horseplay and drinking, indicating a genuinely cordial atmosphere at camp headquarters that goes a long way toward authenticating the sincerity of the many morale-boosting ploys. Keck later wrote effusively: "You surely had a way about you that commanded the respect and love of every officer and man and it seems so peculiar to me that having followed your career all during your service since '98, that at last I should have fallen under your wing. . . . I miss you like the very devil." [39]

Butler's success in winning loyalty can be partly explained by his own loyalty in return. A close personal friend in future years was his superior in S.O.S., General Helmick, but their early encounters were fraught with testiness as Smedley lashed out against hierarchical interference. When Helmick censured a young lieutenant running one of Butler's kitchens, Smedley worked himself into a rage and asked to be detached. The sequel, told in *Old Gimlet Eye*, took place in Smedley's office:

> I lost my temper, pounded on the desk and told Helmick what I thought of him for jumping on a boy. . . . When I had run down, as all hot-tempered people do, he said, 'Now, Smedley, I'll talk. I've let you abuse me, your commander, for two reasons. First, because you've been of such tremendous value to my organization, and second, because I know I didn't do the right thing by that boy. I realize also that you've worked yourself into a state of nervous collapse to make the camp a success. I know you don't mean what you're saying. I never permit myself to be aroused by a tired man's utterances, when that tired man is a good man.'

Helmick then insisted on going to the lieutenant and "made a handsome apology before all the cooks and mess men in the kitchen." Butler was duly impressed; so apparently was the rest of the command.[40]

Brest, the premier American port, was transit point for high-ranking political and military figures. And as a potential scandal, Pontanezen came under particular scrutiny. General Pershing visited the camp monthly in early 1919, and Butler complained to Eleanor Roosevelt of "Army colonels of every variety [who] visit him daily and drive him nearly mad." Josephus Daniels, Jr., was on hand to chat with President Wilson when he and his party disembarked in December 1918. Prominent visitors to Pontanezen included Colonel Edward M. House, Commandant and Mrs. Barnett, Secretary of State Lansing, and numerous generals, admirals, and congressmen. Assistant Secretary FDR came ashore in January to look at captured German submarines in the harbor, and then spent the day touring Pontanezen. He radioed Daniels that Butler had done "splendidly," and also offered to have Josephus, Jr., transferred home in advance of normal procedures, but the secretary declined. The *Duckboard* for 26 March 1919 reported that in the previous two days Secretary Daniels, eleven congressmen, ten generals, and four admirals had been shown around.[41]

Civilian politics were always a factor, with the usual pandering to powerful politicians. Josephus, Jr., reported to his father that he was the object of an intrigue, preliminary to the upcoming crisis over succession to the marine commandancy:

> *Your* friend, Maj. Gen. John A. Lejeune is playing politics over here. When he came over he brought with him as aides, nephews of Senators [Knute] Nelson and [Benjamin R.] Tillman and now that Tillman [head, Senate committee on naval appropriations] is dead the General figures that Lt. Jones can be of no more service to him so he had G.H.Q. [A.E.F. general headquarters] order me from here to the 2nd Division as his aide—but Gen. Butler got Gen. Helmick, the Army Base Commander here, to wire G.H.Q. to revoke the order for I don't want to go and Gen. Butler does not want me to leave . . . . Gen. Lejeune did this without even a hint of any kind to Gen. Butler—so now I am just standing by waiting to see what the outcome will be. When the time comes to pick the next M.G.C. [major general commandant], you will see why this Major General is doing me this way without asking either myself or General Butler. My opinion of this officer has changed quite a bit since I left you back in good old New York. My opinion of a certain Brigadier General, I am not going to mention any names but his initials are Butler, is very, very fine and I think that anything you can do for him will be to your and his and the Corp's benefit.

The transfer orders were killed. But Josephus, Jr., was detached, pursuant to his insistent requests, as his father's personal aide for a tour of France shortly thereafter. Later, Lejeune was Butler's house guest at Pontanezen and there was "much talking." Lejeune referred to this visit as an "unalloyed pleasure," so if there were any difficulties in their long-standing friendship, they were apparently resolved.[42]

Secretary Daniels's visit in March 1919 resulted in a press release glorifying Butler and Pontanezen. He ate "as good as any meal I ever ate in my life," noticed "rosy faced young chaps who came for another plate just as they had been accustomed to do with the food mother used to serve them," and visited tents into which "no drop of water can fall." The "outstanding impression" he came away with was "the buoyant and cheerful spirit of the 50,000 men." Butler was "a steam engine in breeches" whose work would "thrill Americans who take pride in big achievements."[43]

During Butler's last months at Pontanezen he was awarded the Army Distinguished Service Medal, the Navy Distinguished Service Medal, and, subsequently, the French government's Order of the Black Star. But he was not abandoning the warrior faith for any bright prospects as a technocrat; he scorned the latter medal as "an S.O.S. decoration" because it was given for service behind the lines—actually it was an African colonial order now being awarded to noncombatants in Europe. Perhaps the most compelling tribute came in a private letter from Chief of Naval Operations Admiral William S. Benson, who passed through in June: "You have brought order out of chaos and have turned a camp, which promised to be the greatest scandal producer of the war into what virtually amounts to a beautiful residential city. I was particularly impressed with the loyalty to you personally of the Army officers working with you, and there can be no question but that the credit is yours and that it is gladly acclaimed by your associates." "All the same," Butler observed in *Old Gimlet Eye*, "cleaning up a concentration camp was not soldiering. The job could have been handled by any enterprising hotel-keeper or circus manager."[44]

Butler sailed from Brest in late July 1919. Upon arrival in Hampton Roads, he made a memorable farewell speech to his Thirteenth Regiment, which was reunited for the last time after the diaspora of the previous eleven months. Several years later a veteran wrote, "That talk has been remembered by more members of the regiment that I can tell you about. . . . A good many of us never can, nor never will forget the talks that you gave us while in the mud holes of Breast [sic], France." Smedley replied sentimentally that "one of the hopes of my life is to hear the 13th Regiment sing 'Adeline' again, as it was the most gorgeous song I ever heard."[45]

Butler was developing during these years a distinctive style and emotional commitment as an egalitarian commander. To be sure, "democratic" modulation of traditional officer-corps prerogatives was becoming commonplace in wartime mass-conscription armies.[46] During the contemporary revolution in Russia, the officer-enlisted differential was for a time nearly obliterated, and even Kaiser Wilhelm wore relatively unadorned field greys when he turned up at the front. But Smedley's trek with the duckboard was unique. He meant to be a soldiers' general and was not going to forgo personal control and empathy because of large numbers or the remoteness of high rank.

9 The Barnett Putsch

MARINE CORPS POLITICS

As a brigadier general, Butler played a more direct personal role in Marine Corps politics, especially during the early 1920s when he commanded Quantico, the premier marine base, located just south of Washington. For the first time in his career he had daily access to marine headquarters and was involved in staff committees and dealings with Congress.

This chapter will discuss Butler's role in Corps factionalism during the 1910s and 1920s, as well as some personal feuding that extended into the 1930s. He has been stigmatized by several historians as a singularly ambitious intriguer who, using his father's influence as chairman of the House Naval Affairs Committee, engineered the 1920 Barnett putsch and otherwise fomented plots to the detriment of highbrow professionalism in the officer corps.[1] I will argue that, while Butler certainly was ambitious and in the thick of these disputes, he played mainly a secondary and supportive role while others exerted themselves equally or more so, and others were much more effective in attaining political and careerist ends.

The Waller-Butler political disasters down through the years hardly attest to any deft Machiavellian touch—others were more successful at arcane Washington politics, and not for want of trying. In a contest between warriors and corporate technocrats, the latter enjoyed inherent advantages when it came to bureaucratic intrigues at headquarters. Butler's main contributions were not political manipulation but rather his effective liaison work between the marine hierarchy and his father in Congress, his knack for generating colorful publicity for the Corps, and his embodiment of a new style of bulldog marine ethos that projected warrior prowess and physical aggressiveness as an identifying cult.

The Marine Corps had long been rent by factional rivalry and confusion over its mission. Marine leaders had been adept at playing congressional politics in order to survive the awkward transition from the sailing navy to the varied expeditionary and other duties of the early twentieth century, but they were still seeking a secure role that would justify their existence as a separate service attached to the navy. When it came to major deployments, at Veracruz and again during the Great War, marines had been attached to the army to serve as infantry. Crystalization of a distinctive marine mission remained militarily and politically problematic.

Meanwhile, historic cleavages within the Corps pitted staff officers, who did legal, administrative, and supply work at headquarters, against line officers in the field. Line officers resented, as Butler put it, doing "all the nasty jobs that came along," while staff officers were able to curry social and political favor during prolonged service in Washington. Staff officers, admiring education and social refinement, tended to downgrade bushwhacking as marginal and lowbrow in their scale of professional accomplishments (this was before small wars were dignified as counterinsurgency and upgraded with codified doctrine representing formalized professional expertise). Increasingly some line officers, notably Lejeune, were able to play it both ways by alternating service in the field with stints at headquarters and as students at military staff schools. Lejeune was a Naval Academy graduate to start with and later graduated from the Army War College. Yet he could complain, as a lieutenant colonel in the field, about "politicians stationed at Headquarters," and contend that "fortunately the real Marine Corps is elsewhere and consists of the 10,000 officers and men who are scattered around the world."[2]

For many line officers, the recurring demands of expeditionary duty precluded professional advancement through educational preferment. Indeed, the Corps's manpower was often so drained by urgent expeditionary needs that incipient educational programs had to be canceled or suspended. One of the marines' most acute historians, Allan R. Millett, observed that foreign duty prevented the Corps "from filling its quotas to Navy and Army schools, a condition that probably retarded the development of technological and managerial skills within the officer corps and perpetuated Marine Corps anti-intellectualism at a time when the other services were emphasizing formal midcareer training." Butler expressed this view when reminiscing about the Haiti campaign: "At that time [1915] many of us in the Corps were called the uneducated. We did all the bush work and never had time to go to school." Up to 1920, he had spent fifteen of his twenty-one years of service overseas. Of course, in his notoriously recalcitrant case, he did not want to go to these schools either.[3]

By 1920, the cleavages between staff and line, between Washington and service in the field, and between technocrat and warrior were both manifest and subject to sensible mediation. But passions ran high, with many careers and much personal honor at stake. Previous open clashes between factions had left scars and perhaps a few festering wounds: the 1908 shipboard marines dispute; Colonel Barnett's elevation to the commandancy superseding Waller in 1913; the acrimony in Haiti between the bushwhacker Waller and the intellectual Cole; and the 1918 drama on the floor of Congress when

Congressman Butler denounced Barnett and staff as "swivel-chair officers" seeking privileges at the expense of fighting marines at the front. Through all these traumas, the primary Butler father-son conviction had been to thwart headquarters politicos and to insure recognition for field and especially combat service.

The obvious framework for mediation between factions, offering scope to both highbrow and roughneck professionalism, was to develop the advanced-base concept into a formalized expeditionary mission that could embrace increasingly sophisticated doctrine, technology, and training, in addition to field service as occasion warranted. The long-term evolution of just such a program had been in progress, falteringly, for several decades, and was the intellectual domain of staff highbrows in Washington and at the Advanced Base School in Philadelphia, while field marines had campaigned in the Banana Wars as nominal advanced base forces. There had been friction, as when Cole, who was a graduate of the Army War College and commandant of the Advanced Base School, landed in Haiti with his advanced-base regiment and what Smedley Butler took to be effete "million dollar war college" ideas. But even Butler promoted education, although admittedly of an unpretentious sort, such as his efforts in Panama. Now, in the aftermath of the Great War, these various tendencies were due to be reconciled, with some of the Corps's dominant personalities as leading protagonists.

Upon returning from France in the fall of 1919, Butler was assigned to Quantico as deputy to the base commander, Lejeune, who would soon move up to the commandancy in Washington. Quantico was the largest post in the Corps, intended for a brigade of 8,000, but the current garrison was only 1,000. Smedley wrote his army friend General Helmick that his job was "stupifying . . . I really feel ashamed of myself and must find useful occupation soon or rot." He proposed to Roger L. Farnham, still vice-president at National City Bank, that he "find some fresh enterprise for a lot of us Marines to sail to, as life in the service now is more stupid than a Quaker meeting."[4]

Butler was not one to languish in garrison routine, even in the general letdown following demobilization, and he soon threw himself into a new crash program, the first of many that would punctuate his years at Quantico. Coming at the tail end of the Wilson administration, this was to be one of Secretary of the Navy Daniels's culminating reforms and a harbinger of the new peacetime era. With Butler as director, under Lejeune's auspices as post commander and then as major general commandant, Quantico was to become a "great military university." In keeping with the contemporary marine usage of naming facilities to honor reigning commanders, Smedley tentatively dubbed it "The Daniels University of the Marine Corps."[5] Oddly cobbled together out of highbrow aspiration and defensive populist democratizing, it was a Smedley Butler answer to the bugaboo of highbrow professionalism. It was also an elaboration of the staunch Daniels-Butler connection, recently girded by wartime collaboration of the fathers in Washington and the sons in France, and now including General Lejeune.

Daniels throughout his term as secretary had been keen on uplift, but his reforms were generally resisted as fatuous meddling by the naval officer corps. Best known was his banning liquor from navy ships, anticipating national prohibition. He stopped the dispensing of contraceptives to sailors going on liberty. As mentioned, he had been greatly pleased by Butler's 1913 educational efforts in the Canal Zone, and now cited these as stellar examples while testifying to Congress on the merits of the new Quantico program. In a 1914 article, "The Navy's Universities Afloat," he had written urging "every ship a schoolship and every young officer a schoolmaster." Thereafter he issued orders making duty-time schools mandatory for all ships, and developed plans for religious instruction and elementary through postgraduate university education. Now educational uplift, in the interest of training "efficient citizens," was presented as a rationale for continued existence of the military in peacetime.[6] Indeed, all the services were to promote the idea to some extent.

Butler, in loyalty to Daniels, set up the program within severe budgetary constraints on a mainly self-help basis. The scheme was conceived as an egalitarian, communal effort, and bore an unmistakable stamp of iconoclastic resentment of elitist, highbrow methods. Courses were taught by either officers or enlisted men, depending on expertise, and in an early exhortation Butler told the story, possibly apocryphal, of how at Pontanezen he had seen to it that a laggard captain was demoted to private while a private who had stepped in to assume responsibility was promoted to captain. "The same thing is going to exist here. If the Captain can't lead his men and the Private can, we are going to reverse it and make the Private a Captain." At Quantico, privates were to be "in the status of a cadet." Courses included auto, electrical, carpentry, shoe and leather trade, cooking, drafting, English, journalism, forestry, algebra, bookkeeping, Spanish, commercial law, and a small class in basic literacy. Future plans, according to a 1920 press release, included "a collegiate course corresponding to that in some of the better small colleges."[7]

While the method was mainly pulling up by the bootstraps, the long range goal was pretentiously elitist: Quantico was to be "modeled after the U.S. Naval Academy and West Point and of such merit that it will be recognized by the public and educational authorities as ranking among the best." Within the next several years Butler pursued this to the extent of making the Quantico Marines a leading team in national collegiate football, but otherwise the project fell far short and had little to do with contemporary notions of bookish professionalism. Nevertheless, he was personally moving a long way in the direction of appreciating higher educational standards,

construed in populist terms: "This school is a revolution. . . . The old officers of the Marine Corps would turn over in their graves if they knew what
we were doing because in the old days they did nothing but soldier. We want
to make this post and the whole Marine Corps a great university. We want
to find out who our most capable men are and to give them opportunities
accordingly."[8] And from these humble beginnings eventually blossomed
more sophisticated undertakings such as the Marine Corps Institute.

In any case Butler, and Lejeune, who concurred, were squarely in the
midst of Daniels's final reform thrusts as the Democratic administration
limped along with a crippled president to almost certain party defeat in the
November 1920 elections. In the plan Butler sent Daniels in January, he
stressed that "we all feel that this is what you want done and was started by
you years ago in the Navy. We are all extremely loyal and you can depend
upon us to put through your wishes no matter what they are." Quantico
would become the educational mecca of the Corps. The whole program
would be great publicity and would attract high-quality recruits. In March,
Daniels went to Quantico accompanied by the House Naval Affairs Committee to inspect the schools, and recorded in his diary that three-fourths of
the men were voluntarily enrolled in classes. He took special note of the
basic literacy group, feeling that it was "pathetic to see how late in life they
were thumbing their primers." The committee was enthusiastic.[9]

Intertwined with these personal and political affinities connecting Daniels, Smedley and Thomas Butler, Lejeune, and the Naval Affairs Committee were the immediate origins of the most seismic Marine Corps putsch of
the era. The removal of Commandant Barnett can be vaguely traced as far
back as the factional disputes of 1908-10. Relations between staff and line
officers, between headquarters and field commanders such as Waller and
Butler, remained testy thereafter, with Lejeune serving to some extent as
go-between in his role as assistant commandant from 1914 to 1917. As
mentioned, Lejeune had been Daniels's first choice for the commandancy
in 1913, but was too junior in rank. As assistant commandant he became
Barnett's protégé, while performing the delicate task of corresponding "unofficially" with Waller and Butler in Haiti, mediating numerous grievances
in an explicit arrangement that helped keep the Corps in one piece. Lejeune
was clearly heir apparent to the commandancy, generally respected and
well-liked on all sides. During the war he was top marine commander in the
front lines, commanding the army-marine Second Division.

Barnett served his statutory four-year term and was reappointed in
1918 as a matter of wartime continuity. The achievements of getting marines sent to France and of expanding the Corps from 10,000 to 75,000
men, as well as progress in technology, professional training, and advanced
base doctrine can all be credited to him as important administrative suc-

cesses. With many of his Annapolis classmates serving in the upper reaches of the naval hierarchy, marine-navy politics warmed considerably. But he had run afoul of Daniels by going behind Daniels's back in obtaining senatorial support for his own promotion during the 1918 Barnett amendment fiasco. Daniels, steadfastly partial to field and combat service, sympathized with those congressmen, notably Butler, who had denounced Barnett as a "rocking chair warrior." Although he had spent only four of his forty-one years of service in Washington, Barnett had been under fire only once, in a warship that was shelling Santiago in 1898.[10]

Daniels maintained, and Barnett denied, that Barnett gave his word to resign at the end of the war as a condition to the renewal of his expired term as commandant in 1918. Barnett refused Daniels's request for an undated letter of resignation, to which navy bureau chiefs in the same situation acquiesced. The four-year rule had been initiated by Daniels in 1913, and legislated by Congress, to prize loose desk officers who might otherwise acquire undue political influence during prolonged service in the capital.[11]

At the end of the war, according to Daniels, "the consensus of opinion among marines" was that Lejeune should be commandant, but Barnett defiantly refused to resign "in spite of his pledge." Barnett, in his unpublished memoirs, cast aspersions upon Daniels's veracity and presented himself as an upstanding and competent officer who was humiliated by not being allowed to finish a second four-year term. While acknowledging President Wilson's authority to relieve him, he strongly implied duplicity on Daniels's part, citing a story from an unidentified informant that Daniels "told the President that I wanted to be relieved and that the President, who was a very ill man, gave his consent."[12]

What transpired between Daniels and Wilson remains a matter of conjecture, but Wilson did concur in the merit of replacing Barnett with Lejeune, particularly as this was part of a postwar policy to reward those with combat service. Wilson's attitude is best indicated by his personal physician, Dr. Cary T. Grayson, who wrote Lejeune many years later: "I clearly recall a number of General Barnett's friends asking me to intercede with the President in his behalf, and Mrs. Barnett was particularly active and persistent. . . . a number of letters sent to the President by Senators and Congressmen of both parties [were] no doubt inspired by her efforts." This barrage of pro-Barnett lobbying came after his demotion, attempting to turn the tables—but Daniels would have been badly caught out had he lied about Barnett's wishes. To the contrary, there is no evidence that Wilson had second thoughts, and he continued to support Daniels throughout, as attested to by Dr. Grayson's recollections: "I vividly recall the President's comment at the time. He said 'Lejeune's appointment shall be one of merit, and his leadership . . . shall be an inspiration to the other officers of that Corps, particularly to the younger members.' . . . the President backed him [Daniels] to the limit, and afterwards referred to your appointment and record with great pride." [13]

The circumstances of Barnett's relief were fraught with acrimony. In June 1920, he was abruptly sacked by Daniels, with the option of retiring as major general or reverting to his permanent rank of brigadier should he choose to remain on active duty. The notification was delivered by a black messenger who had been instructed to wait for a reply. As told by Barnett and his aide, Captain Clifton B. Cates, this was a rude and sudden procedure implying a strategy of preemptive surprise or deliberate insult. But a draft of the dismissal note in Daniels's papers indicates that Barnett had avoided a personal interview by pleading illness, forcing Daniels to act, as he was leaving for the West Coast and delay was "impracticable." And Barnett's correspondence with friends shows awareness of impending dismissal. Daniels's subsequent absence also discredits at least the time sequence of Cates's 1967 recollection that following Barnett's defiant reply, "there were all kind of conferences going on between Congressman Butler and Secretary Daniels and General Butler. For the next few days, we'd see them go in the office back and forth." This does, however, point to the highly personal and abrasive nature of the infighting. With Marine Headquarters and the Navy Department sharing the same building, few visible nuances of the feud escaped notice. [14]

The actual relief a short time later ended in an ugly confrontation between Barnett and Lejeune in the commandant's office. Barnett, still wearing the two stars of a major general, used his last minutes as commandant to shame his estranged protégé. In 1967 Major General William A. Worton related the episode as it was told to him by an aide whom Barnett had ordered to stay as witness: "'General Lejeune. I am still the Commandant of the Marine Corps, and will be until 12 o'clock noon. Stand at attention, sir, in front of my desk. I have something to tell you.' And he told him of a lifetime of friendship; told him of his disloyalty, as he called it. And then he said, 'They had the nerve, General Lejeune, to suggest that I was ready to retire. It's one minute to twelve, General Lejeune.' Promptly at twelve o'clock he stood up and said: 'General Lejeune, you are the Commandant of the Marine Corps.'" Barnett then had his aide remove one star from his uniform and left the office as a brigadier. [15]

Years later, when asked whether Butler had played a role in the affair, "Torchy" Robinson replied, "There's no doubt about it. . . . I sat in a car with him across the street from the Navy Department Headquarters and waited to see Barnett come out." A month later Smedley wrote Major Vandegrift, still posted in Haiti, that "it was all very quiet; no fireworks, and no one was killed, although the Barnett faction has been making a big noise since and yelling for vengeance, which vengeance I do not believe they will get." [16]

By refusing to retire, Barnett "rather upset their calculations," as he put it, and created the embarrassing spectacle of a commandant demoted and still on active duty, thereby unhinging the Corps's rigid system of lineal rank and precedence. He had been invited to request a new duty station and chose Quantico, the top post in the Corps for a brigadier and the one nearest to Washington. Quantico, he was immediately informed, had already been promised to another officer (Butler). He declined to make any further request, "nor," he wrote his supporter General Pendleton, "shall I ever make one." In the awkward circumstances, and to get him as far away from Washington politics as reasonably possible, Lejeune and Daniels created a new command, the Department of the Pacific, with headquarters in San Francisco. According to Cates, who loyally went along as aide, Barnett "had no authority whatsoever. He couldn't even transfer an enlisted man. . . . In fact, there were only five of us out there . . . it was three years wasted because we didn't have a thing to do." [17]

Mrs. Lelia Montague Barnett, who stayed east, and Republican allies fomented revenge. They appealed in vain to President Wilson and then, as related by Daniels, "they declared that they would—and they did—prevent the confirmation of Lejeune by the Republican Senate and predicted that General Barnett would be reinstated when Harding became President." Upon being relieved, Barnett requested promotion to the major generalship made vacant by Lejeune's elevation, and while this might have paved the way for a more amicable compromise, it was rejected. Daniels cabled Wilson from the West Coast "earnestly" blocking the move, arguing that Barnett should compete with other brigadiers and that "an officer who served with credit at the front as Lejeune did in World War should have first claim." [18]

Barnett made his contribution to Warren G. Harding's victory in the 1920 presidential election by including in his outgoing commandant's report the aforementioned 1919 letter ordering Colonel Russell to stop the "indiscriminate killing of natives" in Haiti. Daniels routinely released the long and otherwise ponderously boring report to the press, just in time for the "indiscriminate killing" gaffe to make national headlines during the closing weeks of the election campaign. Democratic vice presidential candidate Franklin D. Roosevelt's boast that he had personally written Haiti's new constitution had already hurt the Democrats, allowing Harding to promise that if elected he would not "empower an Assistant Secretary of the Navy to draft a constitution for helpless neighbors in the West Indies and jam it down their throats at the point of bayonets borne by U.S. Marines." Barnett's letter now dramatically lent weight to Harding's denunciations of the "rape of Haiti" and charges that "thousands of native Haitians have been killed by

American marines." Disgustedly, FDR wrote Daniels from the campaign trail, "As you know I am slightly prejudiced against Barnett, so will refrain from comments that I would otherwise like to make."[19]

Meanwhile Commandant Lejeune and Smedley Butler were just back from an inspection trip to Port-au-Prince with a glowing report for Daniels telling of "a strong sentiment of gratitude to the marines" throughout Haiti. The trip was intended to preempt an upcoming naval board of inquiry and, depending upon election results, a fullblown congressional inquest into the corvée and 1919 uprising. "On our return home, however," Lejeune recalled, "we found Washington in a ferment and the newspapers filled with great headlines and extracts from General Barnett's report."[20]

Barnett may well have nurtured the Haiti gambit with particular relish. In the October 1920 file in his papers there is an unsigned, undated proposal for interrogating "those having first hand knowledge of affairs in Haiti." The first (and only, at least in the surviving one-page document) projected witness was Smedley Butler, who was to have been subjected to eleven leading questions such as:

1. What were your instructions in regard to Corvee system? Did you institute this system? . . .
5. Were such men ever held in chains?
6. Have you any recollection of having remarked when remonstrated with in regard to such [corvée] methods: 'Hell, I don't care what they do. I want results.'
7. Did you report every step of such actions towards the natives to the Major General Commandant of the Marine Corps [Barnett]?
8. Have you any personal prejudice against Major General George Barnett?[21]

But Republican victory in November 1920 did not turn the tables for Barnett, partly because the Butler connection held fast in the changing political tides. This was probably the key contribution the Butlers made to the entire putsch transaction. The House Naval Affairs Committee, with its Republican majority, continued to favor Lejeune unanimously. Outgoing Secretary Daniels narrated the extraordinary bipartisan exercise in his memoirs: "On the day before Harding's inauguration, Chairman Butler, a grand Old Guard Republican from Pennsylvania, who was resolved to go to any length to keep Lejeune . . . , and other members of the Committee, called at the Navy Department and asked me what I thought they could do to prevent the removal of Lejeune. One member suggested that they go in a body to see Mr. [Edwin H.] Denby, who was to become Secretary in the Harding Administration, and tell him that the one thing they desired above all others was to see Lejeune retained." Denby then sought Daniels's advice, which was to stay in the good graces of the committee if he wanted to achieve anything as secretary. On Denby's recommendation, Lejeune was reappointed and, also on the first day of the new administration, Barnett was promoted to major general. But he remained beyond the pale at his redundant Pacific command until he retired in 1923.[22]

The nature of Smedley Butler's and Lejeune's complicity in the Barnett putsch is suggested by unsigned copies of what purport to be 1932 letters to Mrs. Barnett from a marine officer who was stationed at Quantico in 1919. The officer tells of working alone on Sundays in the post adjutant's office and overhearing conversations in which Butler told Lejeune "that [he?] had everything arranged with Daniels to relieve your husband if Lejeune would take the job. After some little talking and cursing Lejeune gave in." The second letter, upon urging from Mrs. Barnett, provided more details: "I heard Butler refer to Gen. Barnett as a '—— —— old fogy' who had outworn his usefulness. . . . it was said that Mrs. Daniels was jealous of your social position. Almost all of the talking was done by Butler—he was trying to overcome Lejeune's scruples. There was also something to the effect that if he, Lejeune, did not accept someone else would be found. . . . The only exact words I remember are 'g—— d—— old fogy'—I remember them because they were in direct variance to my beliefs." [23]

Mrs. Barnett communicated these charges to Lejeune, and continued to pursue redemption of her husband's honor long after Barnett's death in 1930. In 1935 she took legal action in an attempt to stop circulation of former Captain John H. Craige's book on the marines in Haiti because it referred to Barnett as a "rocking chair warrior." When Lejeune, long retired, replied to her appeal by denying awareness of the book until after it was published, she noted acidly on the letter, "I have personal knowledge that the book was submitted to Gen. Lejeune." In fact Craige, a longtime confidant and currently Lejeune's literary adviser, corresponded regularly with him and it is highly unlikely he would have taken a nasty shot at Barnett had he not known that Lejeune would approve. In 1947 Mrs. Barnett tried to sue Daniels for publishing an anecdote in his memoirs referring to Barnett as "The-Man-Afraid-of-His-Wife." [24] Neither Lejeune nor Daniels nor Craige, who was an accomplished author, were given to gratuitous insults, and these extraordinary incidents can be taken as indications of deeply felt and righteous contempt, probably for Barnett's prima donna performance during the putsch as much as for anything beforehand. The Butlers were not alone in their prejudice against Barnett.

Other reflections on the putsch, shot through with conjecture, blurred memories, and subjectivity that amount to an oral tradition, are the reminiscences of retired marine generals collected in the 1960s by historian Benis M. Frank, director of the Marine Corps's excellent oral history program.

Frank took a special interest in Smedley Butler's role in the Barnett affair. The old generals, harking back to junior officer days, by and large had Smedley hating Barnett and using his father's powerful position to work the coup, with Lejeune more or less an innocent foil. Nobody recalled much substantial detail or seemed to know any inside information, but what does come through is a variety of impressions of Smedley and also some sense that Lejeune, as Robinson put it, was "an outstanding person" and "smarter than hell," while Barnett was "run of the mine." Major General William A. Worton, contrasting Barnett as "a distinguished and learned officer, graduate of the Naval Academy," and Butler as having "little or no schooling," recalled bitter mutual antipathy: "I don't know what the hatred was, and I can vouch for the feeling." [25]

Major General Robert Blake, who liked Smedley, was "very much" aware of the feuding and remembered that Butler made no secret of attempts to get rid of Barnett: "Well, I was at Quantico in close contact with General Butler, and General Butler was 100% extrovert; and anything General Butler believed everybody knew about." Blake hesitated "to put any sort of finger on General Lejeune," who was "a most admirable character," and gave a character sketch comparing Butler with another famous marine firebrand, Lewis B. "Chesty" Puller: "General Butler, with all his political influence and perhaps discreditable attributes, was a very dramatic figure. He may well have saved the Marine Corps then [1920s] when it looked as though it was going to be scuttled. . . . I never knew any Marine who disliked General Puller, and I knew plenty who disliked General Butler heartily. But the two of them had much in common in that they were both dramatic, aggressive and outspoken figures." General Julian C. Smith believed that Butler was "very bitter against Barnett" because of the trouble about getting to France. "Butler was a man who was going to be top dog. I don't think he was loyal to any of his superiors. He was all Butler." [26]

Benis Frank published his findings in "The Relief of General Barnett" (1974), arguing that although Butler's "presence in this affair is shadowy, one can assume that a force in the relief was General Butler's frustrated desire for more rapid advancement. . . . if Barnett retired when Lejeune was appointed, Butler could expect to receive his second star. Butler could also assume that he would be Lejeune's logical successor as Commandant." Other marine historians came to the same conclusion: "We can conjecture that the scenario called for Gen Butler to succeed Lejeune as Commandant," wrote one, while another contended that the putsch "made way for Smedley Butler to be promoted to major general [he was not promoted until 1929] and to assume command at Quantico." But this is far-fetched, because Butler was the youngest temporary brigadier and "lucky enough to hold on to my star," as he wrote a Pontanezen buddy in April 1920, instead of having been one of four marine brigadiers reduced to colonel after the war.[27]

The criterion for reduction and promotion in the Daniels-Wilson era, including most notably Lejeune's elevation to the commandancy, was service in France, preferably in the front lines. Both Thomas and Smedley Butler strongly subscribed to this, and Smedley helped enforce it as a member of the officer selection board that adjudicated rank reductions after the war, largely on the basis of combat service and decorations. Having himself failed to get to the front, Smedley could hardly have expected further promotion. He avoided demotion by just barely having gotten to France; the four brigadiers reduced to colonel had not. Daniels's choice for the vacant major generalship was Wendell C. Neville, who after Lejeune won top laurels at the front.[28] Neville, rather than Butler, was Lejeune's logical successor as commandant, and indeed it was to be so when Lejeune finally stepped down in 1929. There is no evidence that Smedley objected, and his personal ambitions during much of the 1920s focused on getting out of the marines and into a good civilian job, as will be seen.

This is not to deny a major role for Smedley in the putsch. But better that this be understood in terms of hostility to Barnett, who personified highbrow professionalism and Annapolis elitism enhanced by Washington social connections, against which both Butlers had long been implacably hostile.[29] Their alliance with Daniels was a happy one in this respect. Daniels had faced obstruction and ridicule from the same quarters when he tried to introduce his many exotic reforms, which were resented as civilian political interference, particularly his bypassing the officer corps to make a play to the enlisted men. "Never mind about any red tape, either—just come straight to me. I'm your best friend, and I know you're mine," as one derisive critic characterized his approach.[30] His attempts to disrupt cliquishness, cronyism, and insulation of command privilege from civilian scrutiny were likewise strongly resisted.[31]

Barnett represented a cloistered officer corps elite that was subjected to a variety of pressures from the civilian sector, qua Daniels, during the Great War era. The officers' professional aloofness and sense of moral superiority had been forced to give ground to the integrative requirements of wartime mass mobilization. Barnett's memoirs, in contrast, are saturated with narrow professionalism and pristine soldier's honor. He projects himself very much above the battle as regards the treacheries of civilian politics, personified by Daniels, and indicates no sympathy whatever toward the encroachments of populist civilian tendencies in military politics. He no doubt resented Smedley Butler's political influence as unwanted and corrupting, and probably saw Smedley's demagogic tendencies as unseemly, unprofessional. His own political influence was presumably effected on a lofty and discreet social plane, after the putsch notably by his wife's prevailing upon Republican party potentates. In 1921 Barnett's former Annapolis roommate, Secretary of War John W. Weeks, wrote rather apologetically to Secretary of the Navy Denby that he had had a call "from our ubiquitous friend, Mrs. Barnett, who is anxious that in some address to be made tonight" by Denby, favorable mention be made of General Barnett.[32]

The Butlers' spiritual affinity with Daniels is all the more convincing, especially their enthusiasm for his lame-duck maneuvers after the war, in that the Democrats seemed sure to be on the way out. Tom Butler was one of the senior Republicans in Congress, and Smedley was unlikely to suffer during a new Republican national ascendancy; indeed, his relationship with incoming Secretary Denby would be, if anything, tighter than with Daniels. The Butlers' tie with Daniels rather signified definite maverick tendencies. The timing of the Barnett putsch must be seen in this context. Lejeune, from Louisiana, was a Democrat and as Daniels's choice would be best established in the commandancy before the party turnover in March 1921. Lejeune's position would be fragile thereafter, as Barnett's friends calculated in seeking revenge, and this was where the Old Guard Republican Butlers played their key role in midwifing the transition.

As for any reluctance on Lejeune's part, he had good reason—it was after all a rather gross betrayal for unmistakably selfish motives, particularly since Barnett had repeatedly promised his support when it came to choosing a successor.[33] In contrast, there was little love lost between the Butlers and Barnett. It was Lejeune the broker who had long been playing both sides of the street, most recently by negotiating Barnett's skeptical acquiescence to the Quantico university scheme drawn up in early 1920 by Butler, Lieutenant Craige, and Lejeune to suit Daniels.[34] As broker, Lejeune had furthered his own as well as the Corps's interests. It was he who abandoned Barnett at the crucial moment and thereby took upon himself the pivotal role in consolidating the putsch. But arguably, the most bizarre and discreditable aspect was Barnett's arrogance, first in insisting upon a full eight-year double tour and then in spitefully sulking for three years at public expense as the redundant Commander of the Pacific. It was a performance that calls to mind Banana War caricatures of Honduran generals, and was worthy of the enduring resentment evidenced by "rocking chair warrior" jibes from the Lejeune-Daniels camp decades later.

Thus Lejeune, rather than Smedley Butler, can be said to have played the most crucial role in the Barnett putsch. But this is not to say that careerist or partisan interests were furthered at the expense of the larger interests of the Marine Corps. As commandant, Lejeune continued to mediate factional differences adroitly. As late as 1927, Smedley wrote from China describing a marine officer as "a great follower of Barnett's" who was still bitter: "For the last ten years, he has not spoken to me, because I stood up for you and cheered loudly when his friends Barnett and [Charles H.] Lochheimer [Lauchheimer] got the sack." [35] Probably Lejeune was the only one with the stature and skill to contain and heal these grievances, despite his apparent complicity in the putsch. And, as expected, he stepped forth as the architect of new programs and political initiatives that firmly set the Corps to developing amphibious expeditionary warfare as its distinctive mission. This entailed increasing emphasis on highbrow professionalism, particularly formalized officer education, and with a big-war bias, but there was also plenty of scope for Smedley Butler's colorful warrior-style exploits, as will be seen.

In the ongoing factional differences, officer promotions were the most sensitive issue. Immediately after the war, Commandant Barnett set up a board headed by Colonel John H. Russell to decide which wartime temporary officers would be retained, demoted, or discharged. Russell, according to historian Robert H. Williams, "was said to have advised the members of the board to bear in mind that they were selecting the young officers whom they would invite into their quarters and whom their daughters might marry." Educated men of good family were preferred over former enlisted men, especially those with "little formal education." The Russell Board, none of whose members had served with the heroic Fourth Brigade in France, proceeded to ignore combat records in favor of peacetime criteria, notably education. Louis Cukela, a combat hero up from the ranks who spoke broken English, was demoted from first lieutenant to second lieutenant. [36]

These proceedings were reversed with the Barnett putsch. Anticipating the putsch by just a few weeks, Congress passed legislation that nullified the Russell Board. Three days after taking over as commandant, Lejeune convened a new selection board headed by newly promoted Major General Neville, former commander of the Fourth Brigade, and including Brigadiers Smedley Butler and Harry Lee. The Neville Board strongly favored combat service over education and other elitist criteria. Cukela was promoted a complete rank. But, according to General Williams, while some of those favored "except possibly Cukela . . . were officer material by any criteria," many promoted from the ranks "were either too old or without the formal education needed to be effective career officers." [37]

This turning of tables confirmed the Wilson-Daniels-Butler emphasis on rewarding field service, with Lejeune and Neville as signal beneficiaries. Smedley played his part as a member of the Neville Board, and continued to promote the warrior cause thereafter. But this did not mean that the new regime was hostile to highbrow technocratic trends, or that any objections by Smedley Butler would count for much. Lejeune had been and continued to be a strong proponent of officer education and related merit-based reform in the naval promotion system.

The problem, as a marine brigadier wrote Lejeune in 1932, was that reform "would run counter to the always present sentiment of the Senate and House in favor of the former non-commissioned officers. You will remember how strong that was in 1920, and it still persists." What role Congressman Butler played in all this and whether Smedley significantly influenced him are uncertain. The Naval Affairs Committee under his leadership did pass the various reforms based on meritocracy enacted during the 1920s. In fact, the 1928 revision of the Navy percentage system, which called for mandatory retirement after an officer served a number of years without earning promotion, was referred to as the "Butler bill." [38]

Thomas S. Butler was a powerful figure in Congress, and it is easy to postulate an ongoing manipulation of Marine Corps affairs by his son. It had often been assumed, by President Taft among others, that Smedley was being indulged. General Barnett's biographer, Merrill L. Bartlett, states that "often affecting the outcome of legislation concerning the Marine Corps was the influence of [Tom] Butler's son." [39]

But this was up to 1920, and can be substantially documented in instances such as congressional deliberations over Haiti. Afterward, the extant Butler Papers, insofar as they deal with congressional politics, are concerned mainly with budgets and personnel strength. These were the perennial problems, tantamount to survival, faced by the Corps throughout the 1920s. Smedley's role in 1920s marine-congressional politics was to serve as liaison between Lejeune and Congressman Butler, with Lejeune often asking Smedley to do so. There is no substantial indication of Smedley grinding axes or fueling staff-line feuds, or that he was anything but loyally subordinate to Lejeune. Staff-line infighting was now subdued in any case, thanks to Lejeune's ascendancy and deft leadership. Throughout, he and the two Butlers worked in close harmony to generate favorable Marine Corps publicity and to marshal congressional support.

Unfortunately, Thomas S. Butler's personal papers were destroyed, so evidence of any further collusion between father and son, or of Tom Butler's private ruminations, is lacking. He was, indeed, the dominant figure in congressional naval politics during the 1920s. At the time of his death in 1928, he was eulogized as the "Dean of Representatives," being the senior member in years of service. The *Baltimore Sun* commented that "few men in the House were more influential than the chairman of the Naval Affairs Committee." Moreover, he was best known as an "ardent big-navy advocate" who fought hard for the eight-cruiser bill of 1924 and, it was said, "went down fighting" in quest of what ultimately became the 1929 fifteen-cruiser bill. [40]

But his personal style differed markedly from Smedley's. Future Speaker of the House Joe Martin, who arrived in Congress in 1925, remembered Uncle Tom cautioning him, "You're a young man, Joe, and I hope you'll stay here a long time. But let me give you a bit of advice: don't talk too much. The fellows that talk, talk their way out of Congress."[41]

Tom Butler's position as chairman of the Naval Affairs Committee was formidable. While secretaries of the navy, navy bureau chiefs, and marine commandants usually came and went at intervals of four years or less, congressmen built up considerable expertise and mastery during decades of tenure on the committee. In Butler's case this amounted to thirty-two years, the longest stint excepting only Carl Vinson's combined thirty-five years on Naval Affairs and its successor Armed Services Committee. And Pennsylvania was historically the best-represented state on Naval Affairs, with proprietary interests in the Philadelphia Navy Yard, Marine Corps logistic and training facilities, armor plate manufacture, and shipbuilding. During Butler's reign as chairman from 1919 to 1928, there were large Republican majorities, outnumbering Democrats fifteen to six in 1921. A 1923 story illustrates his power. When presented with an urgent navy request for deeper battleship servicing facilities in San Francisco Bay, Butler replied: "I am sorry, Admiral, but after all these years I can't go back on Charlie Curry who has represented Vallejo so long." The battleships did not get new facilities until many years thereafter.[42]

During Thomas Butler's chairmanship, irrespective of any putative interference from Smedley, the development of the Marine Corps proceeded steadily in the direction of professional upgrading. Lejeune vigorously affirmed that the mission of the Corps was to "supply expeditionary forces for service with the fleets in the event of war." This was the big-war mission, not colonial expeditions which were relegated to marginal status, in theory if not in practice. Or, as Lejeune testified to Congress in 1920, the average of one expedition per year for the previous twenty years showed that "in time of peace, these expeditionary forces have their uses also."[43] The new push was for increasingly rigorous organization, big-war planning, and amphibious training exercises with the fleet. In 1920, the Advanced Base Force was moved from Philadelphia to Quantico and was renamed the Expeditionary Force, joined in 1923 by a fledgling West Coast counterpart in San Diego. The ancillary Marine Officers' School in Quantico offered a sequence of courses, and Lejeune intended that eventually all officers would graduate from the respective courses before being promoted to higher rank, with senior officers going off to the Army and Navy war colleges.[44]

To what extent these developments offended Smedley Butler is uncertain. Historian Allan Millett implies that they did, stating that Lejeune's "position was not shared by all other senior Marine officers, particularly Smedley Butler; the Caribbean occupations and the war in France had convinced some officers that the corps flourished in direct relation to its distance from the Navy."[45] To the contrary, Smedley played an energetic part in developing both the East and West Coast expeditionary forces. Under

Lejeune's aegis, he worked very closely with the navy on the China Station in the late 1920s.

In any case, despite the earnest big-war emphasis, colonial light-infantry expeditions remained the Corps's operational mainstay. There was still a good deal of scope for Smedley's acknowledged expertise. Reasons were enumerated by Secretary of the Navy Curtis D. Wilbur in a 1924 memorandum to President Calvin Coolidge: "At present, unrest is seething in these countries [Cuba, Haiti, Dominican Republic, Nicaragua]. . . . Intervention by U.S. Marines under the comity of nations does not constitute an act of war. Normally, if the Army was used, it would be tantamount to a declaration of war. . . . The Marines are Presidential troops, in that the Executive may order them as a part of the Navy to foreign countries without concurrent Congressional action." Thus, the old Banana War subterfuges coexisted uneasily with grander strategy: "War Plans contemplate, upon the declaration of war, the assembly of the U.S. Fleet with an Expeditionary Force of about 22,000 Marines for immediate projection against the enemy." [46]

But colonial operations themselves were changing. Bushwhacking and outright coercion were giving way everywhere to mediatory policies stressing indirect control. And Smedley Butler was a key figure in one of the pivotal transitions, in which carefully modulated relationships with an indigenous client regime emerged as the preferred solution. In 1921 it was decided to retain a predominantly military-colonial emphasis in the ongoing American occupation of Haiti. Butler, with his local experience, requisite brigadier's rank, and extensive background in colonial affairs, was the obvious choice for the post of U.S. high commissioner to Haiti.

In the aftermath of Harding's election victory, a special Senate committee had investigated the corvée, alleged atrocities, and American colonial administration in Haiti. Waller and Butler testified at length. In formulating recommendations, the committee settled upon the quasicolonial device of establishing an American high commissioner to oversee both the resident marine brigade and the Haitian client government. There was disagreement as to whether the high commissioner should be a civilian or a marine. Then came the issue of which marine. Secretary of State Charles Evans Hughes suggested Butler, who he said had been "exceedingly successful" during his previous stint, and Smedley was also Lejeune's and the Navy Department's choice.[47]

As tentative designee, Butler insisted on selecting his own colonial administrators to supervise the various departments of the client government, and "insisted on the right to discharge them if they proved unsatisfactory." His close friend Quartermaster Colonel Cyrus Radford was to be financial adviser, previously the top civilian post, and all the other administrators, except for navy medical support, were also to be marines. This was tantamount to military government, and, as Butler pointed out later, would have afforded the Harding administration few places for civilian office seekers. Radford was keen on the prospect, Smedley decidedly less so, which probably explains his tough demands. Secretary of the Navy Denby repeatedly confirmed the proposition, including President Harding's endorsement, during November and December 1921. Then, while Denby and his family were spending Christmas as the Butlers' house guests at Quantico, the secretary hedged.[48]

In January, Butler was superseded by Colonel, shortly Brigadier General, Russell. The senators on the Haiti committee had come to the conclusion that Smedley was wrong for the job. Joined by Secretary Hughes, they pressured Denby and Harding to back down. Dana Munro, chief of State's Latin American Division, argued that "there does not seem to be an urgent need for coercive measures at the present time," and summarized objections based on "accounts of General Butler's methods in dealing with the Haitians" which suggested "that he would lay us open to well justified attacks from the other Latin American countries and from the press in this country." The State Department and the senators preferred, as Munro put it, "seeking to attain our ends by persuasion rather than by dictation."[49]

Denby held out for Butler, but Harding switched to Russell after conferring with the senators. Butler was told that if he "would not go to Haiti with a civilian Financial Adviser, and other civilians selected as a cabinet, all by the State Department," that he would not go at all. He stood fast when Denby approached him in an attempt to negotiate a compromise. So the job went to Russell, who served as high commissioner until the post was abolished in the aftermath of the 1929 uprising. Butler predicted that Russell would be nothing but a housecarl for the State Department, and this was by and large true. But as such, Russell ran a rigidly authoritarian administration, with Haitian collaborators punctiliously in tow, that was increasingly resented not only by Haitians but by liberal American civilian officials as well.[50] Ironically, Butler soon proved flexible and adept at handling an important diplomatic mission in China.

The Haiti shuffle signified a move toward conciliation and tentative demilitarization on the American colonial circuit. Implications for the current run of peacetime Marine Corps politics were also clear. Butler and the warrior style were being eclipsed in the command hierarchy by timeserving, relatively civilianized, highbrow professionalism. Reversal of the 1919 Russell Board during the Barnett putsch had been a provisional setback. Russell, an admiral's son and Naval Academy graduate, went on to become commandant and Butler did not. Each personified opposite career strategies: Smedley was the bushwhacker representing the fighting Corps, and Russell was the staff-political type who now went off on an eight-year tour of detached diplomatic duty in mufti, and was rewarded as the State Department's candidate for the commandancy in the 1930s. The contrast was dramatized when Smedley came out of retirement to heatedly oppose Russell's Senate confirmation in 1935.

But the contrast should not be exaggerated, particularly during the 1920s when Butler also played the game according to prevailing trends, as in China. Smedley too was involved in big-war technological development, particularly aviation but also the Christie amphibious tank. And Russell was by no means a bloodless conciliator or panderer, surely not when it came to Haitians. Smedley himself once commented that Russell had "done so well" in Haiti as brigade commander from 1917 onward, that he might be kept on.[51] The differences between them, apropos Haiti, were a matter of willingness to adapt and style, with Butler losing out largely because he was identified with the earlier period of rude political repression.

And Butler too was a timeserver during the 1920s. He enthusiastically worked at such odd peacetime projects as marine mail guards, historic Civil War reenactments, and military involvement in civilian sports. Butler, more than anyone else, went to great lengths with bold experiments to introduce the military into civilian life. He did so with warrior panache, but the essential point was adaptive: to popularize and justify the military by articulating with civilian trends.

10 Pep and Pride

QUANTICO

Postwar demobilization meant retrenchment, rank reductions, and fights among the military services for survival in the face of shrinking budgets. In presidential politics, the postwar norm of honoring victorious generals was bypassed in favor of what Harding called a return to "normalcy," making this the first American war not capped by presidential apotheosis. Militarism, however, survived in various mutations, and throughout the 1920s, military leaders were called upon as figureheads for civilian law-and-order campaigns, and the marines were twice used to guard the mails. As a famous and colorful marine with a knack for publicity, Smedley Butler moved with seeming ease to kindred civilian modes, popularizing the military and, on hazard, introducing military style and methods into civilian affairs. On the military side, he launched brash public relations enterprises that not only helped sell the Marine Corps to a reluctant Congress, but also substantiated a new fighting-leatherneck image. The bulldog allegory was both pleasing to the public and credible to marines themselves as their broadcast image in the new era of mass-communications hyperbole and fetishism. This chapter and the next explore Butler's contrivances and achievements amid these trends.

Even as he promoted Secretary of the Navy Daniels's educational schemes and helped work the Barnett putsch, Butler was pursuing civilian options. He professed to Roger L. Farnham of National City Bank, "nor have I such a particular love of the service now that the war is over that I am unwilling to get out, but am practically useless in any other walk of life, so don't dare take a chance." A 1919 possibility as director of Philadelphia's police and fire departments at double his marine salary fell through for the time being.[1]

This left Butler at Quantico for what would be the longest tour by any of its commanding generals. The 1920-24 stint plus his return in 1929-31 made him the dominant figure in the base's early history, as Quantico developed into the Marine Corps's elite focal point for training and maneuvers and a showplace for Washington politics. Home of the Expeditionary Force, it also served as staging area for Caribbean amphibious exercises and was always on standby for expeditionary duty. Butler concentrated on self-help

construction schemes, on aviation, and especially on politics and public relations. The promotional aspect featured annual expeditionary maneuvers
into surrounding states, historic Civil War battle reenactments, and celebrated Quantico football teams.

In fact, public relations figured in everything, either for the public at
large or specially pitched to influential politicians. All this was effectively
orchestrated between Commandant Lejeune, Secretary of the Navy Denby,
Thomas S. Butler as congressional linchpin, and finally Smedley running
the circus at Quantico. Merwin H. Silverthorn, a junior officer at Quantico,
recalled that "once a year before the budget" congressmen came down for
tours, with several assigned to each marine company for eating in unit gal-
leys, truck rides around the base, maneuvers, and parades: "Tremendous
good will was generated, and the Marine Corps, fighting for its life then,
always got by pretty good as a result of those personal visits from Members
of Congress. General Butler occupied the center of the stage—there's no
question about that. But I'm sure General Lejeune was delighted to have
him do that." [2]

In 1922, as coordinated by Denby and Tom Butler, invitations were sent
to all members through the Speaker of the House. Thanks to Denby's efforts, it could be announced that President Harding had made the presidential yacht *Mayflower* available for transport. Senators were approached
through the chairman of the Senate Naval Affairs Committee. [3]

Denby was also influential in getting Harding to embellish Smedley's
Civil War reenactments with presidential attendance and in securing the
1921 mail guard, both significant publicity coups for the marines. One winter Smedley took 500 marines up to Washington to dig Union Station, just
down the hill from the Capitol, out of the snow. Quantico became a site for
veterans' and Shriners' convocations. When Second Division veterans came
in 1922 they messed and bunked with their hosts at no expense, and were
feted with a full program of parades, baseball, boxing, a ball, and memorial
ceremonies. A boy scout troup invited down after Christmas in 1920 ended
its visit with a fathers' and sons' meal for half the boys—those who were
sons of congressmen. Smedley unabashedly wrote one father: "I think it of
great benefit to both members of Congress and the Marine Corps to get
acquainted on the human side, because we need the benefit of your experience and knowledge . . . and it is good for the Corps to be able to present
the facts informally. None of us secure much from formal hearings." [4]

The pace was strenuous. Several of Butler's officers wrote back that they
missed the "hustle and bustle" (both used the phrase) when they moved to
other posts, and the one in Haiti was pointedly told by his new mates to take
it easy, "that I am not in Quantico now and that if the work is not done today,
it can be done tomorrow." Butler kept up the pressure while pushing his
projects, and would intercede at all levels. His children remembered driving

around the base in the family automobile with their mother and father sitting up front, and passing three marines walking on the sidewalk; when only two saluted, "old gimlet eye" stopped the car, got out and rebuked the third.[5]

Perhaps all this tenacity was pathogenic. In 1922 Butler was hospitalized with symptoms of Bright's disease that turned up in his annual physical, but after a week it was dismissed as "nervous dyspepsia." He was dyspeptic all his life and smoked excessively. "Personally, I am feeling pretty tired all the time," he wrote a friend, "but there doesn't seem to be any way of slowing up." Notoriously zealous, he nevertheless got along well with his immediate staff and maintained lengthy and affectionate personal correspondence with cronies—unaffectedly so with several much junior in rank. This was at a time when deference and formality were prevalent; the son of a peer recalled, "General Butler was the only person my father called by his first name . . . . He didn't call anybody by his first name until after he retired, really, except for Smedley Butler. They were very, very close friends."[6]

If everything in Butler's commands seemed to bear his personal imprint, this was mainly achieved through effective delegation and cooptation. "Deacon" Upshur, his administrative aide at this time, wrote home, "I know his ideas pretty thoroughly, write up what I think should be said, and usually get an o.k. on the rough draft without his making a pencil mark on the original." Another officer, eventually a lieutenant general, recalled a conversation with Smedley at a dinner party in China in the late 1920s: "He said, 'Young man, if you want to get along in this Marine Corps, when you get in a position of command, surround yourself with good officers and let 'em do their job.' That was something I never forgot." It was also said that Butler "never played favorites."[7]

Leadership was his strong point, emphasizing physical command presence in the warrior style. "I remember how he would pace back and forth and yell at us," recalled one junior officer. At Quantico and on the expeditionary marches, sometimes with journalists present, he harangued the troops to greater effort. True to the Duckboard precedent, he carried enlisted men's knapsacks to project a populist, egalitarian ideal. He accosted enlisted men individually at random to solicit grievances. On the sentimental side, akin to the Thirteenth Regiment's wartime "Mother," Mrs. Daniels, Butler instituted "Mother De Boo" at Quantico—Mrs. Katherine De Boo held open house, was available for motherly talks with enlisted men, and was duly honored on Mother's Day.[8]

The ambitious education program started under Daniels fared poorly. Commandant Barnett's skepticism that it would "create great dissatisfaction" among men who enlisted expecting big opportunities proved justified. Marine recruiting in early 1920 advertised education to the extent that one recruiting officer wrote Butler that the Institute at Quantico "has, without doubt, been the most attractive inducement offered by any branch of the service to the young men of America." But by December Smedley reported to headquarters that lack of books was causing "a great deal of unrest among the men down here; so much that it is quite a serious question as to whether the school will stay or fall. . . . for God's sake send us some books and help us out."[9] The academic program collapsed, and in 1921 the various efforts were consolidated into a military curriculum. A separate Marine Corps Institute offering general education was moved to Washington and survived primarily as a correspondence school.

Although only thirty miles south of Washington, Quantico was isolated by wretched roads and, comprising mainly humid woodlands set in a depression along the Potomac, was prone to debilitating summer heat waves. Butler built up the base, using marine labor and substantial quantities of cadged materials. Construction was an all-hands effort. Fritz Wise remembered that the command was "nothing but a labor force. . . . There was damned little drill. . . . Butler had made carpenters and plumbers out of the whole outfit." Engineer and sapper units were commonplace elsewhere in the contemporary military, and Butler had no qualms about marines degrading themselves doing manual labor. Especially analogous to Butler's Quantico regime might be the French Foreign Legion precept, *démerdez vous*, shift for yourself. During the 1920s the Legion built roads in North Africa and even hired out legionnaires locally as common laborers. In the marines, Butler was the lineal precursor to the *gung-ho* (work together) spirit that Captain Evans F. Carlson picked up from the Chinese Communists during the late 1930s and introduced into marine lore through his Raider Battalion in World War II. Carlson served under Butler and thought highly of him.[10]

Construction work included officers, who were encouraged to pitch in alongside their men. A young second lieutenant, George F. Good, Jr., happened to be down on the floor showing an enlisted man how to fit parquet blocks when Butler walked in: "General Butler thought I was a fair-haired boy right then. And it was pure chance; I suppose I hadn't done that with respect to any other phase of the construction of the house, but he thought that was wonderful." Parquet floors for officers' quarters were made out of scraps left over from cutting tent pegs in Philadelphia. The lieutenant, ultimately a lieutenant general, recalled in 1970, "Incidentally, I spent my whole career in the Marine Corps, I think, preaching personal leadership, and if there was a man who was a past master at personal leadership in our Corps it was Smedley Butler." Noting "the level of enthusiasm and the level of professionalism" that Smedley demanded and got from the troops, Good commented, "Lots of people didn't like General Butler, they thought he had many undesirable qualities, but I was always a great admirer of his."[11]

Sometimes his demands were eccentric. In 1923, he managed on short notice to invite the patrician Chevy Chase Club to stage a tennis tournament at Quantico, so the marines worked day and night (under floodlights) to build courts in the woods. Everything was ready when Secretary Denby, his wife, the assistant secretary of war, and about seventy-five guests arrived by Eagle Boat on a Sunday morning for their outing.[12]

The biggest construction effort, with no funding from official sources, was a football stadium integral to Butler's hopes for putting Quantico on the map as an athletic spectacle. The plan called for an amphitheater to be gouged out of a hillside so that grandstands could rest directly on graded earth slopes. Smedley boosted the project to a civilian donor with the same fervid sentimentality that he had used to rally his regiment during the war: 33,000 seats might seem excessive for a base with only 2,500 personnel, but this was "a tribute to the memories of all of the 33,000 marines who have died in the uniform of their Corps since its organization on November 10th, 1775." Each seat was to have a bronze plate with the name of one of the dead. "Not only have the men voted to build this with their own labor, but, also, to pay for it from their own funds, and it, therefore, behooves me, as the father of this family, to do it as cheaply as possible."[13]

Such cash as was needed for this and for equipping football teams came out of post exchange revenues, which were normally consigned to welfare and recreation and therefore "belonged" to the troops. To what extent the troops spontaneously volunteered for all this is problematic, but since the whole sports program was pitched in terms of pep and pride, and the troops worked hard and then responded vociferously from the grandstands to Smedley's cheerleading, it seems there was general enthusiasm.

Civilian donors caught some of the spirit, too. President Eppa Hunton of the Richmond, Fredericksburg and Potomac Railroad responded to Butler's appeal by acclaiming "this spirit and desire" as "unlike anything I have ever seen elsewhere, the invariable rule being an effort to impose on the government." In this case Butler was exploiting leverage which the marines had as foremost customers of the RF&P line through Quantico. But Hunton not only donated fishplates and rails for the grandstands but became "intensely personally interested in the Marines," went along on football weekends as Smedley's personal guest, and used his influence to schedule games with college teams such as Virginia Military Institute. Cement was donated by the Dixie Portland Cement Company, sand and gravel were quarried on the base. The labor was already on the government payroll.[14]

Within a year, 60,000 cubic yards of dirt had been sculpted out of the hill and 13,000 seats installed. Concrete slabs reinforced with steel rails served as bench seats, propped up on rail and fishplate supports. It was a big project, much of it hand labor working with pick and shovel, and Butler could be an impulsive taskmaster. General Silverthorn, fondly dubbing Smedley "one of my favorite Marines," remembered working all summer on half the stadium: "We had almost finished and General Butler came out and went up on top. We were just doing the final grading. He said, 'You know, we're going to make it bigger,' and he marched into the woods about 50 yards, turned on his heel, dug a hole and said, 'I want it to come all the way back to here.' So all the work we'd done easing it had to be done again."[15]

A fellow officer, telling of a similar experience while laying concrete seats, recalled, "Well, when Smedley Butler had an idea you had to be in sympathy with it!" Another of the many stories connected with the project had three bandsmen telling Butler they could do no manual labor lest they damage their hands; he agreed, but saw to it that henceforth whenever even a handful of men were working on the stadium there was musical accompaniment to boost morale.[16] The stadium, eventually named Butler Field, survives with its improvised railroad hardware down to the present.

Once during the fall football season, and twice otherwise, Butler launched annual expeditionary overland maneuvers. "Thanks to the Lejeune-Butler credo of survival by keeping the Marines in the news," wrote Vandegrift, "these maneuvers, one of Butler's brainstorms," culminated in the "military pageant" of Civil War battles reenacted at the original sites. While primarily for publicity, the marches were also, as another marine reminisced, "a good thing, you know, because otherwise they would have just sat down at Quantico. Without something like that, troops tend to go to seed a little bit." On the march the troops ran tactical problems that were kept simple so as not to congest the public roads.[17]

The first outing in 1921 was the Wilderness campaign staged at the battlefield near Chancellorsville, about thirty-five miles southwest of Quantico as the crow flies. Along with over 3,000 men, including drafts from other East Coast commands sent for practice mobilization of the Expeditionary Force, went "every bit of our equipment" which Butler intended to display as an awesome modern counterpoint to the historic reenactment. This included 155 mm guns weighing nineteen tons, sixty-inch searchlights, antiaircraft guns, seventy caterpillar tractors, an armored car, a tank, eighteen airplanes, a captive balloon, and over a hundred trucks. The procession strung out three and one-half miles along the Washington-Richmond highway. Leading the column on foot, Butler was called to the rear when about twenty men dropped out because of the heat, and shamed them by carrying one of their knapsacks in addition to his own. After marching the stragglers in, he apparently had a minor heart attack, but recovered quickly under medication and once again had made his point with the troops.[18]

Smedley felt, as he wrote his father, that the exercise would "make a bigger show than the army pulled off in their bombing tests to show Congress that we have, in addition to our big building program here, a highly trained emergency force" which could be rapidly mobilized "for international police work." It was to be "the biggest show any military crowd has pulled off in the United States in peace times." Congressman Butler helped provide the audience. The marines furnished air and surface transportation, and more than a hundred congressmen and senators participated.[19]

The schedule of events, aside from the Civil War piece, which was run first as a historic recreation and then as a modern battle problem, included night air raids against forty searchlights and antiaircraft guns firing blank ammunition, air attacks on a mock aircraft carrier deck with twelve pursuit planes on it, and a battleship layout defended by searchlights and antiaircraft guns. As a break from the military show, there were movies and singing in the woods.

Night flying was new to marine aviators, and conditions, with no night instruments, were primitive. "Smedley had a searchlight battery, and he wanted to see if the searchlights could pick up planes," one aviator recalled. The lights proved unable to follow the planes, but one flyer, diving down into the lights as a technique for eluding them while practicing at Quantico, "never came out. He went right into the Potomac, wide open."[20]

The Wilderness show was thus quite daring, at the forefront of current tactical experimentation. With Harding, Denby, and the congressmen looking on, the display of naval and air warfare was the marines' answer to the controversy raging between the Army Air Service's Billy Mitchell, who had spectacularly sunk a battleship in a bombing demonstration several months before, and the Navy, which was variously defending the battleship as unsinkable and promoting its own separate naval air service. One of the Wilderness exercises featured a noon bombing formation attacking the mock battleship only to be driven off by antiaircraft fire and pursuit planes, "all of this to demonstrate that the battleship, with proper overhead protection, is not an obsolete weapon as General Mitchell would have the country believe."[21] Mitchell, promoting a single air service that would, in one draft version, be equipped with its own aircraft carriers, was getting some comeuppance in the public relations game, while the general cause of military aviation gained from the controversy.

Butler originally hoped to stage two expeditions each year, but this was too expensive. In 1922, the site was Gettysburg in south-central Pennsylvania. The month-long trek by 5,000 men started in mid-June, passed in review through the south grounds of the White House, and proceeded to Gettysburg where elaborate preparations were made, including erection of Camp Harding for housing the many dignitaries expected as guests. Harding came up from Washington in a six-car motorcade with his wife, General Pershing, and an entourage of secret servicemen and reporters. The governors of Pennsylvania, Virginia, and Maryland were on hand to welcome him.

A sixteen-room temporary mansion made of canvas and wood, complete with what the *New York Tribune* described as "luxurious furniture," was ready for the presidential party, as well as lesser buildings for senators and con-

gressmen. When asked whether there was no suitable accommodation for
Harding nearby, General Louis R. Jones, a junior officer at the time, recalled, "Well, it was one of those things for Marine Corps publicity, you
know, General Butler was in command of our outfit, and he always got publicity, so he had Harding there." Irrespective of prohibition, Harding and his
associates indulged in the well-known presidential taste for liquor. Jones
remembered tearing down the mansion afterward: "You'd be surprised at
the number of bottles that were underneath there!" When Pennsylvania
Governor William C. Sproul's plane landed with a case of whiskey, it was
turned over to a marine sergeant who "went through the [presidential]
building and came out the back, and the case of whiskey wound up with
us." [22] Butler was surely aware of this contempt for prohibition in high official circles, and could reflect thereon later when he became a leading civilian
prohibition enforcer.

The Civil War reenactment featured Pickett's charge, led by "Deacon"
Upshur, who gallantly ran his sword through his hat and held it aloft to rally
his Confederate troops at the climactic moment. It was extravagant enough
to please the newsreel moving picture crews and estimated hundred thousand spectators. Guns fired black powder that beclouded the battlefield, and
marines fell at prearranged points in simulating the decimation of charging
troops, leaving only a handful alongside Upshur at the stone wall crest. That
night, a series of heavy thunderstorms blew down many tents, but Harding's
mansion held fast. During the airplane demonstrations, there was another
fatal crash. A De Havilland bomber stalled and burned in front of the crowd
as it came in to land. [23]

The fall 1923 outing, another month-long effort, was to the Shenandoah Valley in western Virginia for the Battle of New Market. According to
Vandegrift, twenty-eight of thirty days "featured a driving, cold rain." The
3,000 men and 150 trucks with their hard-rubber tires mired in the terrible
Virginia backcountry roads. One officer remembered that "practically the
whole motor train was bogged down" so that for a week he scarcely went
to bed. [24]

Maneuvers again included airplane innovations, such as air-ground
pickup with a plane sweeping low to catch a message suspended on two
poles and then carrying it from the outlying unit to Butler at headquarters.
But despite the showmanship and the attractions of Camp Coolidge with its
vertical boiler, "a huge monstrosity being hauled [from Quantico] solely to
provide hot water for the important guests," the new President, Calvin
Coolidge, failed to make an appearance. Harding, a Civil War buff, had died
in office several months before. The crowd watching the Civil War reenactment was estimated at more than 150,000. [25]

After the New Market spectacle, the expedition headed south for a football game with Virginia Military Institute, setting up camp in a field outside

town. General Good remembered Butler's rousing the troops the morning of the game, so that despite mud and rain they marched into Lexington with marine élan: "And it was General Butler that did it. Everybody was disgruntled, wet, we only had minimum clothing with us—just what we could take on our back—but somehow or other, under his inspiration people made the extra effort that makes a Marine different from anybody else." Six years later a former enlisted man, for whom Smedley was helping to secure citizenship papers, reminded him, "Once on the hike through Virginia in 1923 you made a speech to us Marines and you said you would do anything for us even roll in the mud in your clean uniform none of us wished to have our general do so." [26]

After losing to V.M.I., the itinerant leathernecks marched back up the valley and and beat Washington College 19 to 0, thence to the capital for a march-past through the White House grounds and along Pennsylvania Avenue. President Coolidge took the review alongside Denby and Lejeune. The marines parked their artillery overnight on the Ellipse south of the White House and defeated Georgetown University in football the next day. Smedley's friend Eli Helmick, currently inspector general of the army, sent a glowing report ("naturally I did not make any critical remarks") of the parade to Lejeune, but privately pointed out flaws to Smedley which indicated that the troops were showing wear and tear after a month on the road: some field officers on horseback "had a slouchy seat," some men were not properly shaven, and "some of the bayonets were rusted, and one or two I noticed had been stuck in the ground and not properly cleaned afterwards." [27] That was Butler's last Civil War campaign, although the marines staged Antietam as a modern attack in the summer of 1924 without him.

During these years he pushed aviation development at Quantico and by being personally flown to a number of distant extracurricular engagements. On one occasion, recalled by an aviator years later, he went up in "putrid" weather and "evidently had a damn good scare, because he didn't get out of the plane when he first came back, and I kidded him about it later, because he had green twigs in the landing gear." Another early flyer, Ford O. Rogers, remembered "that slow, hit and by miss, program of training, which started during Smedley's regime at Quantico." As a "big aviation fan," Butler promoted many "little progressive steps" such as air photography with the picture developed in the plane, ready to be sprinted across the field to the commanding general after landing.[28]

Rogers once flew Smedley up to West Chester for a veterans' parade, landing in a cow pasture. Smedley came wearing civilian clothes and a Spanish American War marine hat: "He had that hat on, leading the parade, and Uncle Tom [Smedley's father] and I were standing on—they had one of those old-fashioned Pennsylvania houses with a little stoop in front and we were standing on the stoop watching the parade go by. And Uncle Tom looked at Smedley. He turned to me and said, 'Isn't Smedley a damn fool, though. Look at him strutting around."[29]

Smedley's determined promotion of marine football highlighted the other quasimilitary allurements emanating from Quantico. The objective was to strive for football supremacy within the services and then, with superior teams, attain recognition in civilian college football. Here was an enterprising blend of red-blooded Americanism, marine chauvinism, self-help aspiration, and a fair-field-and-no-favor challenge to prestigious civilian and service counterparts, all appealingly couched in high morale and pitched to the thriving mass communications media of the day. Barnstorming publicity and smart, aggressively intrusive politics may not have suited staid professionals like Barnett, but for the moment the national mood was receptive to boosterism, and when couched in patriotism so much the better.

And for the peacetime military, it was devil take the hindmost. Sports, especially those involving brute force, stamina, and virile pugnacity, provided an obvious continuum in which the military might build rapport with civilian society. The marines were not alone in thinking so. General Douglas MacArthur, for instance, promoted athletics at West Point and, on the urging of the army chief of staff, who thought it would be good publicity, became president of the American Olympic Committee in 1927.[30]

Football at Quantico started in 1919 and built up to a crescendo under Butler, although he seems to have had no special interest in the game as such. "I don't give a damn for a football game," he once wrote his father, and neither before nor after the Quantico years was he ever a football fan. But he threw everything he had into promoting the marine teams. A Quantico football player later recalled Smedley's "tremendous love for the game," and how losing the V.M.I. game had hurt him.[31]

From the start sports were linked with the idea of boosting Quantico on a par with West Point and Annapolis. This fit the ambitious plans for a marine university, "securing the true college spirit," as Secretary Daniels put it after a December 1920 game, even as the educational program was collapsing for want of books.[32] Later, the goal of parity with the service academies and top civilian schools survived as a morale and public-relations gambit. Over the next three years, Butler built up teams and increasingly formidable baseball and football schedules with rival service units and civilian colleges. Football was the primary effort, winning greater publicity and much more suitable as a mass spectacle in which the entire Quantico command, indeed the entire East Coast Marine Corps, could take part. Away games at Baltimore, Washington, and Philadelphia brought out thousands of marines, and Butler formed them into colorful cheering sections, drilling them beforehand to shout, wave specially issued semaphore flags, clack together tent pegs, and otherwise make their presence felt.

An adjutant wearing a white sweater with a red "M" was cheerleader, aided by Smedley himself when he was not preoccupied with the game on the sidelines. Asked what the marines thought of Butler's football stunts, General Rogers replied, "Well, everybody was highly amused by him. Nobody—I never got, I never could get mad at him, he was so funny." Silverthorn remembered "a tremendous amount of enthusiasm." In 1921 Butler bought a bulldog, "Jiggs," to be team mascot, and formally enlisted him as a sergeant major. Besides evoking physical aggressiveness, this was an allusion to the "devil dogs" nickname that marines had earned fighting Germans during the recent war. And there was plenty of military fanfare. The large Quantico band was always on hand for games, and for marching formations and massive military parades, depending on the circumstances.[33]

The Quantico team recruited from the entire Marine Corps and thereby fielded some of the great athletes of the day. By 1922, Smedley was able to claim that there was not "a man on our team who has not been a college 'star.'" Nevertheless, it was difficult for the marines to break into civilian sports. They did not charge admission for games, and raised money from the ranks to support the team and sometimes pay opponents in lieu of gate receipts. On the road, the marines paid all their expenses and took none of the gate receipts. When Philadelphia fell through as a site for a big game with the army, Smedley wrote his father not to get upset, that "Baltimore is as good a town as Philadelphia and we are going to make it a liberty area for Marines if they treat us well over there this time."[34]

All the blandishments and high-powered football helped get big games, but of course were also rather menacing as a formula for long-term athletic relationships from the civilian colleges' point of view. The marines were really more in their milieu against army teams, which also played ex-college stars. Among the marine greats were Walter V. "Boots" Brown, formerly of Washington State College, Frank Goettge of Ohio State, Johnny Beckett of Oregon, and Harry Liversedge of University of California. With Beckett as head coach and bulwark of the line, the Quantico Marines won thirty-eight, lost two and tied two in four years. Notable among the great games was a 13 to 12 victory over the Army's Third Corps in 1922 before 60,000 spectators in Baltimore. Most of the army team were former West Pointers, including several all-Americans. "I have never known such excitement," Smedley wrote a marine in Cuba. Six thousand marines came from posts as far away as New London and Parris Island. The army had 6,000 soldiers, "their cheering was really good this year although we beat them to it again."[35]

By 1923 Quantico had penetrated the ranks of civilian college football, playing George Washington University, Villanova, and the University of Michigan in addition to the games played during the Shenandoah expedition. There were, however, problems within the Corps, as pride in Quantico was tempered by resentment from the other posts that had to give up their best talent, thereby forgoing local successes. Butler tried to emphasize the varsity aspect of the big team and "make the newspapers stop referring to Marine Corps Teams as 'Quantico Teams.'"[36]

The other posts were also dunned for levies of spectators to send to the big games, and local post exchanges were tapped for travel expenses. Butler himself would complain about the Quantico monopoly when he tried to build up football in San Diego in 1926, by which time Corps headquarters in Washington had taken over control of the big team and resorted to systematic exactions. "If you will look back," he wrote Lejeune, "I think you will find that in the years 1920-21-22-23-24, the rest of the Marine Corps did not pay the bills of this team, nor did we go outside the Corps and hire professionals at large sums to coach this team."[37]

The 1924 team, based on Smedley's organization and scheduling prior to his departure, went undefeated and overwhelmed the Army's Third Corps 47 to 0. Thereafter, things went downhill. But the loss of amateurish spontaneity was clearly foreseeable in Butler's hard-driving methods. The clumsy, semiprofessional takeover by headquarters only confirmed that success was elusive. The crusading martial spirit could not be sustained as an institutionalized ascendancy. The military as underdog and potential prey was exciting and lovable, but not as sated juggernaut. Victory, or even protracted intrusive publicity, bore sinister connotations and could be pushed only so far against civilian ambivalence.[38]

The climax of Butler's quest for national football stature was the 1923 loss to the University of Michigan, reputedly the best team in the country. All stops were pulled in arranging cut-rate travel expenses, and some of Butler's automobile industry friends got the Detroit City Council to help pay for the 185-piece marine band. Smedley described the extravaganza, a 1,600-man onslaught in five special trains emblazoned with Marine Corps insignia, as having "made an impression on the Middle West which they have never had before from anything." Costs of $90,000 came "out of our own pockets," and "a few of us sports" hired a private Pullman car for Secretary and Mrs. Denby. In Detroit they rented a big hotel and all the marines chipped in to give Denby "a dinner which was a beauty."[39]

The Michigan game also involved Secretary Denby's network of local business associates and their concerted effort to recruit Butler as head of the American Automobile Association. Contemporary military leaders did attain prominence in big business—for instance, Smedley's A.E.F. superior, General James G. Harbord, who now headed Radio Corporation of America. Denby, a former Michigan football star and a wartime marine, had made a fortune in Detroit as an automobile dealer after the war. The Marine-Michigan game, with attendant parades, banquets, and hoopla in Detroit, was something of a triumphal homecoming—Butler suggested "Denby Day," but the secretary modestly declined. A month earlier Smedley and his wife had come to Detroit for an interview with the consortium of auto moguls, and he was apparently serious about the proposition, writing an intermediary, "I don't believe this crowd has enough money to get me out of the service. However, if they have I am ready to do their bidding any time." [40]

Smedley described the negotiations to Denby in a long, flippant letter uncharacteristically interspersed with unctuous Babbitry—quips about a welcoming speech "evidently written by a funeral director," "your filthy but hustling city," "these predatory rich men," and himself treating their offer "with as much scorn as my emaciated financial condition would permit." The *Detroit Free Press* reported that he was taking a position with Packard Motor Car Company, but, as he explained to Eppa Hunton, "while the offer made by these gentlemen is almost staggering, I cannot make up my mind to leave the Marine Corps." Civilian and military friends congratulated him for his idealism—indicating contemporary perceptions of the gap between military and business ethics. General E.W. Nichols of V.M.I. was scornful of Detroit capitalists: "I am glad you have not yielded to the tempter and it is very refreshing to see a man of your prominence actuated in your life's work by higher considerations than those that mere money can offer." Smedley replied to the Jesuit athletic director at Georgetown, "I think your example has helped me to push the tempter aside." [41]

The job, essentially public relations, would have made him rich and allowed him to indulge fully his passion for expensive cars. But the work did not appeal to him "in the slightest degree," as he confided to H.L. Roosevelt, who wrote asking for a job if the Packard rumors were true. To Denby, he implied that Mrs. Butler made the decision. Despite his efforts as middleman coming to naught, the secretary replied that he would "keep on loving you whatever you do," but their warm relationship was soon to lapse, victim to yet another political misadventure. [42] Revelations by congressional investigations into the Teapot Dome naval oil scandal, in which Denby was centrally involved through incompetence rather than venality, forced him to resign in disgrace.

Probably crucial to Butler's turning down the Detroit offer was the alternative of having his cake and eating it too. During the preceding months there were a number of references in correspondence with Colonel Cyrus Radford, his Philadelphia intermediary, to matters best not discussed in writing that would await their next meetings. Six weeks before the Detroit proposition, the mayor-elect of Philadelphia offered Smedley the city's top police post. Apart from adventure more in keeping with the martial, crusading way of life he admired, this meant that he could grope his way into civilian life without cutting himself off from the marines. [43]

In the four years since he had first been bruited as a candidate, he had kept in touch with local affairs through marine football, frequent after-dinner speaking engagements, at least one radio address, Haverford alumni functions, and veterans gatherings, much of this complementary to Marine

Corps publicity. In 1923, Quantico hosted several thousand Shriners during their national convention in Washington, after which the Philadelphia contingent gave a luncheon for Smedley. This was his first and only personal contact with Potentate W. Freeland Kendrick of Lu Lu Temple prior to Kendrick's election as mayor. Kendrick, despite his background as an organization Republican, bypassed professional politicians in putting together a reform cabinet and sought Butler as a famous military figure with constabulary experience and local roots, in addition to a reputation for getting things done or at least (taking the cynical view) generating effective publicity while trying.

Smedley accepted the job on condition that Kendrick give him a free hand and procure President Coolidge's consent to a four-year leave of absence from the marines. Kendrick and the Pennsylvania congressional delegation including both senators visited Coolidge and told him of a "dangerous" situation in Philadelphia, where "banditry, promiscuous sale of poisonous liquor, the sale of dope, viciousness and lawlessness of all kinds are rampant." Pennsylvania Governor Gifford Pinchot sent a telegram emphatically urging approval, and the president, with apparent reluctance, granted a one-year leave, possibly renewable.[44]

There had been a significant precedent in 1918, when Secretary Daniels complained about rampant, officially tolerated prostitution in Philadelphia that was affecting military personnel, and briefly initiated federal government intervention. By 1923 the police were again at a low ebb, to the point that Kendrick was able to ride the public outcry into office. In reporting Butler's appointment, the *New York Times* referred to Philadelphia as "wide open," with 1,300 saloons defying both reform Governor Pinchot and the helpless federal prohibition director. The *Philadelphia Record* stated editorially that Butler's post, the directorship of public safety, was "the most important executive officer of the city" next to the mayor.[45]

Smedley privately characterized the job as "a terrible one and I will probably be cut to pieces." His wife and father both disapproved. To a marine officer in Guantánamo he wrote: "It's a big job Tommy and the people of Philadelphia are expecting a whole lot of things that neither I nor anyone else can accomplish. However, in Marine Corps style, I will do the best I know how."[46]

Before leaving the marines he arranged the secret introduction of an experimental amphibious tank to surprise defenders at Culebra during upcoming maneuvers, in which he was to have commanded the Expeditionary Force. The Christie tank, which proved unseaworthy, was forerunner to World War II amphibious tractors used extensively by marines in the Pacific.[47]

Butler's assault on Philadelphia, while itself an amazing intrusion of marine panache into civilian affairs, came at a time when postwar military and paramilitary insinuations into American civilian life had lost momentum. For the marines, lacking any urgent mission or capability to suit isolationist military policies during the postwar years, Butler's Quantico circus had perhaps saved the day until the late-1920s overseas expeditions provided further respite. Thereafter, the big-war expeditionary mission gained credibility to provide the Corps with a secure role in the 1930s. Amid recurrent threats of being absorbed into the army, the marines held their own in the 1920s with about 20,000 men, while the navy was cut back from 133,000 to 95,000, and the army from 231,000 to 137,000. Meanwhile, diverse initiatives, such as the army's Reserve Officer Training Corps in civilian colleges, universal military training promoted as educational uplift, and soft-sell appeals to civilian interest in military technology, all met with resistance and frustration. Congress stolidly curbed the military with stringent budgets, and after Harding's somewhat pliable administration Presidents Coolidge and Hoover reasserted civilian discipline to squelch unwanted military solicitations.

Through all this, the marines and Butler in particular maintained the old "first in the fight" élan, catching on for such scraps and odd jobs as opportunity presented. In his enthusiasm, showmanship, and even flamboyant exhibitionism, there was a popular appeal that served the Corps well. The brash public relations exercises not only helped sell the Marine Corps to Congress, but projected fighting-leatherneck imagery in a telling way. At Quantico, Butler further articulated and popularized the new bulldog marine ethos, giving the marines both a convincing public image and a credible warrior ideal to suit contemporary notions of manliness. At a personal level, his growing mastery of the politics of media manipulation gave him a sense of prowess for new skirmishes to come.

11   Smashing Crime and Vice
PHILADELPHIA

The history of full-time urban police forces dates back to the mid-nineteenth century. Meanwhile in many countries state-controlled military and paramilitary forces, such as the Irish *Gardai*, the *Guardia Civil* in Spain, and the German *Staatspolizei*, continued to maintain domestic peace. Even in America, where hostility to standing armies and meddling with local liberties was strong, the military continued to intervene frequently in civil crises such as labor wars and urban riots. But military intervention often resulted in brutal class repression at variance with increasingly egalitarian political and legal standards.

American urban police developed as independent local institutions in response to the tensions of ethnically segregated urban class society. By 1900, big-city police forces had acquired uniforms and professional status as law enforcement agencies, and cast aside collateral duties such as street cleaning and boiler inspection. The issue of political control was paramount from the start, with city political machines rooted in immigrant and lower-class communities pitted against middle-class and patrician reformers in the suburbs and upstate. To reformers, notorious police inefficiency and corruption were linked to urban politics, and became the prime target for clean government crusades that were the most consistently identifiable hallmark of the progressive era in American politics.

In pressing for efficient administration, reasonable standards of honesty, apolitical professionalism, higher recruiting standards and other innovations, the movement for police reform coalesced in what urban historian Robert M. Fogelson has identified as the "military analogy" prevalent from 1890 to 1930. By the 1920s, according to Fogelson, "the military analogy was the conventional wisdom of most upper middle- and upper-class Americans too." Police were considered to be, "in the words of Commissioner Theodore Roosevelt, Captain Alexander R. Piper, and Major Frederick Ebstein, respectively, a 'half-military,' 'semi-military,' and 'quasi-military' body." Public officials referred to police chiefs as analogous to commanding generals, and President Wilson stated that policemen were the moral equivalent of soldiers.[1] Patrolmen were transformed into privates, roundsmen into sergeants, and superiors became lieutenants and captains. Military command structure matched the reform ideal of effective centralization in order to overmaster ward politicians.

After 1900, paramilitary state constabularies were established in New York, Pennsylvania, Texas, and elsewhere, adding another dimension to the reform push for militarization. Constabularies, used effectively in American overseas protectorates as instruments of domination and to impose "progress" upon benighted subject peoples, might serve similar purposes domestically and upon similar subjects—the un-American immigrant polities that peopled American cities. While state constabularies ultimately reverted to mainly rural functions and the militarization of big-city police proved a dubious remedy, the movement for military intervention in domestic affairs was a revealing facet of the contemporary reform impulse, embodying elements of both corporatism and elitist (qua nativist) coercion. Reformers saw themselves launching a "war on crime," a kind of domestic pacification in which a number of military officers were recruited as police chiefs, Smedley Butler being both the most prominent and the one most closely identified with colonial expertise.

Butler brought certain advantages to the job. His brash egalitarian manner was the antithesis of dread aristocratic Prussian-style militarism, much despised in recent wartime propaganda. He might thus be militaristic enough for the reformers and at the same time appealing enough as a popularizer to impel a reasonable tightening of discipline on the police and the general public—an ideal front man for politicians seeking token reform and accommodation. And yet, for all his well-known hoopla, Smedley was hard-driving and quite serious about honor, integrity, and means achieving ends. Would he loyally support his superiors in city politics, such as they were, in the same spirit in which he had obeyed orders, more or less compliantly, as a U.S. officer? In fact, he was to be the most aggressive and determined of the military police chiefs, notable, according to Fogelson, for having "followed this [military] analogy to its logical conclusion."[2] Both the reformers and organization politicians were getting more than they bargained for.

Philadelphia in 1924 had a population of almost two million, making it the twelfth largest city in the world. A quarter were foreign-born. Lower-class and immigrant communities were concentrated in the city's core, the middle and upper classes having moved to the periphery. Under national prohibition, bootlegging had become an adjunct of gambling, prostitution, and other vice rackets, intricately connected with ward and machine politics based in immigrant communities in and adjacent to the tenderloin district. The tenderloin had survived as an intact, thriving district longer than in other cities, to the extent that a 1913 vice commission found over a hundred houses of prostitution. Now, as elsewhere, paramilitary police reform peaked along with the most ambitious reform of all, prohibition, by which reformers hoped to clean up urban lower-class morals while striking a death blow to bosses and gangsters who preyed on vice and suborned the police.

Prohibition at the national level had by this time turned the corner from early optimism and widespread public support to disillusionment, cynicism, and growing backlash in favor of modification and repeal. Gangsterism was romanticized in the mass media as an aspect of the new bootleg liquor industry, a type of crime widely supported by popular collusion extending into the middle and upper classes. On the other hand, however unsupported by hard data, the idea of a rising crime wave excited reformers to redouble their efforts, ergo the timing of Butler's adventure in Philadelphia and the quite remarkable press coverage, locally and nationally, that fixed upon his battle with demon rum.

Butler approached the problem head on as a matter of enforcing the law irrespective of legal intricacies, meanwhile cleaning up the police by dint and bluster. It was quite a show. As reported in the *New York Times*, which gave the story front-page coverage most of the first week, he started off with a bang: "POLICE GET 48 HOURS TO RID PHILADELPHIA OF VICE OR QUIT JOBS." His methods recalled crash programs for driving his commands at Pontanezen and Quantico. He assembled the 4,000 city cops in the Metropolitan Opera House in several shifts, and subjected them to pep talks heavily laced with threats. Saluting and formalities were banned, corrupt lieutenants were to be replaced by sergeants and if that failed, then by marines. Police were to be on the streets at all hours of day and night, and Butler and the superintendent would sleep at police headquarters in City Hall until the campaign succeeded. It was not necessary to wait for saloons to violate the law because they were a nuisance and bred crime; therefore, he would call on the fire department "to use pick-axes to break open their doors and then order the men to wreck the bars." Police were to use their guns more freely and would be backed up by the authorities afterward: "I don't believe there is a single bandit notch on a policeman's gun in this city. Go out and get some." He promised a promotion to the first cop to kill a bandit.[3]

The first forty-eight-hour shock assault featured raids on speakeasies, cabarets, candy stores, brothels, poolrooms, and cider saloons throughout the city. Butler toured the tenderloin, made surprise visits to station houses, and personally directed raids. Police statistics released afterward tallied 973 of 1,200 saloons selling illegal beverages as closed, and Butler estimated that 80 percent of vice dens had been eliminated, at least temporarily. Equipment was wrecked and several dozen saloons were padlocked. Butler dramatically suspended eight lieutenants for shirking duty.

The entire melee made great publicity that reverberated in neighboring cities in headlines such as in the *New York Times*: "BUTLER BEGINS WAR:

UNDESIRABLES FLEE FROM PHILADELPHIA." The New York police commissioner predicted an "exodus of crooks, prostitutes, gamblers and bootleggers," and New York and Baltimore reportedly posted police "strong-arm" squads at railroad and ferry terminals to fend off the rumored influx.

Butler announced more forty-eight-hour vice drives at the rate of one a week to keep the lid on, and extravagantly boosted Kendrick as presidential timber on the strength of having cleaned up Philadelphia. Kendrick responded with praise and a salary increase for Smedley from $12,000 to $15,000, up from the previous director's $10,000. The *Times* editorialized, "LOUD TALK MAY BE EFFECTUAL," noting that "while some of his talk has seemed the reverse of wise—to contain too many threats and too many boasts—still he has made all Philadelphia, its good citizens and its bad ones, thoroughly aware of his presence."

A checkup by a reporter several days after the first push revealed that most of the saloons mentioned in Governor Gifford Pinchot's earlier investigation were now locked up and those still open had no signs of liquor available. Bookmakers on Broad and Chestnut Streets were closed down, narcotics dealers were off the streets, and waiters and cabbies confirmed the general cleanup.[4]

The second week's drive began on Friday in order to catch weekend revelers. "Its just like war," said Butler. "Since the forty-eight hour drive last week we've been 'entrenched.' Our position is what is called 'consolidated' in military language. Now we'll advance again." He was on the streets almost constantly, catching a few hours' sleep after 4 A.M., on Saturday before starting in again, visiting all forty-two districts to check on his minions. But there were problems. Many police thought the raids were "just a show, something spectacular to fool the people at the beginning of a new administration." Many raids were faked, after advance warning. He had no authority to sack anyone. Suspensions and demotions would be subject to reversal by his successor once the reform push had run its course.

After the second week's raids he found hundreds of places supposedly closed still operating in broad daylight. He pronounced doggedly, "This is going to be stopped at once," and ordered the first of a series of shakeups, shifting 400 men in four central districts. Entire units were exchanged one for the other on the following midnight. Mary Roberts Rinehart, visiting Butler's office, commented that this was similar to surgical practice "for breaking up adhesions." Meanwhile the underworld provided occasional dramatic counterpoint, as when eight men, four armed with sawed-off shotguns, hijacked a truck loaded with commercial alcohol.[5]

Along with the vice raids came a profusion of stylistic and operational innovations. Unlike his predecessors, who wore civilian clothes, Butler was sworn in wearing his marine uniform and then reappeared a half hour later in a personally designed blue paramilitary uniform with two gold stars (one up from brigadier), gold insignia, and cap visor trimmings. This symbolized bestowal of military prestige upon civilian police, here inimitably expressed by Smedley himself and true to the military analogy for police reform. On a scale of condescension, one is reminded of the colonial subspecies and his grossly inflated rank from major to major general in the Haitian Gendarmerie, and to his references to serving on a "nigger police force." For special occasions in Philadelphia he added a dashing blue cape with red lining borrowed from his marine mess uniform. The police eventually were done up in dark gray outfits with military Sam Browne belts, large holsters at the side, and prominent well-filled cartridge belts.

Butler announced a comprehensive antibandit program with armed guards and observation posts, including twenty-one traffic gates at entrances to the city, described in the press as "an 'iron ring' of semi-military police posts around the city."[6] Bandit-chasing squads in six armored cars were equipped with sawed-off shotguns and radios so that while the driver wore earphones the gunner was free to shoot out the window, as was done in practice runs against a human figure target board.[7] Other novelties included colored lights and signs to guide traffic through the city, avoiding congested corners by routes Smedley charted himself. A powerful red searchlight on City Hall tower, functioning as a prototype traffic light, pointed up Broad Street so that motorists had to stop in their tracks wherever they were up and down the street whenever it lit up.[8]

Press coverage was lavish throughout and, irrespective of editorial brickbats, was largely the result of his own cultivation of reporters and deliberate efforts to mobilize public opinion through flamboyant showmanship. To his many wet enemies much of this was subject to ridicule, but many drys loved it, feeling they had a colorful and intrepid champion. A *New York Times* story of a confrontation with a thug exemplifies the highly personal and florid tone frequently attained: "'Stop,' snapped Butler. Without a word he walked to the curb and addressed the flashily dressed gunman. 'They tell me you're a bad actor,' the General said. 'Well, see this?' his hand pointed to a service stripe he wears. 'I got this for killing your kind. Now get out of this town quick. Hear? Get out, and don't come back, or I'll get you myself.'"[9]

E.Z. Dimitman, then a twenty-six-year-old rewrite man for the *Philadelphia Public Ledger*, attributed Smedley's popularity with reporters to his openness. Any reporter could walk into his office anytime, and he would answer any question. After working until midnight, he often went over to Child's restaurant on Chestnut Street with reporters on the night beat and chatted for an hour, allowing them to come up with fresh news for the morning papers instead of rewriting material from afternoon editions. Such courtesies, and the fact that he was good copy and a straight shooter, compensated for misgivings about the dry crusade. According to Dimitman, before

Butler came, high-quality imported liquor was unloaded right on the water-front, with city editors of the big papers always getting a case to pass around to the boys. This vulnerable supply line was quickly severed.[10]

An aggressive press campaign was by no means tactically inane. Color-ful publicity was the best means Butler had to make an impact enforcing unpopular sumptuary laws, and Mayor Kendrick, beholden to election promises, could not renounce him so long as he projected heroic images of virtue. Nor were the bosses necessarily displeased; this would not be the first reform crusade that made a big noise without really accomplishing much.

Nor was Butler naively unprofessional in his openness and propagan-dizing. As in the marines, his brazen antics went against the grain of con-temporary bookish professionalism, where straitlaced decorum was scru-pulously maintained to support claims to expertise that had not yet attained general credibility. But the scope of professionalism was broadening. Chief August Vollmer of Berkeley, the father of incipient police science, allowed the half dozen reporters covering his department to share the squad room with working police officers, gave them access to police files, arranged planted stories, and otherwise systematically cultivated the fourth estate. Like Butler, Vollmer took every opportunity to address civic groups on be-half of his cause. Community relations was to become an important com-ponent of modern police professionalism.[11]

But Smedley's advantage as a gruff marine, which enabled him to out-face his cops and invade the tenderloin as a red-blooded warrior untainted by middle-class sanctimoniousness, proved to be a two-edged sword. Among reformers and drys, who tended to bourgeois propriety and church affiliations, were many who did not care for his style. One Philadelphia mother, who professed to have been an admirer at first, complained to the secretary of the navy: "I hope when Mr. Butler's leave expires that you will try and teach him that a General should be a gentleman and a leader such as Pershing and Wood and not a common soldier. We teach our children it is low and vulgar to swear, and they listen to Butler over Radio and say, 'Mother, General Butler swears all the time.' He should set an example of his own conduct."[12]

Others bemoaned the diminished dignity of the office and trampled property and civil rights. He was blamed for conducting "hysterical raids" and for using "military tactics which might do in Mexico and other places and has no place in the administration of civil affairs." He should not be allowed to act like a "Military Dictator . . . yet in these disgraceful raids, he wares [sic] his Marine cape of blue lined with red . . . and it has been said in the papers that many Marines are out securing information for him and they have no right to act and be used." A legend of military intervention emerged far in excess of what Butler, a lone marine, ever achieved. According to one apocryphal magazine story, published decades later, he deputized marines as special police and marched at their head to a bootleg warehouse. The marines, in uniform brandishing rifles with fixed bayonets, crashed through the door and confronted naked dancing girls performing for an audience of the city's leading social and political personalities.[13] But his style and rhetoric did suggest similarities between Philadelphia and the cleaning-up of a Caribbean protectorate.

Apart from public controversy, there was opposition from official quarters, including problems of conflicting jurisdictions in the chaotic politics of prohibition enforcement. In 1931 during Butler's court-martial, a U.S. Treasury agent in Philadelphia ingratiatingly submitted a poison-pen attack to President Hoover, recalling that as director Smedley surrounded himself with "a bunch of 'slickers'" about whom the agent had "learned plenty," with no specifics mentioned. The explicit accusation was that when the agent offered confidential information about a blackmail operation, Butler called in a city attorney and stenographer so that the agent "just smiled and showed him a lot of counterfeit money that I had brought along for such an emergency as I saw that he through his ignorance was a dangerous man to talk to . . . . That was the last time I saw Butler and congratulated myself on my narrow escape."[14] Was Butler a naive bungler? Or did he, being isolated and vulnerable, have good reason to suspect federal authorities and force everything out into the open for his own protection? Witness such "slickers" as the agent himself.

The federal record on prohibition enforcement on a national level was ignominiously weak until the Hoover administration took over in 1929, and the Prohibition Bureau (under the Treasury Department) in particular had a long record of dereliction as a political football outside civil service jurisdiction. In fact while Butler was in Philadelphia, President Coolidge appointed retired Army General Lincoln C. Andrews to militarize and depoliticize the service. Other military officers were brought in, but Andrews resigned in frustration in 1927, at which time Major Chester P. Mills of the New York branch estimated that three-fourths of Bureau personnel were "ward heelers and sycophants named by the politicians."[15]

In 1924 when Butler had been on the job for six months, Major R.A. Haynes, federal prohibition commissioner, reported after a visit to Philadelphia that for the first time "great progress" was being made in "that city which has been one of the most difficult in America." Without Butler's "energetic, sincere, and hearty cooperation," the situation "would be almost, if not altogether, hopeless." But Butler's police were often at odds with Prohibition Bureau agents on jurisdictional grounds, and by persistent harassment he shut down breweries that had thrived under federal purview. In late 1925 he wrote Governor Pinchot that eleven breweries had been closed, "while our friends, the Federal Government, still delay," and at one point he suspected that the federal marshal was involved in a nighttime brewing operation, but was unable to prove it.[16]

After the first month Butler called off the forty-eight-hour drives and shifted to routine ongoing intermittent raids. Already the major obstacles were identified. Padlockings and arrests by the thousands had little impact so long as the courts did not back up with convictions. Butler increased liquor arrests sixfold, but after twenty months in office convictions declined to less than pre-Butler levels. Convictions usually meant token fines.[17] The problem with Philadelphia's courts, or their advantage if one prefers elements of community control, was that magistrates were political appointees beholden to ward politics. Of ninety who held office from 1900 to 1924, only three were attorneys, the rest being of diverse backgrounds such as salesmen, bartenders, butchers. Enforcement of public morals laws was wildly uneven from district to district.[18] Butler also had to battle constantly against boss William S. Vare's influence with Kendrick, to protect his honest cops from reprobate ward politicians, and to maintain public support, as against offensive intrusions such as his dress-suit squad that mingled with crowds in clubs and hotels on the lookout for hip flasks.

The door-crashing, ax-wielding excesses of the first weeks gave way to legal circumspection in the face of resistance from the magistrates, but the emphasis on harassment remained: "It cost the proprietors money to refurnish their gambling places; it cost them money for legal talent; and it cost them money to fix things even with the friendly magistrates. This constant drain, we knew, eventually would put them out of business."[19]

Several judges and magistrates backed him, and it was through them that Butler got most of the important convictions. There was also support from prominent dry spokesmen, such as Josephus Daniels, who urged that he be made national prohibition enforcer. Pinchot, who became a political ally and personal friend, openly mentioned him as a likely successor for the governorship—a long shot that held no interest for Smedley.[20]

After six months of raiding and hectoring with mixed results, Butler executed a major police reorganization. This would, if hopes were realized, be decisive in breaking ward-heeler control over precinct police, just as the marine gendarmerie in Haiti had replaced indigenous power matrices with a centralized system impervious to local manipulation. In Philadelphia the forty-eight wards had been paired almost identically with forty-two police districts, reinforcing the relationship as a mainstay of ward and machine politics. Butler's scheme, put into effect in the summer of 1924 against a great outcry from the bosses during which Butler and Kendrick did not speak to each other for three months, was to reduce the number of police districts to twenty-two. Each new district had two lieutenants and one captain, "brought in from a different part of the city, with different political affiliations." This meant that several ward leaders would be in conflict over control of each new district, with three new police officers for them to deal with. And that hostile magistrates could be played off against each other.[21] He also introduced a new emphasis on mobility with squad cars, and juggled special details, eliminating some "pussyfooting squads," such as detectives, while establishing others, such as his own shoe-fly squad to police the police. One policeman remembered something called an "Alcoholic Expeditionary Force," on which he served as a "Buy Man" in speakeasies.[22]

Butler's programs were unique mainly in style and extremity. Elsewhere reformers were using similar methods with similar, usually disappointing, results. In Detroit, where bootleg liquor became the city's second largest industry, a 1923 police survey estimated 3,000 illegal retail liquor dispensaries, and one reporter found 150 "blind pigs" in a single city block. Successive mayors and police commissioners relied on the illegal "tip over," in which police raided and destroyed blind pigs with axes and sledgehammers, making no arrests because they had no warrants, as the only practical means of introducing some element of regulation. Aside from hitting "school pigs" that enticed minors and disrupted education, serious effort to categorically enforce prohibition in Detroit was considered hopeless even by reformers.[23]

On the West Coast, August Vollmer, president of the International Association of Chiefs of Police, was lured from his relatively serene post at Berkeley by a reform-bent 1923 Los Angeles Crime Commission. As chief in Los Angeles, he introduced the technocratic professionalism that was his trademark: an Academy of Criminology, extension courses in police administration, beat analysis, and in-service intelligence testing. But he ran afoul of the politicians and the underworld, and was forced out after a year by harassment including a public scandal in which a woman accused him of breach of promise and compulsion to suicide. Vollmer concluded that vice law enforcement was at the heart of the problem "in all our large cities," and that it was "absolutely impossible for any chief of police or any police department, however well it may be organized and equipped, to eliminate gambling, prostitution, and bootlegging in the City of Los Angeles." He was finally driven from office when the City Council thwarted his proposed reorganization of the police, a problem Butler overcame by legal circuity. Even in Berkeley, Vollmer's haven of police efficiency to which he retreated, he probably only "pushed crime north and south," as one of his protégés put it, into adjacent urban areas such as Oakland.[24]

Despite police tribulations nationwide, Butler has been singled out for criticism by partisans of nascent professionalism. Scholar Samuel Walker, defining police professionalism as mastery of "a complex and esoteric body of knowledge," deplored Smedley's instinct for "direct action" and his heroic "style of furious and dramatic activity."[25] This was similar to the dispute with military highbrows in the Marine Corps. But at this point police professionalization was relatively behindhand, being concerned largely with bureaucratic rationalization as a first step. Hence the relevance of militarization, with its centralized command structure, as the prevalent model for police reform.

Walker was particularly offended that Smedley "summarily abolished the School of Instruction, declaring that 'from now on . . . every cop will learn his job right on the beat.' Thus, in a single gesture, he destroyed one of the most hard won of all police reforms." His "comic approach to police administration" and disregard for "established procedures" undid much of the good work of his predecessors. But the "semimilitary" reform that Walker scorned was a serious attempt to shake up obviously deficient police institutions so that rationalization would be possible.[26] In the circumstances, militarization was construed to be professionalization. Ironically, Butler was the arch-enemy of highbrow professionalism in the marines, where he represented anti-intellectual populist interference, and was at the same time a leading purveyor of military professionalism in the police! The contrast signified a time gap and also the relatively closet nature of military professionalism. Butler considered himself more professional than his "pussyfooting" police predecessors, and was a nationally recognized expert on paramilitary police reform over the next decade. Of what use were police schools and in-service intelligence tests when the whole force was systematically suborned? There was, of course, public pressure for immediate action.

Not that Butler's methods were a smashing success. His demise in Philadelphia involved a losing war of attrition with the politicians set against a backdrop of public apathy. After fending off importunities from the bosses, he settled down to a long game of hide and seek with Mayor Kendrick. "While the mayor did not interfere," said Butler in his post mortem, "he did not help." The first open break between the two coincided with the aforementioned redistricting scheme. Butler requested $25,000 from the City Council for rewiring communications systems, was refused, and proceeded to do the work using electrical bureau employees and ripped-out old wires. This was followed by a heated exchange of insults and accusations between Butler and the Council, and the three months of "great silence" between Butler and Kendrick, toward the end of which the mayor stated to the press, "I had the guts to bring General Butler to Philadelphia and I have the guts to fire him."[27]

With his imminent dismissal widely bruited in the papers, support from civic groups, churches, and other pro-enforcement organizations culminated in a mass meeting of 4,000 in the Academy of Music. Several intermediaries negotiated a truce behind the scenes that apparently confirmed Butler's status as before. Support from civic groups now emphasized the war on crime, and little was said in favor of prohibition specifically.[28]

During the "silence," Butler wrote General Lejeune to arrange his likely return to the marines, but the reconciliation set the stage for another year in Philadelphia. Kendrick again publicly supported the crime-fighting crusade and requested extension of Smedley's leave. President Coolidge acquiesced but for one more year only, commenting that the loan of military officers for civilian duties was of "doubtful propriety and should be employed only in cases of emergency." On this basis Butler entered his second year, 1925, with an impressive statistical record of upgrading law enforcement for murders, armed robberies, and other felonies, but he was confounded by buoyant vice and bootlegging.[29]

And he was starting to show signs of wear and tear. In April, on the anniversary of the Battle of Veracruz, he declared that "I have never seen a war that was as wearing and continually annoying as the fight against vice in this city has been. . . . In fighting vice your enemies are everywhere, and you never know where you are going to find them next." Replying to rumors that Pinchot was setting him up to run for governor, Smedley told reporters, "I would not accept any other public post, nor would I be a candidate for any other office except maybe martial law commander of Philadelphia with 5,000 marines under me. Then I would not be hampered by writs and magistrates' hearings." But several hours later he said this was "purely facetious."[30]

In fact, Butler's militarization of the Philadelphia police fell far short of military command authority. Militarization of civil police involved fundamental contradictions, after all. Effective police work, whether in Philadelphia or in overseas protectorates, required mediation, co-optation, and community collaboration in maintaining shared standards of social deviancy, all of which were seriously compromising to any military system attempting rigorous coercion. Butler himself compromised on key points, as a matter of political survival. The conventional hidebound military response, "get in or get out," was apt but irrelevant, and militarization proved to be largely a vainglorious facade.

Butler kept on fighting. With six months left he announced, "I am going to war," and launched a crackdown on the police—suspending forty, demoting lieutenants to patrolmen, and otherwise straining to stop "men taking money to protect gambling houses and rum sellers if I have to turn the department inside out to do it." But time was running out. He still had another two years to go on his term as director of public safety, but his leave from the marines expired 1 January 1926. In September and October Kendrick came out strongly for another renewal. Butler, after a meeting with Lejeune, announced he had been assigned to the marine base at San Diego. Then he equivocated, saying he would stay in Philadelphia if there was sufficient public support. Kendrick picked this up with the promise, "I am going to go the limit to keep General Butler," and raised the specter of a disastrous crime wave in speeches at keep-Butler mass meetings.[31]

Nearly 1,500 churches and Sunday schools in Philadelphia adopted resolutions. Kendrick and Pennsylvania Senator George Wharton Pepper conferred with Coolidge in an attempt, ostensibly, to change the president's mind, but later Butler learned "on pretty good authority" that Pepper prearranged the interview as a charade, "that they really did not wish it granted but must go through with this visit for publicity." Governor Pinchot requested extension, but Coolidge announced his definite refusal in early November. Navy Department and congressional leaders, minus Tom Butler, were called in for conference by Coolidge and all registered opposition. From another perspective, the director of Women's Activities of the National Liberal Alliance objected to federal use of the military to enforce the eighteenth amendment while neglecting the fourteenth, fifteenth and nineteenth.[32]

After Coolidge's rejection, Kendrick announced Butler's replacement by his assistant, George W. Elliott, whom Smedley had recommended and whom he now praised to Pinchot as likely to "make a better job of it than I have," being "better balanced, more conservative, [and] will not talk much." He also confided that he himself was "completely worn out and am unable to see how I fit in to the scheme of things in any way." But with respect to the remaining possibility of resigning from the marines in order to stay on, he would "let this gang guess until the last in an effort to keep the police standing up."[33]

This was the situation, his departure seemingly fixed except for routine lame-duck maneuvering, as he squared up for his last six weeks in office. Nor did his final moves indicate anything but righteous determination and a burning-of-bridges contempt for the consequences. Political wile and far-flung experience aside, he was now clearly showing physical and emotional strain from an exhausting struggle against insurmountable odds. At a testimonial luncheon given by a ladies club, which he tried to but could not avoid because his mother-in-law was a member, he rose after an hour of eulogies and harangued the audience: "Why not one of you women here could get up and say that you never violated a law in some way. . . . I have learned a lot in my two years in public office. I have learned to believe nothing that anybody says about me and to say nothing that I mean. . . . You have taken me and kicked me and dragged me to death."[34]

His last move was against the big hotels, in effect throwing down the gauntlet to Kendrick and finally coming to terms with the telling criticism that he had been hitting small places in working-class areas while avoiding big-time operators and the rich. Having until now bent to political expediency, he must have relished the chance to expose this hypocrisy and thereby exit on a triumphant note of credibility. Afterward he was able to charge that it was "disregard of the 'divine' rights of the privilege-demanding classes, a lack of differential between the cheap saloons that violated the laws and huge hotels that violated the same laws, often more openly, defiantly and brazenly, that brought about my dismissal." [35]

In collaboration with Magistrate Edward P. Carney, who had long been criticizing him on precisely this issue, Butler raided the Hotel Walton, the Bellevue-Stratford, and the Ritz-Carlton, finding substantial quantities of liquor, drinking parties, and drunks. In the Bellevue-Stratford there were over fifty bottles of liquor in a checkroom adjoining the ballroom. Carney went into the Ritz-Carlton with the police in early December and raided a "400" debutante party, finding blatant violations. Butler publicly castigated "feeding young girls wine and punch at fashionable hotels. Jazzing them up a bit, they call it. I call it a disgrace, and I believe the American people would see the Ritz-Carlton torn down stone by stone rather than allow such conditions to go on. I am going to make an issue of it and see if the people of Philadelphia will stand back of me." [36]

Under the law only the mayor could institute padlocking proceedings. Kendrick had authorized litigation in numerous instances involving small cafés, but now rejected Butler's explicit written requests for action, telling him, according to Smedley, to "lay off the big places" and that there was "a difference between a $7,000,000 investment and a cheap place which blackmails people." Moreover the city, said Kendrick, needed the big hotels for the upcoming sesquicentennial. This altercation, subsequently aired in the press by Butler, lasted from mid-November to 18 December. [37]

As told by Butler, the final spasm began on the 21 December when he learned that an eleventh-hour appeal, delivered to the White House by his father, was refused. He wanted to return to the marines and lacked only two years for retirement with pension. But then he heard that the big hotels were preparing for gala Christmas and New Year festivities on the understanding that he was all but gone, and wrote two more letters to Kendrick demanding action. At home that night he left the dinner table without eating, and by midnight his mind was made up. He would sacrifice everything to stay and "finish my job—my training as a marine demanded that I do so. A few minutes later a newspaper man called me on the telephone to ask about another matter, and I told him of my decision." His wife supported him in the quixotic, last-minute reversal. The family's household effects were already packed and waiting on the front porch for shipment to San Diego. [38]

The news, aired with due prohibition-era theatricality, must have given Kendrick quite a jolt as he simultaneously read the headlines and received Butler's letters demanding a crackdown on the hotels. At their mid-morning confrontation, apparently to Smedley's surprise, Kendrick demanded his resignation. The mayor explained to the press: "I sent for Director Butler immediately upon reading the headlines in the morning paper and frankly told him that I did not think he was treating me with proper respect . . . and that as a resigned officer I did not want him as Director." He also emphasized the prior arrangements with Coolidge and Smedley's successor.[39]

At first Butler defied the order to quit, telling waiting newsmen, "Now we see who is smoked out. . . . If the Mayor fires me, I'll be nothing after January 1st. I'll be neither a marine nor a policeman. But I can still spit in their eye." He returned to his office saying he would hold down the job until pulled out. On the twenty-third, however, he relented when faced with Kendrick's formal edict dismissing him. He sent his resignation to the marines several hours after the session with Kendrick on the twenty-second; now he withdrew it.[40]

His final act while leaving City Hall was to distribute copies of a memorandum addressed to Kendrick and signed by himself, his successor (Elliott), and the counsel for the police bureau, blasting the mayor for having failed to prosecute the big hotels "controlled by your friends." The next day he left Philadelphia to spend Christmas in West Chester, promising more revelations to come: "I know in my heart that I have played the game with all that was in me. . . . Not only the Mayor, but others of prominence will be mentioned in the documents which I shall make public." Kendrick said nothing except to pledge law enforcement with "all my power and strength."[41]

The day after Christmas Butler left for a rendezvous in Pittsburgh with Governor Pinchot. Wearing his marine uniform the following night, he was introduced by Pinchot as "the outstanding figure in law enforcement in the United States" to 3,000 members of the Adult Bible Classes Federation of Pennsylvania, an archetypal dry audience. He spoke, as described on the front page of the *New York Times*, with "characteristic vehemence, dramatic instinct, picturesque expression and sense of humor." Defying Kendrick, the "disloyal chief," to prove his sincerity by closing the big hotels, he posited as fundamental "whether we Americans are to be governed by a lot of bootleggers and naturalized foreigners . . . whether we law-abiding American citizens intend to enforce the law or drop it." Men had been found making young girls drunk: "This is not a matter of law. . . . Any person who permits a minor to have liquor ought to be horsewhipped." America needed "a rope age" in which decent citizens would, "figuratively speaking," drag corrupt officials out of office. He exhorted Pinchot's Bible-toting, nativist constituents. There was "no more reason why you should allow a cesspool in Philadelphia than that the United States should have allowed one in Cuba. You have a cesspool in Philadelphia, and if necessary you should pass laws taking their government away from them if they don't know how to run it."[42]

Assessments of Butler's two-year stint in Philadelphia varied. The *Christian Science Monitor* credited him with having reduced major criminal offenses by 40 percent and robberies at gunpoint by 70 percent, while prohibition enforcement had failed. A *New York Times* survey showed transformation rather than eradication of illegal drinking: "Before General Butler's time a stranger could walk out of his hotel, turn a corner and find plenty of old-fashioned saloons with swinging doors, mahogany bars and brass rails, where the only password needed was 'whiskey' or 'beer.' Nothing like that exists today." There were 200 saloons running openly according to police figures, plus "innumerable" speakeasies, but liquor was mainly sold behind locked doors or privately delivered to homes, offices, and hotel rooms. Regarding his acrimonious departure, the *Times* editorialized that he had been inconsistent in wanting to serve another year, then turning around and kicking Kendrick when the mayor forced him out: "If the Mayor did not play the game, why did General Butler fail to denounce him before? . . . But the General is nothing if not temperamental." A year later in a private letter, Smedley claimed to have been "gagged"—"I knew where my bread was buttered. If I walloped those fellows, and told the truth about them, I would get my block knocked off. But next time there are going to be no strings. They will find out whether or not they can lick marines." [43]

Philadelphia papers took into account his well-deserved reputation for earnestness and zeal, but none defended the last fling. And the *Times* credited Coolidge with having "shrewdly judged" that he "was not saving Philadelphia and his work was not reflecting credit on the Marine Corps." [44] From the military and federal government points of view, having a senior officer chewed up in the maw of big-city politics was an indignity.

Law enforcement in Philadelphia suffered no dramatic relapse despite alarming initial reports. During his first five months in office, Elliott increased arrests by 7,000 and raids on saloons and speakeasies by 1,750 over the previous year, but convictions declined by half. The big hotels, Pinchot apologetically mentioned in a farewell telegram, were not closed because the new director felt there was insufficient evidence. On Christmas Day 1926, Butler's old "mop-up squad" celebrated by conducting its 10,000th raid; they were expected and found a small quantity of liquor. [45]

But by mid-1927 Smedley's father could write, "Thee did not ruin thyself while in Philadelphia, thee only proved an impossibility. Conditions there are frightful, thee is very lucky thee did not remain." The new mayor in 1928, Vare protégé Harry A. Mackey, campaigned for office as a reformer, charging Kendrick with massive police corruption including payoffs from bootleggers who could allegedly buy police lieutenants for $200 a week. Kendrick faded into political obscurity while Mackey, after announcing he would halt "spectacular raids" in favor of "an untiring, ever-increasing challenge to crime," in turn was presently accused, amid damaging disclosures, of chicanery and collusion. Mackey reversed the 1924 redistricting, Butler's most significant structural reform, on the pretense of shaking up the department; the number of station houses was increased from twenty-eight back to forty-three. A friend wrote Smedley describing how the current director of public safety, soon to resign amid scandals, had "shimmied our constabulary! Behind it all is a most commendable motive, which, in slogan form, has been: 'A captain for every ward leader.' The old order return-eth. . . . But you can afford a chuckle, for there could be no more convincing proof of how hard you actually struck when you scrambled the districts."[46]

In August 1928 a series of gangster street killings led to grand jury investigations which revealed scandalously extensive underworld ties with politicians, big banks, and the police in a massive and highly organized bootlegging industry. Crime syndicates policed their own operations, often using suborned city police as operatives. Some of the smaller saloons reportedly formed a union against police rapacity, limiting protection payoffs to a routine $75 per week. Philadelphia again appeared to be one of the wettest and most corrupt cities in the country, and in retrospect Butler's efforts seemed less decisive.[47] At the end, Butler felt he could succeed if given a bit more time. In fact, the meager results of big-city police reform in the 1920s were related to a distinct national trend of short terms for chiefs who, on average, lasted in office two-and-a-half years in the ten largest cities. Vollmer had only a year in Los Angeles, General Francis V. Greene lasted a year in New York, and Detroit's chaotic intrigues begot four chiefs in a single year. The chiefs who held on for longer terms were usually complacent political stalwarts.[48]

Butler never penetrated either ward politics or patrician reform circles, and came and went as a knight errant whom everyone wished to use for disparate ends but no one wished to allow an enduring influence. Nobody wanted 100 percent law enforcement, various patterns of selectivity being the key to police politics. In this Byzantine setting Butler's approach was too rigid to permit many inroads: "I am not, never was, and never will be a professional reformer. There is no creature I despise more than a professional reformer. I was simply a United States officer . . . serving to enforce laws already on the statute books." As such he was sure to antagonize everyone and to isolate himself accordingly. If his integrity and zeal were his great strengths, they were also serious weaknesses in tackling the intricacies of civilian politics. On the eve of his departure a group of his newspaper friends gave him a midnight dinner and a small silver token—"square money," the only kind he would take.[49]

But the following December, after an interlude of even grimmer demon rum traumas in San Diego, Butler wrote Pinchot that "with all the unhappiness and suffering it [Philadelphia] *was* exciting and well worth while." The two years at high salary had also allowed the family to live in suburban Overbrook on the Main Line, and his daughter to spend a year in Europe. Nevertheless, at the end Butler could proudly assert that his bank balance had actually gone down, from $880 to $650, testament to his honesty.[50]

In fidelity to the struggle just passed, he announced that he would hereafter be a teetotaler: "I've fought for a principle and I'm going to stick to that principle. Right now I feel as I did with the marines back in China. We had been marching and fighting for days, when I was shot and forced to go to the rear. Nobody could say I had quit. I had to go to the rear because of the sniping of the enemy. I'm going to get a good rest now, and I'll do no more talking." [51]

12 Devil Dog and Demon Rum

SAN DIEGO

Smedley Butler, accompanied by his wife, three children, and journalist E.Z. "Dimmy" Dimitman, sailed from Brooklyn in late January 1926 on a twenty-six-day cruise to San Diego. Dimitman was to draft the serialized Philadelphia crime story, in which Butler told New York reporters he would be "brutally frank." The trip was also intended to give Smedley a much-needed rest. A week and a half out he wrote his father, "The fever is gradually getting out of my blood and the two years nightmare becoming more and more indistinct, however a great hurt is still present and I imagine always will be and I now realize what a terrible mistake I made in ever getting into that awful mess."[1]

The ship stopped in Colombia, giving him a chance to contrast Latin American mores, of which he had much previous experience, with his more recent insights into North American politics. Yankee smugness yielded to a more ironic view. He commented in a letter to Governor Pinchot that he was "amused to find their Municipal Officials have the same lofty ideals of public service as our Philadelphians, they are not quite as brazen in their methods and their list of prices is somewhat lower but really just in proportion to the value of their currency." A Colombian official's price, mentioned by an American contractor, "compared favorably with those prevailing in the Cradle of Liberty." The ship also put in at Corinto which, like Panama, brought back memories of colonial light-infantry adventures.[2]

The thirty-part series, "Smashing Crime and Vice," ran in over a hundred newspapers around the country. Butler donated 50 percent of the royalties to a fund for prosecuting politicians who interfered with the Philadelphia police force.[3] Dimitman, who got the other half, corrected it in sessions with Smedley, Mrs. Butler, and their daughter. In conclusion the series recommended "a single, state-controlled force, organized somewhat along military lines" similar to the Pennsylvania State Constabulary, to replace all municipal police. Young men, "recruited from every section," would be enlisted for four years during which they would be forbidden to marry. There would be constant shifting of units to prevent political liaisons. This general scheme, to which Butler remained attached and indeed personified for the next decade as a police consultant, public speaker and author, represented the militaristic extreme in contemporary law-and-order polemics. It amounted to an almost explicit domestic interventionism modeled after marine and army colonial constabularies overseas.[4]

The ship arrived in Los Angeles in late February and the Butlers were escorted to the marine base in San Diego, where Smedley assumed command. One of his first acts was to dismiss the personal orderly assigned to him; as always, he would shine his own shoes and brass. A remote and unimpressive post, San Diego was definitely a comedown from Quantico. Lejeune had made a special point of emphasizing growth potential in his *bon voyage* message: "The West Coast is gradually becoming the center of naval activity . . . and I believe that eventually San Diego will become the most important Marine Corps post," an astute prediction considering the coming wars in the Pacific and East Asia. Smedley wrote a friend he would stay until retirement two years hence. First, however, he was in for a nasty encore in his battle with demon rum.[5]

Within the Corps there was hostility to Butler's prohibitionist fervor. Drinking and alcohol abuse were endemic. In an interview, Butler's former aide, General Ray A. Robinson, described his commanding officer in Bremerton in the mid-1920s as having had delirium tremens. When asked "A number of people were heavy drinkers in the Marine Corps at that time, were they not?" Robinson replied, "Everybody." Wet resentment wounded Butler because, except for efficiency and discipline, he did not see alcohol as a moral issue, only law enforcement as such. But having drastically extended himself in Philadelphia, he could hardly equivocate on the central symbolic issue without compromising his personal honor and integrity. And as the outspoken "stormy petrel" of the Corps, he was more vulnerable to any taint of hypocrisy than conventional officers. His integrity often made the difference between respect and ridicule. So he never drank again for the rest of his life, although he condoned subordinates drinking overseas and, after prohibition, sat by while his wife drank cocktails and once served alcohol to houseguests.[6]

Butler's arrival was a big event in the lackluster, upstart Southern California realtors' valhalla of San Diego.[7] Several days in advance the *San Diego Sun* ran the banner headline "ARRIVAL OF MARINE CHIEF TO SPEED UP SOUTHLAND GAYETIES." Civilian and military receptions highlighted a week during which "society folk of the service contingents found themselves in a veritable whirl of brilliant social events." He was heralded as "GEN. BUTLER FIGHTING QUAKER," the "Leatherneck's Friend," "The best known Quaker in America," "famous fighting marine," and "Old Gimlet Eye." The *Sun* estimated that more than a thousand feet of film were shot in two minutes during the change-of-command ceremony at the base. In interviews, Butler said he would not try to clean up Tijuana, the decadent liberty area across the nearby Mexican border, and he repeatedly denied interest in the Los

Angeles police chieftainship. The *Sun* alerted readers to its forthcoming "big newspaper scoop!"—Butler's "Smashing Crime and Vice" series.[8]

The euphoria, masking serious unfriendliness, insofar as San Diego was a wet town, lasted two weeks. Recoil was sudden and severe. Smedley, Mrs. Butler, and their daughter were guests of honor at a dinner party attended by a large number of marine and navy officers, hosted by Colonel Alexander S. Williams at his home off the naval reservation. Williams commanded the Fourth Regiment at San Diego and was acting base commandant pending Butler's arrival; now he was Smedley's ranking subordinate. Previously, their paths had crossed in Haiti where Williams had been Smedley's second in command and recommended successor, serving as commandant of the gendarmerie in 1918-19 during the corvée uprising. They were not particularly close, but had always been on good terms.

Williams was four years older than Butler, but both had the same time in service. As pointed out by the *New York Times* during the subsequent spate of publicity, he was the son of Police Inspector Alexander S. "Clubber" Williams, "Czar of the Tenderloin," who claimed to have coined the term for New York's vice district when he was put in charge of the West 30th Street Station and told a friend he had been eating chuck but would now eat tenderloin. The elder Williams gained notoriety during the 1894 Lexow Committee Investigations of New York police corruption when the committee's star witness, a turncoat police captain, described 30th Street ward-level gambling and prostitution payoff rackets, testifying that he had served as Williams's bagman. On the stand Williams admitted owning extensive property, including a yacht, but said that he got his wealth from real estate in "Ackadady," Japan, that had appreciated in value. He was never tried on the charges against him, and died in 1917 leaving an estate of fourteen dollars. How this family background may have colored his son's perception of Butler, or fueled Marine Corps gossip, is a matter of interesting conjecture.[9]

In Butler's version, Colonel Williams greeted the Butlers at the door of his home accompanied by a maid carrying a tray of cocktails, which Williams plied upon his guests: "Williams continued to press cocktails on me. When I shoved them aside, he drained the glasses he brought me as well as his own. The situation was becoming embarrassing." The Butlers then left the party and went to the Saturday night dance at the Coronado Hotel. An hour later Williams also turned up at the hotel and created a public scene, "reeling from side to side, giggling, mumbling and staring at me." The Butlers again left, and Smedley spent Sunday pondering what to do, torn between honoring the social conventions of the officer fraternity on the one hand, and defending his integrity as commander on the other.[10]

With the support of the commander of the naval district, who said he would press charges if Smedley did not, Butler went for a court-martial. The newspapers picked up the story immediately and for the next six weeks it was national news as the "Cocktail Trial," part of the 1920s' fascination with theatrical litigation—in the genre of the Sacco-Vanzetti and Leopold-Loeb murder trials, the Scopes trial, and the 1925 court-martial of Colonel Billy Mitchell. Butler's renown as a dry reformer set him up as a prime target for sport. He was neatly trapped between the formal law, with all its absurdities, and informal rules of social etiquette. His ordeal was all the more fascinating because it exposed a military subculture normally concealed in the seclusion of garrison life.

Speculation in the press during the first few days reflected the wide-open scope for moralizing. Butler emphasized the public spectacle at the hotel, strenuously maintaining that "whatever happened in his home had nothing to do with my actions," thereby acknowledging the baleful issue of a guest's obligation to his host. The *New York Times* editorialized that there were "certain rules of conduct and friendly intercourse which . . . make it certain that any one who tramples upon them will be socially hanged as high as Haman." The *Sun*, on the other hand, brought up the subtle prohibition era "ethics of an officer offering drinks without first 'knowing his guests.'" In Washington, congressmen issued statements defending and attacking, dividing predictably as drys and wets.[11]

It was a bad time for Smedley, coming right after Philadelphia and coinciding with debilitating dental work. He went into the hospital two days after the Williams story broke and was bedridden for three weeks with extremely low blood pressure while twenty-two teeth were pulled. The *New York Times* described this as a "nervous breakdown following the extraction of ten infected teeth," all of which added drama to the upcoming trial and broadcast Smedley's agony far and wide.[12]

Commandant Lejeune in Washington backed him throughout, but there was little support from the local marine establishment. His loyal protégés Vandegrift, who in heeding Smedley's call to San Diego turned down a prize assignment to the Army Command and General Staff School, and "Torchy" Robinson were on hand, but having "no experience of the outside world," were of little help. Lifelong friend (Olongapo, Nicaragua) General Joseph H. Pendleton had founded the San Diego base and, living in retirement locally, remained influential in civilian circles. He could have been a big help, but "neither old Pendleton, nor his wife," Smedley wrote plaintively, "came near Mrs. Butler or my children when we were bleeding. . . . In fact, we have been ostracized as if we had smallpox."[13]

In late March, Secretary of the Navy Wilbur formally ordered Williams court-martialed. From then until the trial started on 12 April, many newspapers ran advertisements for Butler's "Smashing Crime and Vice" serial which ran concurrently throughout the judicial extravaganza, a neat piece of promotional exploitation. This intensified the pressure of publicity on Williams, and on Butler as he emerged from the hospital to testify. The *Sun*'s full-page notice on 1 April, under the banner "A Devil Dog and Demon Rum," referred to him as "America's fightin'est Devil Dog" who had won "more ribbons and medals than any other Marine." Williams protested to Wilbur when the *Seattle Times* used his name in advertisements for the series. April twelfth was a family field day; the papers also ran news of the Butler bill, a five-year naval aviation building program passed by the House.[14]

During and after the trial, which was covered by fourteen reporters, newspaper commentary and private communications to Butler intensified. The *Helena Independent* railed that "the cheapest stool-pigeons of the Anti-Saloon League would never stoop to Butler's heinous breach of assailing the man whose guest he was." Crank letters denounced him as "Meddly Butler," "Saint Smedley," and a "thoroughgoing rotter." "Smelly Butler" seems to have attained some general currency, implying, according to one columnist, that he was "nosey, prying, unpleasant, sniffling." Dry support came from the governor of Oregon who cabled, apparently without facetious intent, "If you were the general of the Dry Legion of America now being formed the end of the prohibition fight would be in sight." The manager of a theater in Philadelphia, well outside the tenderloin, told of his "audience en masse" applauding Fox newsreel footage of Smedley taking command in San Diego.[15]

The trial itself was a farce, centering on the thorny question of whether Williams had actually been drunk or just appeared to be. Butler himself had not sampled the cocktails so was in no position to say what was in them. Other mostly junior officers, testifying before a very senior court, tended to dissembling and obfuscation—a display that reduced the honor and dignity of the Corps to the level of commonplace civilian prevarications over the same issues.

Captain Clifton B. Cates, previously encountered as Barnett's aide and here serving on Williams's staff, assisted as a defense counsel and testified as a witness, saying he did not think the drinks were alcoholic, having had two himself without effect. Williams, moreover, was not drunk, but ill, acting as if he "had been drinking, was doped, or sick, or had something else the matter with him. Really, after hearing him say he was sick, I knew him to be sick." This view was supported by most of the other witnesses and by expert naval medical opinion brought in to corroborate Williams's illnesses and impugn Butler's testimony. Williams, according to a naval surgeon, had been ill with an intestinal disorder since January. Another surgeon had put him on medication, hexyl resorcinol, for a urinary infection, and testified that Williams had come in two days after the incident "and told me the drug had made him sick." Half a dozen doctors testified that hexyl resorcinol was apt to produce dizziness. There were also allusions to aftereffects from fevers contracted during his several tours in the tropics.[16]

Butler, on the other hand, was "physically unqualified" to tell whether Williams was drunk because he was "suffering from a near nervous breakdown," was "easily excited," and saw poorly out of his left eye when examined several days after Williams's arrest. Naval dentists affirmed that he had been having plenty of trouble with his teeth, allowing the defense to develop the hypothesis that bad teeth poisoned his system and caused hallucinations. Williams's chief counsel, who as a civilian had special indulgence for casting aspersions on a general officer, summed up: "I ask the court to take into consideration General Butler's—I won't say imagination—but his wonderful ability to convince himself that he can determine instantly the right and wrong of any situation." [17]

The prosecution had only one effective witness, Butler himself. "Of the nine or ten witnesses called," reported the *Sun*, "only one witness testified to seeing Col. Williams actually drink a glass of punch grapejuice, orangeade, lemonade, colored water, cocktail, or whatever it has not yet been proved to be." Butler "seemed right at home on the battleground" and launched into an unequivocal attack stressing his reluctance to prosecute and Williams's outright drunkenness: "Colonel Williams was incoherent. He was loquacious, he giggled, his eyes were bloodshot; they had a queer, vacant stare. . . . when he left the hotel I got the impression he was being carried out." He stuck to these points, at times shouting angrily, particularly during cross-examination by Captain Cates: "I know what I saw. This is not the first time that he has done this. He has been drunk before and I had to go through with it." [18]

Cates's main rejoinder was that Butler as senior officer had tried to bully him and other witnesses before the trial, a spurious point considering the vagueness of their ultimate testimony, but in keeping with the repeated insinuations that Williams was the victim of unremitting cadishness. Smedley related his pretrial session with Cates as follows: "'Cates, that statement of yours doesn't mean anything. Do you mean to tell me that an officer of your length of service in the Marine Corps doesn't know when a man is drunk?' I told him that I realized his embarrassment . . . but that I wanted the truth about the case. 'Was the colonel drunk or sober?' I demanded of Cates. 'He was drunk,' Cates replied." [19]

The verdict, guilty as charged, was hardly in doubt since Williams had clearly transgressed the bounds of "good order and discipline," and public drunkenness by an officer in uniform was an offense regardless of the eighteenth amendment. Williams, who was praised in the *Sun* for maintaining a "soldierly silence" throughout the trial, was dropped four numbers on the colonels list, which meant he would probably never make brigadier, and was subsequently transferred from command of his regiment to recruiting headquarters in San Francisco. The *Sun* reported that, "like an earthquake, the trial has split the grounds at the base into two or more camps, and if trans-

fers are not volunteered by Washington, transfers will be requested by certain officers themselves." Cates was transferred to Seattle for recruiting
duty, a career setback similar to his earlier voluntary exile as Barnett's loyal
aide in the then-perfunctory Department of the Pacific, all of which did not
prevent him from eventually becoming commandant of the Marine Corps in
1948. Nor did it preclude Butler's initiating a commendatory letter for his
work supervising mail guards shortly thereafter.[20]

Butler gained nothing from the Williams episode, his reentry into the
marines from front-page prodigality in civilian life had not been auspicious,
and his own sense of the military as a haven from civilian decadence must
have been diminished. The cocktail trial was little different from perfidies
in Philadelphia, where one columnist quipped, "The whole liquor question
in America ought to be turned over to a military tribunal." There was also a
sense that enemies in the Corps were out to get him. Ray Robinson, in his
reminiscences, said, "Williams was challenging him, that's what he was
doing, he was rubbing it in." An admiral wrote relating a conversation with
Congressman Butler: "I told him that I thought they were trying to put the
collar on you, and he replied that he considered it a frame-up, which is
about the same thing." Smedley replied, "Of course, there are various reasons why people take a shot at me, but, as far as I am personally concerned,
they can all go to hell." But he dropped plans to do a book and magazine
articles on the Philadelphia story, being "tired of scrapping for the time
being . . . . It doesn't get you anywhere and only brings down on your head
a tremendous mass of abuse from everybody."[21]

Instead, he produced the autobiographical boys' adventure story *Walter
Garvin in Mexico* (1927), including personal touches such as Mexican soldiers—"greasers"—tearing his shirt away so that his Marine Corps tattoo
betrayed him as a spy. This escapist warrior saga, with its triumphant vin-
dication of good and its utter vanquishing of evil, was in almost complete
contrast to his present fortunes. Vandegrift commented in his memoirs that
"from the black-and-white challenge presented by the banana wars," Butler
"had come up against the gray challenge of public-versus-private interests
and did not know how to cope—an ignorance that hurt him as much as the
experience infuriated him."[22]

Meanwhile, events in Pennsylvania compounded his despair. Pinchot,
running as a dry reformer for the U.S. Senate in the Republican primary
against Boss Vare and incumbent patrician George Wharton Pepper, came
in a poor third, a severe repudiation for a sitting governor. In Philadelphia
he got only 28,000 votes as against 334,000 for Vare and 114,000 for Pepper,
and was obviously not helped locally by publicity flyers quoting Butler: "The
men of political prominence who helped me were few indeed. Governor
Pinchot from the first was most active, sympathetic and friendly." Voters who
did not believe in law enforcement "should adopt means immediately to get

rid of him, for he will fight them to the end." The flyer also cited Butler's denunciations of Vare and Pepper. Commiserating with Pinchot, Smedley pontificated, "I sometimes believe the only cure for rottenness and total disregard for law by our citizens, is a reign by Mussolini," although any infatuation with Mussolini was soon dispelled.[23] Vare won statewide and in the general election but was never seated, being excluded by the Senate for corrupt campaign practices.

Back in California, Colonel Williams drove his coupe off the Embarcadero between piers 38 and 40 in San Francisco in the middle of the night and drowned. Witnesses said he drove straight onto the pier and into the water without slowing down. An autopsy found no traces of alcohol and police were satisfied that it was an accident—perhaps he had fallen asleep at the wheel—but the Associated Press reported that "the most tenable of all the theories advanced is that the colonel may have committed suicide." The mystery was never clarified. His widow bitterly told reporters, "He was never a drinking man and everyone knew it, including Smedley Butler"— the "cocktail colonel" publicity was "all so unfair." In its front-page coverage the *Sun* reported phoning Butler and getting a reaction of shock: "What's that? Repeat that again. Oh my! Oh my! That's perfectly terrible. Perfectly awful."[24]

At the conclusion of the trial, Butler, despite weariness with the cause with and continuing poor health, announced to the press that he would dry up the marine base. Work discipline was stiffened. According to Vandegrift this made him even more unpopular, "that being Southern California and they had been used to a more or less lax schedule, they resented a strict schedule of training and work."[25] The base at San Diego had its origins in expeditionary service in 1915, when marines were twice sent down the west coast of Mexico on standby for intervention. By 1926 there was a complete set of barracks, a power plant, ice plant, laundry and other facilities, and the Fourth Regiment, "San Diego's own," in garrison. Mail guard duty in the fall and then expeditionary calls at the end of the year cut short Butler's contributions, but he nevertheless improved the base considerably with a self-help landscaping program, recalling his previous efforts at Quantico. Everyone turned to, including officers, to the accompaniment of the post band playing in the middle of the parade ground.

Butler also pushed some of the schemes that had generated so much publicity at Quantico. Back East, Lejeune had abandoned the annual Civil War reenactments as too expensive. Now Butler planned a Mexican War reenactment, the 1846 Battle of San Pasqual, to be staged forty miles north of San Diego as part of a combined hike and football excursion. To cut expenses he arranged that Metro Goldwyn Mayer film studios furnish all uniforms, horses, saddles, and other equipment necessary for "a very correct reproduction" that would be part of "another big film around the Marines." Previously, he had established liaison with MGM in making *Tell It to the Marines*, a garrison picture starring Lon Chaney which was filmed on the base. In return, MGM lent a steam shovel for the landscaping effort. Lejeune was delighted with the Hollywood connection and did his part arranging previews and publicity in Washington, including a showing in the House Office Building. A keen cinema enthusiast, Butler loved the film. He enjoyed the movie people and once sat between film beauties Eleanor Boardman and Norma Shearer as guest of honor at a dinner party given by Louis B. Mayer, commenting afterward, "they are good to look upon, but dumb as hell." When he left for China in 1927, MGM gave him a 35 mm movie camera to take along.[26]

The Battle of San Pasqual was canceled when the marines dispersed for mail guard duty, and the football season was a mixed bag. On the East Coast, the Quantico Marines still had hopes of collegiate standing, and Butler now asked that the team be transferred to San Diego for 1927. He would "guarantee a rip snorting college schedule" based on feelers he had made to the University of California, Stanford, University of Arizona, and University of New Mexico. But in fact the college game was running out on the marines. In 1926, the local State Teachers and Junior College declined to renew its game with San Diego Marines, explaining that henceforth it would only play "college teams representing just about the same degree of physical development and maturity that our own boys show."[27]

Despite intentions to avoid public controversy, Butler's travels throughout the western states in connection with running mail guards toward the end of the year kept him in the limelight. He testified as a character witness for Colonel Ned M. Green, former federal prohibition chief in San Francisco, who was acquitted of embezzling confiscated government liquor stores. In January 1927 he made prohibition news in a bigger way through a speech to the Oakland Lions Club, in which he obliquely referred to the "silly" and "foolish" Volstead prohibition act. According to a complaint read into the *Congressional Record* by a dry congressman, this was broadcast in "flaming headlines" as far away as Washington.[28]

The outcry by drys, who looked to Butler as a national champion, included a letter from the Philadelphia Law Enforcement League intimating that a monument the group was erecting for him would now be reconsidered. Butler's response was excerpted in a front-page story in the *New York Times*. He had just spent New Year's Eve in San Francisco and "never before witnessed such an orgy," following newspaper notices that there would be no raiding of the big hotels. Afterward, the papers carried stories of "liquor seized by the prohibition forces from Chinamen! Now, if that isn't class legislation, what is it, when it is publicly announced that there will be no raiding of the rich and powerful, while a lot of Chinamen are harassed?" With this in mind, "and filled with hearty contempt," he spoke at a police official's behest to the Lions Club regarding the current marine mail guard, emphasizing that the marines would guard the mails 100 percent, shooting anyone rich or poor, "not as in the case of this silly Volstead Act, which is enforced only thirty per cent." Prohibition was "the greatest piece of class legislation ever passed in this country."[29]

Guarding the mails offered Butler a 100-percent, wholesome civic mission, and he rather desperately made the most of it. As in 1921, there had been violent gang-style mail robberies, and the federal government called out 2,500 marines, with Butler in command in the West. Marines armed with pistols and riot guns rode the trains and mail trucks in teams of two, three, and four, guarded post offices, and were otherwise present wherever large sums of postal monies were being handled. The Fourth Regiment at San Diego was dispersed throughout the western states as far east as Texas, Colorado, and North Dakota. From his headquarters in San Francisco Butler issued "shoot to kill" orders, widely publicized for public relations and morale purposes, and to intimidate bandits: "I want the mail brought in or dead marines." As in 1921, robbery attempts abruptly ceased.[30]

Smedley threw himself passionately into the new assignment. The mail guard might be built up into a public relations coup for fending off the Corps's threatened personnel cuts, and simultaneously vindicate the "military analogy" and recoup his personal reputation and somewhat battered crusader's prospectus for paramilitary police reform. Here the troops, real marines instead of knavish Philadelphia cops, had a great opportunity to demonstrate all the advantages of discipline, centralized command, high morale, and apolitical efficiency. Butler formulated this as a "war with bandits" and "imbued these officers and men out here with the idea that a perfect performance of this duty will help save our Corps. . . . Perfect appearance, perfect behavior, perfect attention to their duty, cheerfulness, willingness, everything perfect."[31]

He drove himself hard, traveling the inspection circuit and making speeches, and returned exhausted and "as nervous as a cat," but satisfied that discipline was excellent and that the marines were making a big hit with the civilian population. He paraphrased for Lejeune comments made by the mayor of Portland at a luncheon: "His police assured him that the simple moral effect of the presence of these soldiers, the direct representatives of the supreme authority of this country, had had a very quieting effect on all the people; that women were not afraid now to go out in the streets, and that everybody slept better. General, I think I see the first step towards a national constabulary." The governor of Montana "spoke of the quieting effect of these dignified, well dressed guardians of the federal law," and "hoped some day they might have a northwestern police in Montana, that the presence of fifty in that state would make life much more secure"—apparently an allu sion to Canada's national constabulary, the Northwest Mounted Police. People Smedley met all over the Northwest were alarmed, the "more timid are terror stricken . . . the bolder ones are constantly talking about vigilante committees."[32]

After all the dissembling and hypocrisy in Philadelphia and San Diego, Butler was exhilarated by these forthright rugged "frontiersmen." Here at last was seemingly fertile ground for law-and-order militarization. He wrote his father, fervidly offering grist for the political mill: "Father we are coming to a national constabulary. I have been all over states with a combined population of close to ten millions of people; not the mongrels like we have in a city like Philadelphia, with a population almost one third of foreign blood, but men and women who were born out here and who have had to fight with the elements." Everywhere he found people obsessed with suppressing lawlessness, "and I cannot help but feel that the presence of our marines among these people is almost providential."[33]

To Lejeune he reported that he had just written his father a fifteen page letter that would "help us keep our twelve hundred men." The whole project was sincerely and inextricably both selfless duty and political puffery. On the same page that he told of having "poured out everything that was in me" and being "so wrought up I can't sleep," he offered a précis of their past successes at political seduction, which a cynical reader might wrongly dismiss as sheer opportunism: "Members of Congress are like other people. You can pick their pockets when their eyes are full of tears. We demonstrated that year after year at Quantico. The little white tablets in the bunkhouses; the shabby looking buildings but magnificent men . . . . No business argument will save our Corps. It has to be sentiment. Twenty-seven hundred little white crosses in France, as you well know, kept our strength for the first six years of your tenure of office." Now the "lonely mail guards in the snow" who were "upholding the dignity of this republic, against all the forces of evil" also had a sentimental appeal.[34]

No doubt all this was overheated. But there was also a strong instinct for public sentiment, rooted in his own personal faithfulness to popular creeds and his by now extensive experience at evoking them. This was a far cry from General Barnett's aloof managerial style and patrician ways of political wire-pulling, yet there was real insight into the emotive mass-media manipulations that were becoming increasingly important realities of contemporary politics.

Sentimentality, a trait that enlivened his sense of duty throughout his life, here surfaced as publicity, as rapport with his men, and not least as a means by which he convinced himself. And he knew it, apologizing to his father for seeming to "have lost my mind and become very sentimental," but he was so impressed by the "loyalty and devotion, together with the cheerfulness, of all these youngsters, that I cannot help slopping over." Marines were helping old ladies across slippery streets, starting women's cars stalled in traffic, and making a hit with "nice people" everywhere.[35]

This was not to be anything like an ordinary oppressive military occupation. He wrote Lejeune, "You and I can remember the day when the appearance of regular soldiers in a little town would have been the signal to put up all the burglar-proof windows." In the present exercise there had been "practically not one instance of drunkenness" since the initial shakedown period. "This is a great problem; a problem of popular military occupation; and I think we are on the high road to establishing it and making it a part of national life. . . . The stakes are high. One or two false moves and the nation turns against us."[36]

But how might there be "popular military occupation" that would also work as a coercive force for reform, if the troops qua police were constantly having to ingratiate themselves and avoid making "false moves?" It was a delight for Butler to promote the mail guard as a meal ticket for the Corps, since it provided a useful service while threatening no one. But this only marginally addressed the historic American resistance to paramilitary and federal police. Apolitical centralization, the key component of military professionalism as regards police reform, required a degree of public consensus and homogeneity that reformers sought to enforce as an end result. Butler wishfully thought his vigilante "frontiersmen" were already there.

At the same time, he was alluding to a civic-soldier ideal that was becoming abundantly evident elsewhere in twentieth-century militarism. Civil administration had already been undertaken by American military in frontier and conquered areas, as with Butler's gendarmerie in Haiti. The tendency can be seen in colonial administration that was increasingly accommodating rather than punitive in method, and in Butler's various peacetime military insinuations into civil affairs. In Philadelphia and again with the mail guard, Butler himself was tending to see leadership and morale more as embodying matters of conscience and social responsibility. Attuned to mass-media acclaim, he wanted to be loved and respected for doing the right thing and not just to be admired as a bold and efficient commander.

The mail guards were recalled for want of bandits and, more pressingly, because overseas crises had outstripped the State Department's precarious strategy of demilitarization. Adolfo Díaz, pro-American stalwart from Butler's 1912 intervention, resumed the presidency of Nicaragua in the wake of disturbances and requested reinforcements. The East Coast Expeditionary Force was dispatched from Quantico, and West Coast units were mobilized, to the point of stacking seabags under the arcade in San Diego, for shipping out to Nicaragua. At the last minute new orders changed the destination to China.

13 The Marines Who Wouldn't Fight

CHINA

The China expeditionary force, soon nicknamed "exhibition force" by wags in the ranks, sailed from San Diego in mid-February 1927. Its quartermaster later reminisced that the outfit was equipped more for parade competition with international units garrisoning China's treaty ports than for fighting. "All machine guns were nickel plated, our mortars were nickel plated, and the 37 millimeter tank guns, in those days, were also nickel plated." [1] In fact the nickle plating came later, but the characterization was apt. This was military intervention intended to assert American interests by masterful peacekeeping rather than belligerency.

Brigadier General Smedley Butler, left behind on the dock, had strenuously tried to attach himself. The government did not want to send a general lest it "unduly magnify the importance" of the expedition or be taken as indication that a second regiment would soon be added to comprise a brigade. These factors were considered in the light of "an undesirable effect on public opinion both at home and abroad"—a reference to the prevalent anti-imperialist and antimilitarist trend. [2]

But the pressure of events in China, where Americans and other foreign nationals were being evacuated from the interior in the face of violent Chinese nationalism, led to the decision in late February to send more marines and Butler. President Coolidge felt that to send a "large force of the regular army" would probably provoke war, and Secretary of State Frank B. Kellogg also identified army intervention as fraught with unwanted aggressive connotations. So too the international aspect: the American embassy in London was instructed to tell the British that the United States was "not contemplating sending ['troops' crossed out in the message draft] soldiers to Shanghai." "Marines," as Butler later put it, "are international troops and no one objects to their presence for they have a right to visit countries under international law, but that is not so with the Army." [3] These subtleties were probably lost on the Chinese, but they were the form and substance of American policy seeking conservative yet opportunistic responses to war and revolution in the colonial world.

Butler's widespread reputation as an aggressive, outspoken devil dog likewise served as an effective gesture to hawkish Americans, just as sending marines instead of infantry was projected as a trimming option. Marines headed by Butler could project either hawkish leatherneck belligerency or the relatively dovish odd-job transiency of naval diplomacy.

His departure occasioned reminders in the press of his heroic combat record and colorful personality. The *New York Times*, in a full-page spread under the lead "BUTLER OF THE MARINES GOES TO WAR," ballyhooed him as "a wiry man of average height, sloping shoulders, strong wrists and the face of an adventurer." He was "A Theatric Soldier." Humorist Will Rogers, referring to demon rum skirmishes, gibed, "Smedley Butler has arrived in China. The war may continue, but the parties will stop." *Time* magazine put him on its cover over the caption "takes trouble by the whiskers," and reported the "Return of Butler" to Tientsin with a synopsis of past exploits, remarking that "a volume of 'dime novel' flavor might be compiled out of similar true stories." He was "'Old Gimlet Eye' the 'Fighting Hell-Devil Marine'" and "the premier 'Fighting Devil' among 'Devil Dogs.'"[4]

For Butler this was the first expedition in which he held top command, and the responsibilities in this diplomatic mission were quite different from Banana Wars and colonial military occupations. Lejeune gave him a free hand in developing the marine presence in China, sending few instructions, and Smedley acknowledged the trust by promising to write daily a diary of all his actions.[5] He arrived in Shanghai on 25 March 1927 in the midst of one of the great turning points of the Chinese Revolution. The day before at Nanking, 160 miles in the interior, Chinese Nationalist (Kuomintang-KMT) armies advancing down the Yangtze Valley had gutted American, British, and Japanese consulates, looted foreign property, and besieged fifty-two foreigners on Socony (Standard Oil Company of New York) Hill. American and British gunboats laid down barrages on the attacking Chinese. The Nanking Incident, prelude to an imminent advance by KMT armies toward the major concentration of foreign interests in Shanghai, forced the powers to react.

International cooperation, however, was complicated by diehard versus liberal infighting. American, Japanese, and British naval commanders on the Yangtze joined together in calling for a punitive campaign. "Die-Hards," as their liberal opponents referred to conservative businessmen, diplomats, and missionaries, urged military intervention rather than permit erosion of privileges guaranteed to foreigners under the unequal treaties. They made the most of the fact that the KMT was supported by the Soviet Union, with Bolshevik rhetoric much in evidence. A veteran China Coast journalist recalled that "as a result of the self-administered propaganda, foreign areas of Shanghai immediately went on a war basis, and thousands of coolies were employed day and night constructing trenches, barbed-wire barricades, and concrete blockhouses." Liberals, such as visiting U.S. Senator Hiram Bingham, countered the red-baiting by denouncing the racial arrogance of

Americans who ran segregated social clubs and otherwise treated Chinese as "social pariahs" in their own country.[6]

Arriving in Shanghai in the midst of the Nanking crisis, Butler was therefore commanding a colonial relief expedition clamored for by resident American diehards, and making sure that the intervention be as unbelligerent as possible so as to lend credibility to liberal U.S. rhetoric. President Coolidge issued an aggressively pro-Chinese statement, proclaiming that "the friendship of America for China has become proverbial." But there was no mention of the obvious expedient of evacuating the American colony in the face of antiforeign hatred. Withdrawal of Americans from Shanghai, according to a State Department memorandum, "would, of course, paralyze American business interests there and would be most disastrous."[7]

As a famous Leatherneck and Old China Hand carrying battle scars from the Boxer campaign, Butler had unique advantages in foisting a soft policy on the diehards. The *North China Herald* observed that his arrival with a "crack" corps of marines had "shown to the local American community perhaps more than anything else that their interests" were being taken into account. On the other hand, his frequent pronouncements about protecting American lives, while soft-pedaling the usual imperialist "lives and property," was hardly what the diehards wanted to hear. In a rambling interview, he "candidly labelled the American nation as an emotional one" with a strong "sense of chivalry," and dismissed the "few millions of dollars" of American capital in China as "only a drop in the bucket." When people had to pay taxes for battleships and marines to protect this capital they protested. "Not a man, though, but would be willing to shoulder a gun, probably given him by one of his own women-folk, to protect the lives of American women and children out here." This neat formula, presented with "personal magnetism" and the "peculiarly vigorous gesture with which he punctuates his speech," covered the Coolidge administration with respect to defense of the flag, women and children, while placing the onus on the diehards to make a case for a punitive campaign.[8]

Butler was alluding to the venerable frontier ethos of rescuing innocent women and children from menacing savages. With anti-imperialism now a major trend in American domestic politics, he was probably right that it was the only acceptable rationale for U.S. military intervention halfway around the world. Banana War exercises, involving American takeovers of Nicaraguan and Haitian banks, would no longer do. And he was prescient in seeing that the old cavalry-to-the-rescue theme was one aspect of racist-colonial lore that would survive into the postcolonial era. In China, in 1927, that issue was in the forefront, and the United States would soon tentatively renounce military intervention as a means of protecting American citizens abroad. China Coast diehards were well-advised not to press their case and to be thankful for the gunboats and marines they had.

Related to the equivocal stand on American property rights was Butler's reply to the question of how many troops he thought would be necessary to suppress the Nationalist movement: "I would not dream of starting an armed invasion of China without a half million troops, and it probably would require a million more before the end of the first year." As the journalist who asked the question remarked in 1945, it was not a bad estimate—the Japanese tried with two million a decade later and failed.[9] The days when a 25,000-man Boxer expedition could turn the tide were gone.

Shanghai in 1927 was the major international entrepot and industrial center on the China Coast, and one of the world's great cities. Here were the China headquarters of over a hundred American firms, the largest American school overseas, and imposing European and Japanese banks, trading houses, and factories. The foreign settlement was now in near panic, anticipating the approach of KMT armies following their rampage in Nanking. The anchorage off the Bund was crowded with warships carrying troop reinforcements, including the flagship *Pittsburgh* of the U.S. Asiatic Fleet and, moored at the Standard Oil compound, the transport *Chaumont*. About 30,000 foreign troops were on hand to man barricades and patrol the international concessions. The U.S. Marines, however, were held back in keeping with the American policy of reticence, and remained crowded aboard the *Chaumont* or confined to a tent encampment on the pier until the KMT vanguard reached the perimeters of the city.

Butler's first contact with Admiral Clarence S. Williams, commander of the Asiatic Fleet, turned sour when he recommended doubling the number of marines. Williams replied, with "half a chuckle" according to Smedley's diary report, "so you're one of these fellows who wants to build a big job for himself and get a promotion."[10] Butler took the clue and quickly adjusted to the measured, low-profile presence that suited U.S. diplomacy. When the troops were put ashore on emergency standby, this meant keeping them out of the lines manned by the British. Under no circumstances were American troops to come under orders of foreign commanders or associate themselves with the defense of the foreign concessions. They were supposed to protect lives only, a perplexing task should the lines break and thousands of Chinese soldiers come pouring into the settlement.

Butler's solution was to set up a "mobile second line of defense" consisting of motorized officer patrols on the streets behind the British lines, allowing the Americans to watch and make their own decisions, calling upon motorized support from nearby billets as necessary. The scheme was no doubt maddening to all concerned with serious preparations for defense, and, according to Major Vandegrift, the marines eventually did join the perimeter defense, despite orders to the contrary from Washington.[11] But the charade suited perfectly the cunning diplomatic nuances required by American policy. The motorized patrols were also more active and visible, and therefore less embarrassing to American prestige, than distantly aloof interior posts. Butler the showman was catching on, and continued to play the game with panache. Public relations gambits in Philadelphia had failed to impress gangsters and machine politicians. Here they were the substance of American diplomatic initiative, and Admiral Williams was delighted.

In the crisis atmosphere, American Minister John V.A. MacMurray in Peking recommended an army brigade to supersede the marines in Shanghai, which, as Smedley observed, would have left "us Marines no place in the sun at all." As he won Admiral Williams's confidence with dexterous restraint, the admiral delivered what Smedley thought were the crucial endorsements that confirmed the China intervention as a navy-marine show. Since the State Department already favored the use of marines, the army's "Yellow Plan" figured only as an emergency measure, army units being close at hand in the Philippines. According to Butler, the admiral left it for him to estimate whether the situation was safe enough to risk delay, upon which Williams promised to stand by the marines. Against a general background of hysteria, with MacMurray and the treaty port diehards clamoring for immediate massive intervention, Butler and Williams acted coolly and, as things turned out, correctly. Smedley came to admire the admiral and praised him to Lejeune, by no means *pro forma* between marines discussing naval officers: "He is a fine, clear headed thinker, with plenty of nerve." [12]

With foreign troops "so thick you can hardly walk around in the streets," the possibility of a repetition of Nanking was greatly diminished. Butler felt that increased foreign strength was making all the difference, and on 2 April he and the American consul voted, with Williams as arbiter, to recommend a further American buildup.[13] But with the threat of battle dissipated, military effort was redirected to parade competition with rival foreign units, especially the elite British Coldstream Guards, who particularly excited the marines' competitive instincts. This shifted the military focus away from confrontation with the Chinese, while at the same time presumably reinforcing Western prestige. It also afforded the local American colony a chance to take some pride in its own troops. Spit and polish quickly became the name of the game.

Highly polished brass paper fasteners were stuck in the eyelets of web belts, and eyelets of shoes and leggings were burnished, as were entrenching tools, canteens, and bayonets. Helmets were refinished in glistening paint. Colonel Henry C. Davis, enroute from Olongapo with reinforcements, wrote Lejeune that he was preparing his regiment "to knock their eye out when we arrive" by burnishing and then polishing helmets with a buffer, so that his men looked "like some German guard regiment with silver helmets on." [14]

As mentioned, Butler could ridicule Honduran generals for looking like drum majors in a college band. Yet he provided the main driving force behind all this, much of it contrary to regulations and "unsound if we had ever had to engage in combat," as a marine officer later recalled:

> However, General Butler loved anything flashy. My first lieutenant, Lieutenant Rosecrans, commanded my machine gun platoon. He had removed parts of the machine gun and had them nickle plated and the bands around the cooling system had been polished to their basic metal color, which made them look almost golden. The day General Butler came to the billet to inspect our battalion, I was standing on the third floor level where my company was quartered and I had a machine gun with these brightened parts right outside the squad room door. As General Butler climbed the steps and his eyes raised above floor level, he spotted this machine gun and I saw his eyes enlarge. I was taking a deep breath wondering what was going to happen and then he asked, "Who made that machine gun that way?" I told him with great pride, "Lieutenant Rosecrans." He turned to Colonel "Jumbo" Hill, Commander of the 4th Regiment, who accompanied him and said, "Charlie, I want you to make every machine gun in your regiment just like that one."[15]

Butler rallied the troops to the cause. In 1945, columnist George Sokolsky harkened back to one of Butler's pep talks on leatherneck pride: "With a mighty and ear-splitting oath, the wrinkled, hard-boiled Quaker told them to go out and prove to the 'Limies,' even if they were dukes and lords, how Americans can march. . . . In about three months, these boys were marching and their band was playing and every American was stirred to national glory."[16] From various accounts, they outshone all rivals and, at the next international review, were proclaimed best.

Not everyone was enthusiastic about being an "exhibition force." One young lieutenant later remarked, "It sort of burst the balloon about being a big expeditionary force" sent out to save Shanghai. But the rivalry helped keep up morale and, with movie newsreel teams keen for anything topically military, was good publicity. "We are always showing off for their benefit," Smedley related to Lejeune; "this gets every boy's picture on the screen at home and adds to our success." Eventually Washington headquarters pointed out that dazzle betrayed combat doctrine, and more attention was paid to regulations. Smedley himself took to carrying a swagger stick. Indeed, the U.S. infantry garrison at Tientsin required all its officers in uniform and not under arms to carry either a riding crop or stick.[17]

Spit and polish concealed seedier aspects of garrison life in a city Butler called "the cesspool of the world." Bad liquor and diseased Russian refugee women, both abundantly and cheaply obtainable, were creating havoc among the foreign garrisons. Some foreign units were said to have venereal rates of 75 percent. Butler's answer was parades, frequent inspections, sports, and strict discipline. But spit and polish came easy in this troopers' paradise; the lowest enlisted man could afford Chinese servants to do the menial work. Almost anything could be fiddled in an enveloping and highly sophisticated ambiance of corruption and degeneracy. A marine quarter-master in charge of navy purchasing remembered having to "inspect every piece of coal, otherwise it was going to be mud covered with black paint." Marines buying brand-name whiskey in seemingly unopened bottles got river water. A cholera epidemic in the settlement that summer was rumored to have been started by Chinese injecting water into melons to make them heavier. Marines got theirs back by taking advantage of the "chit" system by which they could buy virtually any commodity or service on credit, signing a variety of spurious names including commonly "Smedley Butler." [18]

Meanwhile Butler, in his diary letters to Lejeune, made an effort to evaluate informally the surrounding civil war. While his attitudes were often naive and uninformed, he managed to construct independently the same hard-headed, skeptical prognosis as was being pieced together by policy-makers in Washington. In early April, after less than two weeks in Shanghai, he wrote: "If Shek [Chiang Kai-shek, the KMT leader—Butler persisted in this gross misnomer for several months] is defeated by the Red Element in the Cantonese party, we will probably have more trouble, but if you read the history of China, as I am trying to do in a small way, you will find that no movement of Cantonese, not even the Tai Ping Rebellion [1850s] reached further north than the Yangtze River. However, all estimate of the political situation in this country is the purest guess work." The Nationalists had "adopted some catchy ideas" from "cute foreigners" (Russian advisers), but would not effect any reforms "if by so doing, they would themselves, be in the slightest bit incommoded." On punitive campaigns: "If you say to the Canton bunch that General Fun Dung committed these outrages, they either say Dung is not one of us or that we can't control Dung. . . . General, it is all shadow boxing. There is nothing to hit. It will positively do no good to shoot a lot of Chinese coolies." [19]

He dismissed resident American expatriates, with their "personal axes to grind," as self-serving troublemakers. "If you took them seriously and tried to review all they tell you, you would be hopelessly muddled." His own views, expressing sympathy for Chinese suffering and their overriding cause of self-determination, placed him among the liberal American China watch-ers, if not among the erudite: "The Chinamen must settle, among them-selves, their own form of Government and their own ruler. But, that while they are doing it, they must not molest our citizens. I think that is enough of a policy for Marines. If you tried to keep track of the movements, or even remember the names, of their war lords, you would not be any better off, and would eventually become a dribbling idiot." [20]

At this juncture, however, the Chinese Revolution underwent a crucial transformation that formed the basis for accommodation between conservative Chinese nationalists and the foreign powers. In the north on 6 April, police under the nominal Peking national government, controlled by warlord and Japanese client Chang Tso-lin, raided the Soviet embassy. In the south on 12 April, Chiang Kai-shek, with Japanese foreknowledge, executed a bloody coup against Communist labor unions in the Chinese city at Shanghai, initiating a purge of Communists from the KMT. The final clash between the KMT Northern Expedition and Chang Tso-lin's defensive alliance of northern warlords would thus be anticommunist by exclusion, lessening the impetus for foreign military intervention. A year later, the chief of the State's Far Eastern Division still found "little to choose between the southern military leader [Chiang] and the northern military leader [Chang]." [21]

Military operations now shifted north to Tientsin-Peking, where large foreign communities were vulnerable in the midst of the northern warlords' regional power base. It was to Tientsin that Butler and the bulk of his brigade were shifted in June 1927 to protect the American colony and keep open evacuation routes to the sea for the foreign legations in Peking. But with all Chinese factions now cooperating with the foreigners, and little to choose between them, priority shifted from protecting American interests from the Chinese to appeasing the Chinese and thwarting the Japanese. This involved a significant new departure in that American troops, not just Open-Door diplomatic maneuvers, were directly engaged to support a contentious political initiative. The buildup of American military forces in North China, close by the Japanese sphere of influence in Manchuria, was a positive assertion of American interest at a time when the outcome of the struggle between Japanese confederate Chang and potential confederate Chiang looked to shape the nature and extent of future Japanese expansion.

In 1927-28 the Tientsin region was the focal point of Japanese-American confrontation, and Butler, paired with the diehard MacMurray, carried the escutcheon of the Open Door into this cockpit of future wars. Butler sailed north in mid-May to make a preliminary inspection and to confer with MacMurray regarding instructions to move the American legation from Peking to Tientsin "in the event of serious danger in order to avoid repetition of 1900 situation." MacMurray had been chief of State's Far Eastern Division since 1919 and then minister to China since 1925, and was a hardliner committed to sustaining America's position in China by military force, most recently by advocating military sponsorship of Chang Tso-lin. With Washington now conciliatory to Chinese nationalism and willing to commit military force only to check the Japanese and hold Tientsin as a temporary refuge for foreigners, MacMurray was left representing a policy he loathed. [22] But as a diehard, he served Washington as an excellent foil by absorbing the direct impact of China Coast diehard resentment. He also played the waning Chang Tso-lin card while it lasted, keeping American options open until the civil war was resolved.

Butler found MacMurray well-versed, sincere, but "weak" in that after a series of long talks he still would not make up his mind to withdraw the legation to Tientsin. Smedley advised him to follow orders and evacuate: "He has been informed, in no uncertain terms, and under no considerations, to permit himself to be cut off and thus repeat the blunder of 1900 with its consequent necessity of large and expensive relief columns." [23]

As for resulting loss of prestige, constantly bemoaned by MacMurray and diehards faithful to the tradition of colonial imperiousness, Butler was emphatically irreverent. And he too could argue from the perspective of an Old China Hand: "It is solemnly and blunderously stated by the stick-it-out section that we will lose 'FACE' if we withdraw our Legation to Tientsin. Now there is a difference of opinion as to what our national 'FACE' is and with whom we are to lose it. . . . However, from the angle of thinking men, even out here, the whole standard, WHITE MANS FACE, is pretty well BATTERED ANYHOW and therefore cannot be saved along the lines of good old standards in effect out here twenty five years ago." [24]

In an addendum headed "SECRET STUFF," Butler described Mac-Murray as "a nervous wreck" who felt discredited because the State Department had not "adopted his plan, which meant an invasion of China, followed by intervention and military Government." Smedley suggested he be recalled for consultation and that Admiral Williams be "placed in diplomatic charge during his absence, say as High Commissioner?" Even before going north, Butler had anticipated this in view of MacMurray's diehard recalcitrance: "Ministers do not always do as they are told, but Officers of the Army, Navy, or Marine Corps do. They submerge their own personalities beneath their sense of duty and loyalty. Admiral Williams has certainly handled this delicate situation here to the entire satisfaction of the administration and has kept the American Minister in Peking within bounds." Williams's appointment as high commissioner might also lead to marine regiments being permanently stationed in Tientsin, Peking, and Shanghai, so as to "give our Corps a wonderful reason for existence and increase in size." [25]

Before long the United States, and Britain as well, would set up alternate diplomatic channels through their top military commanders, thereby eclipsing their diehard China-side diplomatic establishments. This resulted in a good deal of infighting over prerogatives, but it provided flexible representation and access to information beyond that available from the limited perspective of the diehards. With both China and American policy in a state of flux, it also allowed several parallel strategems to be explored. To some extent this simply involved "running with the hares and chasing with the hounds" among rival Chinese warlord factions. It also set American military and diplomats, plus several itinerant civilian politicians, at cross-purposes thereby disrupting bureaucratic procedure and maximizing potential for innovation. Interestingly, the military predominated. In this shuffle, Mac-Murray remained minister to Chang Tso-lin and the China Coast diehards, but was superseded by the military in dealings with the Nationalists.[26] Butler was astute in predicting this, and then served as intermediary between MacMurray and successive senior naval officers.

Having established contact with MacMurray and other Americans in the north, while Vandegrift and Robinson looked into logistics, Butler returned to Shanghai to organize 3,200 marines for dispatch to Tientsin. The British, French, Japanese, and Italians were also sending reinforcements to join their permanent garrisons. The American force under Butler, counting the 500 marines in the legation guard at Peking, the 900 army protocol troops under detached command in the Fifteenth Infantry, and marine aviation units, came to about 5,000, the largest national aggregation and about half the total foreign troops in North China. The marines were also by far the best equipped, with tanks, artillery, and three aviation squadrons.

Butler and units of his Third Brigade sailed north in late June. The Fourth Regiment remained in Shanghai under his distant authority, while the rest of the brigade now converging at Tientsin incorporated bits and pieces of units and equipment from as far away as Quantico. Going along with the marines on the transport *Henderson* was anti-imperialist Senator Burton K. Wheeler, who recorded in his memoirs that he was "fascinated by that famous Marine veteran's personal stories of international trouble-shooting by the Leathernecks. General Butler took a very materialistic view of American foreign policy and was cynical about its fine phrases and idealism. I could understand the feeling by a man with his experience."[27]

The marines arrived in the middle of the hot North China summer, with temperatures reaching 109 degrees during the first week, and set up camp on Woodrow Wilson Boulevard, main artery of the former German concession. The Chinese had been using the field "pretty much as a bathroom" according to the engineer in charge, and he "couldn't get them to move without taking some of my men and tossing a few rocks at them."[28] But eventually duty acquired the comforts of garrison life.

The military situation remained uncertain pending the onslaught of KMT forces. Tientsin was both the key strategic center on the southern approach along the railroad to Peking, and the rail junction through which Chang Tso-lin's northern armies would have to retreat on their way north to their home base in Manchuria. It was also the focal point of foreign economic interests in North China and the marshaling point for escape to the sea, or if things suddenly went wrong, for relief of the legations in Peking. Memories of the epic siege of 1900 had been revived by events in Hankow and Nanking. The Peking-Tientsin area had itself recently figured as the region in China with the most intense combat between huge warlord armies, whose capacity for destruction had increased markedly with the introduction of modern logistics and weapons. In the December 1925 Battle of Tientsin, several hundred thousand troops of two northern factions fought it out nearby for two weeks with ferocity and slaughter that belied derision of warlord politics as being long on intrigue but short on actual bloodletting.

Internal divisions among the Nationalists delayed their progress northward through the summer and fall of 1927, leaving the foreign garrisons a whole year to evolve their respective political postures. The arrival of Butler's marines at Tientsin, henceforth pivot of diplomatic and military maneuvering, had the effect of carrying the State Department's militarized mediation policy right into MacMurray's back yard. Butler, on fortnightly trips to Peking and occasional rendezvous with the admirals in Tientsin, off Taku, and in Shanghai, acted as go-between and man on the spot, parrying the council of foreign commandants at Tientsin. In this role, and with the confidence of successive admirals who were busy preempting MacMurray's diplomatic functions, Butler worked out the adaptive nuances of the North China intervention. He worked harmoniously with MacMurray, who was forced to accept the low military profile and appreciated marine preparations for the relief of the legations. Authority to make the decision to evacuate was shifted to the admirals in what Smedley termed "a terrible slap to the Minister." He himself indignantly rejected MacMurray's appeal for a battalion of marines to be posted at Peitaiho, the seaside resort 150 miles east of Peking where Americans and other foreigners normally escaped the summer heat: "This proposition on top of all made me mad and I positively stated that no Marines would be used to protect a Coney Island." [29]

In August, MacMurray went on four months' home leave, and Williams was replaced as commander in chief of the Asiatic Fleet by Admiral Mark L. Bristol, moves obviously laden with political import. The *New York Daily News* commented, "Admiral Bristol will probably be the President's chief advisor in the Far East." While this was not the Williams high commissionership Butler had proposed, it involved a similar eclipsing of the diehard China-side diplomatic corps in the interests of an opportunistic soft-line policy. Bristol came to China from seven years in Turkey, where he had been U.S. high commissioner to the revolutionary nationalist regime of Kemal Ataturk. According to Colonel Davis, upon arrival Bristol told fellow officers "that he knew nothing about running a fleet." Exercising his diplomatic talents, he left expeditionary affairs in the north largely to Butler. [30]

Bristol concentrated on making contacts with a wide spectrum of Chinese including H.H. Kung, T.V. Soong, C.C. Wu, Sun Fu, Chang Tso-lin, and Chiang Kai-shek. He attended Chiang's wedding to Soong Mei-ling. "I am trying," he wrote a friend, "to cultivate the Chinese without regard to the North or the South or any of the factions." [31] In effect, since this was a civil war and the United States maintained formal diplomatic relations with Chang's national government in Peking, he was developing informal, but official, relations with the southern rebels, who appeared more and more likely to win.

MacMurray, meanwhile, was being personally apprised of official policy in Washington. He returned to Peking in December and confided to his fellow diehard, British Minister Sir Miles Lampson, that the trend in the United States was liberal to the point, as Sir Miles paraphrased him, "of readiness to throw in their hand completely, e.g. even over such things as extraterritoriality." But Lampson, too, was being curbed by his superiors and shunted aside in favor of military agents and informal diplomacy in an attempt to reach accommodation with the rising Nationalist movement. In January 1928 Admiral Bristol reported that Commanding General C.J. Duncan, his British counterpart and an "old friend" from Turkey, was doing diplomatic chores reflecting a policy change "very much resented by the British [China-side] community." Bristol introduced Duncan to prominent Nationalists, including the three famous Soong sisters, "and he cultivated their acquaintances very assiduously. . . . My private opinion is that he rather overdid it, but that is the British method—from the extreme of over-bearing forceful attitude to the opposite."[32]

The Japanese were also establishing contacts with the Nationalists, while they too maintained *de jure* relations with the national government in the north. In August 1927, Colonel Davis reported, "Who has bought off Chiang Kai Shek is not at present known by the intelligence departments but they all say it will come out soon and many people suspect the Japanese of having paid Chiang Kai Sheks price."[33]

On the American side, several civilian politicians visited Chinese factional leaders. Among these was Senator Hiram Bingham, who discussed his impressions with Smedley and Admiral Williams aboard the flagship at Shanghai in June 1927. Bingham had just returned from a two-week journey up the Yangtze during which he held talks with, among others, the Soviet agent Mikhail Borodin and Chiang Kai-shek. Butler described Bingham as having "spent considerable time with all northern and southern generals," and "like all the rest of us is convinced the southern movement [KMT] will be successful." Smedley reported to Lejeune: "Bingham, whom we suspect of being the President's representative out here, strongly urges the presence of a certain number of our officers with Shek, ostensibly as military attaches but really as military advisers. It appears, that Shek at present has no foreigners assisting him and the Senator feels that it is a golden opportunity for us to get in on the commercial ground floor of this movement. Shek is anxious to have us and Bingham says he will so recommend to the President, when he returns to America."[34]

Bingham, in a private family letter written the previous day, argued that the United States should court emerging Chinese factions, not just maintain relations with the Peking national government, and should place diplomatic and military representatives with all contending leaders. This might be of great value in furthering American interests in China.[35] The idea had been mooted in the State Department dating back to the first successes of the KMT Northern Expedition. Butler commented to Lejeune, "I agree with Senator Bingham that if we can, without raising too much of a storm, back Shek, peace will come to China many years before it will if this row is allowed to continue without our guidance." He also had the "feeling that perhaps Bingham may have his own way when he returns to Washington and some of us may be sent to Shek's Headquarters," which Smedley thought "would give us a lead over all other foreigners."[36]

But Bingham was not President Coolidge's representative. The first contact between the two regarding China took place only upon Bingham's return, when the senator offered to stop off at the president's Black Hills retreat. At that point Coolidge listened at length to Bingham's detailed account and appeared to be quite interested.[37]

But if Coolidge, who was famous for suppressing novel ideas, was presented with any military-adviser scheme, he never followed through. The idea was certainly germane and the matter of foreign military advisers for the KMT, to replace the recently departed Russians, remained a lively issue. This involved precisely the transition from coercive military intervention to oblique mediatory devices that made China in the 1920s a laboratory for new styles of foreign manipulation.[38] Butler had relevant experience in the Caribbean and Central America. At a staff conference in Shanghai in November, Admiral Bristol related that, according to best information, Chiang had made a great effort to obtain Japanese advisers and failing this might revert to Russians whom Chiang now felt he could handle in the aftermath of the Communist purge.[39] That same month Colonel Max Bauer arrived, first of a long line of Germans who instructed and helped reorganize the Nationalist army. Americans, notably Generals Claire Chennault and Joseph Stilwell, moved in a decade later.

Butler was well aware, after six months of arcane diplomatic maneuvering, of the intricacy of U.S. purposes and options. Admiral Bristol's arrival emphasized the mediatory nature of the exercise. One of his favorite expressions was that he preferred to catch flies with honey rather than vinegar, and he further discouraged belligerency by U.S. forces, for instance, the shooting of "bandits" by sailors of the Yangtze Patrol serving as guards on American merchant ships. Bristol believed that the marine brigade should not have been placed in Tientsin, where it could easily become involved in fighting, and he later commented that it had "been a source of great concern to me from the day I took command."[40]

At first Bristol did not trust Butler, and even eight months later commented to another admiral, "I am inclined to believe that your idea in regard to Butler is correct. I find him a pretty difficult proposition to handle, but I will attend to that in the end." After a conference with Smedley, he wrote to his wife, "A good deal—a great deal of personal ambition stands in the way of deciding things according to right and wrong." But Bristol was himself something of a prima donna. Colonel Davis remarked that he was "very touchy about his rank and prerogatives and he seems to have brought from Turkey the idea that he is on the right hand of God." Davis liked to "play him up to himself and he has more grease on him now than any channel swimmer ever had." [41] Bristol was put off when Butler, apparently at Lejeune's behest, tried to get him to request more marines on the grounds that this would favorably impress Congress. [42] But Smedley eventually won him over with a very effective and loyal performance at Tientsin, and Bristol wound up praising him extravagantly. Actually, Bristol ventured up to North China only just prior to the KMT invasion in late spring 1928, because of a mutual desire to avoid confrontation between himself and MacMurray. The chiefs of the American military and diplomatic establishments did not come face to face until then.

As Bristol's intermediary with MacMurray and man on the spot in Tientsin, Butler was duly apprised of the admiral's wishes, particularly the admonitions to ingratiate himself with the Chinese. Smedley subsequently parroted this back as "*Nothing* but protection of American lives, and that by the 'handshaking method' if humanly possible," and "playing a lone hand" with respect to the other powers. [43]

At Tientsin the marines kept their distance from the other garrisons. Relations were governed by the Boxer Protocol, and the commandants of the Allied Forces met frequently to adjust them. Despite being second highest in rank and commander of the largest contingent, Butler refused to attend these sessions, sending his chief of staff instead. The ranking American member was therefore the colonel commanding the Fifteenth Infantry, committed under the protocol to collective defense under orders of the senior officer, a Japanese lieutenant general. Butler was careful to disassociate himself and the marines from the Fifteenth and from the protocol, although there was a covert understanding whereby the Fifteenth would abandon the treaty commitment and obey Butler in any crisis. The marines thus remained independent of the whole treaty structure and free to ignore treaty stipulations such as defense of the neutral zones around the city and the railway line to the sea—and to effectively thwart allied initiatives by simply refusing to cooperate. [44] Under the circumstances, relations between the allies were necessarily fretful—quite deliberately so from the American standpoint.

The operational role assigned to Butler's brigade at Tientsin was to rescue Americans in the event of sudden danger in Peking and to open an escape route to the sea. At the outset, in May 1927, when danger seemed imminent, he envisioned a rescue operation in purely military terms, complete with a "Hollow Square" of marines protecting the American minister in embattled retreat. He wrote Colonel Davis, who was standing by at Olongapo, to be ready to blast his way inland from the landing at Tangku all the way to Peking, with airplanes and artillery providing cover: "I am desperately anxious to get both of your columns to Tientsin without loss and will not hesitate to bomb and shell everything within five miles of your line of march." This was to be done "expertly, and without loss of life" rather than by "a blundering-through performance," but "loss of life" referred to marines, not Chinese.[45]

Six months later, with enough time to work out tactics appropriate to the diplomatic mission, he wrote Lejeune with an entirely different emphasis. This would not be "a cruelly bungled, bloody job, but . . . a neat snappy job with a minimum of bloodshed on all sides." His past exploits in the reliefs of Peking and Managua, and the projected Mexico City commando scheme, added up to considerable expertise which he now adapted to the present low-profile exercise—an "emergency flying column."[46]

The marines, with their several light tanks, airplanes, and large number of trucks, were well-equipped for a mechanized operation, and Butler planned accordingly. Dependence on the railroad with all its uncertainties was avoided. Instead, 700 marines could go on their own trucks and another 2,000 on trucks available on option from civilian sources. Most of the latter were truck chassis for which the marines built wooden bodies, ready to be bolted on in ten minutes so that the vehicle could carry twelve men plus ammunition and rations. When the alarm sounded, two hundred drivers collected the trucks at various garages and drove them to the billets, where each squad attached its body and jumped in. Constant drills reduced preparation time so that Butler could get a force of 2,000 men and a battery of artillery, supported by eighteen airplanes, ready to hit the road in two hours. The U.S. military attaché in Peking marveled at Butler's "ability to keep some 3,500 men on their toes who normally would question the utility of carrying boxes to hypothetical trucks and back again day after day." No wonder there was grumbling in the ranks. Butler himself "thought so much about it that I can almost go thru' every move in my sleep."[47]

The ninety-mile road to Peking was improved under marines supervision, partly as a gesture of goodwill to the Chinese, and bridges were strengthened to bear the weight of the tanks. In winter, fires burned day and night to keep oil and fuel warm for planes, tanks, and trucks.[48]

Any obstruction by the Chinese would be dealt with by persuasion rather than force. As in the Banana Wars, there was contempt for local standards of political consciousness. Circulars were prepared in Chinese announcing friendly American intentions and offering to buy rifles for $5

Mexican each and ammunition for $2 more, with generals getting $100 for their swords. Then everyone was promised a hot meal. These circulars were to be weighted with coins and dropped from airplanes onto any Chinese troops along the road, the planes trailing off away from the road as they dropped more circulars so that Chinese soldiers would chase them "to pick up the coins regardless of any order from their commanders," thereby clearing the road for the marines. To disperse crowds blocking the streets of Tientsin, Butler arranged "to secure three tons of native copper cash which we had intended to use as 'bait' to attract the crowds away from the route of our column thru' the city." The cash would be dribbled out of the back of a truck. Using small amounts in a trial run, the marines had "no difficulty," and Smedley was "confident we would not have had any trouble at all in buying off all the armies in China." In all, he planned to take along $200,000 Mexican (US $100,000) for bribes.[49]

The marines could, if all went well, make it to Peking within twelve hours. Once there they would seize the Temple of Heaven as a staging area for evacuating American civilians, who would be rescued from their homes by the legation guard's "suicide squad," forty men riding Mongolian ponies.

The most useful of Butler's projects was his air force. He parried initial concern over possible incidents involving Chinese air space, and gradually extended flights beyond the Boxer protocol zone two miles either side of the railway from Peking to the sea. During the next year and a half, the aviators ranged far and wide over the Tientsin-Peking area, flying 3,818 sorties, mostly on reconnaissance. Seven planes were holed by ground fire from itinerant Chinese armies. A challenge from the Japanese, who at one point brought planes to observe marine ground maneuvers outside Tientsin, was deflected, according to Vandegrift, by marine flyers screaming down out of the sun to disperse the surprised Japanese formation. Perhaps the Japanese pulled back in deference to the pivotal role the marines played in the international military structure on the ground. In any case, the marines enjoyed absolute preeminence in the air, with exclusive advantage in surveillance of Chinese military movements.[50]

The marines built their airdrome on the Hai River five miles inland from Tangku at Hsin Ho, where the flyers and accompanying battalion of troops protected the otherwise vulnerable Standard Oil compound. It was a fifteen-minute flight from marine headquarters at Tientsin. The company, as in Shanghai, allowed the marines to use its buildings for billeting and stores. Indeed, at Tientsin the only position the marines manned and rigged with permanent barbed-wire defenses was the Standard Oil installation. Elsewhere they maintained the low profile consistent with U.S. diplomacy, and at their own quarters built wire entanglements on sled runners that were kept inside the billets, to be dragged out only in time of crisis. Protecting Standard Oil gasoline stores was to some extent a practical military consideration, but this close symbiotic relationship between the marines and the major American commercial enterprise in China lent strong credence to Butler's anti-imperialist rhetoric of the 1930s—"I spent 15 years of my service, Mr. Chairman, running around the world guarding Standard Oil tins." One of the aviators, echoing Butler, later commented, "We were protecting the Rockefeller oil interests along the Hai Ho River. Otherwise there was no need for any military presence there at all."[51]

In Tientsin, the brigade settled into cramped quarters in the former German concession, facing a difficult climate and the degenerate allurements of treaty port garrison life. Most crucial was to avoid provocations that might compromise friendly American overtures to the Chinese. During the first months there were complaints in local newspapers and from diplomatic sources about marine drunkenness and rowdiness, including an incident in which marines went into the French concession in rickshaws and fired pistols. The Japanese police chief thought the marines were the worst foreign troops.[52]

But this soon changed. Butler was quoted acknowledging that troops on foreign soil tended to be arrogant, but that "this country belongs to the Chinese, and I tolerate no clashes between my men and the Chinese people. If a man so much as slaps a rickshaw coolie or lays a hand upon a servant, he gets a general court-martial." Assisting him in setting a severe tone was Lieutenant Colonel Ellis B. Miller, "the best Chief of Staff I have had," who according to Vandegrift and others was "one of the sternest disciplinarians in the Corps." If Miller thought he was right, he would tell Butler so, "right straight from the shoulder," which was definitely not an easy thing to do. Miller was a "tough character," and forty years later Robinson remembered him as "the only fellow I ever disliked in the Marine Corps." Butler and Miller took away disciplinary authority from regimental commanders and instituted a "star chamber summary court." A number of officers were sent home or court-martialed.[53]

There were complaints, but these were tempered by appreciation of the overall mission. At the start of the Tientsin stint, Captain Adolph B. Miller recorded in his diary, "No liberty for men. Much AWOL [unauthorized absence] and drunkenness. Morale low." The most caustic public criticism came from Private John P.S. Mahoney, who went home and wrote a twenty-eight chapter serial in his father's newspaper, the *Lawrence Telegram* (Massachusetts), entitled "Touring the Orient at Uncle Sam's Expense." According to Mahoney, "If ever one man made 5,000 others suffer, for his eccentricity and peculiarities, Smedley Butler certainly did." Butler made all the marines "suffer for the sins of a few." Liberty was cut back to 10:00 P.M., military police arrested "any man with the sign of liquor on him," and offenders were turned over to brigade headquarters for punishment, "which he [Butler] certainly did ruthlessly." Morale was "at a very low point," and there were incessant inspections, reviews, and maneuvers: "A good many of them no doubt were of military value, but the majority of them were simply because General Butler lost track of the fact that enlisted men are 'Human Beings' and not simply 'Tin Soldiers' to do with as he pleased." [54]

On a more positive note, *New York Times* correspondent Hallett Abend, who often visited Butler in Tientsin and thereafter invited enlisted marines to dinner on Thanksgiving and Christmas for the remainder of his long China beat, wrote that Butler "spared himself less than he spared his men, and his popularity in his brigade was immense. He was a profane, quick-thinking, tough-talking teetotaler, and his officers and men felt that he knew his job thoroughly." Butler's adjutant at this time, William A. Worton, recalled that "the men loved Smedley. Smedley was a born leader of men, and the enlisted men worshipped Smedley Butler, there's no doubt about it." [55]

Tensions and animosities were inherent in the circumstances. During the first summer, Smedley was down to 138 pounds, and two marines, possibly a third, died of sunstroke. Later Butler was troubled by recurrent nervous indigestion that was serious enough to warrant several week-long sessions in the Rockefeller hospital in Peking. He apparently had nothing to do with the stunning suicide of Colonel "Jumbo" Hill, his subordinate commanding the Fourth Regiment in Shanghai, who shot himself pursuant to what an official inquiry termed "a service induced mental condition." And Smedley tolerated marine drinking, so long as it was within disciplinary bounds. Worton remembered that "he'd stand up against the fireplace drinking ginger ale, and he'd argue with these fellows who drunk all the time, argue them like [inaudible], and they got to like him. Because he was a very lovable character when he wanted to be." This was in a situation in which another officer recalled "notorious bottle men" interspersed among the officer ranks, and Smedley, wondering who might replace him at Tientsin, quipped to his father, "there are a choice lot of generals in the Marine Corps to pick from when sending one out here where liquor runs wild." [56]

Butler kept liquor and venereal disease under control through stiff disciple, and established a demarcation line separating marine and Fifteenth Infantry areas in town, to curtail brawling. The Fifteenth, meanwhile, sent free rickshaws around to the bars at closing time as a means of holding down venereal rates, and was in the throes of a feud in which officers tried to force the removal of General Joseph C. Castner, overall army commander in North China, on charges of mental incompetence. Castner has been described by one scholar as "of that irritating breed of military men who pride themselves on being simple, rough, and blunt soldiers. . . . [He] was convinced that the way to turn out a well-disciplined, rugged command was by hard drill and long hikes, the latter led by himself at a pace that forced the men at the end of the column to run most of the time." Butler predictably got along well with Castner, his junior and *de facto* subordinate, and considered him "a fine old type of Army officer [who] has been through all their schools and colleges but remains unspoiled."[57]

Life in Tientsin had its attractions. This was the beginning of the "golden age" of the Marine Corps, China in the early and mid-1930s. Tientsin in 1927-29, according to Robinson, "was golden enough, but— Lord, on a captain's pay I could live better there than you could here [U.S.A.] on a full general's pay." Johnnie Walker scotch sold at 97 cents a bottle, gin for 62 cents. A 1928 Tientsin prospectus in the *Marine Corps Gazette* recommended at least two servants for an apartment, and three or four for a house. Garden coolies were paid $5.70 per month and fed themselves. For officers there was club life, including golf and polo, and constant rounds of parties.[58]

Mrs. Butler, a "very lovely lady" according to Worton, came out for visits in 1927 and 1928, and in keeping with Admiral Bristol's hand-shaking policy, the Butlers attended Chinese official dinners. Often they were the only foreigners, which Smedley attributed to concerted efforts at restraining the troops and the impact of the garrison's large payroll on local commerce. Social events, including invitations for large numbers of Chinese to airplane demonstrations and other outdoor entertainments, sustained the goodwill initiative, although early on Smedley had confided to Lejeune, "You understand that we will not be particularly excited by social contact with Chinese." Relations with the Japanese garrison were mainly formal and quite polite, but the Japanese were insulted, according to Robinson, by the marines' inability to distinguish them from Chinese.[59]

On Christmas Eve in 1927, there was an exciting break from garrison routine when a huge fire broke out in the Standard Oil compound directly across the river from the international settlement in Tientsin. The previous day an explosion had ripped the provincial Chinese ammunition depot and at night there had been several large fires in the British concession, raising suspicions of sabotage. The Socony fire spread from the candle factory to an adjacent kerosene facility, threatening gasoline godowns nearby. Streams of burning oil and wax gushed into the river, covering it with sheets of flame which spread across to the bund, endangering shipping, especially wooden junks.

The main fire in the compound burned for three days, generating intense heat and leaving a horrible mess afterward. Socony firemen managed to contain the worst danger, then Butler arrived with 2,000 marines. His experience in Philadelphia, where he had charge of firefighting as well as police, served him well. He personally directed, according to newspaper reports, not only marines but also Chinese, British, French, and Italian fire brigades that responded to the company's alarm.

Marines worked long into the night and the following day building firewalls, hosing down the blistering side of a gasoline storehouse adjacent to the blaze, and carrying out drums of gasoline and kerosene. At 3 A.M. on Christmas morning a sewer blew up, releasing a stream of burning oil that spread, halfway across the river. Five hundred marines built a cofferdam across the mouth of the sewer, thereby forming a huge cauldron of burning oil which held until that night when an ice-jam broke up river and carried away part of the dam. Through all this, Butler was highly active, and American newspapers gave him prominent coverage as the focus of attention, including photographs showing him with a riding crop directing his men. Smedley acknowledged in a letter to his father that "we are charged with an inordinate desire for publicity," but dismissed this as jealousy on the part of the Fifteenth Infantry, which had not taken part, and pointed instead to the mid-winter boost the fight had given marine morale.[60]

Private Mahoney picked up the publicity-seeking charge in a chapter of his newspaper serial entitled "General Butler Needlessly Exposes Men To Danger For His Own Glory." The piece documents the resentment that Smedley's aggressive theatricality could excite. Mahoney felt that the fire, being across the river, presented little danger to human life, but that Butler's sending marines into a place where "flames were licking hungrily" around thousands of gallons of gasoline did. The marines suffered from being overheated close to the fire and then froze as they carried tins of gasoline out into the winter weather. There were "plenty of coolies available" for this, and coolies were "the cheapest labor in the world and the Standard Oil company, one of the wealthiest concerns." Meanwhile Butler was displaying himself, "first placing a gasoline can on his shoulder, then having his 'CAMERA MAN' snap his picture. Next he would go to where the engineers were digging an entrenchment to prevent the burning oil from spreading, and he would pick up a shovel while his photo was snapped. He even had himself photoed helping to hold one of the fire-hose."[61]

Whether one liked Butler depended to a great extent on how far one went along with the marines' "First in the Fight" ethos, and in particular his rendition as a style of leadership. Many considered him self-important and self-serving. But with his notorious energy and wholehearted commitment—including publicity seeking—it is hard to make him out a phony. Sincerity was absolutely crucial to this style of leadership, witness Mahoney's dissent pointing to vulnerability. In Tientsin, Butler placed that credibility on the line by pushing tough discipline and tedious training exercises.

The fire consumed $1 million in petroleum stocks and an estimated $25 million in plant and equipment. Standard Oil donated $10,000 for a marine recreation hall and gave a new uniform to each man who fought in the fire.

During these months, from the marines' arrival in June 1927 until the spring of 1928, the military showdown between advancing Nationalist armies and the northern warlords remained in the offing. Butler kept track of the motley and ill-fed northern armies that dominated the Tientsin region, and negotiated with the Peking government under Chang Tso-lin regarding the marines' various projects. He looked askance upon the "pathetic slaughtering of innocent people by a lot of brutal war-lords," and thought the Peking government was hardly better: "When bandits roam around in bunches of five thousand they cease to be bandits and . . . the only reason they are so classified by the Chang-so-Ling crowd is because it has not yet been possible to determine what side they are on."[62]

According to Colonel Davis, Butler made a great success at the diplomatic game, so that "those who decried sending Smedley out here have been proved wrong." But Butler's own account of negotiations to parry protests and request privileges, such as barracks and airspace extensions, betrays a blundering naiveté reminiscent of his tangles with politicians in Philadelphia and Haiti. During a "uselessly formal" session with the Chinese minister of foreign affairs, he challenged the minister directly: "Your political difficulties are the same as ours, and if you will permit me, I will point out to you the 'jam' in which you now find yourself. You, personally, wish to have American troops in Tientsin because it stabilized the situation . . . . [But] as an official of the Chinese Government you feel it your duty to make protest in order to quiet such oppositional political parties as you may have." After this, the minister's "face broke into a broad smile," followed by "perfectly straight talk" between the two for the next fifteen minutes while the American chargé and other conventional diplomats sat by agape.[63]

More likely Butler was being taken in. The minister invited him to meet "Chang-so-Ling, the dictator," but when he turned up for the appointment, the Old Marshal proved "indisposed" and the Americans left after half an hour's formal conversation with his chief of staff. Since Butler's instructions at this point were to minimize contact with Chinese officials "in order that we may not be charged with favoring one of the two factions," Chang gained face at American expense. The purpose, to obtain former German barracks in a Chinese district of Tientsin, came to naught.[64]

Both Chang Tso-lin and Chiang Kai-shek had every reason to cultivate Americans as counterweights to the Japanese, but not so blatantly as to compromise their respective reputations as Chinese nationalists. To the south the KMT, reunified under Chiang, launched the second phase of its Northern Expedition in April 1928, thereby finally joining the issue of whether it could dispose of Chang and come to terms with the heavy-handed Japanese presence in North China.

Tokyo, signaling a new "positive policy," had in 1927 dispatched a 6,000-man military expedition to Shantung province, several hundred miles south of Tientsin, and then withdrawn it when KMT armies failed to appear. Following explanations by the Japanese commandant at Tientsin, Butler commented: "They justified this invasion on the ground of protecting their interests along that road [Tsingtao-Tsinan railroad], but in reality, they are suspected of making the movement to stop the advance of the Nationalist or Southern army. At any rate, that was the effect." [65] Now, in early 1928, the Japanese reached an understanding with the KMT that Chang would retreat without a fight to Manchuria while the KMT, in keeping with prior commitments, would respect Japanese interests in North China and not venture north of the Great Wall. This extremely tenuous arrangement was contingent upon transit of several hundred thousand northern and southern troops through Shantung and Tientsin, on the avoidance of clashes with foreign nationals and their protecting military forces, and on the discipline of the Japanese army in China, with its seditious officer corps increasingly intent upon outright Japanese military occupation. Butler would now play a crucial role in limiting Japanese military initiatives in pivotal Tientsin.

The contrast between Butler's calculated defusing of Japanese and other foreign military activities in Tientsin and the potential for mischief by aggressive or insubordinate commanders was vividly demonstrated by a preliminary incident 175 miles to the south. There, KMT armies advancing northward along the railway in the spring of 1928 confronted Japanese forces ostensibly sent to protect the Japanese civilian colony in Tsinan. After retreating northern armies had left, an incident involving KMT and Japanese soldiers sparked a serious firefight. The Japanese attacked and drove all KMT forces out of the city, which thereafter was held under Japanese military government for the remainder of the year. Sixteen Japanese civilians and 230 soldiers were killed, while Chinese casualties totaled 2,000. The government in Tokyo supported this independent action taken in the field by sending additional reinforcements to Shantung and Tientsin, building up the force at Tsinan to 23,000 by July. Admiral Bristol, writing from Tsingtao in Shantung, observed that the Japanese had "certainly made a military occupation out of their so-called use of military forces for simply protecting Japanese interests in this part of China." [66]

The Tsinan Incident, 3-5 May 1928, is commonly interpreted as a major turning point, the commencement of Japanese military expansion in China that ultimately led to the Pacific War. A week later at the council of foreign commandants in Tientsin, Japanese Lieutenant General K. Arai, the ranking commandant, explained events in Tsinan in terms of Communist-inspired Chinese troops run amok slaughtering Japanese civilians: "Eyes out, noses cut off, burned alive, buried alive, and women violated and murdered." This meant that existing plans for Chinese troops to pass through Tientsin, sealing off only the international settlement, were no longer acceptable. Arai proposed that the foreign garrisons expel northern troops and establish a defensive perimeter seven miles out, surrounding Tientsin, to which they were entitled under existing treaty concessions. The marines declined to participate, thereby in effect vetoing the proposal. General Castner, speaking for the Fifteenth Infantry, likewise refused. The British favored the seven-mile perimeter and otherwise preferred to go along with Japan, but as a Foreign Office annotator wrote on one of Minister Lampson's dispatches, "If the Americans refuse to agree to any action based on juridical right, it would be madness for us to join with the Japanese alone in such action." Lampson was instructed that it was "of the highest importance at this moment especially to secure the co-operation of the American commander if possible," reflecting Butler's central role at Tientsin. The Japanese at this point said they had 2,000 troops plus another 2,000 on the way, while the British had 1,000, so the marines remained the premier force in any projected international scheme.[67]

Advancing southern armies reached Tientsin a month after the inauspicious clash at Tsinan. In the interim Japan prevailed upon Chang Tso-lin to withdraw peacefully to Manchuria where, as a Japanese client, he and his army might be useful in containing any anti-Japanese insurgency. Chang left Peking by rail, via Tientsin, in advance of his retreating army but was killed in Manchuria when his train was blown up by insubordinate Japanese officers. During the first week in June northern armies proceeded along the same route. Troops traveling by rail passed through Tientsin without detraining, while those on foot avoided the city by several miles.

There remained, however, three to five thousand northern troops inside the "native city," plus several local warlord armies, allied to the northern coalition, variously strung out in the environs. Admiral Bristol, after last-minute conferences with MacMurray in Peking and with Butler, barely managed to get away on 2 June in a special car and locomotive, "through the influence of General Butler and the foreigners running the railway." The station was jammed with Chinese troop movements. There were rumors of restlessness and possible friction between elements of the disintegrating northern alliance.[68]

Events in Tientsin took a decisive turn as the Nationalist armies drew near. Several northern armies prepared to make a stand in the city and to the north and west, and there was rifle firing across the Pei River. Serious battle was averted by the critical defection of a northern general who was reassigned a KMT command and took control of Tientsin on the twelfth, raising the Nationalist flag on government buildings. But this transitional force lacked sufficient discipline to prevent disorders in the Chinese city that night. The French consul reported widespread pillaging and barbaric killings, "but at a safe distance from the foreign concessions, although firing could be quite distinctly heard." In the following days regular KMT troops entered the city and restored order through an "energetic repression." The remaining northern armies retreated in disarray.[69]

From the marines' vantage point, as Butler put it, "there was considerable excitement around here for about ten days but the Chinese passed us without so much as a belligerent look," this perhaps because "the Tsinanfu incident was still fresh in their memory." He estimated that for about a week there had been at any time 150,000 Chinese troops of the several factions within a radius of ten miles of the foreign settlement, mostly passing through on uninterrupted transit. The passive 15,000-man foreign garrison proved sufficient deterrent: "Had we not been in such strength we would have had trouble."[70]

Marine aircraft maintained aerial surveillance over Chinese troop movements throughout the region, tracking retreating armies almost as far north as the Manchurian border. Several were holed by rifle fire from passing KMT armies as they took off and landed at Hsin Ho. Butler sought conciliation behind the scenes, and sent Vandegrift to negotiate with General Feng Yu-hsiang, who proved most cooperative regarding overflights and also promised to keep his main units seven miles outside Tientsin. "The Southern crowd," Smedley wrote Lejeune, "is, if possible, even more friendly than the others and our relations are of the very best." At the same time he continued to view the KMT coalition as predators indistinguishable from their northern counterparts. The three "Southern war lords" were now holding conferences "to divide up the spoils and still maintain friendly relations toward each other (a thing impossible for any great length of time) and which will eventually, I imagine, result in a split among them and another civil war."[71] This was the prevalent view among foreign observers.

The American presence at Tientsin thus had the effect of politically and militarily easing the conflict, specifically by neutralizing the threat of further Japanese army adventurism. It was a delicate position, perilous in that, as summarized in a mid-June naval intelligence report, there was a "constant danger of our forces becoming involved in a clash with the Chinese, brought on by Japan's 'positive policy.'" Butler reported to Lejeune that the Japanese had done "everything in their power to provoke an incident," but had been prevented by the "passive attitude maintained by this Brigade." On three occasions the Japanese sought American support for "offensive movements toward the Chinese," but had been thwarted. "All the other nations were willing to join the Japanese but because we would not, on each occasion, the Japanese cautiously withdrew from their position." The occasions were the seven-mile perimeter, an ultimatum in the name of the "Allied Forces" which Butler quashed by saying he would inform the Chinese he was not party to it, and his refusal to extend allied lines into the Chinese city.[72] Local Japanese officers, whatever their inclinations, were given little opportunity to exploit the situation aggressively.

The Peking-Tientsin area thus passed over to the Nationalists without, for the time being, significant Japanese military inroads. To the south, in Shantung, which MacMurray described in mid-June as under Japanese control and "avoided by all Chinese militarists," this was not the case.[73] To the north, Japanese domination was consolidated in a comprehensive military occupation following insubordinate action by the Japanese army in the 1931 Manchurian Incident. In retrospect, Butler's 1927-29 stint at Tientsin marked the last tenuous collaboration between Japan and the United States in monitoring developments in China. Thereafter, Japanese military invasion extended past Tientsin far south into China, precipitating the Pacific War.

Butler's role may be seen as an important instance of military achievement of an official policy of peaceful mediation, all the more striking when contrasted with momentous military insubordination by the Japanese. And it was the American military, led by Williams, Bristol, and Butler, that persevered in appeasement and neutralization as against zealous demands for a militaristic "positive policy" by MacMurray and civilian American diehards. And it had been a strenuous clash of wills. In August 1928 a bitterly resentful MacMurray complained to the chief of State's Far Eastern Division: "Does the Department realize that it has worked its China Service, diplomatic and consular, as a nigger works a second-hand flivver—no oil for the crank-case, no juice in the battery, no water in the radiator?" [74]

Smedley's own feelings about all this were mainly expressed in appropriate mediatory terms—avoidance of bloodshed, sympathy for the Chinese people, and development of American commerce. But the old devil dog peeked through the web of goodwill and modulation. Reporting the anticlimactic turnover at Tientsin to Lejeune during the letdown afterward, he confided in a handwritten postscript that "while, as an official, I did all in my power to prevent a conflict here, I am just personally a little bit sorry that some excitement was not rammed down our unwilling throats." He felt that he had "lost my standing with the men," and recommended turning over the "inactive and monotonous garrison duty" at Tientsin to the army: "We *can* do this traffic duty better than anyone else and direct the Chinese to their various camping grounds, but we do not like it." The marines were the "'Nation's bloodhounds' [kept] in leash for real 'rough and tumble' service," and the government had "inferior forces which can do this 'missionary work' and should use them." [75]

With the crisis passed, the issue of withdrawing the marines pitted Admiral Bristol, who was always nervous about their being dangerously exposed, against MacMurray who held fast to the diehard axiom of always wanting as many troops as possible. MacMurray's major arguing point, humoring Washington in its intent to appease the Chinese, was the marines' reported popularity! Butler sided with MacMurray, but having "fought and fought for ten months" with the admiral over keeping the marines until the turnover, he "played fairly" and promptly recommended reduction when the danger was passed. Thereafter, the issue was complicated, as highlighted in a naval intelligence report in mid-June, by the likely continuation of friction between American and Japanese commanders which had already received "considerable publicity" in the Japanese press.[76]

In arguing rapid withdrawal, Bristol pointed to substantial risks already taken, which made continuation at Tientsin unacceptably perilous. He was greatly relieved when tanks, artillery, and aircraft squadrons departed, leaving a "more mobile force." By contrast, marines at Shanghai could be removed anytime by ship on short notice if it became "necessary politically or otherwise to withdraw them." Tientsin was particularly vulnerable for an American garrison, being inland "and located at a strategic cross-roads which is the focal point of military operations by armed forces in North China," where foreign armies were "bound to find themselves between contending native armies striving to occupy this place." In other words, the advantages of occupying Tientsin from an old-fashioned imperialist viewpoint were decided disadvantages if one was avoiding hostile confrontations and entanglements. Given China's development, any future relief expeditions "would be necessarily much more extensive than those of the Boxer incident." And the "idea that the mere presence of Marines in numbers would over-awe the Chinese" assumed "that a show of foreign force would bluff them." In sum, times were changing and the basis for colonial diehardism was hopelessly undermined. Butler's stint at Tientsin, with all its caution and cajolery, had been a rather close-run thing.[77]

For the marines, Tientsin involved an awkward regression back toward their colonial light-infantry heritage, in the midst of big-war amphibious pretensions. Commandant Lejeune responded to Bristol's critique of equipment tables for Marine Corps expeditionary forces by conceding that he had "fully realized for sometime" that the marines in Tientsin "had too many heavy trucks and too much heavy equipment," and was "convinced that light trucks would be more advantageous for expeditions" of this type. Earlier, Admiral Williams lost his temper over 8,000 tons of freight accompanying the marines, commenting, as paraphrased by Butler, "that he had no use for this 'god damned' organization of the Marine Corps. That he wanted soldiers and not trucks. That we had gotten so top heavy, we couldn't move." And roads outside the cities were so bad Butler planned to use Chinese carts.[78] But the point was not that the marines might be called upon for colonial bushwhacking requiring speed and mobility with minimal firepower, but rather that they should be lightly equipped and mobile in order to get out fast according to the volatile political considerations of mediatory intervention.

In his final six months at Tientsin, Butler broadened the public relations initiative to include a joint road-building project reminiscent of gendarmerie days in Haiti. The initial impulse was to facilitate rescue of Americans in Peking, but when local villagers expressed enthusiasm after the marines replaced a washed-out bridge on the Tientsin-Peking highway, Butler pursued it further. Chinese authorities provided between 600 and 1,500 soldiers daily to work under marine supervision, and twenty miles of dirt road were dragged and raked, aided by marine tractors and trucks. "Butler Bridge" and the "Sino-American Highway" were effusively commemorated in ceremonies attended by Chinese and American dignitaries. The KMT provincial governor said the bridge symbolized the joining together of the Chinese and American people in friendship. Two six-foot granite monuments were erected at Yangtsun, each bearing bronze placards with Chinese Nationalist and American flags, and Butler was presented with a Ten Thousand Blessings Umbrella by the village of Peichang.[79]

Apparently everyone was pleased, but behind the scenes Admiral Bristol reacted sourly. He was represented at the ceremony by the U.S. naval attaché, who reported that Butler took all the glory for himself and the marines without mentioning Bristol and the navy. Bristol noted, "Butler is quite a character and most of his qualities are very admirable, but there is one thing that he cannot to save him eliminate from his feelings, and that is his desire to eliminate the Marines entirely from the Navy." It was regrettable that "a junior officer does not realize that loyalty to a senior will increase the credit due him and lack of loyalty will always detract from his most brilliant achievement." Besides which the admiral mentioned resentfully, "For your information only, this work of the Marines was a suggestion of mine." Nevertheless, Butler still rated "a pretty large plus sign" in his overall estimation: "It is remarkable how Butler handles any situation when he makes up his mind to do it. He has untiring energy, brilliant imagination, and original ideas."[80]

Previously Butler had reported to Lejeune that Bristol was "at last on friendly relations with us," and the admiral had written the attaché that he had gotten to like Smedley, referring to him as "the best man of his corps that I could have to handle this delicate situation" at Tientsin. In the aftermath of the successful June turnover, Bristol commented to the secretary of the navy that he was "deeply impressed with the ability and with the minute manner in which he [Butler] has thought of every possible thing which might happen and tried to make preparations to meet every emergency," pointing out that "our forces at Tientsin had a very decided restraining effect upon the Japanese."[81]

Butler was given a second Ten Thousand Blessings Umbrella by the village of Ta Chi Ku outside Tientsin for having, as wryly recalled by Robinson, inadvertently been caught up in a passing Chinese army while driving out to the golf course: "They said if he hadn't been there in his car the Chinese brigade would have stopped in their town and they would have had to feed them." The large, cylindrical red silk umbrellas, on fifteen-foot poles, were appended with tags bearing names of village elders plus inscriptions: "You have saved a part of Tientsin from trouble; Your kindness is always in the mind of the people; The Chinese love General Butler as they love China; General Butler loves China as he loves America." [82]

Butler did acquire a respect for the Chinese which he mentioned for the rest of his life, and also an updated perspective on American military intervention. Publicly boosting the mercantile Open-Door creed, he described himself as having been an "unofficial good will ambassador and trade envoy." Friendliness and tact were the best ways to deflect anti-imperialist hatreds, in what he characterized to Lejeune as "a struggle for commercial supremacy." The American "bloodless invasion" contrasted with Japanese and British arrogance that provoked serious boycotts against those nations' goods in 1927-29. He now renounced a longtime bias against business interests dating back to the Boxer campaign, when "in common with many others I had the hard-boiled idea that if Americans didn't like it in China, or felt unsafe there, they should get out and come home." [83]

Similarly, in the flush of the successful China expedition, he pointed out to Lejeune implications of the debacle in Nicaragua where another brigade of marines was bogged down in a bloody counterinsurgency campaign. U.S. foreign policy regarding "occupation of weaker nations" was increasingly problematic: "As long as we occupy these countries without great uproar and particularly, without the loss of our own men, little attention is paid to our movements by the [American] public at large. We may even kill a lot of natives of such countries without much comment . . . but, as soon as our losses begin to grow there is a big 'hubbub,' as you no doubt know, and the Corps comes in for unfavorable criticism." [84]

Butler thus came away from his final overseas expedition with a fairly complete appreciation of contemporary American military interventions. He had covered the full spectrum, with China 1900 and 1928 as felicitous anchor points, from colonial punitive warfare to mediation characteristic of formal empire in retreat. An old warhorse, he bowed out with a widely admired diplomatic performance at Tientsin.

As the senior brigadier in the Corps with nearly double the foreign service of any other general except Russell, who was still in Haiti, Butler had to his credit a distinguished fighting career, proven administrative ability, and now a signal diplomatic success. And yet he denied ambitions to succeed to the commandancy, explaining to Lejeune, "I can do no good in the Marine Corps after you have gone. . . . And I would never be any good as Commandant myself, as I simply could not get along with politicians. Their insincerity and duplicity would eat my vitals out, and there would be nothing but fighting, with the consequent decimation of our Corps." Major General Neville was "without doubt" the only worthy successor. In early 1928 Smedley wrote his father that if there was a chance for promotion he would hang on for the extra retirement pay; otherwise he would get out. [85]

In any case, his prospects within the naval establishment received a severe setback in May 1928 when his father died in Washington at the age of seventy-three, three weeks after a severe heart attack in his office at the Capitol. Personally, this was a big shock for Smedley, and he was greatly upset at not being home during the critical time. Thomas S. Butler was the senior member of the House in point of service, and his *New York Times* obituary photograph bore the caption "Father of the House of Representatives." A committee of the House consisting of seventy-eight members went as a body to West Chester for the funeral. There were "innumerable unconfirmed rumors" in Washington that Smedley would resign upon coming home from China and that his "popularity in his home district would undoubtedly sweep him into office" as his father's replacement.[86]

14 To Hell with the Admirals

WASHINGTON

Returning home in early 1929, Smedley Butler was assigned to Quantico, where he took over from Major General Wendell C. Neville. Neville succeeded Commandant Lejeune, who retired after nine years in office, his prolonged tenure being partly attributable to a "firm stand" by Congressman Butler.[1] In July 1929 Smedley was promoted to major general upon the death of Eli K. Cole. At forty-eight years of age, he was the youngest major general in the American services, and this was the top rank excepting only the army chief of staff. He was now the senior general in the Marine Corps after Neville, and ten years younger than rivals in line for the commandancy.

With the raise in salary, he disregarded a civilian job prospect. Quantico, with most of the command off on expeditionary duty in Haiti and Nicaragua, was undemanding. Butler again pushed athletics, and there were self-help construction schemes using stone and lumber cut on the base. He collaborated with his two younger brothers, who had finally made headway in the Texas oil industry, to obtain high-grade aviation gasoline for marine races. After seventeen years' overseas service, Smedley could write an old crony that he now had "a big house, a fine automobile and enough to live on, so my worries are over as Major Generals in our Corps don't have to go on foreign duty." The car was a new $4,500 Stutz sedan with custom fittings. The Butlers bought an old farmhouse in Newtown Square, Pennsylvania, near West Chester, and began refurbishing it at great expense. The architectural feature that attracted Smedley was an open central axis which he remodeled into a two-story living room-hallway big enough to accommodate the Thousand Blessings Umbrellas, brought home from China, that served as conversation pieces and dominant motif. The Butler sons were off at college—Smedley, Jr., at M.I.T. and Cal Tech, and Tom Dick at Swarthmore.[2]

These expenses absorbed the salary increase, and Butler was soon on the lookout for extra income. This meant cashing in on sidelines open to him as a public figure of some repute in military and police affairs—public speaking, journalism, and potboiler adventure stories. A $3,000 offer to make another Marine Corps feature film fell through. Instead, he teamed with his old partner E.Z. Dimitman in producing "The Marines Who

Wouldn't Fight," a chronicle of the North China intervention serialized and published nationally by North American Newspaper Alliance in the fall of 1929. He used the same material, reworked in various ways, for magazine articles and speaking engagements. Dimitman, now an editor on the *Philadelphia Inquirer*, continued to ghost Butler's political articles and radio speeches, based on a fifty-fifty royalty split, for the next half-dozen years in close collaboration true to Butler's style. Smedley roughed out preliminary drafts and corrected Dimitman's fleshed-out enlargements.[3]

For the pulp adventure stories, Butler turned to Arthur J. Burks, co-author of *Walter Garvin in Mexico*, who had resigned from the marines and was hacking out popular military fiction at a prodigious rate, 125 stories in the past year and a half, much of it at two cents a word. Burks, acting as unpaid agent and collaborator, rewrote some of Smedley's material, absorbed some into his own stories, and gave advice. The object was strictly commercial: "I take it you are more interested in money than in fame, and if I can whip a yarn out of the Honduras material, I'll use whichever name brings the most money, yours or mine." Regarding style, he cautioned Smedley that a "conscious effort on your part to 'write' may impair the worth of your material." Better to dictate to a stenographer, "DON'T TRY TO BE LITERARY! JUST TALK." Butler cranked out chapters for an autobiography, "Adventures with the Marines," of which fragments appeared in various guises.[4]

The public speaking circuit, which at this time was enjoying national revival as a cultural and entertainment medium, proved more substantial. By his own contacts and then with professional booking through the Alber Bureau, he appeared before veterans' groups, Rotary and Lions Clubs, civic associations, colleges, and dollar-a-ticket public forums. This was done on his own time, either on leave or by dashing off on weekends. From October 1929 to May 1931 his schedule listed ninety-eight performances around the eastern United States. His standard fee was $250, and he was not reticent about the mercenary motive. Nevertheless, his extemporaneous speeches on crime fighting and Marine Corps adventures, plus topical discursions, were highly opinionated and naturally tended to iconoclasm, hyperbole, and irrepressible showmanship. He urged a police audience, "Don't fiddle with these thugs! Kill 'em!" As a serving U.S. officer he flouted discretion, denouncing the government of China for "planning to spend millions building a modern capital while 70,000,000 Chinese are starving. The Nationalist Government is nothing but three or four war lords eating up the country."[5]

Pithy political invective was part of his appeal and also pointed to possibilities of elected public office. In the fall of 1929, American Legionnaires in Chester County, Pennsylvania, started a "Butler for Governor" boom with a dry reform bent. Smedley was wary, and his aunt Isabel Darlington, a lawyer experienced in public affairs, reported rumors that the "McClure gang" which "kept thy father in Congress, as thee knows, for many years," wanted Smedley for the Chester-Delaware congressional district. To this Smedley replied heatedly that he "would never tie myself up with that lousy low-brow [John] McClure . . . . I won't accept anything from him or his kind. In fact the only thing that would tempt me to enter a political contest would be to wipe out such animals as that fellow." He was above conventional party politics, despite knowing the odds from personal and cumulative family experience. Aunt Isabel also noted that state leaders may have "called upon McClure to sidetrack thee from *governor* to *Congress*." [6]

In the ensuing months he gauged his chances while traveling around the state giving lectures, and it became apparent there was little basis for an independent insurgency. His political posture at this point was a rehash from previous battles, emphasizing gang busting, suppression of crime, clean politics, and, as a general cathartic, prohibition. The dry commitment resurfaced as national news in September when he shut down the town of Quantico by declaring it off limits to his troops. After a strenuous week-long effort to drive out bootleggers, Butler and the mayor declared the town dry. He also testified before the presidential Wickersham Commission on Law Enforcement, and he was quoted in the press as having denounced existing liquor laws as class legislation while calling for a crackdown on big operators. He was again put forward by drys to be national prohibition enforcer. [7]

By December 1929 Butler had thus reestablished himself in the domestic American arena and in the Marine Corps as a colorful, outspoken public figure. With both his father and Lejeune departed from the scene, he had come back from China to find a comfortable niche within the Corps. A marine general at headquarters wrote Lejeune that Smedley was "still full of energy and of plans of all kinds. He has not changed." [8] Considering his strong position for succeeding to the commandancy as against dubious civilian political prospects, there seemed to be no compelling reason for him to burn his military bridges through acts of public defiance. And even if he wanted recklessly to test his Pennsylvania gubernatorial prospects, attacking U.S. foreign policy was hardly the right note. His first major public recantation must therefore be seen as spontaneous, emanating from the provocative, straight-shooting, impulsive candor with which he assailed his audiences on the lecture circuit.

Butler dropped his anti-imperialist bombshell on 5 December 1929 in an after-dinner speech before 700 guests at the Pittsburgh Builder's Exchange. Several days before, he declared that disarmament was "bunk," prompting a nationally syndicated columnist to remark, "He Goes Too Far." Now he told, topically, how marines had cynically rigged elections in Nicaragua in 1912, and how they had controlled the client president and manipulated politics in Haiti. The government was acutely sensitive to criticisms regarding its Caribbean protectorates because of a month-long uprising against the marine occupation in Haiti which, the next day, culminated in a ghastly massacre when a marine detachment was surrounded and ostensibly rushed by 1,500 angry peasants armed with stones, machetes, and clubs. Butler's statement received wide publicity and was strongly resented by the tightly reined Hoover administration, now much embarrassed by worldwide reaction to the Cayes massacre, which included calls for an investigation by the League of Nations and anti-imperialist attacks in Congress that compared America's role in Haiti with British and Japanese imperialism in India and Korea. President Herbert Hoover's Latin American "good neighbor" policy, which had been his cardinal diplomatic initiative, was in jeopardy. Strong measures were taken both to curb marine operations in Haiti and, more circumspectly, Butler.[9]

Newspaper reaction to Smedley's charges was generally favorable, reflecting prevaling anti-imperialist sentiment, and hostility toward administration moves to censure him. Under the lead "Butler Tells the Truth," the Reading, Pennsylvania, *Times* quoted him denouncing U.S. interventions in the Caribbean as "hypocritical and oppressive . . . a policy imposed by force and fraud," and then went on to editorialize that he had only "said what we all know. . . . the general is merely stating the facts when he says that in Latin American elections 'our candidates always win because their opponents are designated "bandits."'" A nationally syndicated editorial asked "Did He Spill The Beans?" and argued that "an inquiry is in order," but not into the speech, rather "into the actions of those responsible for the state of affairs that General Butler described." On the negative side, the Charleston, South Carolina, *Post* called him a "Master Blowhard" who had "let himself loose again," recalling the dastardly Williams court-martial in San Diego.[10]

Following veiled public indications of displeasure, Secretary of the Navy Charles Francis Adams called Butler on the carpet and gave him a stiff oral reprimand. The *New York Times* observed that the administration was apparently anxious not to magnify the incident further, and Adams announced that he was convinced the speech had been misrepresented. Behind the scenes, Marine Corps headquarters approached Smedley for an explanation to furnish friendly congressmen, and in an American Legion speech he said that "God made us the most influential nation in the world for a purpose . . . it is our duty to keep our neighboring nations from murdering one another." He would no longer get "stewed up" over the presence of marines in Haiti and Nicaragua, lest he be "called in to do some more explaining."[11]

His partial retraction was followed by a long period of discretion which confirmed that the Pittsburgh speech was reckless. He remained basically responsive to the official hierarchy, and in the months that followed went to great lengths trying to neutralize the damage done and reestablish himself within naval and administration circles.

Commandant "Buck" Neville, whose anticipated four-year term started in 1929, suffered a stroke in early 1930, and it soon became apparent that he might not recover sufficiently to resume his post. Already in April he observed that "the rumor has gotten around that I am down and out for good, particularly at that nest of rumors—Quantico." Word also reached Haiti, whence General John H. Russell wrote Admiral Mark L. Bristol, "If you receive any news verifying this, please take the opportunity of boosting me and my qualifications for the position among your friends in the Navy Department." [12] Bristol was currently sitting on the navy's General Board. As Neville's recovery dragged on with lingering partial paralysis, there were other maneuvers among rivals to the succession.

In late June, General Logan Feland, one of the four ranking aspirants, passed on to a friend with inside connections in the White House a letter from an unnamed "reliable" source to whom Neville had revealed his doctor's intention of surveying him for physical disability. The source predicted a fight for succession between Butler and Russell, with Russell supported by Adams, Secretary of State Henry L. Stimson, and most of the navy but otherwise politically discredited by the uprising in Haiti. Butler was reportedly backed by admirals from the China Station, and had "intimated that he would not object to [General Ben H.] Fuller getting the job for two years; after that he would take it." Feland commented that Fuller would have "sympathy from the Navy people, as an Annapolis graduate, but has never done anything to warrant his serious consideration." Feland concluded that he himself was "in a pretty good position with the struggle among the others getting more acute, especially as Mr. Ritchey [presidential secretary Lawrence Richey] will see that no decision is hastily made." But he did not want to make "a false move now" by approaching his navy supporters, presumably because it would be bad form with Neville still on the scene, "though I do not want to delay too long." Neville died on 8 July 1930. [13]

Butler and his supporters were not idle. A delegation from Pittsburgh went to the White House accompanied by Pennsylvania Senator David A. Reed and Secretary of Labor James J. Davis, and then called on Secretary Adams. According to Smedley, they brought "statements from many of the prominent men who attended this [Pittsburgh] dinner to the effect that I had not said one disloyal thing." Hoover assured them he knew Smedley's record well. Davis indicated that he would remain in Washington as cabinet-level liaison until the appointment was made. An officer in the Navy Department reported that Adams received 2,500 letters and telegrams on Butler's behalf. Supporters cabling Hoover included Josephus Daniels, Gifford Pinchot, and Lejeune. Smedley estimated that twenty-one senators and over a hundred congressmen acted on his behalf in what he characterized as "a show down between the Naval Academy element and those from civil life and the ranks." [14]

The odds were insurmountable. Fuller and Russell were both Academy graduates and had strong Navy and State Department support respectively, which counted for more than all Butler's congressional and public backing. He got an indication of his low standing in the naval establishment when Adams disparagingly inspected Quantico during the interregnum. Butler reportedly lost his temper and introduced him to a group of officers with the statement "Gentlemen, I want you to meet the Secretary of the goddam Navy." Smedley wrote his brother that "a well confirmed rumor has it that the Navy crowd believe that, if Fuller is named, I will retire—then they will offer to the Secretary of State my Major General's vacancy for General Russell and, in that way, the two favorites will be rewarded." While he would like to "get away from all this," if these were their plans he would not retire, but would "hold onto this commission for the next 15 years and block every Naval Academy man who comes around. Or at least, I will keep it long enough to block their little game." He had fifteen more years to mandatory retirement. It would take a court-martial to strip him of his rank and, subsequent misadventure to the contrary, he did "not intend to make any false steps and give them any loophole." [15] Had he been alive, General Barnett would no doubt have relished this moment.

Within the administration deliberations focused on Russell and Fuller. The State Department recommended Russell, acknowledging that longtime close collaboration resulted in his being correspondingly disliked in the navy and marines. A White House memorandum based on "contacts at the Navy Department" stated that both navy and marines "seem to be unanimous for General Fuller," with Feland second and no backing for Butler. Fuller was an Annapolis classmate of the new chief of naval operations "which can only tend to good results." He was senior to all the others in years of service but junior in rank. Within the Corps, unlike Butler, he probably had few enemies; one marine congratulating Fuller commented, "I know that many have heaved a sigh of relief, if you get what I mean." [16]

Fuller's selection was also characteristic of a trend to appoint what sociologist Morris Janowitz called "almost completely unknown organization men" as service chiefs during the peacetime era of the late 1920s and 1930s. Novelist C.S. Forester, in a 1936 characterization of British military politics, evoked the warrior viewpoint in referring to "the pliant subservient bootlicking type of general who always wins promotion under civilian command." [17] Bold resourceful aggressiveness, valued in wartime, was now anathema. The exception was Douglas MacArthur, who was installed as army chief of staff the same day as Fuller and was similarly promoted over a number of seniors, but even MacArthur in office acted like a timeserver. Butler, despite his disciplined and sensitive political performance in China, was still too much the "stormy petrel" to suit peacetime bureaucratic tendencies toward deferential mediocrity, particularly under President Hoover who personally disliked militarism. Smedley was hardly the ideal choice to represent, cap in hand, a curtailed and humbled military.

Denied the commandancy, Butler did not dig in for a prolonged sulk as major general *manqué*. In the letter in which he vowed to block Naval Academy rivals for the next fifteen years, he also alluded to a resilience that precluded anything like General Barnett's last stand as commander of the Pacific: "We must keep our faces to the Sun and out of the shadow. Keep our tails up and go on and what ever comes of this, it will be for the best in the end." Several months later he was making up his mind to retire. He met with Arthur Burks for advice, after which Burks wrote him thoughtfully summarizing the pros and cons. Burks observed that "the mental uncertainty which prompted you to ask me to that conference was totally unlike you," and came down in favor of early retirement and an offer from Joseph Alber's lecture bureau. Smedley had said that now he would never be commandant, and that the Corps was being ruined. Burks argued that he might stay in to try and save it. But there was the prospect of "leaping" from the "top of the heap" in the marines to "a neighboring heap which may be higher, if your legs are springy enough—which they won't be at sixty four." And if Smedley were to succeed his father in Congress, he would "be back in the driver's seat," with no military regulations to hamper him.[18]

With what he thought was almost half his life ahead of him, Butler decided to retire. The decision preceded the Mussolini incident. Being beaten at the top rung of command politics did not, however, mean he would go out quietly. Now definitely an outsider in Corps and navy politics, he continued in command at Quantico and resumed his extracurricular public speeches. Recent developments freed him from careerist constraints and from any need to defer meticulously to superiors. Despite not going out of his way to foment trouble, this fragile situation soon broke down, and he again ran afoul of brittle and maladroit chiefs in the Hoover administration.

In a speech on "how to prevent war" delivered to the Philadelphia Contemporary Club in January 1931, Butler related an anecdote about Italian Prime Minister Benito Mussolini while making the point that "mad-dog nations" could not be trusted to honor disarmament agreements. Butler recounted a story told him by an unnamed friend who had been taken by Mussolini for a high-speed automobile ride through the Italian countryside, in the course of which the dictator ran down a child and did not bother even to slow down: "My friend screamed as the child's body was crushed under the wheels of the machine. Mussolini put a hand on my friend's knee. 'It was only one life,' he told my friend. 'What is one life in the affairs of a State.'"[19]

The Italian government protested, Rome newspapers denounced the speech as "insolent and ridiculous," and Mussolini issued a categorical denial: "I have never taken an American on a motor-car trip around Italy, neither have I run over a child, man or woman." Secretary of State Stimson issued a formal apology to Mussolini for "discourteous and unwarranted utterances by a commissioned officer of this government on active duty." Smedley was placed under arrest and ordered court-martialed by President Hoover.[20]

The *New York Times*, in its lead story, characterized this as surprisingly severe and as yet another instance of the State Department dominating the navy. It was the first time a general officer in the U.S. services had been court-martialed since Major General Fitz John Porter was cashiered for disobedience of orders following a Union Army battle loss in 1862. More recently there had been the famous 1925 prosecution of Colonel Billy Mitchell, and the upcoming Butler trial promised similar fireworks. A cabinet officer warned Hoover that he could "see no profit in putting the Admirals up against a dashing Marine with a unique flair for publicity." And in a bizarre non sequitur, the Navy Department released a brochure, "The United States Navy in Peace Time," which included the commendation: "Probably no finer example of successful arbitration by American officers has been demonstrated in recent years than the peacemaking achievements that crowned General Butler's efforts in China in 1927 and 1928."[21]

With Butler and Mussolini as principals, public discussion was intense and replete with moral posturing. Senator James T. Heflin flaunted his congressional immunity, making Butler's court-martial seem petty and vindictive by contrast: Mussolini was a "red-handed murderer" to whom "General Butler must bow down and crawl in the dust and apologize to." Heflin entered into the *Congressional Record* three pages of mail backing Butler ("Don't let them degrade one of our finest and most courageous generals") and condemning the apology ("What we need in Washington are more Americans and less diplomats"), along with reportage from the New York antifascist newspaper *Il Nuovo Mondo* substantiating the hit-and-run charges.[22]

In Washington, according to the *New York Times*, the Butler case occupied "first rank in public interest." Theater crowds applauded heartily when his picture came on in newsreels, and showed "signs of disapprobation" at Mussolini and Stimson. The *Washington Daily News* featured an autobiographical series on Butler's life and ran doggerel championing "that blunt, outspoken devil-dog . . . the Ace of our Marines!" Ten days after the original speech Mussolini, now attempting to play the issue down, wired his ambassador in Washington to communicate "that I consider closed the incident, which, for my part, I have already forgotten." The episode, according to the historian of American reaction to Mussolini, "cast a shadow over the dictator's heretofore almost immaculate image."[23]

Outlook magazine, in a gossipy "Backstage Washington" survey of military staff officers, came up with solid pro-Butler sentiment, "except the bu-reaucratic bell boys." But few had "any personal sympathy for the famous 'devil dog,' since most of them look upon him as a bit of a braggart and a limelight lover." Two weeks later the same magazine, in an article entitled "The Bad Boy of the Marines," reported that the privates loved him. The author also dug up a quotation from Theodore Roosevelt referring to Smedley as "the ideal American soldier." [24]

Butler's informant turned out to be socialite journalist and world traveler Cornelius Vanderbilt, Jr. A lecture bureau chief declared that the story, based on what Vanderbilt had said to a meeting of the Affiliated Bureaus of America in New York, "was just as Vanderbilt told it to the last detail." Another bureau head agreed, as did members of the Reno Rotary Club and classes in journalism at the University of Nevada, who had heard essentially the same story during a recent Vanderbilt visit. The Italian Foreign Office, having denied Mussolini ever met Vanderbilt, searched its records and conceded that Mussolini received him in 1926 but "emphatically" reiterated that there had been no car ride. Vanderbilt himself refused comment and then evasively accused Butler of having "garbled" the story.[25]

Years later Vanderbilt substantially confirmed Smedley's version in *Farewell to Fifth Avenue* (1935) and *Man of the World: My Life on Five Continents* (1959). In the latter he related a four-day boisterous rip with Mussolini through northern Italy: "A small child standing on the right tried to beat the Fiat across the road. The car shuddered, and I felt the car wheels go up, then come down. I turned quickly to look. I can still see the little crumpled-up body lying in the road. Then I felt a hand on my right knee and I heard a voice saying, 'Never look back, Mr. Vanderbilt, never look back in life.'" [26] In effect, Butler's version was essentially correct, although based upon a somewhat shifty source. All this, however, was irrelevant to the court-martial, which focused on Smedley's deportment as an officer and gentleman, not on Mussolini's driving habits.

While under house arrest at Quantico, Butler procured Major Henry Leonard as counsel. Leonard had lost an arm in the Battle of Tientsin in 1900 shortly after rescuing Smedley and was now a successful Washington attorney, circumstances which made good press copy. A junior officer at Quantico went to see Butler at this time and was told a choice Tientsin anecdote: "One of the American civilians was hiding with the women under someplace or other. So they went and saw who it was, and it was this engineer chap. They hauled him up out of the hideout and put him on the wall and treated him rough. He [Butler] says, 'You know who that was? Herbert Hoover.'" Leonard reminded Smedley of the story. This tidbit, for what it was worth, was apparently bruited about as part of the deepening Butler-Hoover antagonism. After Smedley's release from arrest, the *Washington*

Herald reported him and Leonard playing "hide and seek all day with eager crowds that sought to catch a glimpse of the famous general." New York Governor Franklin D. Roosevelt, Josephus Daniels, and General James G. Harbord offered to testify in his behalf.[27]

Within the Cabinet, Secretary of State Stimson took the lead in pressing for maximum severity. In his diary he recorded having "made it rather uncomfortable for poor little Adams, who apparently was rather timid about ordering a court-martial on account of Butler's political influence. The President felt the way that [Secretary of War Patrick J.] Hurley and I did, and, if there is any backbone there, we will put something into it, I think." Several days later Stimson found Hoover "rather alarmed and worried about it . . . afraid it would make a great mess . . . some of the Boy Scouts [military?] had gotten hold of him and gotten him scared." Stimson urged firmness. When Hoover drafted a statement seeking to give Butler "an opportunity to let himself down easily, and opportunity for amends," Stimson advised him to stay out of it. But after two weeks, with hostile public reaction continuing to build up, Stimson himself came around to dropping the court-martial and pressured Adams, who was understandably concerned "that it might be thought a weakness," to back down.[28]

Negotiations between the State Department and Leonard started with an offer to drop formal charges in return for Butler's accepting a reprimand, detachment from command, and indefinite status awaiting orders. Leonard rejected this and subsequent more lenient offers. With the trial little more than a week away, Butler held the whip hand and State finally accepted his terms, which were that he and Leonard write the reprimand and that in all other respects he be restored to rank and privileges. He was also asked to submit a letter of apology, and this became the ultimate quid pro quo. Conspicuously, at no point was there any apology to Mussolini. When releasing the documents, Adams announced that Smedley had received milder punishment because of his "long record of brilliant service."[29]

Literary Digest ridiculed the reprimand in an article entitled "Our Comic Opera Court-Martial." In a private comment, Captain John H. Craige wrote Lejeune, "It is a little difficult to imagine the type of genius that thought of the plan to courtmartial a prominent and brilliant officer on such a charge." Craige was in Philadelphia, which had "been much excited over the Butler case, just as has the rest of the country only more so."[30]

Several months later the tables were turned when Butler asked Adams and the State Department to demand an apology from Haitian Minister Dantès Bellegarde. Bellegarde, commenting on one of Smedley's autobiographical articles, had pronounced that Fort Rivière did not exist. Behind the scenes, in a remarkable moment of smugness at the seat of American imperial power, Hoover discussed the incident with Stimson:

When I saw the President at the White House, he brought up that subject himself and told me confidentially that he had received a full account of the battle of Fort Riviera [sic], in Haiti, in which Butler got his Medal of Honor, and that the account he had received was not very flattering to Butler. It had come, however, from Dr. [Joel T.] Boone, and both the President and I know how accurate and trustworthy Boone is. The worst thing about the story was that after the fort had been captured, under Butler's orders fifty of the Haitians were put to death in cold blood. Boone was present and saw it, and the thing took place without any casualties on the part of the Marines; Boone being the medical doctor knew of that from personal contact.

Bellegarde was corrected by a spate of public denunciations, including one by Governor Roosevelt, who recounted the whole saga of the Medals of Honor.[31]

After the Mussolini affair, newspapers published long-standing rumors that Butler intended to resign and run for the Senate. He announced his retirement, to take effect in the fall, and set out on a lecture tour, with half his earnings committed to Philadelphia unemployment relief. In May he took a leave of absence to help organize the new Oregon state police on the principles of an apolitical, militarized, motorized, radio-equipped force to be composed of young unmarried men. Similarly, he continued to advocate a federal police force in his many speeches on crime and gangsterism.[32]

On 22 September 1931, with tears in his eyes and flanked by Governor Pinchot and Mayor Harry A. Mackey of Philadelphia, Smedley faced the troops at Quantico for the last time. A large number of friends and public figures were on hand for a brigade mobilization, air review, boxing smoker, dinner, dress parade, and the climactic lowering of his two-star flag. He loved the marines and had passionately involved himself in Corps affairs, to the extent of being able to recite from memory the names of all its commissioned officers.[33] But he had gone as far as he could.

He fired a parting shot in an article entitled "To Hell With the Admirals! Why I Retired at Fifty," published in *Liberty* magazine. He specified to Dimitman, who ghosted it, that he intended to "do a little swatting of some heads of some low-down-bums who tried to ruin my life for me." The article reviewed his long career, quoting from the many commendations and excellent fitness reports, and came to the conclusion, "Because I am not a Naval Academy man, a clique of admirals-without-ships determined that I should never be commandant of the Marine Corps." The chief of naval operations warily expressed admiration for Butler's record, and then replied, "It's all piffle—this talk about 'desk admirals.' . . . I can't think of a single one who would come under that category." President Hoover, in an earlier comment on Butler's retirement, had characterized him as "a very distinguished and gallant officer."[34]

In retirement he mainly avoided Marine Corps politics, and as a public figure dwelt upon larger issues of crime, gangsterism, imperialism, war, and peace. But on several occasions he made gestures to uphold the warrior ethos in the Corps that he saw being eclipsed by highbrow bureaucratism. In 1933 he wrote President Roosevelt supporting Brigadier General Harry Lee and the "class of Marines which is fast passing out, discouraged and broken in spirit." The Academy clique had destroyed his own career; now the "clique of favorites" was plotting to promote Brigadiers Dion Williams, who could make "no claim to soldierly distinction," and Russell, with Russell then favored for the commandancy. Both were junior to Lee, who in contrast had strong combat credentials as a regimental commander in France. Lee had written Butler complaining that the Academy faction had for years "been working to navalize the Corps, . . . hurdling the Academy men over our heads to retire them as Major Generals, not caring a damn what became of us."[35]

His efforts to thwart Russell's 1935 confirmation fixed Butler as the leading symbol of old-guard, anti-intellectual recalcitrance, just as Russell symbolized to Smedley and others all that was going wrong with the Corps. The central issue was Russell's 1934 success in obtaining a Marine Corps personnel act that allowed for "plucking" overaged and ostensibly incompetent officers and retiring them to make room for younger officers on the basis of merit—most readily attested to by educational credentials. Commandant Russell presided over the Selection Board, and inevitably made enemies, as had been the case with the 1919 Russell Board. Most victims were World War combat veterans up from the ranks who were deemed professionally unqualified for promotion and had created "humps" in the junior officer grades. The chance to turn the tables came in 1935 when Russell, a temporary major general as commandant, was up for promotion to permanent major general, which required confirmation by the Senate.

Butler came out of retirement as the most prominent marine opposing Russell, but he was probably not the instigator. There had always been opposition to Russell because of his long diplomatic stint in Haiti and favored status as the State Department's protégé. Harry Lee, one of Russell's rivals, wrote Lejeune in 1933 referring to "anticipated opposition from the Senate" to Russell's confirmation as commandant. Lejeune, from retirement, apparently played it both ways, backing Lee while later variously supporting and kicking Russell. He got Josephus Daniels, now ambassador to Mexico, to support Lee. Butler was in touch with Lee, but could do little. Then, a month before Russell's 1935 confirmation hearings, Smedley received an appeal from retired Colonel "Fritz" Wise asking, "Are you willing to help me chew John Henry Russell whose permanent Maj. Gen. is being held up.

I want the Water Works Vera Cruz brought out. Sens [Senators] King Utah & Black Ala [Alabama] are after him."[36]

Vera Cruz meant the El Tejar incident in 1914, which Smedley narrated to the hearings. The "Battle of Russell's Run" was widely disputed in the press and on the floor of the Senate. Senator Hugo Black stated that Russell had "surrendered or was about to surrender his battalion to one Mexican with a white flag," and Black's rendition reportedly "convulsed the Senate." Butler's version was supported by other eye-witness evidence, including a passage from Lejeune's memoirs in which he described rushing nine miles with reinforcements in answer to Russell's distress message, only to find no Mexicans. In response to repeated urging, Lejeune now wrote Senator Black that when he and Butler arrived, "everything was quiet and no hostile troops were in sight," and that "according to my recollection of the El Tejar incident, we considered it a joke." On Russell's behalf, an officer he had sent on reconnaissance cabled a statement that he and Russell had initially encountered "at least a squadron" of Mexican cavalry, but that they subsequently disappeared. Russell's daughter, assisted by *New York Times* reporter Arthur Krock, dug up and distributed 1914 newspaper clippings with headlines such as "Major Russell Defies Mexican."[37]

On the real issue, the decimation of overage officers who rose from the ranks, Butler testified in support of the egalitarian warrior ideal, defending Captain Cukela, the Medal of Honor winner who had figured prominently in the 1919-20 controversy and was now threatened with forced retirement: "To be sure his table manners are not good, but it was my impression we were not running a knitting society." Lejeune supported Russell, praising merit selection and denouncing the old seniority system as one in which "the meritorious, the energetic, and the able have been smothered, very often, by the worthless, the lazy and the stupid."[38]

Butler felt he had done everything he could to "end this outrageous regime," but his attack on Russell was ineffective, a last hurrah for warrior standards that were diminishing in importance at marine headquarters and as a factor in congressional politics. And it is doubtful that Smedley expected to reverse the trend. For him it was a brief digression from other commitments, and not part of any elaborate vendetta. Afterward, he wrote to General Lee's wife: "What I did before the Senate Naval Committee was in the interest of my old friends. I only wish I had the power to help them all but I am entirely out with this administration and in fact—have no political friends."[39]

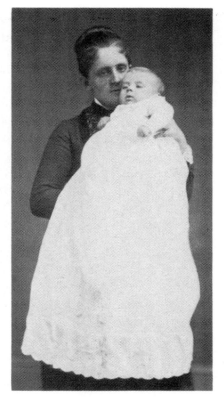

Above left, Pennsylvania Congressman Thomas Stalker Butler, father of Smedley D. Butler, about 1890s. Above right, Maud Mary Darlington Butler holds her infant son Smedley, probably in his christening robe. Left, Smedley at about age eight.

Unless otherwise indicated all photos are courtesy of Thomas R. Butler.

Above, Smedley, center, is surrounded by the family of his maternal grandfather, Smedley Darlington. Directly behind him stands his father. At right in the second row are his mother and his brother Samuel. Left, the newly enlisted cadet, 1898.

Above, Butler's company at Portsmouth, New Hampshire, upon return from Cuba, 1898. Captain Goodrell is at left (with mustache), Lieutenant Butler at right. Below, Butler (rear center) is surrounded by naval officers aboard the USS *Brooklyn,* about 1900.

Captain Butler in dress uniform, about 1900.

Left, Butler and his fiancée, Ethel Conway Peters ("Bunny"), pose for their engagement picture, 1904. Below, Captain and Mrs. Butler with their wedding party, Bay Head, New Jersey, June 1905. The best man, Lieutenant Colonel Waller, is behind and immediately to the left of Butler.

Above, Camp Elliott, Panama, 1910, with officers' bungalows in the background. Below, rebel soldiers march in the streets of León, Nicaragua, 1912. Both from National Archives.

Above, marines move mule-drawn artillery through Veracruz, Mexico, in 1914. Below, marine officers in Veracruz: from left, front row, Wendell C. Neville, John A. Lejeune, Littleton W. T. Waller, Butler, and R. C. Berkeley. Both from National Archives.

Left, two marines guard a captured Haitian during the *caco* campaign, 1915-1919. Below, Haitian President Philippe Sudre Dartiguenave and his cabinet are flanked by U.S. marines, 1919. Both from National Archives.

Above, soldiers on their way home to the States await chow at Camp Pontanezen, France, 1919 (National Archives). Below, mud at Camp Pontanezen was made passable by laying sections of duckboards. Butler carried one in himself, earning the nickname "General Duckboard."

Ethel and Smedley Butler at home in West Chester, Pennsylvania, about 1920, with their children: Ethel "Snooks," Thomas R. (center), and Smedley, Jr. (in front).

Below, a crowd of onlookers on the run at the Wilderness battle reenactment near Chancellorsville, 1921 (National Archives).

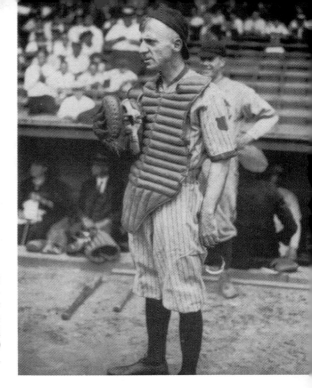

Butler encouraged sports by playing on the police baseball team in Philadelphia, 1924-1925 (right), and by leading cheers (below) at a Marine Corps-American Legion football game, Philadelphia, about 1930 (Defense Department photo).

Left, Generals Butler and John A. Lejeune at a marine baseball game, Griffith Stadium, Washington, D.C., 1923 (National Archives).

Below, Butler, in charge of Philadelphia's police force, 1924–1925, confers with Superintendent William B. Mills.

Butler reviews British troops in Shanghai, April 10, 1927.

Butler and a Nationalist Chinese general congratulate each other at the 1928 ceremonial opening of a joint Sino-American highway project supervised by marines.

Presentation of the Thousand Blessings Umbrellas, Tientsin, September 1928.
National Archives.

Butler with General Wendell C. Neville addresses the troops at Quantico, 1929.
National Archives.

Above, Philadelphia Mayor Harry A. Mackey attends Butler's retirement ceremony at Quantico, 1931 (Defense Department photo).
Below, one of Butler's many antiwar speeches during the 1930s.

Above, a relaxed Butler at home in Newtown Square, Pennsylvania, Christmas 1933. Below, Mrs. Butler presents her late husband's sword to General Lemuel C. Shepherd, Jr., Marine Commandant, at Sundown Parade, Marine Headquarters, in 1953. Behind her are sons Thomas R. Butler and Smedley D. Butler, Jr. Daughter Ethel Butler Wehle is behind Smedley, Jr.

15 Renegade Marine

AMERICA IN THE 1930s

During his final months on active duty in 1931 and continuing into civilian life, Butler worked the lecture circuit with urgency and vigor. Publicity organized by professional lecture bureaus touted him as "one of the most picturesque and dynamic personalities in American life today." A flyer signed by radio personality Lowell Thomas ballyhooed him as "a stick of human dynamite . . . [a] Major General who would as leave spit in your eye as look at you." He used his own material, based upon "unique and thrilling experiences," and scorned subterfuge. "He indulges in none of the circuitous and tortuous manner of speaking that passes, in these days of compromise and straddle, as diplomacy." An Indiana paper announced his imminent arrival with the headline "Gen. Butler, Marine Firebrand, Soon to Speak Here, 'Wears No Man's Collar.'" His two set topics, open-ended because of his discursive style, were "Blowing the Lid Off Crime," and "Thirty-two Years with the Marines." [1]

His mannerisms were appropriately histrionic. He roamed the stage, sat on the lecturn table, flailed his arms, and one listener recalled that "he would scratch his head with the left hand and rub his backside at the same time with his right unknown to him." At home he complained his jackets were too tight in the shoulders, and he often spoke in shirtsleeves. [2]

Half his earnings went to Philadelphia unemployment relief during early 1931; charity receipts in his papers totaled $3,315 for April to June, a substantial sum during the Great Depression. After retirement in the fall he reverted to paying his mortgage. But politics remained in the offing. In an interview set against rumors of his candidacy in the upcoming 1932 elections, he outlined a plan for coping with the depression. Predicting violent revolution otherwise, he called for taxing the rich to finance unemployment relief through national school and road construction programs, plus government subsidies for inventions and budding industries. [3] He then set out on a western tour, making sixty speeches across the country.

He returned home for his daughter's marriage to marine aviator Lieutenant John Wehle, the only occasion after retirement that he wore his marine uniform. In March 1932 he announced his candidacy in the Republican primary for the Senate seat held by James J. Davis, who was running as a

wet supported by the Vare machine and the regular Republican state organization. Butler entered the fray "as a dry and you can spell it out in capital
letters, 'D-R-Y,'" and described his candidacy as "a Pinchot-Marine Corps
baby."[4] Governor Gifford Pinchot, serving his second term as an independent Republican, was trying to build up an insurgent state organization,
possibly as basis for an attempt to topple President Hoover at the Republican National Convention in June. He was also interested in leading a national third party along the lines of Pennsylvania's "Little New Deal"—a
program of welfare spending and reform, plus familiar attacks on boss rule,
concentrations of wealth, and demon rum, that Pinchot had kept up since
Bull Moose days. Davis, a former Cabinet member, was loyal to the president. Prohibition remained a lively issue in Republican politics and was the
main point of contention at their upcoming convention, despite the urgency
of the depression. Butler led the Pinchot ticket in the present exercise,
which also featured Mrs. Pinchot running unsuccessfully for Congress. The
Republican primary was tantamount to election; no Democrat had been
elected to the Senate from Pennsylvania since the 1870s.

The campaign was brief and the voters' verdict emphatic. In addition to
rallying the dry crusade at a time when *Literary Digest* polled 70 percent of
Pennsylvanians favoring repeal, Butler came out strongly for the veterans'
bonus, a losing issue with this economically conservative electorate. He
campaigned hard, making 167 speeches in less than four weeks—hitting out
at unemployment and "big New York financiers," urging government aid for
the poor, and opposing war. The *Philadelphia Record* reported him returning
from a statewide swing spouting "damns" and "hells" and looking tired, "his
hair . . . disheveled, his voice near the breaking point." He lost decisively, by
a two-to-one margin statewide, and by 280,000 to 98,000 in Philadelphia.
He himself termed it a "big drubbing."[5]

There were a few twists and turns in this seemingly straightforward
disaster. On the one hand, Smedley was the unalloyed Pinchot candidate.
The governor stumped through the state with him and he received almost
all his financial support through the Pinchot organization. After the election
regular Republicans raised charges of improprieties, and Philadelphia's
Democratic newspaper alleged that the "famous 'Two-Percent Club,' made
up of state officeholders" had contributed $250,000 to Butler's campaign.
In response to a U.S. Senate inquiry, Smedley replied he had been off on a
speaking tour from the outset until election day and "was not in any way in
touch with the campaign chairman," nor did he recall having even been told
the name of the treasurer, and he knew nothing about monies contributed
or spent. This is plausible. He was not a professional, had no organization
of his own, and had previously been on the lecture circuit for many months.[6]

But his total dependence upon the Pinchot organization raised the suspicion, in view of the severe defeat, that as the election approached Pinchot

scuttled Butler to cut his losses. Throughout the state Butler trailed lesser Pinchot candidates and in some districts state senators won while Smedley lost, prompting the *Philadelphia Record* to mention "evidence that the local Pinchot leaders had concentrated on an attempt to take control of the party organization rather than on the election of Butler." In the same vein, alluding to "Pinchotism, with its despicable political chicanery," the head of the Pennsylvania Division of Women's Organization for National Prohibition stated, "This poor, futile, misguided soldier, floundering in the midst of political maneuvers he could not understand, was never anything but a straw figure raised by Pinchot and labelled 'dry.'" A Pinchot county leader wrote Smedley that "real men like yourself were sacrificed by meddling with local affairs." The "slimy brood" with which Pinchot had cast his lot remained in control.[7]

Butler thought he had been sold out, and privately referred to a "sordid tale of desertion on the part of my backers." He wrote his former aide Ray A. Robinson that Pinchot had shifted votes to Davis in return for electing Pinchot delegates to the National Convention. "No, Torchy, it was a mystifying affair and I was like a sheep being led to the slaughter." Next time he would battle on his own behalf, "without any strange flag flying over the advancing army."[8]

The rather dismal defeat was Butler's lone run for elected office. As with earlier setbacks, conclusive defeat in civilian politics freed him from another tangle of demands and constraints. Raiding Philadelphia's big hotels after his break with Mayor Kendrick, and "To Hell with the Admirals" after denial of the marine commandancy were harbingers of defiance to come. To Robinson he professed, "Just between us, I don't like politics as it is now played; and it actually made me sick to think of being U.S. Senator." He had let it be known that he did not want to be governor or anything beneath senator.[9] More and more he was an outsider beholden only to his own beliefs, to the audiences that attended his lectures and read his writings, and to the broader public credibility necessary to keep him afloat as an entertainer and free-lance dissident. His political views shifted ever more outspokenly toward a radical critique of contemporary events.

This meant defiance toward the powers that be, and the chance to enunciate maverick tendencies previously hedged. His natural audience were the enlisted ranks, whom he could reach by leadership that had made him a famous soldiers' general. Now he could fully indulge in the egalitarian rapport in which that style of leadership thrived, attacking the hypocrisies of rank and power that he had long resented. This was not failure, but the living realization of a romantic ideal. Was the "stormy petrel" of the Marine Corps going to fade away into respectable old general's retirement? Answering mail in the aftermath of his election defeat, while his wife puttered around the house, Butler complained to Robinson that he was "bored stiff.

I guess Torchy, you and I were cut out to be pirates and the civilized drone-like life is not to my liking." [10]

In July he denounced the "Tory Group" which, "through its wealth, its power and its influence," controlled the government, and went to Washington as guest of the veterans' Bonus Expeditionary Force (B.E.F.). Encamped in squatter hovels on the Anacostia flats, the 1932 Bonus March was an attempt by 20,000 destitute veterans, many accompanied by their families, to pressure the government into immediate payment of World War veterans' cash benefits not due until 1945. The Senate overwhelmingly defeated the enabling Patman bill, but the veterans stayed on much to the consternation of the beleaguered Hoover administration. Butler's arrival in mid-July, by which time tensions had built up considerably, came on the eve of the official eviction, which nine days later culminated in the famous military rout. Smedley, according to the *New York Times*, "evoked tremendous applause when he mounted an improvised stand," and with a "damn" and "hell" every few words, urged the vets to stick it out: "You hear folks call you fellows tramps, but they didn't call you that in '17 and '18. I never saw such fine soldiers. I never saw such discipline. . . . You have as much right to lobby here as the United States Steel Corporation. . . . This is the greatest demonstration of Americanism ever seen." [11]

According to the War Department's intelligence report, the speech was somewhat demagogic and inflammatory, but he also "carefully advised the men to obey all the laws." A transcript included brief allusions to class conflict: "One class believes that the country was made for them. The other class would like to come in some how. A few people on one side, and the great masses on the other." Butler and his son Smedley, Jr., spent the night in a tent and shared meals with the men. The general gave another pep talk the next day, cautioning the veterans to "keep your sense of humor" lest belligerence cost them the considerable public sympathy they had already won. [12]

On 28 July army units including cavalry marshaled on the Ellipse outside the White House, where Butler's marines had parked their artillery during a football game a decade earlier, and proceeded to break the B.E.F. Soldiers ran down ex-soldiers in a travesty that cast doubt upon current official standards of loyalty and legitimacy, and raised the specter of anti-government paramilitarism akin to fascist prototypes in Europe. Callous statements afterward by President Hoover and other high officials marked a low point in public disrepute for the Hoover administration.

In the days that followed, 6,000 disillusioned veterans set up a rump B.E.F. camp at Johnstown, Pennsylvania, and newspapers carried rumors that Butler might assume leadership of the Khaki Shirts, a paramilitary force for economic justice. He denied any knowledge or inclination, and urged the veterans to go home for the safety of their families. But he continued to support the bonus staunchly in speeches and articles, writing in late 1932 that the real "treasury raiders" were not the soldiers, but the industrialists who during the war had pocketed "millions of dollars worth of patriotism . . . on a ten per cent plus cost basis."[13]

Declaring himself a "Hoover-for-Ex-President Republican," Smedley used the bonus issue and the army's gas attack in routing the B.E.F.—recalling infamous gas warfare during the Great War—to disparage Hoover during the 1932 general elections. He came out for the Democrats "despite the fact that my family for generations has been Republican," and shared the platform when Republican Senator George W. Norris opened a coast-to-coast stump for Franklin D. Roosevelt in Philadelphia. Butler made about forty speeches abusing the Republicans, but mostly outside Pennsylvania; his recent defeat in the Senate primary made him a dubious asset to the Democrats.[14]

Butler also figured in the contest in a more obscure way. A file in Hoover's papers entitled "1932 Presidential Campaign, General Smedley Butler's smear and facts" contains testimonials to Hoover's bravery at the siege of Tientsin in 1900. A draft document, dated 2 September 1932 but unsigned, begins: "I have observed General Butler's reckless and malicious statements as to Mr. Hoover's conduct during the siege," and goes on to give an eye-witness account attesting to "Mr. Hoover's courage and devotion." It is unclear whether Butler publicly revealed the allegations of Hoover's cowardice or whether Hoover was getting ready just in case.[15]

Butler was pleased with election results that saw Hoover crash to defeat. He had exerted himself in the campaign more "to get rid of Hoover than to put in Roosevelt," and to "square a debt." FDR, his old Haiti ally, was a "nice fellow" and might make a good president, but Smedley did not expect much influence with the new administration. In a reflection on the many years when he had been a political insider, he did offer to try and help his marine son-in-law: "I was a fool for not getting everything I could while your Grandfather Butler lived and had power. Instead of which I did all the nasty jobs that came along. Never had a day's duty in Washington from the time I was a Second Lieutenant in 1898 until I retired."[16] But he was now beyond the pale politically, a renegade from an insurgent faction of a defeated party.

In 1933 Butler published the book-length autobiography *Old Gimlet Eye: The Adventures of Smedley D. Butler as Told to Lowell Thomas*, written in the first person in collaboration with the popular adventure writer and radio commentator. Thomas first made his mark by discovering and promoting Lawrence of Arabia, and his collaboration promised that *Gimlet Eye* would be a similarly genuine epic. While often extravagant, it was based to a great extent on Butler's letters which his family had saved over the years. Butler had, indeed, long been mining this material. The collaboration involved one of Thomas's research assistants who spent three weeks at Quantico in 1931 taking Smedley's dictation. Thomas did the rewrite.[17]

Old Gimlet Eye, like the rest of Butler's adventure writings, was part of a genre literature that romanticized military exploits and strident manliness against a backdrop of exotic settings. Little attention was paid to political or material interests being served, or to the implicit misfortunes of invaded peoples, who were often ridiculed and patronized. There was little sense of spreading progress and civilization that to some extent leavened the popular literature of British imperialism—and Butler's own private letters and congressional testimony regarding colonial affairs. *Old Gimlet Eye* was somewhat circumspect, but other Butler pieces, such as the aforementioned *Walter Garvin in Mexico* (1927), were not. The *New York Times* reported all Honduras aroused to wrath by his 1931 article "Opera-Bouffe Revolts: What Usually Happens When the Marines Have Landed."[18]

Butler was producing for a highly articulated and competitive potboiler market, access to which was controlled by commercial publishers who demanded salability. He did fuss over accuracy, as when he deliberated with Dimitman over who shot a Haitian *caco* at Fort Rivière, but his motives were unabashedly mercenary.[19] His collaborators were all professionals who knew the game and produced to the required formulas. This explains the ongoing production of pulp swashbucklers into the early 1930s, overlapping with the serious purposefulness, particularly the antiwar stance, that marked his output thereafter. Nor was the contradiction as great as it might seem.

Butler retained an aura of red-blooded American heroism that reinforced his credibility throughout the strenuous anti-imperialist apostasy that followed. This was sustained by his thorough familiarity with and faithfulness to popular military mores, as demonstrated in the pulp adventure stories and by his ongoing personification of the warrior style in speech and action. His ongoing commitment to the warrior style was also crucial in helping him keep his bearings in the confusing flux of 1930s popular politics, and in crystalizing his own presentation of basically traditional military values.

Butler was also "quite a character," and he can be seen moving the hero archetype away from the strong, silent, emotionally aloof type to a more voluble and, for the times, politically relevant gadfly activism. This was particularly true as he attacked elite cliques in the American Legion and elitist managerial trends in the military. The warrior champion had to be seen effectively battling vested interests and entrenched bureaucrats. Butler was thus recasting popular military values even as he helped sustain them. Of course, stolidity remained a viable popular ideal, notably in the Hollywood escapist sense: to suffer quietly and loyally and not rock the boat. In the Marine Corps Butler's devil-dog updating of the warrior image had similarly introduced a new assiduousness that was rather more colorful and contentious than the traditional strong, stolid type. As a renegade in the 1930s, he went on to turn the patriotic-warrior rite, of which he was a leading popular exemplar, into a convincing vehicle for dissent against the seriously compromised social-class hierarchy. Butler the radical antiwar crusader had found a new cause worthy of his romantic-warrior prestige and battling instincts. That was still quite recognizably "Old Gimlet Eye" the dime novel hero up there on the peace platform, hectoring his audiences.

In his speeches he presented himself as military adventurer and crime fighter, a man of action true to the Victorian heroic ideal. But the heyday of the imperialist adventurer was passing fast, and Butler's credibility before skeptical, sullen audiences of the 1930s demanded straight talk, the ring of truth that, from a decorated high official of a tarnished regime, came most naturally and cleanly through defiant apostasy. This, for the times, was integrity, and the role suited Butler perfectly. His bravery as a soldier was beyond dispute. As a firebrand who had recklessly burned himself in a long succession of public controversies, he spoke with obvious conviction. As a former insider and ranking military proconsul, he was an authoritative critic commanding attention and respect.

Lecture-circuit publicity and press notices highlighted his two Congressional Medals of Honor and high military rank. Trappings of conventional authority were necessary to legitimize dissent, given the dearth of intrinsic working-class leadership or American tradition of respectable class conflict. Workers shied from identifying themselves as such in a political culture dominated by bourgeois norms. Bonus Marchers were first and foremost veterans clinging to the flag. Unemployment remained a personal disgrace. Even trade unionism, narrowly committed to self-interest in accordance with prevailing business ethics, was held in general disrepute as a form of unseemly agitation from below. Radical mass leadership in the 1930s remained inhibitively construed in terms of middle-class condescension, or even, if one includes President Roosevelt, upper-class noblesse oblige. All the notable popular demagogues were conspicuously dignified by tokens of bourgeois respectability: Father Coughlin, Dr. Townsend, Reverend Gerald L.K. Smith, Senator Huey Long, and Major General Smedley Butler. Just as the others flouted conventional proprieties of rank and stature to embrace the masses, so did Butler the soldiers' general.

Butler addressed himself particularly to the four and one-half million veterans who, with their vested interest in unredeemed bonus certificates, their memories of military service and camaraderie, and their several patriotic fraternal organizations, constituted a potential political and paramilitary force. This was popular politics, not militarism—certainly a far cry from amoral, elitist, authoritarian military professionalism. But it was militaristic to the extent that the American Legion, Veterans of Foreign Wars (VFW), and similar organizations indulged in uniform caps, medals and service ribbons, flags, parades, paramilitary command hierarchies, and patriotic self-justifications. In a society in which government and political parties tended heavily to preclude and preselect choices offered to the general public, the veterans organizations offered the possibility of direct democratic participation and perhaps concerted action by a national mass membership consisting mainly of former enlisted men. As the Bonus March suggested, popular politics and things military were not stark alternatives, but fortuitous conjuncts given the right time and circumstances. Mass propaganda and popular mobilization during the recent Great War had established numerous precedents, of which the veterans movements were living reminders.

Butler appealed to the vets with gruff directness punctuated by "damns" and "hells," offending obscenity standards to the extent that sometimes he was cut off the air during radio broadcasts. He repeatedly reaffirmed his commitment to the rank-and-file and to physical bravery, consistent with his lifelong preference for roughneck soldiering. This now took on definite class-conflict overtones. Taking swipes at the current top brass—a vulnerably pompous lot, at least by contrast with Butler—struck a resonant chord during these hard times. So did his ongoing fight for the bonus, which he and others justified as back pay for soldiers who had gone off to fight and die while civilians enjoyed high salaries at home. "This is just a two-cent medal," he said as he decorated thirty veterans with Purple Hearts during Memorial Day ceremonies at Passaic, New Jersey; "the great advantage is that even [financier J.P.] Morgan can't buy one." He told a veteran who was getting $10 a month compensation for a battlefield wound, "How many of the 'favorite crowd' would sell their legs for $10 a month?" [20]

It was true that he made a good living off the veterans' circuit with speeches at several hundred dollars each, but he was also plunging boldly into their factional disputes. In doing so, he incited them with his famous command presence, reviling them as the "dumbest crew on earth" for allowing themselves to be manipulated and used. This was a sore point, because whether or not his rousing projection that the veterans and their families could muster twenty million votes was true, it was apparent that until now they were a quite marginal political force, and even as such had served mainly as occasional strong-arm auxilliaries for ultrapatriotic, reactionary, and antilabor causes. American Legion units had been conspicuous as strikebreakers, nativist vigilantes, and antipacifist, antisubversive bullies, dating back to the Legion's origins under right-wing auspices in 1919. Butler objected to this—except in his role as crime-fighting expert where, perhaps facetiously, he advocated organizing unemployed veterans into an "Anti-Crime Legion" so that the federal government could employ them in "an offensive war against the underworld." [21]

Tackling the political issue, he blasted the so-called Royal Family of financiers that controlled the Legion. Speaking to members of the more restive and openly dissident VFW in New Orleans in December 1932, on the same platform with Huey Long appealing for "share the wealth," he repeated a mutinous attack he had made at a Legion convention in Cincinnati: "I said that I had never known one leader of the American Legion who had never sold them out—and I mean it." The Royal Family was maneuvering the Legion into supporting the gold standard, then advocated by certain Wall Street interests in opposition to inflationary New Deal monetary policies. Butler told the New Orleans veterans not to be taken in; "What the hell do you know about the gold standard? You stand by your friends and to hell with the rest of them." As for Wall Street, it should pay their bonuses: "I believe in making Wall Street pay for it—taking Wall Street by the throat and shaking it up."[22]

A year later in Atlanta, he began a tour of VFW posts on the invitation of its commander, fellow-Pennsylvanian James E. Van Zandt, whom he boosted as honest in contrast to Legion leadership. Denouncing war as "largely a matter of money" to profit the privileged classes, he cautioned the vets not to believe "the propaganda capital circulates. Capital owns all the newspapers." Politically, he advised skepticism: "Democrats take care of you, keep them in—if not, put 'em out." The speech was reported to FDR's political adviser Louis Howe by an operative who made behind-the-scenes inquiries into Butler's schedule of twenty VFW speeches around the country at $250 each. Butler had been "approached by a representative of the bankers gold group" and offered $750 extra per speech if he would make favorable references to the gold standard. "This would have meant an additional ten thousand dollars to General Butler, but he told the representative of the gold group that even if he were offered a hundred thousand dollars to do this, his answer would be 'no.'" While he did not personally know Butler, the operative commented that rejection of the bribe "shows him to be a man of exceptional character."[23]

Butler's dealings with the "bankers gold group" extended from the summer of 1933 until September 1934, and climaxed in his November exposé of an alleged plot by Wall Street interests to topple President Roosevelt and establish a dictatorship. The story broke in the *New York Post* and *Philadelphia Record* under the banner headline "GEN. BUTLER CHARGES FASCIST PLOT," and revealed what purported to be Butler's testimony to a closed session of the House Un-American Activities Committee (HUAC) in New York. Financiers led by broker Grayson M.-P. Murphy and Singer sewing machine heir Robert Sterling Clark had raised $3 million, with more in the offing, and approached Butler to lead an army of 500,000 veterans to overthrow the government in a bloodless coup. FDR would be persuaded to put Butler in charge of Civilian Conservation Corps camps which were to serve as support facilities during a paramilitary phase. Had Butler declined the role of man on the white horse, Chief of Staff Douglas MacArthur and then

Hanford MacNider, a former American Legion commander, were said to be next in line. Other former Legion commanders were mentioned as co-conspirators.[24]

The *New York Times* added rumors, heatedly denied by Butler, that he had told friends that General Hugh S. Johnson was slated to be dictator and that J.P. Morgan & Company was involved. The *Times*' brief sketch of Butler's charges was followed by an authoritative "chorus of denials" which took up most of the two-column front page lead, conveying an impression of skepticism. An editorial the next day dismissed the whole story as "a gigantic hoax." Morgan partner Thomas W. Lamont called it "perfect moonshine." MacArthur referred to it as "the best laugh story of the year." Murphy said it was a "damned lie," and Clark threatened a libel suit. Gerald C. MacGuire, a Murphy & Company employee whom Butler named as intermediary, called it a "publicity stunt." On the other hand, Van Zandt, head of VFW, stated in Helena that Butler had told him about the plot two months previously, and that he had also been approached. Congressman John W. McCormack announced that HUAC had been investigating for five weeks. Co-Chairman Samuel Dickstein, dismissed by *Time* magazine as "publicity-loving," said that "from present indications, General Butler has the evidence. . . . We will have some men here with bigger names than Butler's before this is over."[25]

The sensation in the news media discouraged systematic investigation or discreet procedures, and everyone involved played to the galleries from the start. Moreover HUAC, even in these relatively scrupulous early days—stalking both Communists and Fascists—was itself engaged mainly in trial by publicity. There was no serious prospect of formal legal proceedings. The committee was powerless, Dickstein acknowledged privately, to compel witnesses to appear or produce documents. When McCormack was asked whether Robert Sterling Clark, who was in Europe, might be extradited to testify, he replied, "There's no question of extradition. No crime has been committed. Under our law, you can go ahead and form any organization you want."[26]

From Butler's perspective, the flourish of publicity suited his militant extrovert style and limited outsider's options—although later he told J. Edgar Hoover of the Federal Bureau of Investigation (FBI) that he informed HUAC he had reported the plot to the Treasury Department's Secret Service, apparently to no avail.[27] Butler was a loner with no organizational base. He was well aware of the extent to which public facades of propriety and calm masked manipulations by the rich and powerful. But during the 1930s, revelations of failure and scandal had tended to discredit many conventional illusions. From the perspective of more complacent times, Butler might have seemed a disgruntled loser; now there was something wildly heroic in his defiance. His protagonists in the present scrap—Wall Street brokers, their legal counselors, and shrewd political operatives—were backed by a supporting network that extended into veterans' affairs, politics, and the right-wing press. For Smedley this had become a war of attrition. In September he told the story to Paul Comly French, investigative reporter for the liberal J. David Stern newspapers—the *Record*, *Post*, and two Camden sheets. French interviewed the intermediary, MacGuire, and appeared before HUAC as a corroborating witness.

The story that Butler and French told under oath to the committee necessarily centered on MacGuire. Smedley related in impressive detail how MacGuire, first accompanied by another legionnaire, William H. Doyle, had contacted him repeatedly over the previous year and a half regarding Legion political intrigues. Initially, Butler was to accompany several hundred Pennsylvania legionnaires to the Chicago national convention, where they would be strategically placed on the convention floor to start a demonstration while he read a speech favoring the gold standard. MacGuire gave Smedley a copy of the speech and showed him bankbooks with deposits of $42,000 and $64,000. He offered to pay all expenses, and subsequently identified his sponsors as Murphy, by whom he was otherwise employed as a $100-a-week bond salesman, and multimillionaire Clark. In September 1933, when Butler refused the offer and accused him of bluffing, MacGuire threw down a wad of $1,000 bills on a Newark hotel bed, saying it was $18,000. Butler countered that this was an ensnarement, numbered bills to implicate him, and insisted on dealing directly with MacGuire's superiors.[28]

Several days later Butler wrote MacGuire that the Newark proposal was "a great idea" and he would have no difficulty getting a hundred legionnaires. There must be "positive assurance of financial support" and no "slip-up in the arrangements, particularly in the matter of paying their expenses and treating them properly." He proposed that MacGuire stage a fight on the convention floor to have him invited to speak, in which case he would fly to Chicago. "If I am to be of any value to the cause you sponsor, I would necessarily have to have some position. All of this would be lost if I force my way into this part through an imitation delegateship."[29] This letter is one of the few relevant items in Butler's papers. In the light of his subsequent testimony and HUAC documentation, he was presumably playing along with the scheme in order to draw out its sponsors.

Whereupon Clark, according to Butler's HUAC testimony, made the pilgrimage to Newtown Square. Smedley had known him briefly during the Boxer campaign in 1900 as the "millionaire lieutenant" serving with the army. Clark offered to pay off the mortgage on Butler's house and provide a private railroad car to take him to Chicago for the gold speech. The rationale for the veterans was that their bonuses would be paid in sound money.

Smedley refused and berated Clark for trying to bribe him. Clark backed down, and using Smedley's phone gave instructions that neither he nor Butler would be at the convention, and to send telegrams instead.[30]

Butler noted that the Legion convention, after receiving a flood of telegrams, endorsed the gold standard but not the bonus. MacGuire turned up again to offer $1,000 and a private car for making a gold speech in Boston, but Smedley declined. MacGuire went to Europe in early 1934, then the two met in August and MacGuire allegedly unfolded plans for a coup. He had observed European veterans' movements, particularly in France, and proposed something similar. There would be $3 million to start with and $300 million later. Destitute captains would be paid $35 a month, privates $10. After the coup, a Secretary of General Welfare would supersede FDR in the national interest; all was to be patriotic and there was no need for violence. MacGuire, according to Butler, described Smedley's pivotal role: "The Morgan interests say that you cannot be trusted, that you will be too radical, and so forth, that you are too much on the side of the little fellow; you cannot be trusted. They do not want you. But our group tells them that you are the only fellow in America who can get the soldiers together. They say, 'Yes, but he will get them together and go in the wrong way.'"[31]

French testified that during their interview MacGuire baldly advocated a Fascist government to save the country from communism. As for the existing government, "we might go along with Roosevelt and then do with him what Mussolini did with the King of Italy." Butler could organize a million men overnight; half the Legion and half the VFW would join.[32]

A great deal obviously depended upon how much the committee could get out of the middleman MacGuire, and to what extent he could be convincingly linked to alleged sponsors. He was a slippery witness. A short, pudgy, middle-aged man with what the *Record* described as "a plaintive voice with a faint East Side accent," MacGuire repeatedly perjured himself. He admitted meeting Butler eight or nine times, initially as a member of the Legion's distinguished guest committee to see if Smedley would favor the sound dollar and run for commander of the Legion. Together with Doyle, he proposed the gold resolution at the Chicago convention and sent ninety-nine telegrams. But he flatly denied just about everything else and was badly compromised by the committee's investigations into his bank accounts, by his movements as traced by hotel bookings, and then by the testimony of Clark's attorney who ran MacGuire as legman for the Committee for a Sound Dollar and Sound Currency. For instance, HUAC investigators established that MacGuire was in Newark and in possession of a large number of thousand-dollar bills on the date specified by Butler, and not in Chicago as MacGuire had testified in his alibi. Having denied ever having access to more than the $30,000 above-board capitalization of the Committee for a Sound Dollar, he was now shown to have been in possession of $64,000 at the convention and to have spent $24,000 for what Clark's attorney called "entertaining."[33] HUAC also produced letters written by MacGuire from Europe reporting favorable impressions of the Croix de Feu, the right-wing French veterans' association, plus a few references to fascism, but this evidence was weak.

Clark's attorney, Albert Grant Christmas, testified frankly as to how he had run MacGuire as an agent in Legion politics. This clarified the conspiratorial workings of the Committee for a Sound Dollar, which was funded by Clark, but most of this was already known from Butler's testimony substantiated by HUAC investigations. Christmas offered extra tidbits that dramatized MacGuire's deceitfulness; while MacGuire denied proposing a gold speech to Butler, Christmas said that it was MacGuire's idea to begin with, and that he later received a report of Butler's refusal. In all, he laid everything neatly at the doorstep of the Committee for a Sound Dollar and made MacGuire look like a bungling, third-rate confidence artist. His testimony was limited to what he himself volunteered because of his privileged attorney-client relationship with Clark. Congressman Dickstein remarked to McCormack that there was "no question that MacQuire [sic] told an untruth and that this Committee ought to do something about it," but nothing was done. HUAC was at the end of its current congressional mandate, which was not renewed; Christmas testified on its final day of hearings.[34]

Thus, testimony and other evidence convincingly established that a substantial part of Butler's story was true, but mainly that which dealt with the gold cabal. This involved more details of Wall Street manipulation of veterans' affairs than had hitherto been publicly disclosed, but not so as to fundamentally recast conventional wisdom regarding the "Royal Family" or the stereotype of legionnaire dupes wielding baseball bats as auxilliary strikebreakers. Butler's personal integrity was vindicated insofar as he was shown to have rejected enticements to sell out the rank-and-file veterans. These significant disclosures tended to be lost, however, in the confusion surrounding the larger issue of an alleged plot to overthrow the government. In the HUAC proceedings, the grandiose conspiracy to mobilize 500,000 veterans reduced simply to what Butler and French said MacGuire had told them, supported by very few slender threads of circumstantial evidence.

Even if Butler was telling the truth, as there seems little reason to doubt, there remains the unfathomable problem of MacGuire's motives and veracity. He may have been working both ends against the middle, as Butler at one point suspected. In any case, MacGuire emerged from the HUAC hearings as an inconsequential trickster whose base dealings could not possibly be taken alone as verifying such a momentous undertaking. If he was acting as an intermediary in a genuine probe, or as *agent provocateur* sent to fool Butler, his employers were at least clever enough to keep their distance and see to it that he self-destructed on the witness stand.

But why did Butler publicize the plot in its most lurid scope just on the basis of MacGuire's fantastic pitch? Tactically, the gold cabal did constitute a prima facie case of Wall Street conspiracy, while the coup provided sensational impact to launch the whole package as a major exposé. The *New York Times* editorialized that "Butler himself does not appear to more than half credit it."[35] But there were circumstantial details in MacGuire's pitch that predicted imminent major developments in Wall Street opposition to the Roosevelt administration, demonstrating, as MacGuire no doubt intended, that he had access to high-level inside information. These led Butler to believe, or so he testified, that MacGuire's plot was part of a formidable undertaking. MacGuire apparently made every effort to present the plot in this way. But most of Butler's and French's testimony regarding MacGuire's name-dropping and informed gossiping, crucial ploys in establishing his credibility as intermediary, were omitted as hearsay from HUAC's published extracts of the hearings.

The suppressed testimony was indeed hearsay, and defamatory insofar as it implicated leading Wall Street and government figures in the alleged plot. On the other hand, by the very conspiratorial nature of the undertaking, these circumstantial connections and innuendos provided the most important substantiation of a larger conspiracy. Most significant was the allusion in the published version to an unnamed "society to maintain the Constitution" with "big fellows in it" that, according to Butler quoting MacGuire, would be publicly announced in several weeks. This society was to be the "background" for the veterans plot, its members "the villagers in the opera." Censored out of the published extracts was Butler's comment: "and in about two weeks the American Liberty League appeared, which was just about what he described it to be. That is the reason I tied it up with this other thing about Al Smith and some of the other people, because of the name [names] that appeared in connection with this Liberty League."[36]

Inasmuch as the Liberty League was the major organized right-wing assault on Roosevelt in the mid-1930s, and included in its leadership former Democratic presidential candidates Al Smith and John W. Davis, with both mentioned and Davis actually impugned in the Butler-MacGuire conversations, this was relevant circumstantial corroboration of sorts. More telling was the association between MacGuire, Murphy, and Clark with the Legion gold intrigue on the one hand and the League on the other. Murphy was treasurer of the Liberty League, Clark one of its founding donors.

The fact that HUAC suppressed testimony dealing with the Liberty League and prominent personalities tended to magnify the significance of deleted passages and discredit the integrity of HUAC's investigation. Circumstances of disclosure led to further distortion. Journalist John L. Spivak, researching Nazism and anti-Semitism for *New Masses* magazine, got permission from Dickstein to examine HUAC's public documents and was (it seems unwittingly) given the unexpurgated testimony amid stacks of other papers.

Spivak's two-part feature "Wall Street's Fascist Conspiracy" appeared in early 1935, a month after the hearings closed. He cogently developed a case for taking the suppressed testimony seriously. But this relevant material was embellished with overblown aspersions against "Jewish financiers working with fascist groups"—a mishmash of guilt by association that connected Morgan interests with Jewish financier Felix Warburg, HUAC, and certain members of the American Jewish Committee. Spivak was intent upon grinding his own axes, and elucidation of the plot was obscured. The suppressed Butler-MacGuire conversations could hardly support all this. Moreover *New Masses* was left-wing with a limited readership; the scoop was stigmatized as "red" propaganda and generally not cited elsewhere.[37]

Spivak's pieces contrasted with the treatment the plot received in the right-wing press. *Time* magazine outdid itself in superciliousness, ridiculing the story as its National Affairs lead story the first week with no followup coverage of the many developments until, three months later, brief mention in a footnote to a jaunty Butler-Jimmy Durante "personalities" photo. This curtly related HUAC's final report to Congress that the "story of a Fascist march on Washington was alarmingly true." The extravagant earlier piece featured a burlesque with half a million veterans marching through Maryland on U.S. Route 1 led by Butler on a white horse, accompanied by Johnson, MacArthur, and three former Legion commanders: "Between them and the first squad of marching men glided a shiny limousine. On its back seat, with a plush robe across their knees, were to be seen John P. Morgan and his partner, Thomas William Lamont, deep in solemn talk." *Time* remarked that "no military officer of the U.S. since the late, tempestuous George Custer has succeeded in publicly floundering in so much hot water as Smedley Darlington Butler." The liberal *Nation* and *New Republic* argued that fascism originated in pseudoradical mass movements; therefore Butler's revelations of a reactionary Wall Street plot were no cause for alarm.[38]

Smedley denounced HUAC on national radio for suppressing evidence and stopping "dead in its tracks when it got near the top" by failing to call Murphy, Clark, and others to testify. He denied the plot was Fascist, "except certain newspapers and the Committee itself so termed it," nor had a march on Washington ever been mentioned. In a rejoinder, Dickstein argued that Butler had never "made any specific charges" against the big names. But Dickstein's criticisms were qualified in Butler's favor, reflecting HUAC's final report to Congress: "There is no question that these attempts [the plot] were discussed, were planned, and might have been placed in execution when and if the financial backers deemed it expedient." The committee had verified "all the pertinent statements made by General Butler, with the exception of the direct statement suggesting the creation of the organization." The *New York Times* paraphrased the report in a front-page story: "Definite proof has been found that the much publicized Fascist march on Washington, which was to have been led by Maj. Gen. Smedley D. Butler, retired, according to testimony at the hearing, was actually contemplated." But by this time, with HUAC terminated, there was no apparent means or inclination to pursue the story further.[39]

Butler may have blown the whistle on an incipient conspiracy, and the plot reverberated in contemporary events and down through the years. Nobel Prize winner Sinclair Lewis explored similar themes of collusion between the rich, the military and ex-military, and the right-wing press in his admonitory 1935 novel *It Can't Happen Here*. Silver Shirts, Khaki Shirts and the Black Legion were highly visible reminders, however marginal and strange, that paramilitary strong-arm methods appealed to some Americans. A botched Khaki Shirt march on Washington the previous year served as paradigm for media coverage of Butler's charges, as did Mussolini's 1922 march on Rome.

Probably the most important effect of the Butler episode was to stigmatize right-wing protofascist linkages. The Liberty League proved particularly vulnerable, as noted by its historian, George Wolfskill: "Some people were easily spooked; and with the unthinking ones allegations, no matter how incredulous, were accepted as facts. From the Butler yarn there remained a residue of suspicion. The League was now more vulnerable to future attacks, attacks of perhaps not so serious a nature but no less worthy, attacks against which there was no adequate defense." But then the League itself gratuitously publicized its proneness to cranky right-wing fanaticism in the effusions of its leading spokesmen, such as Al Smith, who wildly attacked the New Deal as cryptocommunism. This was strikingly analogous to attacks on democratic governments by European Fascists. In this sense the gold plot, if not the march on Washington, was both sufficiently concrete and close to the League to justify larger suspicions. The League, as Wolfskill noted, failed to protect itself from associations with right-wing extremists and suffered the consequences in terms of public distrust—and rightfully so.[40]

Butler's attack on Wall Street enhanced his reputation as a champion of the rank-and-file, spitting in the eyes of the rich and powerful, whether he took a drubbing in the right-wing press or not. In the fall of 1935 he was named secretary of war in presidential aspirant Huey Long's shadow cabinet, revealed in *My First Days in the White House*, which was published posthumously shortly after Long's assassination. Long "understood" Butler "more intimately than some of my other appointees to the cabinet." In a chapter entitled "Wherein Rebellion Brews and Fades," he had Smedley putting down a right-wing putsch by Morgan interests intent upon sabotaging Share Our Wealth legislation. Butler, enroute to a VFW convention in New Orleans, commented that the selection was "the greatest compliment ever paid me," but in fact had almost nothing to do with Long except that they made speeches together favoring the bonus. In private letters he praised Long for siding with the underdog, and mentioned that "with Huey Long's death I lost most of my interest in the present political picture."[41]

Otherwise, the plot and its ramifications isolated him further from conventional politics, and he seemed to relish the final burnings of bridges. He was now more than ever a loner, speaking his mind as a free spirit. And he was an emotional man. Spivak, on trudging through the snow to Butler's home in Newtown Square, was amazed to find a general who talked like a radical agitator: "When I saw him he said things about big business and politics, sometimes in earthy, four-letter words, the like of which I had never heard from the most excited agitators crying on streetcorners, from socialists speaking on the New Haven Green or, in later years, from communists." When Spivak reminded him he was from *New Masses*, reputedly "a communist magazine," Smedley replied, "So who the hell cares?" The United States had been founded by radicals. George Washington, after all, was "an extremist—a goddam revolutionist!" In 1936 he voted for Socialist presidential candidate Norman Thomas.[42]

He had started letting loose before retirement. In August 1931, according to Jules Archer's undocumented secondary account, he used the "racketeer for capitalism" epigram that appeared variously in his speeches and writings thereafter.[43] Most frequently cited was the 1935 *Common Sense* article quoted at the front of this book and elaborated here:

> I helped make Mexico and especially Tampico safe for American oil interests in 1914. I helped make Haiti and Cuba a decent place for the National City Bank boys to collect revenues in. I helped in the raping of half a dozen Central American republics for the benefit of Wall Street. The record of racketeering is long. I helped purify Nicaragua for the international banking house of Brown Brothers in 1909-12. I brought light to the Dominican Republic for American sugar interests in 1916. I helped make Honduras "right" for American fruit companies in 1903. In China in 1927 I helped see to it that Standard Oil went its way unmolested. . . . Looking back on it, I feel I might have given Al Capone a few hints. The best *he* could do was to operate his racket in three city districts. We Marines operated on three *continents*.[44]

He was said to have used identical phrases in an unpublished November 1933 letter to *Common Sense*. Archer was probably right. Radical expressions were probably omitted from press reports of many of his speeches and toned down in articles submitted to conventional magazines. Snippets emerged. The previous January, *Nation* reported him characterizing the U.S. military as "a glorified bill-collecting agency" and saying he "wouldn't want to see a boy of mine march out with a Wall Street collar about his neck."[45]

Butler made the analogy between imperialism and domestic crime into an explicit indictment. His argument was rooted in conventional morality that had long sustained overseas and domestic coercion in the names of uplift and reform. When used to conquer injustice and backwardness and to spread the American way of life, the use of force was good. Conversely, force used for evil was all the more hateful when tainted with deceit and hypocrisy. Current popular fascination with gangsterism—witness the stardom of James Cagney and Edward G. Robinson and the dozens of Hollywood gangster films each year—provided convenient jargon which Smedley used to drive home a conviction that had evolved out of a lifetime of military and police experience.

He had been inveighing against gangster-political manipulations since at least 1912, when he was outraged in Nicaragua by predatory client-government officials, the "gang," being allowed to subvert his own "honest" administration in Granada.[46] Now his renunciation of war as a racket and imperialism as gangsterism matched exactly his invective against Capone. Crime fighting at home was sustained by ideals of uplift and fair play—the same as official rationales for intervention overseas. Abuse of the military for corrupt purposes overseas was equivalent to police corruption at home. The logic was inescapable once one had dispensed with the patriotic symbols, pious rhetoric, and specious legalism that had wafted a long succession of overseas military expeditions.

His anti-imperialist, anticapitalist rhetoric was offset neatly by vigorous support for domestic law and order. The issue was justice and morality, boldly asserted in terms of duty-bound American manliness. Likewise, his antiwar theme was complemented by unflinchingly militaristic support for national defense. He was always the patriot and battling marine, never the sniveling pacifist or convoluted ideologue. The marriage of extreme left- and right-wing themes enhanced his warrior method of attack.

The resulting system of contentious arguments was morally consistent and coherent enough to be convincing and, if not, to disarm and placate by its balanced audacity. Butler was careful not to commit himself to the many partisan organizations he encountered as an orator and propagandist, so that he could be taken on merit and be respected for his personal integrity. He thus maintained a degree of credibility across the political spectrum and was able to publish his radical views in such diverse forums as *Woman's Home*

Companion, Reader's Digest, Common Sense, and *New Masses.* Even when tol-
eration for dissent narrowed with the coming of war in the late 1930s, he
remained a popular spokesman on the veterans' circuit. And he collaborated
on friendly terms with such seeming irreconcilables as Earl Browder, Maury
Maverick, James G. Harbord, and J. Edgar Hoover, not to mention ongoing
loyal friendships with a number of Marine Corps officers. In 1936 when
General Harbord, a widely respected military figure, published his *The
American Army in France, 1917-19,* he included a glowing recitation of the
Duckboard saga and referred to Butler as "that Marine of Marines," and "a
great organizer of men, the best I have ever known in commands where
personal contact was possible for the organizer." Smedley wrote a testimonial for the book.[47]

Most surprising, in retrospect, was his reputation in the law enforcement community as an expert and proponent of state and federal constabularies while he simultaneously expounded left-wing views on capitalism
and imperialism. He frequently boosted the FBI as the shining example of
how the federal government should respond to crime. Butler's FBI file contains a half dozen reports by field agents who heard and often shared speakers' platforms with him during the late 1930s. He was reported to have told
an Idaho American Legion convention "to support you [Director J. Edgar
Hoover] and the Bureau in every way," and to have praised the FBI as "the
finest organization in the world today . . . with the possible exception of the
Marine Corps." The agent, who was the only other speaker, noted that
Smedley "spoke along his usual lines, calling on the Legion to keep the
country out of war. His talk was extremely well received and he was congratulated by me at its conclusion." Hoover sent Smedley thank you notes
and invited him to tour the Bureau in Washington. Butler often quoted
Hoover in his speeches, for which Hoover sent pamphlets and copies of his
own speeches, up to 1940 when an agent reported: "He is still a sincere
admirer of you and the Bureau and showed me several of your recent addresses which he carries with him and from which he states he quotes in
every talk."[48]

When Butler told a 1936 dentists' convention in Chicago that the FBI
was one of the few government departments "which did not smell to high
heaven," the agent who was his co-speaker warmly thanked him and reiterated Hoover's invitation to visit Bureau headquarters. That the agent considered the remainder of Smedley's speech, entitled "The Munitions
Racket," to be "rather radical . . . he castigated everybody from the President down, and particularly the present Secretary of War," did not seem to
matter. And he noted approvingly that the speech was "well received" by the
audience. In 1961, when tolerance for dissent was very narrow, someone
sent in a clipping quoting Butler's "racketeer for capitalism" diatribe. The
agent researching the complaint found numerous references to Butler in

bureau files and came to the conclusion that "our relations with him were very cordial." Since he had been dead for twenty years, the case was dropped.[49]

The FBI was aware of the alleged 1934 Wall Street plot but apparently did not investigate. In a curious sequel, while visiting the bureau in 1936 Butler told Hoover about a plot by Father Charles Coughlin to invade Mexico to protect the Catholic Church from harassment. Smedley said that Coughlin, the famous "radio priest" whose voice he recognized, had approached him by telephone and that the call was traced back to Coughlin afterward. It seems that Butler was being hoaxed. In any case, he was clearly wary of becoming involved in another publicized plot exposé. He did mention the Coughlin plot again to an agent in 1940 in connection with what he termed dozens of "screwball" organizations that had invited him to appear as a speaker.[50]

Butler's affinity with Hoover reflected what historian Samuel Walker bemoaned as a trend toward highly centralized authority by which police executives were given "almost complete discretion" to do as they liked: "Like General Butler in Philadelphia and Boss Frank Hague in Jersey City, J. Edgar Hoover proved that the techniques of professionalism and efficiency could easily be perverted." Walker castigated Hoover for manipulating public fears of a crime wave during the 1930s by mounting an FBI "publicity blitz" regarding a few sensational criminals, in which the bureau's press releases "inflated to heroic proportions" its successes. A most disturbing aspect was the "vicious quality of the rhetoric" used, in which Hoover referred to criminals as "vermin" and "Public Rat Number One." The result was reorientation of police professionalism so that the "crime-fighter image" perniciously superseded "social work aspects of policing." Butler, with his fervid warrior-style exhortations to "put the law books in cold storage and bring out the high-powered rifles and machine guns," was a leading exponent of this trend.[51]

At the other end of the political spectrum, Butler wrote five articles for non-Marxist, socialist *Common Sense* magazine in 1935-36.[52] During this period *Common Sense* featured intellectuals, such as John Dewey, Upton Sinclair, John Dos Passos, and Bertrand Russell, and practicing politicians such as Floyd B. Olsen and Maury Maverick, with format and style pitched to the general public. Butler became a prominent spokesman for the League Against War and Fascism, which was considered by many to be Communist-dominated.[53] Local American Legion units occasionally harassed the League for its alleged subversive activities. No matter, Smedley retained his stature as a red-blooded patriot; the Marine Corps League (veterans) pleaded with him to attend its 1936 national convention: "We need you *vitally. . . .* We *must* have the support by *personal presence* of two or more of our Nationally known leaders, such as yourself." In 1941, the Smedley D. Butler

Detachment petitioned President Roosevelt that a Tulsa newspaper was publishing "un-American" editorials.[54]

Following Spivak's 1935 "Wall Street Fascist Conspiracy" articles, *New Masses* published "Where Smedley Butler Stands." The author, Walter Wilson, recalled attending a left-wing veterans' meeting in New York where Smedley spoke after James Ford, a black veterans' leader and Communist Party vice presidential candidate. Butler said New York newspapers had tried to stop him coming: "They told me I'd find a nest of communists here. I told them 'What the hell of it!' In 1917 the government went around drafting boys into the army; they didn't ask then what a man's politics were; they merely asked if he had a sound body and a strong back."[55]

Noting that many of Butler's statements had been vague so that "a lot of people mistakenly considered him a demagogue in the Long or Coughlin class," Wilson tried to pin him down. Smedley replied with his current views. Big Business and Wall Street were the enemies, bent upon "the same tricks used by European dictators to keep capitalism on the top of the economic heap." Workers had an absolute right to strike, and calling them Bolsheviks was just a pretext for repression. Company unions were "a racket." He endorsed the American Federation of Labor but was critical of its leadership: "Why, I'm more radical than most of them." For political affinities, he named Congressmen Maury Maverick and Vito Marcantonio, and Senator Ernest Lundeen, all on the far left of the congressional spectrum. While conceding undemocratic aspects and need for reform, he firmly believed in American democracy. On a personal level, he said he had now given over 1,200 speeches in 700 towns and cities. He needed the money, but recently declined a personnel manager job with a large corporation because "of course that simply meant keeping the workers fooled." Driving Wilson to the station after the interview, Smedley pointed out the homes of his affluent neighbors, and Wilson gathered that many old associates were now hostile. "He told me that even certain relatives had lined up against him. It would seem that he has broken irrevocably with the upper classes."[56]

Butler was indeed moving in different circles from those usually habituated by retired generals mellowing in pensioned comfort. The left-wing veterans' meeting, for instance, took place at the Star Casino on 107th Street in East Harlem and featured Communist Party General Secretary Earl Browder and Congressman Marcantonio as well as Butler, Ford, and radical veterans' leaders. Smedley taunted the vets for supporting FDR: "When he runs again in 1936, you soldiers will be out there voting for him again, too." There was a loud chorus of noes. A year later he joined Senators Gerald P. Nye and Elmer A. Benson, Professor Robert Morss Lovett, and Clarence Darrow in the Non-Partisan Committee for the Re-Election of Representative Vito Marcantonio; Joseph Brodsky, attorney for the Communist Party, presided at the public announcement.[57]

In a series of 1935 radio speeches over Philadelphia's WCAU, a Columbia network affiliate with national shortwave reach, Butler supported the current Camden shipyard strike and the Connery bill banning use of federal equipment by the National Guard against strikers. It was a year marked by vicious antilabor violence. One of the speeches was on the theme "a life is worth less than a pane of glass": "Some thug hired by the mills slams a blackjack across the head of a striker. And someone hurls a rock. Maybe it breaks a 6-cent pane of glass in the factory and maybe it doesn't. The hired thugs or the police—or maybe the national guard—whoever is there to guard the property—gets excited and starts. shooting. And a striker or an innocent victim, maybe a woman or a child, gets shot." The thirteen quarter-hour weekly broadcasts, sponsored by Pep Boys automotive stores, were drafted by Dimitman and then read over the air, an awkward regimen for Smedley, who much preferred ad-libbing in his public lecture style. He complained to another journalist, "I don't like this broadcasting. It irritates me and is rapidly destroying my digestion." [58]

His major collaboration with Dimitman was the 1935 book *War Is a Racket* (52 pages). It was condensed in *Reader's Digest* as a book supplement, prefaced by Lowell Thomas commending Smedley's "moral as well as physical courage .... Even his opponents concede that in his stand on public questions, General Butler has been motivated by the same fiery integrity and loyal patriotism which has distinguished his service in countless Marine campaigns." [59]

War Is a Racket was an expansion of an earlier magazine article. Dimitman said he dictated the draft manuscript to his wife in a single night. Briskly written, it began with the catch phrase, "War is a racket," and ended with "TO HELL WITH WAR!" War and imperialism were functions of capitalists' greed: "Newly acquired territory promptly is exploited by the few—the self-same few who wrung dollars out of the blood of war." America had respected Washington's (actually Thomas Jefferson's) warning against "entangling alliances" before 1898, but had become "internationally minded" thereafter: "It would have been far cheaper (not to say safer) for the average American who pays the bills to stay out of foreign entanglements. For a very few this racket, like bootlegging and other underworld rackets, brings fancy profits, but the cost of operation is always transferred to the people—who do not profit." [60]

Chapters entitled "Who Makes the Profits?" and "Who Pays the Bills" cited data culled from Senate hearings on profiteering during the World War. The victims were taxpayers and a generation of young men whose minds were twisted through psychological manipulation—about which Smedley the charismatic commander could have claimed to be an authority: "They were made to 'about face'; to regard murder as the order of the day. . . . We used them for a couple of years and trained them to think nothing at all of killing or being killed." Many were "destroyed, mentally, because they could not make the final 'about face'" back to civilian life. Men were made to feel ashamed if they shunned military service. War propaganda was "so vicious that even God was brought into it." Clergymen, avowing that "God is on our side," incited the soldiers to "kill, kill, kill." Making the "world safe for democracy," "war to end wars" and other "beautiful ideals were painted for our boys who were sent out to die." They were told it would be a "glorious adventure." And they were paid $30 a month, less deductions for Liberty Bonds which were later sold at discount contributing to bankers' profits "in the hocus-pocus of manipulated Liberty Bond prices."[61]

In the chapter "How to Smash this Racket!" he urged an assault upon capitalist warmongers and their political allies. Capital, industry, and labor should be conscripted a month before any general manpower draft in wartime, to serve for $30. Everyone must "be restricted to a total monthly income not to exceed that paid to the soldier in the trenches!" After thinking it over, the warmongers would change their minds. A law should be passed requiring a plebiscite before declaration of war, with voting lists restricted to young men of military age who had qualified for the draft.

There must be laws restricting the military to defensive functions. Lobbying by militarists must be thwarted. "Swivel-chair admirals" were smart: "They don't shout that 'We need a lot of battleships to war on this nation or that nation.' . . . [first] they let it be known that America is menaced by a great naval power. . . . the great fleet of this supposed enemy will strike suddenly and annihilate our 125,000,000 people. Just like that. Then they begin to cry for a larger navy." Next the admirals stage maneuvers—not right off the Pacific Coast but two or three thousand miles off the coast: "The Japanese, a proud people, of course will be pleased beyond expression to see the United States fleet so close to Nippon's shores. Even as pleased as would be the residents of California were they to dimly discern, through the morning mist, the Japanese fleet playing at war games off Los Angeles."[62]

Much of *War Is a Racket* was stock antiwar, anti-imperialist idiom, part of an American tradition dating back to the eighteenth century. Butler's particular contribution was his recantation, denouncing war on moral grounds after having been a warrior hero and spending most of his life as a military insider. The theme remained vigorously patriotic and nationalistic, decrying imperialism as a disgrace rooted in the greed of a privileged few.

No consideration was given to geopolitical factors by which a Great Power's spheres of influence, hegemony over satellite states, and preemptive military actions might be rationalized. But, especially since the recent extravagant propaganda of the Great War, public discourse over these issues was almost entirely on a moral and idealistic plane. Proponents of overseas military interventions seldom raised cynical justifications, lest they discredit the high-minded crusading purposes that were their rallying cries.

Butler emphasized class interest and a populist projection of the anti-imperialist message. As a renegade warrior and gruff soldiers' general, he had an appeal and authority quite different from the usual run of pacifist intellectuals, reformers, statesmen, and clergy who crusaded on these issues. But then, the 1930s were unique in that antiwar sentiment attained unprecedented popular scope, ranging from national college student strikes to the veterans' resolutions and petitions in Butler's domain.

Apart from the veterans' circuit, he associated with all manner of antiwar groups and presented his case at a variety of levels. In 1935 he began his two-year association with the League Against War and Fascism, a united front of socialists, communists, and various church, college, trade union, and women's groups. In Cleveland in early 1936, he gave a talk entitled "War Is a Racket" as main speaker of the Third U.S. Congress Against War and Fascism, after having given another speech on behalf of the League over the ABC radio network that afternoon. Other speakers included Rabbi Barnett R. Brickner, Langston Hughes, Heywood Broun, and Roger Baldwin. Baldwin, longtime head of the American Civil Liberties Union, who at this time moved furthest left in a lifetime of left-liberal politics, later recalled: "My fears [of fascism] were shared by my colleagues, most surprising of whom was a retired general of the marines, Smedley D. Butler, who often spoke with me at League meetings. The general was the most colorfully outspoken opponent of war, armies, fascism and reaction I'd ever met. He got fairly good fees for it, but conviction was his motive." [63]

In November 1936 the League's local branch in Perth Amboy, New Jersey, was denied use of the high school auditorium by the board of education which said Butler's speaking might incite a riot. He went through with the meeting anyhow. One member recalled: "His coming was on all radio stations with the threat of riot emphasized and we had the largest paid audience ever in a loft with the whole town police force in attendance. . . . Many of his Nicaraguan soldiers came and shook his hand. It was fun. He spoke of colonial warring and said it was not for the flag but for big business. Much applause—no riot. . . . He wasn't very big but he was great and we were very grateful." But Smedley opposed all overseas military intervention, and broke with the League when it favored intervention during the Spanish Civil War. He told one meeting, "What in hell is it our business what's going on in Spain." [64]

By 1936 he had long since abandoned the New Deal. Earlier attacks over the veterans' bonus gave way to criticism of what he took to be FDR's guileful preparations for war. In 1935 he told 4,000 veterans at the VFW annual convention that America was "rapidly drifting toward another war through the medium of dictatorship. The political leaders of this country are for another conflict to cover up their blunders." In early 1936, anticipating FDR's first covert moves toward the World War II alliance system,

Butler advocated requiring the secretary of state to read all diplomatic correspondence over the radio to preclude secret commitments.[65]

He even took a swipe at his old Haiti quartermaster, now FDR's assistant secretary of the navy: "Complacent and credulous Assistant Secretary Henry Latrobe Roosevelt performs his duties as a yes-man for the gold-braided bureaucrats [admirals] with no questions asked." Yet earlier that year, chiding himself for being a "nut or a sentimental old fool," he sent a warm note to HLR recalling the old days: "The sight of you sitting in that Committee Room yesterday brought over me a great wave of affection for you personally." But this was qualified with reference to present disputes: "I don't like your playmates or the gang you run with."[66]

Butler's critique focused particularly on naval expenditures and naval diplomacy, areas in which he had considerable expertise and a strong personal sense of historical perspective. Naval policy was FDR's foremost military passion, and the navy was the first service to undergo extensive rearmament corresponding to an increasingly militaristic foreign policy. The doldrums in military spending were over, and Butler was quick to blow the whistle. In the 1935 *Common Sense* article subtitled "'Happy Days Are Here Again': The Navy," he called FDR "the biggest of the big navy men" who was reversing an anti-imperialist trend maintained by Republican presidents since World War I. None of the Republicans had "shown much concern about protecting our overseas possessions," notably his old adversary Herbert Hoover whom Smedley now lauded for prescribing "that the army and navy should be large enough to prevent invasion—nothing more."[67]

He recalled that half a century ago the navy had built coast-defense battleships "far more responsive to the national will and far more in step with our traditional policies," but then Admiral Alfred Thayer Mahan and Theodore Roosevelt had administered "their respective shots of imperialistic hasheesh." Subsequent naval interventions had "coerced small countries into bowing to the wishes of our commercial interests." Now naval expansion was broached in terms of defense, but in reality it was a recrudescence of imperialism "at direct odds" with current neutrality legislation. The navy did not "possess a single plan that does not contemplate an attack on another country. Its true policy is the bewhiskered imperialistic slogan 'the best defense is the offensive' . . . to be able to sail to foreign waters and attack its enemy of the moment at the first opportunity."[68]

Regarding most of this, he might well have delved into his own efforts as a marine propagandist in the 1920s, and his father's long involvement as a principal architect of the modern "big navy" in three decades on the House Naval Affairs Committee. But he never mentioned his father in public, nor did he publicly discuss Marine Corps politics and personalities except in the 1935 attempt to block Commandant Russell's confirmation. He still considered himself very much a loyal marine and by and large honored the confidentiality of past relationships including his own complicity at the policy-making level. And yet he was an ardent convert, suggesting in his denunciations that he knew whereof he spoke and had been on the high road himself. As an insistent and self-confessed turncoat, he had to maintain his personal dignity or else succumb to ridicule—to which he was, in any case, no stranger. He repeatedly pushed his public credibility to the limits and beyond and took an enormous amount of abuse accordingly.

In opposing the remilitarization of American foreign policy, he called for a viable defense exclusive of imperialistic capabilities. With existing U.S. military capability, no foreign enemy or likely coalition could invade America. It would take a force of at least a million men to invade a nation of 130 million. They would have to arrive all at once to be effective. There was not enough shipping in the entire world to transport such a force across 3,000 miles of ocean in a period of ten days. In the last war it had taken four months, using the enemy's biggest ships as well, to get a million men to Europe. A strong U.S. coastal defense would be a final and insurmountable obstacle. In *Woman's Home Companion*, also in 1936, he advocated a constitutional amendment to prohibit removal of armed forces from the continental United States and Panama Canal, and to restrict warships to within 500 miles of the coast and aircraft to within 700 miles, somewhat extended from distances proposed in *War Is a Racket*. The real danger of war was American military adventurism, not foreign invasion.[69]

Similarly, he was an early and dedicated supporter of Congressman Louis Ludlow's proposed constitutional amendment to require a national referendum prior to declaration of war. Ludlow invited him to testify at Judiciary Committee hearings, where Butler pointed out that he had "invaded country after country, at the direction of the President of the United States, without a declaration of war." A referendum would delay war and thus make presidential circumvention less feasible. He urged restriction of voting to those between eighteen and forty-five years of age and their wives. In November 1935 he spoke favoring the Ludlow bill to a crowd of 10,000 peace demonstrators in Philadelphia following a parade up Broad Street. The crowd chanted "no more war" and "unite for peace," one of many such spectacles in the mid-1930s. In 1937 Ludlow asked him to help form a national committee.[70]

A critical juncture for remilitarization was the 1938 Naval Expansion (Vinson) Act for construction of battleships, aircraft carriers, and cruisers to create a two-ocean navy with long-range attack capabilities. Butler testified at length to Senate Naval Affairs Committee hearings regarding his past career "running around the world guarding Standard Oil tins" and "robbing little Central and South American countries in the interests of Wall Street." He described himself as a "military isolationist" who believed "in having all sorts of friendly contacts and commercial contacts with all other nations on earth," but in keeping military forces "within our own boundaries." This was in opposition to a "very, very small minority that think we should police the world, that we should guard every American wherever he might be, and every dollar wherever it might be." Another group, also a small minority, wanted to police just the Western Hemisphere. The majority, in which Smedley included himself, would guard the continental United States only. There was another small group, outright pacifists, "that thinks we ought to disarm and trust to the 'ring-around-the-rosy' loving each other procedure to insure our safety." [71]

As a military isolationist, Butler did not turn against the military as such. He was isolationist only insofar as he denounced overseas military interventions, which he saw as tantamount to imperialism—or international gangsterism, as he had come to understand and loathe it. Imminently, however, massive overseas military intervention and rampant militarization of U.S. foreign policy during and after the coming World War resulted in drastic reformulation of public debate. Crusading military interventionism was again termed "internationalism," as in the Wilsonian precedent. Again represented as messianic patriotism, it was self-justifying and self-glorifying as against a succession of evil empires that threatened America's global reach. The regime of wartime propaganda, extending to paranoia during the Cold War, redefined tolerable public discourse to exclude Butler's viewpoint. Military expeditions were again equated with making the world safe for democracy—dubious inference that required an extraordinary exercise in ideological distortion. "Isolationism" was relegated to the dustbin of history, exorcised of its anti-imperialist heresy and then ridiculed as rustic, narrow-minded, and xenophobic. [72]

During the height of the Cold War, many interventionist euphemisms that Butler had denounced in the 1930s attained full sway. For instance, the isolationist maxim of strong military defense was usurped and distorted by doublethink such as renaming the War Department the Defense Department and garrisoning "strategic defense perimeters" in the far corners of the world. The marines, for reasons of their own, banned "expeditionary" terminology in the mid-1930s and changed the Expeditionary Force to the politically neutral Fleet Marine Force. [73] Had Butler denounced "robbing little Central and South American countries in the interests of Wall Street" before a Senate committee in the 1950s, he would have been reviled as un-American, an insult he would have furiously resented.

Butler did not live to see the "internationalist" versus "isolationist" debate perverted to this extent. But he could clearly foresee the coming interventionist sanctification of war, and spent his last years trying to demystify it. The mystique of militarism, as he well knew, was largely based on the arrogation of special expertise to imply professional infallibility. "There isn't any secret about this business," he testified to the Senate Naval Affairs

Committee: "My experience was in the bushes, but, nevertheless, I got to be a general officer, and I was one for 14 years before I retired. I sat on these boards and I saw all this stuff. It was as easy as rolling off the logs." Generals, he wrote, "besides being reactionary," were possessed of "the backwardness of the military mind."[74]

Japanese aggression did not impress him: "Japan happens to be the enemy this year. Next year it may be somebody else . . . . The next thing we may be loving the Japanese to death." The 1937 sinking of a U.S. gunboat on the Yangtze in company with three Standard Oil tankers was proof that American forces were posted where they had no business being: "Why don't those damned oil companies fly their own flags on their personal property—maybe a flag with a gas pump on it." Marines, soldiers, and gunboats in China should all be brought home. "United States citizens should get the hell out of China and stay out. . . . let the financial interests who are crying over there run up their own flags and fight their own battles." The United States must abandon the Philippines, Hawaii, Alaska, and Puerto Rico, to which he now added the Panama Canal, rather than war for them.[75]

As for Europe, the United States had nothing to do with "Hitler's landgrabbing" or with "promises Britain and France made to Poland." He elaborated in the 1939 anthology *Common Sense Neutrality*, playing upon presumed American moral superiority but drawing opposite conclusions from the interventionists—America was above the battle: "These are some of the SMELLY things in this pit of European back-alley politics into which we will be sucked if we don't watch our step—if we are fools enough to get all excited about this brawl that is going on over there, as such brawls have, almost since the dawn of history." The anthology, edited by his ally in the 1934 Wall Street plot exposé, Paul Comly French, included pieces by Charles A. Beard, a number of senators, Eleanor Roosevelt, Herbert Hoover, Norman Thomas, and the commander of the American Legion. Elsewhere, Smedley conceded that, along with "90 percent of the American people," he sympathized with the western allies. But this was no reason to intervene or rearm beyond "an iron clad defense a rat couldn't crawl through."[76]

One of his more desperate gestures, at the crest of the peace movement when public pressure still confounded the interventionist Roosevelt administration, came at the 1937 VFW annual convention in Buffalo. The VFW, with 300,000 members as against the American Legion's one million, held that year's encampment under the slogan "Peace for America," and heard speakers including New York Governor Herbert H. Lehman, Mayor Fiorello La Guardia, and Senators Bennett Champ Clark, Josh Lee, and Arthur H. Vandenberg. The press photo of Vandenberg at the convention showed him against a backdrop picture of horse marines in Shanghai over the slogan "Take the Dollar Signs Out of the Battle Flags." "Loudest cheers," according to *Time* magazine, "were reserved for an old V.F.W. favorite, Major General Smedley Butler."[77]

Smedley exhorted the vets, "It's your crowd that's going to do the dying and bleeding, not the Wall Street bunch of flag wavers," and the convention, "lifting chunks from the Vandenberg and Butler speeches," adapted an antiwar resolution calling for mandatory neutrality and withdrawal of all American forces from foreign soil. Then, just before the convention closed, Smedley was reintroduced to make a special announcement. As reported by the *New York Times*, he "amazed the session" by reading a letter ostensibly sent by FDR expressing appreciation of the veterans' "red-blooded, soldierly resolution" and agreeing that "other countries must make their damned wars without our help." The veterans "whooped and whistled in appreciation" until Butler concluded saying, "It ain't signed. Wouldn't it be fine if we did get such a letter from the President?" He predicted that a real letter would be forthcoming, but this rather silly ploy aborted.[78]

As the peace movement waned in the face of totalitarianism and militarism, he met with increasing disparagement in the interventionist press. In March 1939, *Time* ridiculed a performance at Wesleyan University: "Noisy, beak-nosed Major General Smedley Darlington Butler, U.S.M.C., retired, exploded with a characteristic bit of Butlerese: 'If there is another war I intend to make James Roosevelt [FDR's son] go to the front line trenches . . . . I am not afraid! Let them shoot me! I'm all through. Let's get shot here at home if we're going to be shot.'" It was easy to patronize such an outspoken firebrand, particularly when he overstepped the bounds of propriety, as he often did. In private Josephus Daniels, who went against the internationalist grain by praising Butler in a 1937 war monument speech at Brest, wrote apologetically to FDR: "I felt it was due Smedley to pay tribute to his good work here. If he was as wise in speech as he was brave in war, he would not have lost the prestige he deserved."[79]

During these last years, Butler was increasingly cut off from old connections. Of his lifelong friends in the Marine Corps, only Torchy Robinson came regularly to visit, also occasionally Vandegrift, and Smedley came to feel that many of his old cronies had had ulterior motives. Lejeune kept in touch but was reserved. Smedley tended more toward reflection; his son Tom remembered seeing him sitting alone in the back yard for hours on end, staring at the horizon. One of his granddaughters recalled listening from an upstairs bedroom at night to loud arguments going on below, probably about politics.[80] But whatever the private frustrations, Smedley persisted as a magnetic public personality and committed activist.

With war a reality since 1937 in the Far East and since 1939 in Europe, the prospects for keeping America out were fading fast. Butler's radio broadcasts, several on national networks, were delivered in an emotional, hoarse, low gravelly voice, not unlike the intimate style popularized by Gabriel Heatter and other radio personalities of the day. Smedley's speeches were characterized by colorful language and frequent aphorisms, condemn- ing "war dogs" and war as "a mean, cruel, yes filthy racket." In an October 1939 broadcast introduced by Senator Clark, he urged the mothers of America not to let their sons be sent overseas as "cannon fodder":

> Now—*you Mothers*, particularly! The only way you can resist all this war hysteria and beating of tom-toms is by asserting the love you bear your boys. When you listen to some well worded, some well- delivered *war* speech, just remember it's nothing but *sound*. No amount of sound can make up to you for the loss of your boy. After you've heard one of those speeches and your blood's all hot and you want to bite somebody like Hitler - go upstairs to where your boy's asleep. . . . Look at him. Put your hand on that spot on the back of his neck. The place you used to love to kiss when he was a baby. Just rub it a little. You won't wake him up, he knows it's you. Just look at his strong, fine young body because only the best boys are chosen for war. Look at this splendid young creature who's part of yourself, then close you eyes for a moment and I'll tell you what can happen. . . .
>
> Somewhere—five thousand miles from home. Night. Dark- ness. Cold. A drizzling rain. The noise is terrific. All Hell has bro- ken loose. A star shell burst in the air. Its unearthly flare lights up the muddy field. There's a lot of tangled rusty barbed wires out there and a boy hanging over them—his stomach ripped out, and he's feebly calling for help and water. His lips are white and drawn. He's in agony.
>
> There's your boy. The same boy who's lying in bed tonight. The same boy who trusts you. . . . Are you going to run out on him? Are you going to let someone beat a drum or blow a bugle and make him chase after it? Thank God, this is a Democracy and by your voice and your vote you can save your boy.[81]

In early 1940 Butler set out on a grueling six-week western speaking tour during which Germany launched its Blitzkrieg in northern and western Europe. Returning home, he wrote the head of an Independent Republican Women's group that he was tired and in poor health, and so would have to defer a speech: "I hope you realize that I am about run to death making speeches professionally and I feel that I must take a rest this summer as my engagements run clear up into June. Also I feel sure there is no use talking any more about this war business. The people of America are fools. If they want to have their children shot in order to keep Franklin Roosevelt on a pedestal, they will just have to do it."[82]

Appropriately, among what proved to be his few remaining appearances were talks to Quaker Meetings in West Chester and at Swarthmore—close to home and the antiwar taproot of family beliefs. On 22 May he gave a last speech in his usual style to a Temple University Alumni dinner at the Penn Athletic Club, warning that the United States should not get "panicky" over British and French military collapse. England was not finished until its navy was sunk; by then Hitler would be too weak to attack the United States. Americans should defend their own country only, "everything else is a damned commercial racket of some kind." The *Inquirer* noted that he showed the strain of a long illness that had caused him to lose twenty-five pounds.[83]

The next day he entered Philadelphia Navy Yard hospital for what was thought to be a rest. Newspapers were filled with war news, and a cartoon in the *Inquirer* entitled "Break that Stranglehold" showed a snake labeled "Fifth Column Activists" wrapped around a gun marked "U.S. Defense Program." A week before, Congressman Martin Dies of the revamped Un-American Activities Committee had called for a crackdown on fifth columnists.[84]

Butler died four weeks later on 21 June, the day before the French surrender at Compiègne. His doctor described the illness as an incurable condition of the upper abdominal tract, presumably cancer. He was conscious until the end and attended by his family, which brought his new 1940 Oldsmobile, which he never drove, and parked it so he could see it from his hospital window. Later Mrs. Butler wrote Lejeune, "He was working so hard for his country, and came home always so tired. We were afraid of a breakdown but never dreamed there was anything serious." He left an estate of $2,000.[85]

He was eulogized extensively in the press and the *Congressional Record*, but evasively, indicating the extent that antiwar and anti-imperialist dissent had already been shut down. The *New York Times* ran a three-column obituary that made no mention whatsoever of his apostasy or antiwar activities. The *Inquirer*, without naming specifics, commended his "innate honesty and reckless courage," his fearlessness in speaking and acting "with complete disregard of the consequences to himself," and his heroic career as a soldier. The latter point was accentuated by a testimonial from Theodore Roosevelt that he was "the finest fighting man in the armed forces." Ex-Mayor Kendrick said he was "a man of strong character and absolutely a straight shooter . . . we remained close friends to the end." Farmer-Laborer Senator Lundeen, after an oblique reference to "a wild and fantastic [U.S.] defense plan contemplating the rescue of the British Empire" that was the sole veiled allusion to anti-imperialism in all the eulogies, said his "courage and patriotism cannot be questioned . . . if there ever was a patriot, and a noble, courageous warrior, it was General Smedley D. Butler, a man who was unafraid in the presence of kings and presidents, and who dared to speak his mind at all times." FDR sent a personal message to Mrs. Butler, "I shall always remember the old days in Haiti," brushing aside the awkward recent years.[86]

Funeral services took place beneath the Chinese Thousand Blessings Umbrellas in the Butler home. A dozen uniformed marine officers, including Colonels Vandegrift and Ellis B. Miller, attended along with friends, members of the family, several congressmen, and nearly forty Philadelphia police officers. In the absence of an official military guard of honor, the policemen lined up outside the house as the casket was carried away.[87]

Butler's memory was subsequently honored by the 1941 commissioning of the destroyer USS *Smedley D. Butler*. In 1942 he was featured in an episode of the Hearst syndicate's wartime "Heroes of Democracy" newspaper cartoon series: three frames depicted heroic exploits in China, Nicaragua, and Mexico, and one frame showed him in civilian clothes, tie pulled loose and shirtsleeves rolled up, bellowing into a microphone, "1,000 Marines can whip 10,000 of any other soldiers!"—a line apparently lifted out of context from a 1937 VFW antiwar speech.[88] In none of this, needless to say, was there any mention of his apostasy. The marine base on Okinawa is named after him.

A month after Smedley's death, a plaque commemorating his police work in Philadelphia reappeared in City Hall, and it was later permanently mounted on the outside facade. It had been out of sight in storage for the previous decade. Within the family Mrs. Butler, who did not drive, kept the 1940 Oldsmobile until 1956. She could not bear, and refused over the years, to listen to recordings of Smedley's radio broadcasts. The Butler home was kept by her and their children more or less intact the way Smedley left it, complete with Chinese Blessings Umbrellas, regimental banners, and other memorabilia, down to the present.[89]

16 Epilogue

The 1934 Wall Street plot materialized into marching troops in a 1977 Universal Studios film, *The November Plan*, with Lloyd Nolan playing Butler. The scenario, loosely based on Butler's exposé, was presented as plausible.

It was not until the late 1960s that Butler's radical antiwar message again appeared in the mass media. National Public Television broadcast newsreel footage of him walking the parade ground in Shanghai, quoting some of his anti-imperialist rhetoric in the voice-over, as part of a critical documentary on the history of U.S. military interventions. And his example may have inspired another generation of renegade marines who spoke out against American intervention in Vietnam, notably Commandant David M. Shoup, who had served under Butler in China. Decrying a "New American Militarism," Shoup drew an analogy between the "'military task force' type of diplomacy" of the 1960s and "the tradition of our more primitive, pre-World War II 'gunboat diplomacy.'" In 1984, Brigadier General William C. Lemly paid tribute to "the great populist Gen. Smedley Butler" and characterized his own service in Nicaragua as "helping make things safe for the United Fruit Company and the big bankers."[1]

In his well-known critique of U.S. imperialism, *The Shark and the Sardines* (New York, 1961), former President (1945-51) Juan José Arévalo of Guatemala quoted Butler's "I was a racketeer for capitalism" interpretation of Latin American interventions, and introduced these as "words which we Latin-Americans should read to our young people every day at dawn."

Butler's memory has been kept alive in the Marine Corps as one of its authentic warrior heroes. And the warrior style survives as a central theme in the Corps and in popular military mores. In the 1962 film *The Longest Day*, an epic recreation of the World War II landing at Normandy starring Robert Mitchum, with cameo roles by almost all the leading macho actors of the day, Mitchum played the heroic soldiers' general and personally spearheaded the attack alongside a tough old sergeant. The two went out in front of the American lines to blow up a German installation that had Mitchum's troops pinned down (the incident was true). Mitchum wore grimy combat gear identical to the sergeant's, crawled in the sand, and sweated and grunted. In starkly invidious contrast, Nazi officers shown in cuts to the enemy side were depicted as aristocratic, highbrow staff types, immaculately dressed and careful to keep well behind the front lines in their command posts, which were set in effeminate French drawing rooms.

Butler's warrior contempt for "gold braided bureaucrats" and the reciprocal resentment of egoism and populist political interference persist as military prejudices. But the struggle between heroes and military managers was provisional rather than absolute. Butler himself embodied many qualities of a potential synthesis that saw military professionalism attempt to combine the rational and the heroic. He did represent a retreating old guard insofar as democratic political influence, as in the notorious nineteenth-century militia system, was fading fast.[2] Favoritism based on extraneous political connections was anathema to the new breed of merit professionals with their educational credentials. By promoting civilian political intervention in favor of battlefield as against educational criteria, Smedley became a prime target for resentment by highbrows whose reforms were set back. His defiant anti-intellectualism rankled in an officer corps struggling to attain recognition for exclusive, authoritative military expertise. But popular sentiment remained rooted in democratic, citizen-soldier, warrior values.

In the Marine Corps, he was the "stormy petrel" and was seen by some as almost insubordinate. But the picture was not so simple. As a leading proponent of the "military analogy" for civilian police reform, Butler strongly advocated centralization of authority in order to curb political influence. Obedience by cops to an apolitical chain of command was crucial to professional upgrading. Likewise, in the military his achievements as an enterprising leader of small combat units would today be recognized as a vital component of professional warmaking. Butler's enemies—staff officers, desk admirals, and war college intelligentsia—were part of a cloistered officer corps elite that still had much to learn about emerging trends in professionalism. Butler was far ahead of them, and very "modern," in mass leadership skills and in mastering mass-media public relations. Today the armed forces are ridden with public-relations units that might well envy Butler's early publicity coups. In this sense Butler was brilliantly adaptive, turning old-fashioned political contacts to institutional advantage as in orchestrating the Quantico publicity circus during the 1920s. He was also keenly interested in using new military technology, notably airplanes at Quantico and in China.

So the warrior versus rational manager characterization turns out to be not so clearcut. Even in fighting conservative rearguard actions for warrior preferment, Butler creatively explored new dimensions in military-civilian politics. Albeit he wound up a loser; bringing popular civilian-political pressure to bear within the military was at this point not at all smart in the careerist sense. But according to attributes listed for entrance into the "elite nucleus" of top military command by Morris Janowitz in his classic *The*

Professional Soldier (1960), Butler would score many points. He was unconventional, a rule breaker, was "creative" and "prepared to challenge the fundamentals of military organization," and had "adaptive career experiences" with "political overtones" requiring "communications skills." He failed, of course, in not having "an early and persistent propensity for staff work."[3] That so many of his protégés went on to outstanding careers attests to Smedley's worth as a mentor.

Butler's views on imperialism were shaped by awareness of American business interests and client-state corruption in Nicaragua and Haiti. He did partake keenly, especially in Haiti and later pushing the Open Door in China, as a loyal officer and timeserving careerist. But he was always sensitive to manipulative and hypocritical aspects of U.S. policy. His radical 1930s recantation is best understood as evolving from experiences within the military and in civilian police work, rather than from outside ideological influences. Civilian political symbols, by which military officers are deemed "liberal" or "conservative," are thus of dubious relevance. Butler defiantly came to see the military as conservative and himself as radical, but he was really a maverick who staunchly believed in traditional popular military values and conventional democratic fair play. While actually "conservative," these convictions led him to increasingly radical opposition to contemporary elitist trends in military and civilian politics. That this ran parallel to left-wing politics in the 1930s indicates the logic of populist ideals in the circumstances, and is no basis for ideological pigeonholing—which he resisted. His remarkable credibility across the political spectrum implied acceptance as a valid personal testament, untainted by doctrine or partisan politics.

Much of Butler's antiwar, anti-imperialist rhetoric was compelling, and the issues had to be accommodated in internationalist rationales for militarism and war. Nationalism was best served by internationalism! National defense and protection of innocent American civilians, as in racist colonial lore, were projected on the international scale. Butler's "gangster for Wall Street" was unthinkable, and national interest would not be propagandized in economic or even strategic military terms. Future justifications for overseas military intervention would be cast in the very highest moral tones, either as ideological crusades or as emotional vendettas. Weaker enemies, condemned as outlaw bandits in Butler's day, would be similarly condemned as outlaw terrorists. International politics became a contrived morality drama, with righteous warrior patriotism on call, including—selectively— memories of Butler's heroic exploits.

As a politically potent media phenomenon, Butler was a maverick. The obliteration of his 1930s apostasy when the tide turned demonstrated the fragility of this mode. Henceforth, access to mass publicity for political purposes was increasingly institutionalized. Financial and organizational backing became crucial, to the exclusion of maverick volatility. Similarly, his

1920s Marine Corps showmanship was superseded by institutionalized public relations. But today's expensive, skilfully contrived political campaigns still try to project images of personal integrity and populist candor that Butler achieved naturally as a straight-shooting loner.

Abbreviations Used in the Notes and Bibliography

File No.   [893.00, for example] U.S., Department of State decimal file, National Archives, Record Group 59. Frequently cited files are: 812 (Mexico), 817 (Nicaragua), 838 (Haiti), and 893 (China)

AA   Politisches Archiv des Auswärtigen Amtes, Bonn (German Foreign Office Archives)

AD   Archives Diplomatiques, Ministère des Affaires Étrangères, Paris (French Foreign Ministry Archives)

CinC   Commander in Chief

CMC   Commandant, U.S. Marine Corps

CUOHC   Columbia University Oral History Collection, New York

FBI   U.S., Department of Justice, Federal Bureau of Investigation, Washington, D.C.

FDRL   Franklin D. Roosevelt Presidential Library, Hyde Park, New York

FO   Great Britain, Foreign Office Archives, Public Record Office, London

FRUS   U.S., Department of State, Foreign Relations of the United States (Washington, D.C., 1912-15)

HHL   Herbert Hoover Presidential Library, West Branch, Iowa

HI   Hoover Institute for War, Peace and Revolution, Palo Alto, California

LC   Library of Congress, Washington, D.C.

MC   Member of U.S. Congress

MCHC   U.S. Marine Corps Historical Center, Washington, D.C.

MCOHC   Marine Corps Oral History Collection, MCHC

NA   U.S. National Archives, Washington, D.C.

NS   Newtown Square, Pennsylvania

NYPL   New York Public Library, New York City

RG   Record Group in U.S. National Archives. Frequently cited are: 38 (Office of Naval Intelligence); 45 (Naval Records Collection); 59 (Department of State); 80 (Navy Department); 127 (Marine Corps); and 165 (Army, Military Intelligence Division)

SDB   Smedley D. Butler

TSB   Congressman Thomas S. Butler, father of SDB

USA   U.S. Army

USMC   U.S. Marine Corps

USN   U.S. Navy

Notes

CHAPTER 1: INTRODUCTION

1. SDB, "America's Armed Forces," pt. 2, *Common Sense* 4:11 (Nov. 1935).
2. SDB quoted in *Time* 30:11 (13 Sept. 1937), and *New York Times*, 24 Sept. 1939.
3. *Time* 30:11 (13 Sept. 1937).

CHAPTER 2: THE BOY OFFICER

1. Thomas R. Butler interview with author, Mar. 1976, and letter to author, 18 Mar. 1977.
2. Thomas R. Butler interview, Mar. 1976. SDB left Haverford before the end of his final year but was awarded a diploma, 6 June 1898, which states he completed the Scientific Course "with Credit"; Butler MSS (NS).
3. SDB and Martha Strayer, "Smedley Butler was 'Scared to Death' and Homesick on His First Marine Assignment," *Washington Daily News*, 4 Feb. 1931.
4. Henry Clay Cochrane Diaries, 10 and 12 July 1898, MCHC; Cochrane to Pruiosa, 30 July 1898, Cochrane Papers, ibid.; SDB to wife, 26 May 1914, Butler Papers (NS).
5. SDB, *Old Gimlet Eye: The Adventures of Smedley D. Butler as Told to Lowell Thomas* (New York, 1933), 18-21.
6. Cochrane Diaries, 31 Aug., 3 Sept. and endpage 1898.
7. Apart from education, SDB's social background was similar to that of his general-officer peer group; Richard C. Brown, "Social Attitudes of American Generals, 1898-1940" (Ph.D. diss., Univ. of Wisconsin, 1951), 15, 33, 35.
8. Peter N. Stearns, *Be A Man! Males in Modern Society* (New York, 1979), 39, 82 and passim.
9. Kenneth McCaleb, "Life Story of Butler—Fightin' Quaker," ch. 3, series in *Philadelphia Record*, Feb. 1931, clipping in SDB file, MCHC.
10. SDB, *Old Gimlet Eye*, 30-40.
11. SDB to mother, 8 Aug. 1899 and 9 Mar. 1900, Butler Papers (NS).
12. CinC Asiatic to sec. navy, 10 Oct. 1899; Elliott to CMC, 13 Oct., and to CinC Asiatic 13 Oct., NA, RG 127, Entry 26; singing in James Bevan, "From Filipinos to Boxers in 1900," *Leatherneck* 18:4 (Apr. 1935).
13. SDB, *Old Gimlet Eye*, 36-40.
14. Ibid., 42-43; Col. Robert L. Meade to CMC, 19 Mar. 1901, NA, RG 127, Entry 26; SDB to mother, 17 June 1900, Butler Papers (NS).

CHAPTER 3: THE TEENAGE HERO

1. Ragsdale to Hill, 5 Jan. 1900, NA, RG 59, M114/R7.
2. Henry L. Leonard, "The Visit of the Allies to China in 1900," *Military Historical*

Society of Massachusetts, Papers 14 (1918), paper read to the Society 4 Dec. 1900; Waller to Asiatic Station, 6 July 1900, NA, RG 127, Entry 26.

3. SDB, *Old Gimlet Eye*, 50; McCalla memoirs (1910), quoted in Paulo E. Coletta, *Bowman Henry McCalla: A Fighting Sailor* (Washington, 1979), 124-25.

4. SDB, *Old Gimlet Eye*, 34, 57-58.

5. *The Memoirs of Herbert Hoover: Years of Adventure, 1874-1920* (New York, 1951), 52; SDB, *Old Gimlet Eye*, 53-54.

6. Waller rept. (Tientsin), 30 July 1900, NA, RG 45, Subj File 1875-1910, HJ, box 152.

7. Frey, *Français et alliés au Pé-tchi-li: Campagne de Chine de 1900* (Paris, 1904), 21, but hearsay because he did not arrive until 24 July.

8. Waller rept. (Tientsin), 27 July 1900, NA, RG 45, Subj File 1875-1900, HJ, box 152; Cochrane Diary, 16 Oct., and Cochrane to wife, 21 Oct. 1900, Cochrane MSS; Frederick M. Wise, *A Marine Tells It to You* (New York, 1929), 42.

9. Hoover, *Memoirs, 1874-1920*, 53.

10. Leonard, "Visit of the Allies"; Meade to CMC, 17 July 1900, NA, RG 127, Entry 26; Meade rept. (Tientsin), 16 July 1900, NA, RG 45, Subj File 1875-1910, HJ, box 152. For battle maps, see W.C. Davidson, "Operations in North China," *U.S. Naval Institute Proceedings* 26:4 (Dec. 1900).

11. SDB, *Old Gimlet Eye*, 62.

12. Ibid., 62-64; SDB to mother, 23 July 1900, Butler MSS (NS); Richards to CMC, 14 Mar. 1901, and Meade rept. (Tientsin), 17 July 1900, NA, RG 127, Entry 26.

13. SDB to mother, 23 July 1900, Butler MSS (NS); Harry C. Adriance Recollections, State Historical Society of Wisconsin, copy in MCHC.

14. SDB to mother, 23 July 1900, Butler MSS (NS); Ragsdale to Hill, 16 July 1900, NA, RG 59, M114/R7.

15. James Bevan, "From Filipinos to Boxers in 1900," *Leatherneck* 18:4 (Apr. 1935); Adriance Recollections; Wise, *A Marine Tells*, 38-41.

16. Dorward to Meade, 15 July 1900, NA, RG 127, Entry 26; SDB to mother, 4 Aug. 1900, Butler MSS (NS).

17. Daggett (Kansas City, 1903), 41; List of Recipients . . . for Service in China, n.d., ca.1900, NA, RG 127, Entry 26.

18. SDB to mother, 2 Aug. 1900, Butler MSS (NS).

19. Ibid., 2 and 26 Aug. 1900; TSB to Waller, 15 Aug. 1900, Littleton W.T. Waller MSS, MCHC.

20. For informed character assassination of Waller as field commander, ca. 1901, see untitled 15-page MS, n.s., n.d., Ben H. Fuller MSS, MCHC.

21. Gordon Casserly, *The Land of the Boxers or China Under the Allies* (London, 1903), 51; Frey, *Français et alliés*, 72-73.

22. SDB to mother, 4 and 19 Aug. 1900, Butler MSS (NS); James Bevan, "With the U.S. Marines on the March to Peking, China—1900," pt. 1, *Leatherneck* 18:6 (June 1935); Waller rept. (Peking), 20 Aug. 1900, NA, RG 45, Subj File 1875-1910, HJ, box 152; SDB, *Old Gimlet Eye*, 69-70.

23. James H. Wilson, *Under the Old Flag: Recollections of Military Operations in the War for the Union, the Spanish War, the Boxer Rebellion, Etcetera* (New York, 1912), 2: 522.

24. Bevan, "With the U.S. Marines," pt. 1; SDB to mother, 19 Aug. 1900, Butler MSS (NS); SDB, *Old Gimlet Eye*, 73-74.

25. Bevan, "With the U.S. Marines," pt. 1; SDB to mother, 19 Aug. 1900, Butler MSS (NS); Conger to sec. state, 11 June, 16 and 17 Aug., and 1 Sept. 1900, NA, RG 59, M92/R109; overall casualty figures in Victor Purcell, *The Boxer Uprising* (Cambridge, Eng, 1963), 252.

26. Bevan, "With the U.S. Marines," pt. 1; Wise, *A Marine Tells*, 65-68; SDB, *Old Gimlet Eye*, 76.

27. SDB to mother, 26 Aug. 1900, Butler MSS (NS); James Bevan, "With the U.S. Marines on the March to Peking, China—1900," pt. 2, *Leatherneck*18:7 (July 1935).

28. "Butler's Bawl," n.d., 11-page MS attached to envelope annotated J.T. Kennedy to Maj. Gen. Fuller, Fuller MSS, MCHC. Fuller served in the Boxer campaign as a junior officer.

29. Rockhill to sec. state, 1 Oct. 1900, NA, RG 59 M92/R110; Chaffee to Corbin, 30 Nov. 1900, Records of U.S. Army Commands, HQ China Relief Expedition, quoted in Andrew T. Ford, "The Diplomacy of the Boxer Uprising" (Ph.D. diss., Univ. of Wisconsin, 1971), 155; Cochrane Diary, 12 and 21 Sept. 1900; SDB, *Old Gimlet Eye*, 78, 85.

30. Ethel Butler Wehle, Smedley D. Butler, Jr., and Thomas R. Butler interview with author, Mar. 1976; Thomas R. Butler to author, 28 June 1977; SDB, *Old Gimlet Eye*, 79.

31. SDB, *Old Gimlet Eye*, 70-71; Bevan, "With the U.S. Marines," pt. 1.

32. SDB to Paul Voigt, 25 May 1929, Butler MSS (MCHC).

CHAPTER 4: KNIGHT ERRANT

1. SDB comments on the diplomatic implications in *Old Gimlet Eye*, 95.

2. Ibid., 95-101; SDB to mother, 20 Mar. 1903, Butler MSS (NS).

3. *Liberty* 8 (10 Oct. 1931).

4. (New York, 1897), 59-62.

5. SDB, "Opera-Bouffe Revolts," *Liberty* 8 (10 Oct. 1931); "twentieth person" in SDB, *Old Gimlet Eye*, 105.

6. SDB to mother, 20 Mar. 1903, Butler MSS (NS).

7. Wildt to Loomis, 8 Mar. 1903, NA, RG 59, T-545.

8. Alger to Loomis, 12 Feb. and 26 Mar. 1903, ibid., T-661; Richardson to Loomis, 23 Mar. 1903, ibid., T-701.

9. SDB, "Opera-Bouffe Revolts"; Honduras file, MCHC; Wildt to Loomis, 2 Mar. 1903, NA, RG 59, T-545; SDB to mother, 26 Mar. 1903, Butler MSS (NS).

10. SDB to mother, 26 Mar. 1903, Butler MSS (NS); Wildt to Loomis, 2 Mar. 1903, NA, RG 59, T-545.

11. SDB to mother, 2 Mar. 1903, Butler MSS (NS); Eustice to Admiralty, 16 and 25 Apr. 1903, FO 39, No. 72, 6714.

12. "Cupid" clipping, minus logo, n.d., Butler MSS (NS); *Evening Bulletin*, 14 Oct. 1904.

13. Wise, *A Marine Tells* (NeJune 1906, Butler MSS (NS).

14. SDB, *Old Gimlet Eye*, 114-20.

15. SDB file, MCHC; Kenneth McCaleb, "Life Story of Butler . . . Fighting Quaker," ch. 7, series in *Philadelphia Record*, Feb. 1931, copy in SDB file, MCHC; SDB, *Old Gimlet Eye*, 120-21.

16. SDB, *Old Gimlet Eye*, 121-24.

17. Roosevelt to Wood, 28 Nov. 1908, in Elting E. Morison, *The Letters of Theodore Roosevelt* (Cambridge, Mass., 1952), 6:1389; Butt to Mrs. Clara Butt, 19 Nov. 1908, in Lawrence F. Abbott, ed., *The Letters of Archie Butt* (Garden City, N.Y., 1924), 184.

18. Roosevelt to Foss, MC, 18 Feb. 1909, in Morison, *Letters*, 6:1524-25; Dewey to sec. navy, 14 Jan. 1909, in U.S., House, Naval Affairs Committee, *Hearings on the Status of the Marine Corps, 1909* (Washington, 1909), 350-51.

19. Butt to Mrs. Clara Butt, 25 July 1909, in Archibald W. Butt, *Taft and Roosevelt: The Intimate Letters of Archie Butt, Military Aide* (New York, 1930), 1:156-58; Allan R. Millett, *Semper Fidelis: The History of the United States Marine Corps* (New York, 1980), 141-44; Jack

Shulimson and Graham A. Cosmas, "Teddy Roosevelt and the Corps' Sea-Going Mission," *Marine Corps Gazette* (Nov. 1981).

20. SDB to TSB, 5 Dec. 1910, Butler MSS (NS). See also Wayne A. Wiegand, "The Lauchheimer Controversy: A Case of Group Political Pressure during the Taft Administration," *Military Affairs* (Apr. 1976). SDB was hostile to Col. Charles H. Lauchheimer, who is the "Jew" referred to in the 5 Dec. letter, cf. McCaleb, "Life Story of Butler," ch. 6.

21. Butt to Mrs. Clara Butt, 2 Feb. 1911, in Butt, *Intimate Letters*, 2:587-88. For Taft's apologies, see Taft to TSB, 30 Jan. 1911, Butler MSS (NS).

CHAPTER 5: THE AMERICAN KITCHENER

1. SDB, *Old Gimlet Eye*, 126.

2. Ibid., 26; SDB to wife, 15 Jan. 1910, Butler MSS (NS).

3. Lay and Price to Moses, 3 Feb. 1910, NA, RG 38, Entry 98, Naval Attaché Repts., L-3-c, reg. 662.

4. Dana G. Munro, *Intervention and Dollar Diplomacy in the Caribbean, 1900-1921* (Princeton, 1964), 172-75; Harold N. Denny, *Dollars for Bullets: The Story of American Rule in Nicaragua* (New York, 1929), 79; Wilson to Reid, 1 July 1910, NA, RG 59, 817.00/1147.

5. Knox quoted in Munro, *Intervention and Dollar Diplomacy*, 176; Taft quoted in Richard D. Challener, *Admirals, Generals, and American Foreign Policy* (Princeton, 1973), 293; Wilson to Reid, 1 July 1910, NA, RG 59, 817.00/1147.

6. Munro, *Intervention and Dollar Diplomacy*, 164-70.

7. Moffat to sec. state, 12 and 26 May 1910, NA, RG 59, 817.00/947 and 967.

8. SDB to Gilmer in Gilmer to sec. navy, 18 July 1910, NA, RG 59, 817.00/1200; SDB, *Old Gimlet Eye*, 127-28.

9. SDB to Gilmer in Gilmer to sec. navy, 18 July 1910, NA, RG 59, 817.00/1200; but rept. by R.M. Gilson, Nov. 1910, NA, RG 38, Naval Attache Reports, 1886-1939, L-3-d, 707, noted "health record of Bluefields has for years been remarkably good."

10. Rept. by R.M. Gilson, Nov. 1910, NA, RG 38, Naval Attache Reports, 1886-1939, L-3-d, 707; SDB, *Old Gimlet Eye*, 130-31.

11. SDB to Marston, 30 July 1929, Butler MSS (MCHC); SDB, "America's Armed Forces," pt. 3, *Common Sense* 4:12 (Nov. 1935); cf. Munro, *Intervention and Dollar Diplomacy*, 186.

12. Consular reports, NA, RG 59, 817.00/1162, 1166, 1172, 1250, 1304; DeOlivares to sec. state, 19 Aug. 1910, ibid., 1320; Cavendish-Venables rept., 20 Oct. 1912, FO 371, No. 1308, 32888, 54926.

13. Mena had been a top Conservative general. As Díaz's minister of war, he was supported for the client-presidency by some U.S. diplomats and was considered an alternative to Díaz by the State Department. But his election as Díaz's eventual successor was annulled by the U.S.; NA, RG 59, 817.00/1702. For comments on his fortunes under the Americans, see Cavendish-Venables rept., 20 Oct. 1912, FO 371, No. 1308, 32888, 54926.

14. Knox to Taft, 5 Aug. 1912, NA, RG 59, 817.00/1822. See also Lester D. Langley, *The Banana Wars: An Inner History of American Empire, 1900-1934* (Lexington, Ky., 1983), 67-68.

15. SDB to wife, 3, 9, and 11 Aug. 1912, Butler MSS (NS).

16. Campbell to sec. navy, 5 Aug. 1912, NA, RG 59, 817.00/1819.

17. Weitzel repts., NA, RG 59, 817.00/1844, 1853, 1856, and 1868; Wilson, *The Sun* (New York), 6 Oct. 1912.

18. NA, RG 59, 817.00/1863 through 1896.

19. Ibid., 817.00/1915; Taft and Stimson quoted in Foster to Wilson, 27 Aug. 1912, 817.00/1907; Taft to Stimson, 2 Sept. 1912, quoted in Challener, *Admirals, Generals*, 305.

20. SDB to wife, 18 and 22 Aug. 1912, Butler MSS (NS).

21. Brown Seligman Co. to sec. state, and Weitzel to sec. state, NA, RG 59, 817.00/1900, 1891 and 1919; SDB, *Old Gimlet Eye*, 140-43; Vandegrift interview (1962), 133; SDB to wife, 24 Aug. 1912, Butler MSS (NS). The "General Walkemback" ditty is reproduced in Langley, *Banana Wars*, 69.

22. SDB to wife, 25 Aug. 1912, Butler MSS (NS).

23. Alexander A. Vandegrift, *Once a Marine: The Memoirs of General A.A. Vandegrift*, as told to Robert B. Asprey (New York, 1964), 40.

24. Ibid.; SDB, *Old Gimlet Eye*, 146.

25. SDB, *Old Gimlet Eye*, 148-49; Vandegrift, *Once a Marine*, 41; Vandegrift interview (1962), 130, MCOHC.

26. SDB to wife, 28 Aug. and 5 Sept. 1912, Butler MSS (NS).

27. Adm. Harold C. Train, USN, Recollections (1965), 41-43, CUOHC; SDB to wife, 5 Sept. 1912, Butler MSS (NS); cf. SDB, "The Toughest Five Minutes of My Life," *Liberty* (4 July 1931).

28. SDB to wife, 5 Sept. 1912, Butler MSS (NS); NA, RG 59, 817.00/1937 and 1946; Train Recollections (1965), 41-43;

29. Campaign Orders Nos. 4 and 8, Memo for Commanders, 4 Sept. 1912, and Southerland to Pendleton, 12 Sept. 1912, Joseph H. Pendleton MSS, box 1, MCHC; Cavendish-Venables rept., 20 Oct. 1912, FO 371, No. 1308, 32888, 54926.

30. SDB to wife, 14 Sept. 1912, Butler MSS (NS); Pendleton to Southerland, 11 Sept. 1912, Pendleton MSS, box 1.

31. Pendleton to SDB, 14 Sept. 1912, Pendleton MSS, box 1; SDB to Pendleton, 15 Nov. 1912, NA, RG 127, Entry 43, box 3.

32. SDB to wife, 18 Sept. 1912, Butler MSS (NS); Zeledón to Southerland and Long to Zeledón, 18 Sept. 1912, NA, RG 127, Entry 43, box 2.

33. SDB to Pendleton, 15 Nov. 1912, NA, RG 127, Entry 43, box 3; SDB to wife, 23 Sept. 1912, Butler MSS (NS); Vandegrift, *Once a Marine*, 41; Southerland to sec. navy, 20 Sept. 1912, NA, RG 59, 817.00/1997.

34. NA, RG 59, 817.00/1988, 1994 and 1998; for the purported message, see Chamorro to Weitzel, 20 Sept. 1912, Pendleton MSS, box 1.

35. SDB to Mena, 21 Sept. 1912, NA, RG 59, 817.00/2119; SDB to Mena, 21 Sept. 1912, Mary Grist MSS, MCHC; SDB to Pendleton, 15 Nov. 1912, NA, RG 127, Entry 43, box 3.

36. SDB to wife, 23 Sept. 1912, Butler MSS (NS); Vandegrift, *Once a Marine*, 42; Train Recollections (1965), 45.

37. SDB to wife, 23 Sept. 1912, Butler MSS (NS).

38. Ibid., 30 Sept. 1912; Weitzel to sec. state, 29 Sept. 1912, *FRUS, 1912*, 1051-53.

39. NA, RG 59, 817.00/2119 and 2129; Pendleton to Southerland, 11 Oct. 1912, NA, RG 127, Entry 43, box 3.

40. SDB to wife, 30 Sept. 1912, Butler MSS (NS).

41. Ibid.

42. NA, RG 59, 817.00/2018, 2020 and 2023.

43. Ibid., 817.00/2018 and 2025.

44. Wilson to Taft, 23 Sept. 1912, NA, RG 59, 817.00/2003B quoted in Challener, *Admirals, Generals*, 306; Taft memo, 23 Sept. 1912, NA, RG 59, 817.00/2014; cf. Richard W. Turk, "Strategy and Foreign Policy: The U.S. Navy in the Caribbean, 1865-1913" (Ph.D. diss., Fletcher School, 1968), 190.

45. Pendleton to Zeledón, 2 Oct., and Zeledón to Pendleton, 3 Oct. 1912, NA, RG 127, Entry 43, box 2.

46. SDB to wife, 5 Oct. 1912, Butler MSS (NS); Pendleton to Southerland, 11 Oct., and SDB to Pendleton, 15 Oct. 1912, NA, RG 127, Entry 43, box 3; SDB, *Old Gimlet Eye*, 165-67.

47. NA, RG 59, 817.00/2072; SDB to wife, 9 Oct. 1912, Butler MSS (NS).

48. Peter Karsten, *The Naval Aristocracy: The Golden Age of Annapolis and the Emergence of American Navalism* (New York, 1972), passim; James L. Abrahamson, *America Arms for a New Century: The Makings of a Great Military Power* (New York, 1981), 84-86. For a contrasting interpretation of the same theme, see John P. Mallan, "The Warrior Critique of the Business Civilization," *American Quarterly* 8 (Fall 1956).

49. SDB to wife, 23 and 30 Sept. and 17 Oct. 1912, Butler MSS (NS); Weitzel to sec. state, 25 Nov. 1912, *FRUS, 1912*, 1067-68; *Globe Democrat,* 23 Sept. 1912; "blond pigs" quoted in Langley, *Banana Wars*, 75; *Nation*, 112:2903 (23 Feb. 1921).

50. SDB to wife, 9 Oct. 1912, Butler MSS (NS); Southerland to SDB and Pendleton to SDB, 7 Oct. 1912, and petition, Pendleton MSS, box 1.

51. SDB to wife, 9 Oct. 1912, Butler MSS (NS).

52. Ibid., 9 and 23 October 1912; Southerland to Pendleton, 8 Oct., and Pendleton to Southerland, 30 and 31 October, 1 and 2 Nov. 1912, Pendleton MSS, box 1.

53. Southerland to sec. navy, 4 Nov. 1912, NA, RG 59, 817.00/2160; SDB quoted in *Literary Digest* 113:12 (12 Dec. 1929); SDB, 1912, quoted in Jules Archer, *The Plot to Seize the White House* (New York, 1973), 57-58.

54. Pendleton to Southerland, 11 Nov. 1912, Pendleton MSS, box 1.

55. FO 371, No. 1308, 32888, 54926.

CHAPTER 6: THE SPY

1. *New York Times*, 6 July 1912; SDB, *Old Gimlet Eye*, 135-37.

2. Morning repts., Panama Battalion, 1909-10, NA, RG 127, Entry 233; Lt. Gen. Julian C. Smith interview (1968), p. 23, MCOHC.

3. SDB to TSB, 8 Nov. 1913, Butler MSS (NS).

4. Josephus Daniels, *The Wilson Era: Years of Peace, 1910-17* (Chapel Hill, 1944), 256.

5. Smith interview (1968), 24.

6. SDB to mother, 18 Jan. 1914, Butler MSS (NS).

7. Ibid.; SDB to Daniels, 11 Mar. 1914, LC, Josephus Daniels MSS, box 531.

8. Senators' endorsements in Swanson to Tumulty, 2 Dec. 1913, Daniels MSS, box 23; Daniels, *Wilson Era: Years of Peace*, 322-23; Merrill L. Bartlett, "Old Gimlet Eye," *U.S. Naval Institute Proceedings* 112 (Nov. 1986). From 1881 to 1896, the Naval Academy was the exclusive source for new marine officers.

9. Spring-Rice to FO, 23 Jan. 1914, FO 371, No. 2025, 91 5205.

10. Lind to Bryan, 13 Oct. 1913, NA, RG 59, 812.00/11437.

11. Ibid.

12. William S. Coker, "Naval Diplomacy during the Mexican Revolution: An Episode in the Career of Admiral Frank Friday Fletcher," *North Dakota Quarterly* 40 (Spring 1972); NA, RG 59, 812.00/11414; Friedrich Katz, *The Secret War in Mexico* (Chicago, 1981), 222-23.

13. Lind to Bryan, 2 and 8 Mar. 1914, NA, RG 59, 812.00/11032 and 11098.

14. SDB to wife, 1 and 10 Mar. 1914, Butler MSS (NS); Fletcher to sec. navy, 1 Mar. 1914, NA, RG 45, Corresp. Polit. Cond. Mexico, 1911-14, and 5 Mar. 1914, RG 59, 817.00/11180; Lind to sec. state, 2 Mar. 1914, ibid., 11032.

15. Fletcher to sec. navy, 5 Mar. 1914, NA, RG 59, 817.00/11180; Lind to sec. state, 23 Feb. 1914, ibid., 10957; Grey to Spring-Rice, 11 Feb., FO 371, No. 2025, 91, 6537; cf. Lloyd C. Gardner, *Safe for Democracy: The Anglo-American Response to Revolution, 1913-23* (New York, 1984), 56, 62.

16. Lind to sec. state, 23 Feb. 1914, NA, RG 59, 817.00/10957.

17. SDB to wife, 10 Mar. 1914, Butler MSS (NS).

18. O'Shaughnessy (New York, 1916), 212; Lind to sec. state, 8 Mar. 1914, NA, RG 59, 812.00/11098.

19. SDB to wife, 10 Mar. 1914, Butler MSS (NS).

20. Lind to sec. state, 8 and 12 Mar. 1914, NA, RG 59, 812.00/11098 and 11227.

21. Ayguesparsse to Foreign Ministry, AD, NS6, Mexico; cf. Larry D. Hill, "The Progressive Politician as Diplomat: The Case of John Lind in Mexico" *Americas* 27:4 (Apr. 1971).

22. SDB plan, 24 Feb. 1914, NA, RG 45, Subj File 1911-27, WE-5, box 661; Lind plan, annotated by Capt. William A. Burnside, is "Detail of Plans Expeditionary Forces to Mexico City," by SDB, Mar. 1914, NA, RG 165, file 6474-356, box 106F. I am indebted to Timothy K. Nenninger of NA for finding this obscurely placed document.

23. "Detail of Plans," by SDB, Mar. 1914, NA, RG 165, file 6474-356, box 106F; cf. Katz, *Secret War*, 26, 47, 93.

24. Lind to sec. state, 11, 12 and 19 Mar. 1914, NA, RG 59, 812.00/11134, 11227, and 11218.

25. Vandegrift, *Once a Marine*, 43; SDB, *Old Gimlet Eye*, 178; SDB to CMC, 12 Apr. 1914, Veracruz file, MCHC.

26. John A. Lejeune, *Reminiscences of a Marine* (Philadelphia, 1930), 205-06; Wise, *A Marine Tells*, 125-26; SDB to wife, 24 Apr. 1914, Butler MSS (NS); H.O. Stickney customs rept., 6 Dec. 1914, NA, RG 45, Subj File 1911-27, WE-5, box 663.

27. Neville rept., 21-25 Apr. 1914, NA, RG 45, Subj File 1911-27, WE-5, box 663; SDB to CMC, 12 May 1914, Veracruz file, MCHC; Jack Sweetman, *The Landing at Veracruz* (Annapolis, 1968), 123.

28. Kendrick A. Clements, "Mexican Policy, 1913-15," *Diplomatic History* 4:2 (Spring 1980); Arthur S. Link, *Wilson: The New Freedom* (Princeton, 1956), 400-402; Katz, *Secret War*, 197-99.

29. Funston to adjutant general, 7 May and 10 June 1914, NA, RG 94, Entry 25, box 7480; Langley, *Banana Wars*, 105.

30. Katz, *Secret War*, 298-302; Cole Blazier, *The Hovering Giant: U.S. Responses to Revolutionary Change in Latin America* (Pittsburgh, 1976), 106. At one point, the War Department advised that it would take almost 500,000 troops to invade Mexico effectively; Lloyd C. Gardner, "Woodrow Wilson and the Mexican Revolution," in Arthur S. Link, ed., *Woodrow Wilson and a Revolutionary World, 1913-21* (Chapel Hill, 1982).

31. NA, RG 59, 812.00/11598, 11652, 11689; Sweetman, *Landing at Veracruz*, 128-30; Robert E. Quirk, *An Affair of Honor: Woodrow Wilson and the Occupation of Veracruz* (Lexington, Ky., 1962), 108-09.

32. Lejeune, *Reminiscences*, 212.

33. Edith O'Shaughnessy, *A Diplomat's Wife in Mexico* (New York, 1916), 327.

34. W.P. Arbuthnot, Capt., R.M.L.I., notes, 30 May 1914, Littleton W.T. Waller, Jr., MSS, box 1, MCHC; James Leutze, *A Different Kind of Victory: A Biography of Admiral Thomas C. Hart* (Annapolis, 1981), 44; *Collier's* 53:11 (30 Apr. 1914).

35. Newspaper clipping, source unidentified, SDB file, MCHC.

36. "Admiral Dewey was so proud of him [SDB] and his splendid conduct, and so vain of his temerity that he always called him 'the stormy petrel,'" Mrs. George Dewey to TSB, 1 Mar. 1922, Butler MSS (NS).

37. D. Clayton James, *The Years of MacArthur* (Boston, 1970), 1:118-27; Douglas

MacArthur, *Reminiscences* (New York, 1964), 40-42; sec. navy to SDB 18 Jan. and 13 Aug. 1915, SDB to sec. navy, 23 Feb. and 9 July 1916, Butler MSS (MCHC); SDB to mother, 21 Feb. 1916, Butler MSS (NS).

38. Daniels to FDR, 19 Apr. 1933, FDRL, PPF86.

CHAPTER 7: THE HAITIAN GENERAL

1. TSB to Josephus Daniels, 10 Nov. 1914, Daniels MSS, box 531; SDB service record, 9-12 June 1915, SDB file, MCHC.

2. SDB to wife, 19 Aug. 1915, Butler MSS (NS). Most of SDB's letters during the Haiti years are reproduced and copiously annotated in Anne C. Venzon, "The Papers of General Smedley Darlington Butler, U.S.M.C., 1915-1918," (Ph.D. diss., Princeton University, 1982).

3. SDB to TSB, 5 Oct. 1915, Butler MSS (NS); Waller to Lejeune, 21 and 26 Aug., 21 Sept. and 20 Oct. 1915, LC, Lejeune MSS. Lejeune instructed Waller regarding the correspondence, and later told Waller not to write reflecting on the reputations of his officers because Barnett felt this should go through official channels; Lejeune to Waller, 1 Oct. 1915, ibid.

4. SDB to TSB, 5 Oct. 1915, Butler MSS (NS); Bartlett, "Old Gimlet Eye."

5. SDB to TSB, 5 Oct. 1915, Butler MSS (NS).

6. Waller to Lejeune, 21 Sept. 1915, Lejeune MSS; "chicken thieves," ibid., 8 Sept. 1915; "inconceivably miserable," Waller quoted in William B. Caperton, "History of a Flag Career," MS, n.d., ca. 1920, p. 149, NA, RG 45, Subj File 1911-27, ZN Caperton, box 802.

7. SDB to TSB, 5 Oct. 1915, Butler MSS (NS); Caperton, "Flag Career," 150-60; Rameau proclamation in ibid., 406; SDB, *Old Gimlet Eye*, 183-86.

8. Waller to Lejeune, 21 Sept. 1915, Lejeune MSS.

9. Hans Schmidt, *The United States Occupation of Haiti, 1915-1934* (New Brunswick, N.J., 1971), chs. 3, 7, and passim.

10. Waller to Lejeune, 26 Sept. 1915, Lejeune MSS.

11. Waller to Lejeune, 7 and 15-19 Oct. 1915, Lejeune MSS.

12. Adolph B. Miller Diaries, 15 and 16 Oct. 1915, MCHC; Waller to Lejeune, 20 Oct. 1915, Lejeune MSS; SDB to TSB, 23 Dec. 1915, Butler MSS (NS).

13. SDB to Cole, 7 Dec. 1915 (copy dated 8 May 1931), Butler MSS (MCHC); Vandegrift, *Once a Marine*, 47; Miller Diaries, 16 and 22 Oct. 1915.

14. Waller to Lejeune, 15 Oct. 1915, Lejeune MSS; Campbell to mother, 14 Nov. 1915, and Campbell Diary, 5 Nov. 1915, Chandler Campbell MSS, MCHC.

15. Pp. 186ff.

16. SDB to Cole, 7 Dec. 1915, Butler MSS (MCHC); SDB, *Old Gimlet Eye*, 195; Miller Diaries, 24 and 26 Oct. 1915.

17. SDB, "The Fightingest Man I Know" [Sgt. Maj. Dan Daley], *American Magazine* 112:3 (Sept. 1931); SDB to Cole, 7 Dec. 1915, Butler MSS (MCHC).

18. Waller to Lejeune, 1 Nov. 1915, Lejeune MSS; SDB to Cole, 7 Dec. 1915, Butler MSS (MCHC); Campbell Diary and Campbell to mother, 14 Nov. 1915, Campbell MSS.

19. Campbell Diary and Campbell to mother, 14 Nov. 1915, Campbell MSS.

20. Campbell to mother, 14 Nov., and Campbell Diary, 8-17 Nov. 1915, Campbell MSS; Thomas E. Thrasher, "The Taking of Fort Rivière," *Marine Corps Gazette* 15:4 (Feb. 1931); SDB to Cole, 7 Dec. 1915, Butler MSS (MCHC).

21. SDB to Cole, 17 Nov. 1915, in Campbell Diary; SDB, *Old Gimlet Eye*, 207; Campbell quoted on teeth in unidentified newspaper clipping, 29 Apr. 1931, scrapbook "Haiti," vol. 3, NYPL, Schomburg Collection.

22. Campbell Diary, 17 Nov. 1915; SDB to Cole, 7 Dec. 1915, Butler MSS (MCHC).

23. Upshur to mother, 12 Jan. 1916, William P. Upshur MSS, Southern Historical Collection, Univ. of North Carolina; Waller to Lejeune, 1 July 1916, Lejeune MSS.

24. Daniels to Caperton, 20 Nov. 1915, *FRUS, 1915*, 493; cabinet anecdote in Daniels, "The Problem of Haiti," *Saturday Evening Post* 203:2 (12 July 1930); Roosevelt, "Trip to Haiti . . . 1917," MS, FDRL.

25. David Healy characterizes the campaign "not only as a model of military efficiency, but also as relatively economical in human life": *Gunboat Diplomacy in the Wilson Era: The U.S. Navy in Haiti, 1915-16* (Madison, Wis., 1976), 184.

26. Perl to Bethmann-Hollweg, 18 Jan. 1915, AA, 1A, Haiti No. 1, vol. 26. For background to U.S. intervention, see Brenda Gayle Plummer, "Black and White in the Caribbean: Haitian-American Relations, 1902-34" (Ph.D. diss., Cornell Univ., 1981), chs. 3 and 4.

27. "The Bank," Office of Naval Intelligence rept., n.s., n.d., ca. early 1915, annotated by Capt. E.H. Durrell, commanding officer, USS *Connecticut*, in Haitian waters Aug.-Sept. 1915, NA, RG 45, WA-7, box 631.

28. 3 Apr. 1915, NA, Bryan-Wilson Corresp.

29. Capt. Edward L. Beach memos, 10 Aug. 1915, and n.d., ca. 15 Aug. 1915, NA, RG 45, WA-7, box 635; Caperton quoted in Healy, *Gunboat Diplomacy*, 84.

30. U.S., House, Naval Affairs Committee, *Estimates Submitted by the Secretary of the Navy*, 64 Cong., 1 sess. (1916), 2264.

31. Waller to Lejeune, 7 and 26 Oct. 1915; SDB to TSB, 5 Oct. and 23 Dec. 1915, and SDB to wife, 23 Jan. 1916, Butler MSS (NS).

32. Waller to Lejeune, 13 Oct. 1915 and 3 Apr. 1916, Lejeune MSS. I am indebted to Charles A. Wood, chief curator at MCHC, for calling the Nat Turner connection to my attention. The Waller family figures prominently as Virginia slaveholders in Alex Haley's best-selling chronicle of slavery and freedom, *Roots* (1976).

33. Waller to Lejeune, 31 Aug. 1916, Lejeune MSS. Butler's four-star uniform as Major General Commandant of the Gendarmerie d'Haiti is occasionally displayed at the Marine Corps Museum, Washington, D.C.

34. Vandegrift, *Once a Marine*, 49; *Congressional Record*, 64 Cong., 1 sess. (17 Apr. 1916), 53:7, 6306-07; SDB to Lejeune, 4 Mar. 1916, Lejeune MSS.

35. Waller to Lejeune, 1 July 1916, Lejeune MSS; SDB to wife, 16 July 1916, Butler MSS (NS); Caperton to Benson, 20 July 1916, Caperton MSS. Batie to Pinchon, 21 Mar. 1917, AD, NS6, Haiti (cf. B. Danache, *Le Président Dartiguenave et les amèricaines* [Port-au-Prince, 1950], 45); Caperton, "Flag Career," 165.

36. Waller to Lejeune, 26 Aug. 1915, Lejeune MSS; Waller to SDB, 7 July 1916, Haiti MSS, MCHC, quoted in John C. Chapin, "The Marines' Role in the U.S. Occupation of Haiti: 1915-22" (M.A. thesis, George Washington Univ., 1967), 44; SDB to Wright, 13 Oct. 1916, Butler MSS (MCHC).

37. Waller to Lejeune, 3 Apr. 1916 and 13 Dec. 1915, Lejeune MSS.

38. Batie to Ribot, 6 June 1917, and to Pinchon, 21 Nov. 1917, AD, NS6, Haiti.

39. Waller to Lejeune, 1 July and 31 Aug. 1916, and SDB to Lejeune, 13 July 1916, Lejeune MSS.

40. SDB to Lejeune, 13 July 1916, Lejeune MSS; Danache, *Président Dartiguenave*, 60; "socially objectionable" in William B. Seabrook, *The Magic Island* (New York, 1929), 139. As retold by a State Department clerk who arrived in 1920 and "played both sides of the street" socially, Butler confronted the president of the club, a German married to a Haitian woman ("an octaroon of course"), and "turned to him and said, 'I can't shake hands with you. You're a German.'" The German, who was receiving guests at the door, then "very properly said, 'Well, how can you come to my club if you can't shake hands with me?' . . . so Smedley Butler turned on his heels with his officers and he put the club out of bounds for Navy and Marine

Corps"; Lawrence Dennis Reminiscences (1967), CUOHC. This seemingly innocuous incident attained notoriety as a milestone in the breakdown of social relations, probably because it was not overtly racial and therefore was acceptable as an anecdote in Haitian public discourse.

41. G.R. Coulthard, "The French West Indian Background of 'Négritude,'" *Caribbean Quarterly* 6:3 (Dec., 1961); Alexis (Port-au-Prince), pp. 56, 67, 98-99.

42. SDB testimony, U.S., Senate, Inquiry into the Occupation and Administration of Haiti and Santo Domingo, *Hearings Before a Select Committee on Haiti and Santo Domingo*, 67 Cong., 1 and 2 sess. (Washington, 1922), 516-18, hereafter cited as *Haiti Hearings, 1922*; Waller to Lejeune, 1 July 1916, Lejeune MSS; "same race" and "docile," Waller testimony, U.S., House, Naval Affairs Committee, *Estimates Submitted by the Secretary of the Navy*, 64 Cong., 1 sess. (Washington, 1916), 2265, 2268.

43. Caperton to Benson, 18 May 1916, Caperton MSS.

44. SDB testimony, *Haiti Hearings, 1922*, 516; Waller to Lejeune, 26 Aug. 1915, and SDB to Lejeune, 13 July 1916, Lejeune MSS.

45. Upshur to father, 28 Jan. 1917, Upshur MSS.

46. According to the French minister, "all of Port-au-Prince society was invited to the ball, but the Americans, as usual, hardly mixed with them," Batie to Briand, 14 Feb. 1917, AD, NS11, Haiti. Marvin interview (1946) in Frank Freidel, *Franklin D. Roosevelt: The Apprenticeship* (Boston, 1952), 279.

47. FDR, "Trip to Haiti . . . 1917," and FDR to McIlhenny, 14 July 1917, FDRL; Shanton (Puerto Rico) to SDB, 16 May 1917, and Barnett to SDB, 10 Feb. 1917, Butler MSS (MCHC).

48. H.L. Roosevelt to McIlhenny (copy to be shown to FDR), 4 Mar. 1917, HLR to FDR, 17 Feb. 1917, and FDR to McIlhenny, 18 Oct. 1922, FDRL; Schmidt, *U.S. Occupation*, 111-12.

49. SDB to McIlhenny, 29 Jan. 1918, and SDB to Farnham, 11 Feb. 1918, Butler MSS (MCHC). After internment during the war, fifty leading Germans were deported in 1920.

50. SDB in *Haiti Hearings, 1922*, 536-38; SDB, *Old Gimlet Eye*, 216; Daniels, *Wilson Era: Peace*, 178. Sténio Vincent, a staunch nationalist, was elected president when the marines withdrew in the 1930s. SDB to McIlhenny, 23 June 1917, Butler MSS (MCHC).

51. George Marvin, "Healthy Haiti," *World's Work* 34:1 (May 1917); Samuel Guy Inman, *Through Santo Domingo and Haiti: A Cruise with the Marines* (New York, ca. 1919), 68; Wise, *A Marine Tells*, 135; Vandegrift, *Once a Marine*, 58.

52. SDB to TSB, 1 Oct. 1916, Butler MSS (NS); SDB to TSB quoted in TSB to FDR, 29 Oct. 1917, FDRL.

53. SDB in *Haiti Hearings, 1922*, 529-32; TSB to FDR, 29 Oct. 1917, FDRL.

54. Memo for chief of gendarmerie, ca. Dec. 1917, and Fitzgerald-Brown to SDB, 24 Nov. 1921, Butler MSS (MCHC); SDB, *Old Gimlet Eye*, 239; FDR to SDB, 21 Dec. 1917, FDRL; Farnham to SDB, 22 Dec. 1917 and 21 Jan. 1918, Butler MSS (MCHC).

55. SDB to FDR, 28 Dec. 1917, FDRL; SDB to McIlhenny, 31 Dec. 1917, Butler MSS (MCHC).

56. SDB in *Haiti Hearings, 1922*, 535; *The Cabinet Diaries of Josephus Daniels, 1913-1921*, ed. E. David Cronon (Lincoln, Neb., 1963), 553; Schmidt, *U.S. Occupation*, 100-107.

57. McIlhenny to FDR, 2 May 1919, FDRL; Fitzgerald-Brown to SDB, 24 Nov. 1921, Butler MSS (MCHC); Daniels, "Problem of Haiti."

58. Helmick to SDB, 15 Mar. 1920 and SDB to Helmick, 18 Mar. 1920, Butler MSS (MCHC); SDB, *Old Gimlet Eye*, ch. 11.

59. SDB to Eyre, 28 Jan. 1918, Butler MSS (MCHC); Waller to Lejeune, 13 Dec. 1915, Lejeune MSS; Miles, IRS to SDB, 4 Sept. 1917, and lease, 1 Nov. 1916, Butler MSS (MCHC); SDB, *Old Gimlet Eye*, 240; *Le Nouvelliste* (Port-au-Prince), 14 Jan. 1918; *Le Matin*

(Port-au-Prince), 18 Jan. 1918; SDB to McIlhenny, 31 Dec. 1917, and to Radford, 10 Aug. 1917, Butler MSS (MCHC); family details, Ethel Butler Wehle, Thomas R. Butler, and Smedley D. Butler, Jr., interview with author, Mar. 1976.

60. Ethel Butler Wehle, Thomas R. Butler, and Smedley D. Butler, Jr., interview with author, Mar. 1976; SDB to Lejeune, 18 Dec. 1926, Butler MSS (MCHC).

61. Danache, *Président Dartiguenave*, 57-58.

62. William W. Cumberland Reminiscences (1951), CUOHC.

CHAPTER 8: GENERAL DUCKBOARD

1. FDR's allusions in mother to SDB, 25 Oct. 1917; TSB to SDB, 19 Jan. 1918; McIlhenny to SDB, 17 July 1917; Farnham to SDB, 21 Jan. 1918 and 8 Jan. 1919, all in Butler MSS (MCHC).

2. SDB to parents, 6 Oct. 1917, Butler MSS (NS).

3. Ibid., 27 Jan. 1918; Caperton to Waller, 16 Mar. 1916, Butler MSS (MCHC). When Waller objected to Caperton recalling SDB from Washington, the admiral replied, "Of course you do not wish him back. He went there to work for you for [promotion to] brigadier general," Waller to Lejeune, 1 July 1916, Lejeune MSS.

4. TSB to SDB, 19 Jan. 1918, and Walter L. Hensley, MC to SDB, 2 Oct. 1917, Butler MSS (MCHC).

5. *New York Times*, 1 May 1916; TSB to SDB, 19 Jan. 1918, Butler MSS (MCHC). See also ibid., 25 Dec. 1917.

6. Lejeune to Butler, 19 Dec. 1916, Butler MSS (MCHC).

7. Ibid., 24 Apr. 1917; Lejeune, *Reminiscences*, 237.

8. George Barnett, "Soldier and Sailor Too," MS, n.d. (ca. 1920s), ch. 26, MCHC; trainee letter, Aug. 1918, quoted in Albertus W. Catlin, *With the Help of God and a Few Marines* (New York, 1919), 282-84; Lester A. Dessez interview (1970), 20, 43, MCOHC; "Conditions of the Battle Front Reproduced," *New York Times*, 14 Oct. 1917.

9. Catlin, *Help of God*, 19; SDB to TSB, 16 May 1917, urging help for a navy medical officer working in the bush who had failed his promotion exam—"Do what thee can for our comrade in illiteracy and we 'roughnecks' will be again in the ascendancy," Butler MSS (NS); Upshur to father, 7 July 1918, Upshur MSS.

10. SDB, *Old Gimlet Eye*, 243; SDB to mother, 21 Feb. 1916, Butler MSS (NS).

11. Benis M. Frank, "The Relief of General Barnett," *Columbia Historical Records* (annual ed., 1974), Columbia Historical Society, Washington, D.C.; *Congressional Record*, 65 Cong., 2 sess. (18 June 1918), 56:8, see also ibid. (19 Apr. 1918), 56:6, 5360; TSB to FDR, 27 Apr. 1918, FDRL.

12. Dessez interview (1970), 19-20; SDB, *Old Gimlet Eye*, 243.

13. Cronon, *Cabinet Diaries*, 139; Lejeune to Daniels, 27 Apr. 1917, Lejeune MSS; Lejeune, *Reminiscences*, 236.

14. Cronon, *Cabinet Diaries*, 165, 174, 281-82, 320, 324.

15. SDB to Mrs. Daniels, 9 Sept. 1918, Daniels MSS, box 23; Cronon, *Cabinet Diaries*, 334-35.

16. Dessez interview (1970), 21; SDB to Livingston Davis, 3 July 1918, FDRL; SDB, *Old Gimlet Eye*, 244-45.

17. SDB, *Old Gimlet Eye*, 244-45; Daniels Jr. to mother, 20 Sept. 1918, Daniels MSS, box 23.

18. Alfred W. Crosby, Jr., *Epidemic and Peace, 1918* (Westport, Conn., 1976), 133-34.

19. SDB, *Old Gimlet Eye*, 245-46; SDB to wife, quoted in Merrill L. Bartlett, "Ouster of a Commandant," *U.S. Naval Institute Proceedings* 106:11 (Nov. 1980) (Bartlett also explains

marine troops movements, concluding that SDB had "remained in Haiti inexplicably blaming his exile on Barnett"); Millett, *Semper Fidelis*, 293-96.

20. Maj. Gen. Robert Blake interview (1968), 7, MCOHC.

21. U.S., War Department, *The Medical Department of the U.S. Army in the World War*, vol. 2, *Administration A.E.F.* (Washington, 1927), 465-68; "U.S. Naval Air Station, Brest," MS, n.d., NA, RG 45, ZPA, box 810.

22. *Literary Digest*, 8 Mar. 1919.

23. SDB, *Old Gimlet Eye*, 247-48.

24. Thomas Krug, Jr., to SDB, 16 July 1929, Butler MSS (MCHC).

25. Gen. Ray A. Robinson interview (1968), 9-10, MCOHC.

26. Josephus Daniels, Jr., to mother, 28 Oct. 1918, to parents, 13 Nov., and to father, 24 Nov. 1918, Daniels MSS, box 23.

27. SDB, *Old Gimlet Eye*, 249-54. For analogous frustrations of an army colonel dealing with red tape at Brest, see Forrest C. Pogue, *George C. Marshall: Education of a General, 1880-1939* (New York, 1963), 194-95.

28. SDB, *Old Gimlet Eye*, 249-54; "The Duckboard Story," *Pontanezen Duckboard* 1:2 (5 Mar. 1919), MCHC.

29. SDB to Jones, 6 Nov. 1919, Butler MSS (MCMC).

30. Mary Roberts Rinehart, *My Story* (New York, 1948), 277-79; SDB, *Old Gimlet Eye*, 254.

31. Rinehart, *My Story*, 279. Cf. "The Much-Discussed Embarkation Camp at Brest," *Leslie's Weekly* 128:3328 (21 June 1919).

32. *Pontanezen Duckboard* 1:10 (2 Apr. 1919).

33. Mimeographed description of camp, Headquarters Pontanezen, 11 Apr. 1919, HI, Niel R. Allen MSS; *Pontanezen Duckboard* 1:1, 6, 9, 21, and 26 (Mar.-May 1919); *New York Times*, 30 Mar. 1919, sec. 3.

34. War Department, *Medical Department*, 2:467, 469-70.

35. *New York Times*, 30 Mar. 1919, sec. 3.

36. Arthur W. Little, *From Harlem to the Rhine: The Story of New York's Colored Volunteers* (New York, 1936), 354.

37. William L. Langer, *Gas and Flame in World War I* (New York, 1965 repr. of unit history, ca. 1919), 110-11.

38. Niel R. Allen, "Putting 'Em Away," MS, n.d. (ca. Jan. 1919), Allen MSS; Langer, *Gas and Flame*, 108.

39. SDB, *Old Gimlet Eye*, 255; Robinson interview (1968), 1; Keck to SDB, 15 Dec. 1919, Butler MSS (MCHC).

40. SDB, *Old Gimlet Eye*, 257-58.

41. Eleanor Roosevelt to Sara Delano Roosevelt, 1 Nov. 1919, in Elliott Roosevelt, ed., *F.D.R., His Personal Letters, 1905-1928* (New York, 1948), 448-49; FDR to Daniels and Daniels to FDR, 13 Jan. 1919, Daniels MSS, box 94.

42. Josephus Daniels, Jr., to parents, 23 Feb. and 3 Mar. 1919, Daniels MSS, box 23; "talking," SDB to Mrs. Daniels, 17 July 1919, ibid., box 533; Lejeune, *Reminiscences*, 453. See also SDB to Lejeune, 18 Dec. 1926, Butler MSS (MCHC).

43. Daniels, "For the Press," Brest, 24 Mar. 1919, Daniels MSS, box 533.

44. SDB to Harbord, 24 Apr., and to Helmick, 23 Apr. 1920, Butler MSS (MCHC); Benson to SDB, 19 June 1919, LC, Benson MSS, general corresp. 1874-1941, box 12; SDB, *Old Gimlet Eye*, 246.

45. William J. Graham to SDB, 10 May, and SDB to Graham, 23 May 1920, Butler MSS (MCHC).

46. In peacetime too. Admiral Sir Hugh Tweedie, RN, recalled steaming through the Red Sea in 1900: "After Suez we got down to five knots, and everyone in the ship, from the

captain downwards, was taking a spell in the stokehold. The stokers were a young lot and couldn't stand up to the heat for long at a time." Tweedie, *Story of a Naval Life* (London [ca. 1939]), 70.

CHAPTER 9: THE BARNETT PUTSCH

1. Robert H. Williams, "Those Controversial Boards," *Marine Corps Gazette* (Nov. 1982); Frank, "Relief of General Barnett"; Bartlett, "Ouster of a Commandant"; and, most pointedly, Bartlett, "Old Gimlet Eye."
2. SDB to John Wehle, 21 Nov. 1932, Butler MSS (NS); Lejeune quoted in Shulimson and Cosmas, "Teddy Roosevelt and the Corps' Sea-going Mission."
3. Millett, *Semper Fidelis*, 174; SDB, *Old Gimlet Eye*, 189.
4. SDB to Helmick, 14 Nov. 1919, and SDB to Farnham, 6 Jan. 1920, Butler MSS (MCHC).
5. "Plan to make the Marine Corps a great military university," by Lt. John H. Craige, typewritten, n.d. (ca. Jan. 1920), annotated by SDB, Daniels MSS, box 533.
6. Daniels testimony, U.S., House, Naval Affairs Committee, *Estimates Submitted by the Secretary of the Navy, 1920*, 66 Cong., 2 sess. (Washington, 1920), 1841-42; Daniels article, *The Associated Sunday Magazines*, 15 Feb. 1914, copy in Howe MSS, box 5, FDRL.
7. SDB speech at Quantico Schools, *Leatherneck*, 16 Apr. 1920; Navy News Bureau release, 24 Jan. 1920, and "Vocational and Educational Schools at Marine Base, Quantico," ca. 1920, Butler MSS (MCHC);
8. SDB speech, *Leatherneck*, 16 Apr. 1920.
9. SDB to Daniels, 13 Jan. 1920, Naval Affairs Committee, *Estimates Submitted by the Secretary of the Navy, 1920*, 1842-43; cf. Daniels to SDB, 10 Jan. 1920, soliciting the plan, Daniels MSS, Miscellaneous Items; Cronon, *Cabinet Diaries*, 500, 503.
10. Bartlett, "Ouster of a Commandant," provides a sketch of Barnett's career and a convincing analysis of the Barnett-Daniels troubles.
11. Frank, "Relief of General Barnett."
12. Josephus Daniels, *The Wilson Era: Years of War and After, 1917-23* (Chapel Hill, 1946), 155; Barnett, "Soldier and Sailor Too," chs. 29-31.
13. Grayson to Lejeune, 1 June 1932, Lejeune MSS.
14. Barnett, "Soldier and Sailor Too," chs. 29 and 30; Gen. Clifton B. Cates interview (1967), MCOHC; Cronon, *Cabinet Diaries*, 539, 541; Cabinet Diaries, Daniels MSS, box 1, and dismissal note pencil draft, n.d. (ca. 18 June 1920), ibid., box 64; Bartlett, "Ouster of a Commandant"; Frank, "Relief of General Barnett." Awareness of Barnett's impending dismissal in Barnett to Long, 25 June 1918, Fuller to Barnett, 21 June, and Lyman to Barnett, 21 June, Barnett MSS, and in Robert Hugh Williams, "Those Controversial Boards," *Marine Corps Gazette* (Nov. 1982).
15. Maj. Gen. William A. Worton interview (1967), MCOHC, 88-89, as told to him by Charles Murray, who is described as very loyal to Barnett. See also Cates interview (1967), 66, and Barnett, "Soldier and Sailor Too," ch. 30. Cates's version is related in Frank, "Relief of General Barnett."
16. Robinson interview (1968), 12; SDB to Vandegrift, 6 Aug. 1920, Butler MSS (MCHC).
17. Barnett to Mustin, 28 June 1920, Barnett MSS; Barnett, "Soldier and Sailor Too," ch. 29; Barnett to Pendleton, 23 June 1920, Barnett MSS; Lejeune to Daniels, 26 June 1920, Daniels MSS, box 88; Cates interview (1967), 68-69.
18. John W. Weeks to Mrs. Barnett, 2 Sept. 1920, Barnett MSS; for Mrs. Barnett's activities, see Frank, "Relief of General Barnett," and Bartlett, "Ouster of a Commandant";

Daniels, *Wilson Era: Years of War*, 155; Daniels to Wilson, 29 June 1920, Daniels MSS, box 64.

19. *New York Times*, 14 Oct. 1920; Harding quoted in ibid., 29 Aug. 1920, pt. 2, p. 12, and ibid., 18 Sept. 1920; FDR to Daniels, 16 Oct. 1920, FDRL; cf. Barnett, "Soldier and Sailor Too," chs. 30-31.

20. Lejeune to Daniels, 4 Oct. 1920, Butler MSS (MCHC); Lejeune, *Reminiscences*, 468. For Barnett letter, cf. John H. Craige, *Cannibal Cousins* (New York, 1934), 84-87.

21. "Suggestions," n.s., n.d., Barnett MSS; see also E.N. McClellan to Barnett, 11 Oct. 1920, ibid.

22. Daniels, *Wilson Era: Years of War*, 156; Barnett, "Soldier and Sailor Too," ch. 32.

23. Ramond J. Bartholomew to Mrs. Barnett, 11 and 27 Jan. 1932, Barnett MSS.

24. "Copy Letter to Lejeune," n.d., Lejeune to Mrs. Barnett, 10 Feb. 1935, and associated legal correspondence, Barnett MSS; Craige, *Cannibal Cousins*; Craige-Lejeune correspondence in Lejeune MSS; Frank, "Relief of General Barnett."

25. Robinson interview (1968), 9, 13; Worton interview (1967), 90.

26. Blake interview (1968), 35-36; Smith interview (1968), 57.

27. Frank, "Relief of General Barnett"; Williams, "Those Controversial Boards"; Millett, *Semper Fidelis*, 322; SDB to Keck, 8 Apr. 1920, Butler MSS (MCHC).

28. Daniels to Josephus Daniels, Jr., 1 Aug. 1919, Daniels MSS, box 23; Daniels to FDR, 15 May 1936, FDRL; Daniels to Wilson, 29 June 1920, Daniels MSS, box 64, Barnett file.

29. Bartlett, in "Ouster of a Commandant," makes a similar point, characterizing Barnett as "the antithesis of the officer idealized by [Smedley] Butler."

30. Archibald Douglas Turnbull, "Seven Years of Daniels," *North American Review* 212:780 (Nov. 1920).

31. For instance, he introduced a four-point scheme for fitness reports to open up officer evaluation as against immured seniority criteria and sub-rosa cronyism. This was evaded by assignment of 4.0 grades: "The records of many officers, for every grade of service, bore the mark of perfection all the way through." Innis LaRoche Jenkins, "Josephus Daniels and the Navy Department" (Ph.D. diss., Univ. of Maryland, 1960), 169.

32. Barnett, "Soldier and Sailor Too," passim; Weeks to Denby, 30 June 1921, Edwin H. Denby MSS, Burton Collection, Detroit Public Library.

33. Barnett, "Soldier and Sailor Too," ch. 30.

34. Barnett to Lejeune, 10 Feb. 1920, Lejeune MSS; Barnett testimony, Naval Affairs Committee, *Estimates Submitted by the Secretary of the Navy, 1920*, 1850-51.

35. SDB to Lejeune, 27 Apr. 1927 and 23 July 1928, Butler MSS (MCHC).

36. Williams, "Those Controversial Boards." Cukela was an immigrant whose English, as of 1931, Williams described as "so broken as to be barely understandable and sometimes mirth-provoking," Robert Hugh Williams, *The Old Corps: A Portrait of the U.S. Marine Corps Between the Wars* (Annapolis, 1982), 17-19.

37. Williams, "Those Controversial Boards."

38. Rufus H. Lane to Lejeune, 24 May 1932, Lejeune MSS; U.S., House, Naval Affairs Committee, *Hearings, Sundry Legislation Affecting the Naval Establishment, 1927-28*, 70 Cong., 1 sess. (Washington, 1928), reference to "Butler bill" on p. xviii of index, cf. pp. 3215 and 3258-60.

39. Bartlett, *George Barnett, 1859-1930: Register of His Personal Papers* (Washington: MCHC, 1980), 3.

40. Newspaper eulogies quoted in *Army and Navy Journal*, 2 June 1928.

41. Martin, *My First Fifty Years in Politics* (New York, 1960), 236.

42. Vallejo anecdote and other details in Robert G. Albion, "The Naval Affairs Committees, 1816-1947," *U.S. Naval Institute Proceedings* 78:11 (Nov. 1952). See also Michael A.

West, "Laying the Legislative Foundations: The House Naval Affairs Committee and the Construction of the Treaty Navy, 1926-34" (Ph.D. diss., Ohio State Univ., 1980), 74, 80, 96-98.

43. Lejeune testimony, Naval Affairs Committee, *Estimates Submitted by the Secretary of the Navy, 1920*, 2014.

44. Kenneth J. Clifford, *Progress and Purpose: A Developmental History of the United States Marine Corps, 1900-70* (Washington: MCHC, 1973), 30, 36; Richard S. Moore, "Ideas and Directions: Building Amphibious Doctrine," *Marine Corps Gazette* (Nov. 1982).

45. Millett, *Semper Fidelis*, 324-25.

46. Wilbur to Coolidge, 23 June 1924, LC, Coolidge MSS, reel 23, 18E.

47. U.S., Senate, *Haiti Hearings, 1922*, passim; Sen. Medill McCormick to Hughes, 14 Dec. 1921, NA, RG 59, 838.00/1825.5; Hughes to Denby, 18 Oct. 1921, NA, RG 80, File No. 5526-321:37; SDB to Radford, 26 Aug. and 16 Nov. 1921, Butler MSS (MCHC); Schmidt, *The U.S. Occupation*, 123-25.

48. SDB to Vandegrift, 19 Jan. 1922, and SDB to Radford, 26 Aug., 16 and 21 Nov., 14 and 28 Dec. 1921, Butler MSS (MCHC).

49. Denby to SDB, 26 Jan. 1922, Denby MSS; see also Denby to Hughes, 13 Jan. 1922, ibid.; Munro to Fletcher, 5 and 7 Jan. 1922, NA, RG 59, 711.38/175 and 176; cf. Dana G. Munro, *The U.S. and the Caribbean Republics, 1921-33* (Princeton, 1974), 84.

50. SDB to Radford, 13 Jan. 1922, Butler MSS (MCHC); Schmidt, *U.S. Occupation*, ch. 10 and passim.

51. SDB to McDougal, 5 July 1921, Butler MSS (MCHC).

CHAPTER 10: PEP AND PRIDE

1. SDB to Farnham, 6 Apr. 1920, and SDB to Helmick 14 Nov. 1919 and 18 Mar. 1920, Butler MSS (MCHC).

2. Lt. Gen. Merwin H. Silverthorn interview (1969), 115-19, MCOHC.

3. Denby to TSB and Denby to Page, 20 Apr. 1922, NA, RG 80, Sec. Navy Correspondence, 1916-26, serial 7662-569.

4. Upshur to mother, 30 Jan. 1922, Upshur MSS; Eastman to SDB, 25 May 1922, and SDB to Royal C. Johnson, MC, 18 Dec. 1920, Butler MSS (MCHC).

5. Holcomb to SDB, 10 Sept., and Tighe (Haiti) to SDB, 10 Nov. 1922, Butler MSS (MCHC); Ethel Butler Wehle, Thomas R. Butler, and Smedley D. Butler, Jr. interview with author, Mar. 1976.

6. Upshur to mother, 13 and 19 Feb. 1922, Upshur MSS; lifelong dyspepsia, Thomas R. Butler interview (1978); SDB to Radford, 22 Mar. 1922, Butler MSS (MCHC); Robinson, Tighe, Vandegrift and other correspondence with juniors, ibid.; Lt. Gen. James P. Berkeley interview (1969), 10-11, MCOHC—his father was Maj. Gen. Randolph C. Berkeley.

7. Upshur to mother, 20 Feb. 1921, Upshur MSS; Lt. Gen. Thomas A. Wornham interview (1967-68), MCOHC; William C. Lemly interviewed in Tom Valentine, "Retired General Remembers Military Hero Smedley Butler," *The Spotlight for America First* (Washington, D.C.) 10:12 (19 Mar. 1984).

8. Valentine, "Retired General Remembers"; "Mother De Boo" in Charles A. Fleming, Robin L. Austin, and Charles A. Braley, III, *Quantico: Crossroads of the Marine Corps* (Washington: USMC, 1978), 57-58.

9. Barnett to Lejeune, 10 Feb. 1920, Lejeune MSS; Upshur to mother, 17 Oct. 1920, Upshur MSS; Fegan to SDB, 23 Aug., and SDB to Harllee, 1 Dec. 1920, Butler MSS (MCHC).

10. Wise, *A Marine Tells*, 336; John Creigh Hendrickson, who is working on a biography of Carlson, has told me of Carlson's admiration for SDB.

11. Good interview (1970), MCOHC.

12. SDB to Hackett, 24 Apr. and 8 May 1923, Butler MSS (MCHC); Frank O. Hough, "Personalities—Men Who Differed," *Marine Corps Gazette* 34:11 (Nov. 1950).

13. SDB to Hunton, 21 Sept. 1922, Butler MSS (MCHC).

14. Hunton to SDB, 26 Sept. and 16 Dec. 1922, Hunton to McGuire, 17 Nov. 1922, and Hardy to SDB, 17 Aug. 1923, Butler MSS (MCHC).

15. SDB to Hardy, 22 Aug. 1923, Butler MSS (MCHC); Silverthorn interview (1969), 107-08.

16. Maj. Gen. Louis R. Jones interview (1970), 28, MCOHC; Vandegrift, *Once a Marine*, 62.

17. Vandegrift, *Once a Marine*, 63; Lt. Gen. James L. Underhill interview (1968), 43, MCOHC.

18. SDB, *Old Gimlet Eye*, 260-62.

19. SDB to TSB, 2 Sept. 1921, Butler MSS (MCHC); John H. Craige, "The 'Wilderness' Manoeuvres," *Marine Corps Gazette* 6:4 (Dec. 1921).

20. Maj. Gen. Ford O. Rogers interview (1966), 60-61, MCOHC.

21. SDB to TSB, 2 Sept. 1921, Butler MSS (MCHC).

22. Francis Russell, *The Shadow of Blooming Grove* (New York, 1968), 541-42; *New York Tribune*, 1 July 1922; Jones interview (1970), 31.

23. Silverthorn interview (1969), 111, and Gen. Vernon E. Megee interview (1967), 25-26, MCOHC.

24. Vandegrift, *Once a Marine*, 63-64; Megee interview (1967), 29-30.

25. Vandegrift, *Once a Marine*, 63; crowd estimate in newspaper clipping, n.d., Perry K. Dean MSS, MCHC.

26. Good interview (1970), 12-13; Zelinsky to SDB, 15 Sept. 1929, Butler MSS (MCHC).

27. *New York Times*, 6 Oct. 1923; Helmick to Lejeune and Helmick to SDB, 5 Oct. 1923, Butler MSS (MCHC).

28. Lt. Gen. Louis E. Woods interview (1968), 60, MCOHC; Rogers interview (1966), 62, 101, 105, MCOHC.

29. Rogers interview (1966), 105, MCOHC.

30. D. Clayton James, *The Years of MacArthur, 1880-1941* (Boston, 1970), 1:325.

31. SDB to TSB, 16 Nov. 1920, Butler MSS (MCHC); Valentine, "Retired General Remembers"; cf. SDB to Hawthorne, 1 Dec. 1932, Butler MSS (NS).

32. Daniels to SDB, 6 Dec. 1920, Butler MSS (MCHC).

33. Rogers interview (1966), 105; Silverthorn interview (1969), 107; Fleming, et al., *Quantico*, 46.

34. SDB to Richard Peters, Jr., 26 Apr. 1922, and SDB to TSB, 19 Nov. 1920, Butler MSS (MCHC).

35. SDB to Holcomb, 11 Dec. 1922, Butler MSS (MCHC).

36. SDB to Berkeley, 13 Oct. 1923, Butler MSS (MCHC).

37. SDB to Lejeune, 26 July 1926, Butler MSS (MCHC); cf. Lt. Gen. Joseph Charles Burger interview (1969), 89, MCOHC.

38. The Quantico Marines again played "big-time varsity football" after World War II but withdrew because of budget cuts in 1972, when they beat Eastern Illinois University 56 to 14, Fleming et al, *Quantico*, 98, 111.

39. SDB to Fegan, 22 Dec. 1923, and contemporary correspondence, Butler MSS (MCHC).

40. SDB to Denby, 14 Oct., and SDB to Mellett, 19 Sept. 1923, Butler MSS (MCHC); Denby to SDB, 18 Oct. 1923, Denby MSS.

41. SDB to Denby, 14 Oct. 1923, Butler MSS (MCHC); *Free Press*, 22 Oct. 1923; SDB to Hunton, 14 Oct., Nichols to SDB, 6 Nov., SDB to McDonough, SJ, 15 Oct. 1923, and contemporary correspondence, Butler MSS (MCHC).

42. Roosevelt to SDB, 18 Oct., and SDB to Roosevelt, 27 Dec. 1923, Butler MSS (MCHC); Denby to SDB, 18 Oct. 1923, Denby MSS.

43. SDB-Radford correspondence, 1923, Butler MSS (MCHC).

44. Memorandum of interview, ca. 5 Dec. 1923, Coolidge MSS, Reel 23, 18-E; Coolidge to Denby, 12 Dec. 1923, Denby MSS.

45. Samuel Walker, *A Critical History of Police Reform: The Emergence of Professionalism* (Lexington, Mass., 1977), 102-03; *New York Times*, 6, 8, 10, and 14 Dec. 1923; *Record*, 5 Dec. 1923.

46. SDB to H.L. Roosevelt, SDB to Marston, and SDB to Thomas Holcomb, 27 Dec. 1923, Butler MSS (MCHC).

47. Clifford, *Progress and Purpose*, 45.

CHAPTER 11: SMASHING CRIME AND VICE

1. Robert M. Fogelson, *Big-City Police* (Cambridge, Mass., 1977), 54-55.

2. Ibid., 89.

3. *New York Times*, 7, 8, and 19 Jan. 1924. In 1924 the police killed sixteen bandits; SDB in "City Club Bulletin" (Los Angeles), 13 Mar. 1926, copy in Butler MSS (MCHC).

4. *New York Times*, 9-13 Jan. 1924. For an account based on Philadelphia newspapers, see Fred D. Baldwin, "Smedley D. Butler and Prohibition Enforcement in Philadelphia, 1924-25," *Pennsylvania Magazine of History and Biography* 84:3 (July 1960).

5. *New York Times*, 16, 20, 21, and 26 Jan. 1924; SDB, "Smashing Crime and Vice" (30-pt. serial, Bell Syndicate and North American Newspaper Alliance, Apr.-May 1926, copies in SDB file, MCHC), ch. 4.

6. *New York Times*, 13 Jan. 1924.

7. SDB, "Fighting Crime and Vice," ch. 16.

8. Percival M. Sax, Jr., to author, 1 Dec. 1975.

9. *New York Times*, 13 Jan. 1924.

10. E.Z. Dimitman interview with author, 19 Mar. 1976.

11. Gene E. Carte and Elaine H. Carte, *Police Reform in the United States: The Era of August Vollmer* (Berkeley, 1975), 50-52.

12. "A woman" to sec. navy, 9 Feb. 1924, NA, RG 80, Sec. Navy Correspondence, 1916-26, serial 13673-5605.

13. Tobin to sec. navy, 12 Jan. 1924, ibid.; C. Seamus Krone, "'Gimlet Eye' Butler—America's Greatest Marine," *Stag* 11:12 (Dec. 1960).

14. William H. Houghton to Richey, 30 Jan. 1931, HHL, Presidential Cabinet Offices—Navy-Marine Corps, box 36.

15. Andrew Sinclair, *Prohibition: The Era of Excess* (Boston, 1962), 183-86.

16. Haynes to Slemp, 18 July 1924, Coolidge MSS; SDB, "Smashing Crime and Vice," ch. 23; SDB to Pinchot, 1 and 27 Oct. 1925, LC, Pinchot MSS, box 259.

17. *New York Times*, 10 Feb. 1924 and 13 Sept. 1925.

18. Spencer Ervin, *The Magistrates' Courts of Philadelphia* (Philadelphia, 1931), 104-17.

19. SDB, "Smashing Crime and Vice," ch. 19.

20. *New York Times*, 9 Feb. 1924, 24 May and 19 July 1925.

21. SDB, "Smashing Crime and Vice," chs. 5 and 8.

22. SDB quoted in Fogelson, *Big-City Police*, 78; Henchel to SDB, 1 June 1931, Butler MSS (NS).

23. Larry D. Englemann, "A Separate Peace: The Politics of Prohibition Enforcement in Detroit, 1920-30," *Detroit in Perspective* (Autumn 1972).

24. Carte and Carte, *Police Reform*, 58-62.

25. Walker, *Critical History of Police Reform*, ix, 66-67.

26. Ibid., 42, 61-67.

27. SDB, "Smashing Crime and Vice," chs. 9, 11-13.

28. Ibid.; Baldwin, "Butler and Prohibition."

29. SDB to Lejeune, 14 July 1924, Lejeune MSS; SDB, "Smashing Crime and Vice," ch. 13; Coolidge quoted in Baldwin, "Butler and Prohibition."

30. *New York Times*, 22 Apr. and 19 July 1925.

31. Ibid., 16 May and 24 June 1925; Kendrick quoted in SDB, "Smashing Crime and Vice," ch. 24.

32. SDB, "Smashing Crime and Vice," ch. 24; Pepper intrigue in SDB to Pinchot, 22 Feb. 1926, Pinchot MSS, box 259; appeals from organizations in NA, RG 80, Sec. Navy Correspondence, 1916-26, serial 13673-5605, and Coolidge MSS, reel 23, 18E; *New York Times*, 28 May, 31 Oct., 2 and 4 Nov. 1925.

33. SDB to Pinchot, 16 Nov. 1925, Pinchot MSS, box 259.

34. Ibid.; SDB quoted in Baldwin, "Butler and Prohibition Enforcement."

35. SDB quoted in Baldwin, "Butler and Prohibition Enforcement."

36. SDB, "Smashing Crime and Vice," chs. 25 and 26.

37. Ibid.; Kendrick quoted by SDB in *New York Times*, 24 Dec. 1925.

38. SDB, "Smashing Crime and Vice," chs. 26 and 27; *New York Times*, 23 Dec. 1925; wife's support, Thomas R. Butler interview with author, Sept. 1978.

39. Kendrick quoted in Baldwin, "Butler and Prohibition."

40. *New York Times*, 23 Dec. 1925; SDB, "Smashing Crime and Vice," ch. 27.

41. Ibid.; *New York Times*, 24, 25, and 28 Dec. 1925.

42. Ibid., 28 Dec. 1925.

43. *Monitor*, 24 Dec. 1925; *Times*, 27 and 23 Dec. 1925; SDB to Lejeune, 18 Dec. 1926, Butler MSS (MCHC).

44. Baldwin, "Butler and Prohibition"; *New York Times*, 29 Dec. 1925.

45. Ibid., 11 June and 26 Dec. 1926; Pinchot to SDB, 27 Jan. 1925, Butler MSS (MCHC).

46. TSB to SDB, 14 July 1927, Butler MSS (NS); *New York Times*, 9 Mar. and 9 Sept. 1928; Farson to SDB, 4 May 1928, Butler MSS (MCHC).

47. *New York Times*, 9 Sept. 1928; Mark H. Haller in Allen F. Davis and Haller, eds. *The Peoples of Philadelphia: A History of Ethnic Groups and Lower Class Life, 1790-1940* (Philadelphia, 1973), 285-86.

48. Fogelson, *Big-City Police*, 101.

49. SDB, "Smashing Crime and Vice," ch. 30; SDB, *Old Gimlet Eye*, 274.

50. SDB to Pinchot, 20 Dec. 1926, Pinchot MSS, box 272.

51. *New York Times*, 29 Dec. 1925.

CHAPTER 12: DEVIL DOG AND DEMON RUM

1. *New York Times*, 29 Jan. 1926; SDB to TSB, 7 Feb. 1926, Butler MSS (NS).

2. SDB to Pinchot, 7 Feb. 1926, LC, Pinchot MSS, box 259.

3. SDB to Philip Andrews, 24 May 1926, Butler MSS (MCHC).

4. Dimitman interview with author, 19 Mar. 1976; SDB, "Smashing Crime and Vice," ch. 20.

5. Thomas R. Butler interview with author, Mar. 1976; Lejeune to SDB, 25 Jan., and SDB to Andrews, 12 Jan. 1926, Butler MSS (MCHC).

6. Robinson interview (1968), 57, MCOHC; Thomas R. Butler interview with author, Mar. 1976.

7. SDB referred to his local civilian protagonists as "a lot of land speculators, bootleggers and oily politicians, who have simply made a paying proposition out of a painted desert through the simple and inexpensive medium of verbal fertilizer—in other words, oratorical manure"; SDB to Holcomb, 26 May 1926, Butler MSS (MCHC).

8. *San Diego Sun*, 19, 25, 26, and 27 Feb. 1926.

9. *New York Times*, 12 Mar. 1926; Virgil W. Peterson, *The Mob: 200 Years of Organized Crime in New York* (Ottawa, Ill., 1983), 75; cf. New York State, Senate, *Report of the Special Committee Appointed to Investigate the Police Department of the City of New York* (Albany, 1895), 5:5311-84 and 5431-5578.

10. SDB, *Old Gimlet Eye*, 278-79.

11. *San Diego Sun*, 10-12 Mar. 1926; *New York Times*, 12 Mar. 1926.

12. *New York Times*, 14 and 15 Mar. and 6 Apr. 1926.

13. Vandegrift, *Once a Marine*, 66; SDB to Dimitman, 24 Apr. 1926, Butler MSS (MCHC).

14. SDB to Dimitman, 17 April, and Bell Syndicate to C.B. Blethen, 19 Apr. 1926, Butler MSS (MCHC); *San Diego Sun*, 1-12 Apr. 1926.

15. Lt. Gen. Leo D. Hermle interview (1968), 31, MCOHC; clippings and letters in Butler MSS (NS and MCH); SDB, *Old Gimlet Eye*, 285.

16. *New York Times*, 20 Apr. 1926; *San Diego Sun*, 12-15 Apr. 1926.

17. *San Diego Sun*, 12-15 Apr. 1926; "easily excited" in *Seattle Times*, 14 Apr. 1926; summation in *New York Times*, 20 Apr. 1926.

18. *San Diego Sun* and *Seattle Times*, 13 and 15 Apr. 1926.

19. *Seattle Times*, 13 and 15 Apr. 1926.

20. *San Diego Sun*, 17 Apr. 1926; SDB to Lejeune, 22 Apr. and 18 Dec. 1926, and Lejeune to SDB, 7 Dec. 1926, Butler MSS (MCHC).

21. Don Marquis column, n.d., clipping in "Butler Front Page Final" (MS), 1:3 (16 May 1926), Butler MSS (MCHC); Philip Andrews to SDB, 8 May, and SDB to Andrews, 24 May 1926, ibid.; Robinson interview (1968), 29.

22. SDB and Arthur J. Burks, *Walter Garvin in Mexico* (Philadelphia, 1927), 235-36; Vandegrift, *Once a Marine*, 67.

23. Election data, *San Diego Sun*, 19 May 1926; Pinchot flyer in "Butler Front Page Final" (MS), 1:3 (16 May 1926), Butler MSS (MCHC); SDB to Pinchot, 14 Aug. 1926, ibid.

24. Associated Press in *Great Falls Tribune* (Mont.), 2 Oct. 1926; *San Francisco Chronicle*, 1-2 Oct. 1926; *San Diego Sun*, 1 Oct. 1926.

25. *San Diego Sun*, 19 Apr. 1926; Vandegrift interview (1962), 284, MCOHC.

26. SDB to Neville, 27 Sept., and SDB to Irving Thalberg, MGM, 11 Sept. 1926, Butler MSS (MCHC); Lejeune to SDB, 7 Feb. 1927, SDB to Lejeune, 1 Dec. 1926, and SDB to Radford, 30 July 1926, ibid.; Thomas R. Butler interview with author, Mar. 1976. Films of China, 1927-29, are in Butler MSS (NS).

27. SDB to Lejeune, 21 July and 1 Dec. 1926, and Edward L. Hardy, State Teachers and Junior College, to SDB, 23 Mar. 1926, Butler MSS (MCHC).

28. *Great Falls Tribune*, 17 and 22 Dec. 1926; *Congressional Record*, 69 Cong., 2 sess. (10 Jan. 1927), 1395-96.

29. *New York Times*, 7 Feb. 1927.

30. "Marines to Guard the Mails," *Leatherneck* 9:15 (Dec. 1926); *San Francisco Chronicle*, 23, 25 Oct. and 5 Dec. 1926.

31. SDB to TSB, 15 Dec., and SDB to Lejeune, 18 Dec. 1926, Butler MSS (MCHC).

32. SDB to Lejeune, 18 Dec. 1926, Butler MSS (MCHC).

33. SDB to TSB, 15 Dec. 1926, ibid.

34. SDB to Lejeune, 18 Dec. 1926, ibid.

35. SDB to TSB, 15 Dec., and SDB to Lejeune, 18 Dec. 1926, ibid.; cf. Vandegrift, *Once a Marine*, 68.

36. SDB to Lejeune, 18 Dec. 1926, Butler MSS (MCHC).

CHAPTER 13: THE MARINES WHO WOULDN'T FIGHT

1. "Exhibition force," John P.S. Mahoney, "Touring the Orient at Uncle Sam's Expense," *Lawrence Telegram* (Mass.), serial 1 Apr.-13 May 1929, ch. 9; Jones interview (1970), 44, MCOHC.

2. Lejeune to SDB, 7 Feb. 1927, Butler MSS (NS).

3. NA, RG 59, 893.00/8221; Coolidge to CinC Asiatic, 28 Jan. 1927, 893.00/8167; Kellogg memo, 31 Jan. 1927, 893.00/8168; Grew to London, 25 Feb. 1927, NA, RG 59, 893.00/8311; SDB to Lejeune, 11 Aug. 1927, Butler MSS (MCHC).

4. *New York Times*, 13 Mar. 1927, 4:7; Rogers in ibid., 28 Mar. 1927; *Time* 9:25 (20 June 1927).

5. SDB to Lejeune, 1 and 27 Apr. 1927, Butler MSS (MCHC). SDB-Lejeune correspondence, 1927-29, is mostly in Butler MSS (MCHC), with duplicates and additional items in Butler MSS (NS).

6. John B. Powell, *My Twenty-five Years in China* (New York, 1945), 146; Bingham, *Peking and Tientsin Times*, 19 July 1927, clipping in NA, RG 59, 893.00/9325.

7. Coolidge speech in NA, RG 59, 893.00/8802a; Nelson T. Johnson memo, 19 Jan. 1927, quoted in Akira Iriye, *After Imperialism: The Search for a New Order in the Far East, 1921-31* (Cambridge, Mass., 1965), 104.

8. *North China Herald*, 9 Apr. 1927.

9. Powell, *Twenty-five Years in China*, 146.

10. SDB to Lejeune, 1 and 4 Apr. 1927, Butler MSS (MCHC).

11. Ibid.; Vandegrift, *Once a Marine*, 70.

12. SDB to Lejeune, 1 and 5 Apr. 1927, Butler MSS (MCHC); army option, NA, RG 59, 893.00/8945.

13. SDB to Lejeune, 1, 5, and 27 Apr. 1927, Butler MSS (MCHC).

14. H.C. Davis to Lejeune, 9 and 19 June 1927, Butler MSS (MCHC).

15. Maj. Gen. Omar T. Pfeiffer interview (1968), 85-86, MCOHC.

16. Sokolsky syndicated column, *Syracuse Post Standard*, 27 Oct. 1945, clipping in Butler MSS (MCHC).

17. Burger interview (1969), 33, MCOHC; SDB to Lejeune, 12 May 1927, Butler MSS (MCHC); Lejeune to SDB, 22 Aug. 1927, Butler MSS (NS); Barbara W. Tuchman, *Stilwell and the American Experience in China, 1911-45* (New York, 1970), 99.

18. SDB to Lejeune, 27 Apr. and 5 May 1927, and Davis to Lejeune, 12 May 1927, Butler MSS (MCHC); Jones interview (1970), 47-51; Pfeiffer interview (1968), 86. See also Williams, *Old Corps*, ch. 4, "Shanghai." An excellent British garrison memoir is Ralph Shaw, *Sweet and Sour* (London, 1973), published in U.S. as *China Nights* (New York, 1974).

19. SDB to Lejeune, 1 and 5 Apr. 1927, Butler MSS (MCHC).

20. Ibid.

21. Johnson to Bristol, 10 Mar. 1928, NA, RG 59, 893.00/9802.

22. NA, RG 59, 893.00/8508, 8641, 9197.

23. SDB to Lejeune, 31 May 1927, Butler MSS (MCHC).

24. Ibid.

25. Ibid., 12 and 31 May 1927.

26. I am working on a study that will elaborate beyond what is discussed here and below.

27. Wheeler, *Yankee from the West* (New York, 1962), 383.

28. Maj. Gen. John N. Hart interview (1970), 29-31, MCOHC.

29. SDB to Lejeune, 25 June 1927, Butler MSS (MCHC).

30. *Daily News*, 23 Aug. 1927, quoted in Janet S. Collester, "J.V.A. MacMurray, American Minister to China, 1925-29: The Failure of a Mission" (Ph.D. diss., Indiana Univ., 1977), 174; Davis to SDB, 19 Nov. 1927, Butler MSS (NS).

31. Bristol to Thomas, 14 Jan. 1928, LC, Bristol MSS, box 52, 8-27.

32. Lampson to FO, 25 Dec. 1927, FO 371, No. 12412, 2, F9418; ibid., 21 Oct. 1927, FO 371, No. 12410, 2, F8200; FO to Lampson, 12 May 1928, FO 371, No. 13231, 2255, F2306; Bristol to Johnson, 20 Jan. 1928, Bristol MSS, box 52, 19-28.

33. Davis to Lejeune, 30 Aug. 1927, Butler MSS (MCHC).

34. SDB to Lejeune, 16 July 1927, re. session with Bingham on 28 June, Butler MSS (MCHC).

35. Hiram Bingham Family Letter, 27 June 1927. I am indebted to his son, Professor Woodbridge Bingham, for allowing me to cite this very interesting manuscript material which will appear in his forthcoming book-length biography of Hiram Bingham. Woodbridge Bingham, then just beginning his career as a Sinologist, accompanied his father on the 1927 China trip.

36. SDB to Lejeune, 16 July 1927, Butler MSS (MCHC).

37. Woodbridge Bingham interview, Berkeley, Cal., 27 Aug. 1984.

38. J.K. Davis to sec. state, 29 Jan. 1927, NA, RG 59, 893.00/8588.

39. Reported in H.C. Davis to Lejeune, 3 Nov. 1927, Butler MSS (MCHC).

40. Bristol to commander, Yangtze Patrol, 22 June and 11 Dec. 1928, Bristol MSS, box 53, 310-28, and box 54, 539-28; Bernard D. Cole, *Gunboats and Marines: The U.S. Navy in China, 1925-28* (Newark, Del., 1983), 152, 157, 161; Bristol to Enochs, 25 June 1928, Bristol MSS, box 53, 293-28.

41. Bristol to Rear Adm. H.O. Dunn, 6 May, and to Mrs. Bristol, 25 May 1928, Bristol MSS, box 52, 214-28, and box 13; Davis to Butler, 19 Nov. 1927, Butler MSS (NS); Cole, *Gunboats and Marines*, 144 and 154.

42. Bristol to Dunn, 6 May 1928, Bristol MSS, box 52, 214-28; Davis to Lejeune, 6 Dec. 1927, Butler MSS (MCHC).

43. SDB to Bristol, 31 Dec. 1928, Bristol MSS, box 54, 374-29.

44. SDB to Lejeune, 25 June, 16 July, 2 Sept. and 21 Nov. 1927, Butler MSS (MCHC). Several scholars have indicated that there was no definite link between the marines and the Fifteenth, but SDB reported that when asked by Adm. Williams "if he would consider himself under my command in case of emergency, Castner [army commanding general in North China] replied that he certainly would, and that he would carry out all my orders, that he is my junior"; SDB to Lejeune, 16 July 1927, ibid.

45. SDB to Davis, 30 May 1927, Butler MSS (MCHC).

46. SDB to Lejeune, 21 Nov. and 27 Dec. 1927, ibid.

47. SDB to Bristol, 31 Dec. 1928, NA, RG 45, Subj File 1911-27, box 799, ZK-misc.; SDB to Lejeune, 27 Dec. 1927 and Magruder to SDB, 1 Feb. 1928, Butler MSS (MCHC).

48. SDB, "The Marines Who Wouldn't Fight," 8-pt. serial, North American Newspaper Alliance, starting Sept. 1929, ch. 6, copies in SDB file, MCHC.

49. Ibid.; SDB to Bristol, 31 Dec. 1928, NA, RG 45, Subj File 1911-27, box 799, ZK-misc.

50. SDB to CMC, 25 July 1930, and SDB to Lejeune, 16 July 1927, Butler MSS (MCHC); Vandegrift, *Once a Marine*, 73; Gabrielle M. Neufield and James S. Santelli, "Smedley Butler's Air Corps: The First Marine Aviators in China," *U.S. Naval Institute Proceedings* 103 (Apr. 1977).

51. SDB to Davis, 30 May 1927, Butler MSS (MCHC); SDB to Bristol, 31 Dec. 1928, NA, RG 45, Subj File 1911-27, box 799, ZK-misc.; SDB testimony, U.S., Senate, Naval Affairs Committee, *Hearings, Naval Expansion Program*, 75 Cong., 3 sess. (1938), 143; Valentine, "Retired General Remembers" (interview with Brig. Gen. William C. Lemly).

52. E.C. Long to SDB, 24 Aug. 1927, Butler MSS (NS); Cole, *Gunboats and Marines*, 138-39 and 201. Cole quotes the U.S. consul describing Butler as "evidencing no disposition to care for Chinese susceptibilities," but this, as the preceding part of the sentence states, "concerns the airplane flights," not marine rowdiness; Gauss to Mayer, 25 Aug. 1927, NA, RG 84, Tientsin, Class 834.8. For Chinese newpaper clippings, see Gauss to SDB, 18 Aug. 1927, ibid., Class 830, and NA, RG 127, Entry 38, Box 4.

53. *New York Times*, 15 Apr. 1928; SDB to Lejeune, 16 July 1927, Butler MSS (MCHC); Vandegrift, *Once a Marine*, 71; Vandegrift interview (1962), 331, MCOHC; "tough character," Megee interview (1967), 52, ibid.; Robinson interview (1968), 39, ibid.

54. Miller Diaries, 7 June 1927, MCHC; Mahoney, "Touring the Orient," chs. 8, 9, and 14 (Apr. 1929).

55. Hallett Abend, *My Life in China, 1926-41* (New York, 1943), 71; Worton interview (1967), 92, MCOHC.

56. SDB to mother, 18 Aug. 1927, Butler MSS (NS); SDB to Lejeune, 5 and 27 Apr., 5 and 31 May, and 23 July 1927, Butler MSS (MCHC); inquiry in Pfeiffer interview (1968), 87. Just before the suicide, SDB commented to Lejeune regarding revocation of Hill's orders to command the prestigious Peking legation guard: "You have mortally wounded Charlie Hill and I am sorry," SDB to Lejeune, 5 May 1927; Worton interview (1967), 92; Megee interview (1967), 58; SDB to TSB, 31 Mar. 1928, Butler MSS (NS).

57. Demarcation in Charles G. Finney, *Old China Hands* (New York, 1961), 163-64; feud, Tuchman, *Stilwell*, 99, 117; Forrest C. Pogue, *George C. Marshall: Education of a General* (New York, 1963), 241; SDB to Lejeune, 16 and 23 July 1927, Butler MSS (MCHC).

58. Robinson interview (1968), 43; prices in Jones interview (1970), 51; "Living Conditions in China," *Marine Corps Gazette* 13:1 (Mar. 1928).

59. Worton interview (1967), 92; SDB to Lejeune, 27 Aug. and 21 Nov. 1927, Butler MSS (MCHC); Robinson interview (1968), 38.

60. SDB to Lejeune, 27 Dec. 1927, Butler MSS (MCHC); *New York Times*, 26 Dec. 1927; SDB to Bristol, 28 Dec. 1927, Butler MSS (MCHC); Gauss to sec. state, 31 Dec. 1927, NA, RG 84, Tientsin Consular Records, vol. 25; SDB, "Marines Who Wouldn't Fight," ch. 7; *China Illustrated News* (Tientsin), 31 Dec. 1927; SDB to TSB, 31 Dec. 1927, Butler MSS (NS).

61. Mahoney, "Touring the Orient," ch. 15. *China Illustrated News* (Tientsin), 31 Dec. 1927, has a 4-page spread on the fire, featuring SDB.

62. SDB to Lejeune, 16 July 1927, Butler MSS (MCHC); SDB to Bristol, 26 Oct. 1927, Bristol MSS, box 51, 59-27.

63. Davis to Lejeune, 30 Aug., and SDB to Lejeune, 2 Sept. 1927, Butler MSS (MCHC).

64. SDB to Lejeune, 2 Sept. 1927, Butler MSS (MCHC).

65. Ibid.

66. Bristol to MacMurray, 13 July 1928, Bristol MSS, box 53, 355-28.

67. Notes of conference of foreign commandants, Tientsin, 11 May 1928, Butler MSS (MCHC); NA, RG 59, 893.00/9964; Lampson to FO, 10 May, and FO to Lampson, 12 May 1928, FO 371, No. 13231, 2255, F2306.

68. NA, RG 59, 893.00/10038 and 10130; Bristol to Courts, 7 June 1928, Bristol MSS, box 84, 273-28.

69. Saussine to Paris, 14 June 1928, AD China 238.

70. SDB to Lejeune, 23 July 1928, Butler MSS (MCHC). A marine aviator recalled returning to SDB with a count of 30,000 to 50,000 at which SDB "got mad as hell and yelled that such a number was impossibly large." Later, when SDB learned that there were 100,000, "he sent me a letter apologizing for his outburst. That's indicative of what a fair man he was." Valentine, "Retired General Remembers."

71. Lt. Gen. William J. Wallace interview (1967), 35-39, MCOHC; NA, RG 59, 893.00/10062 and 10155; Vandegrift missions in CinC Asiatic to sec. navy, 11 June 1928, ibid., 893.00 AFReports/11, and Vandegrift, *Once a Marine*, 74-75; SDB to Lejeune, 23 July 1928, Butler MSS (MCHC).

72. NA, RG 59, 893.00 N-I Reports/20; SDB to Lejeune, 23 July 1928, Butler MSS (MCHC); SDB to Bristol, 7 July 1928, NA, RG 45, Subj File 1911-27, box 799, misc.

73. NA, RG 59, 893.00/10089.

74. MacMurray to Hornbeck, 10 Aug. 1928, Stanley K. Hornbeck MSS, HI.

75. SDB to Lejeune, 23 July 1928, Butler MSS (MCHC).

76. NA, RG 59, 893.00/9789; SDB to Lejeune, 23 July 1928, Butler MSS (MCHC); NA, RG 59, 893.00 N-I Reports/20.

77. Bristol to sec. navy, 6 Nov. 1928, NA, RG 59, 893.00 AFReports/38; Shanghai in Bristol to Neville, 21 May 1929, Bristol MSS, box 55, 272-29.

78. Lejeune to Bristol, 22 Jan. 1929, Bristol MSS, box 54, 112-29; SDB to Lejeune, 27 Apr. 1927, Butler MSS (MCHC).

79. *L'Impartial* (Tientsin), 31 Oct. 1928, clipping in NA, RG 127, Entry 38, box 4; *China Weekly Review* (Shanghai), 24 Nov. 1928.

80. Bristol to Powell, 12 Dec. 1928, Bristol MSS, box 54, 548-28.

81. SDB to Lejeune, 23 July 1928, Butler MSS (MCHC); Bristol to Powell, 7 June 1928, Bristol MSS, box 53, 271-28; Bristol to Wilbur, 23 June 1928, ibid., 313-28.

82. Robinson interview (1968), 41; SDB, "The Umbrella of Honor," *The Illustrated Blue Book of Fiction* 65:2 (June 1937); *Sentinel* (Tientsin), 6 Oct. 1928, copy in NYPL; *New York Times*, 21 Oct. 1928; "Umbrella Presentation," MS, 5 Sept. 1928, Butler MSS (NS).

83. SDB, "Marines Who Wouldn't Fight," chs. 1 and 2; "struggle for commercial supremacy," SDB to Lejeune, 11 Aug. 1927, Butler MSS (MCHC).

84. SDB to Lejeune, 31 Jan. 1928, Butler MSS (MCHC).

85. SDB to Lejeune, 23 July 1928, and quotes, 18 Dec. 1926, ibid.; SDB to TSB, 31 Mar. 1928, Butler MSS (NS).

86. Lejeune to SDB, 2 May 1928, Butler MSS (NS); *New York Times*, 27 and 29 May 1928; rumors, *Army and Navy Journal* 65:40 (2 July 1928).

CHAPTER 14: TO HELL WITH THE ADMIRALS

1 SDB to TSB, 31 Mar. 1928, Butler MSS (NS).

2. SDB to Keck, 22 July 1929, ibid.; Thomas R. Butler interview with author, Mar. 1976.

3. Movies, Wilson, Tiffany-Stahl, to SDB, series of letters Feb.-Mar. 1929, Butler MSS (MCHC); Dimitman interview with author, Mar. 1976.

4. Burks to SDB, 21 Mar., 6, 10, and 13 Apr., and 2 May 1929, and SDB to Burks, 16 May and 7 June 1929, Butler MSS (MCHC); MS articles and related correspondence, Butler MSS (NS). Burks eventually wrote over a dozen substantial books—*Land of Checkerboard Families* (New York, 1932) being an interesting memoir of his experiences as a marine in the Dominican Republic.

5. List of Engagements, and SDB to Boyd, 25 Oct. 1929, Butler MSS (MCHC); *Philadelphia Evening Public Ledger*, 1 May 1929; *New York Times*, 9 Oct. 1929.

6. Governor boom, *Washington Post* and *New York Times*, 4 Sept. 1929, and *Philadelphia Public Ledger*, 2 Oct. 1929; Darlington to SDB, 9 Sept., and SDB to Darlington, 10 Sept. 1929, Butler MSS (MCHC).

7. *New York Times*, 20 Sept. 1929; *Philadelphia Public Ledger*, 5 Oct. 1929; *Times*, 25 Sept. 1929.

8. Lane to Lejeune, 4 June 1930, LC, Lejeune MSS.

9. "Bunk" clippings, 30 Nov.-5 Dec. 1929, SDB file, MCHC; *Post-Gazette* (Pittsburgh), 6 Dec. 1929; *New York Tribune*, 7 Dec. 1929; *New York Times*, 15 Dec. 1929; Schmidt, *U.S. Occupation*, 199-205.

10. Reading, Pa., *Times*, 20 Dec. 1929; "Beans" clippings, SDB file, MCHC; Charleston, S.C., *Post*, 18 Dec. 1929. Cf. Sinclair Lewis in *Nation* 129:3363 (18 Dec. 1929).

11. *New York Times*, 18, 22, and 30 Dec. 1929; SDB, *Old Gimlet Eye*, 300; Brig. Gen. Rufus H. Lane to SDB, 27 Dec. 1929, Butler MSS (MCHC).

12. Neville to Lejeune, 12 Apr. 1930, Lejeune MSS; Russell to Bristol ("Dear Mark"), 28 Apr. 1930, LC, Bristol MSS, box 56.

13. Feland to Mark L. Requa (a friend of Hoover's), 27 June, Requa to Richey, 28 June (forwarding Feland's letter with recommendation "Butler can wait"), and Richey to Requa, 7 July 1930 (saying he passed on Requa's 28 June to Hoover), HHL, Presidential Papers, box 36.

14. SDB to Samuel Butler, 28 July 1930, Butler MSS (MCHC); cables to Hoover in HHL, Presidential Papers, boxes 471 and 36.

15. *New York Times*, 29 Jan. 1931; "Gentleman" in *Outlook* 157 (25 Feb. 1931); SDB to Samuel Butler, 28 July 1930, Butler MSS (MCHC). A year later when SDB was about to retire, the State Department recommended Russell be appointed to the vacant major generalcy; W.R. Castle to Hoover, 3 July 1931, HHL, Presidential Papers, box 36. SDB apparently singled out Admiral Bristol and the General Board as his main adversaries; Snodgrass to SDB, 20 Aug. 1930, Butler MSS (NS).

16. White to Stimson, 10 July 1930, NA, RG 59, Francis White MSS; C.R. Train memo, 21 July 1930, HHL, Presidential Papers, box 36; Col. George C. Reid to Fuller, 11 Aug. 1930, Ben H. Fuller MSS, MCHC.

17. Janowitz, *The Professional Soldier: A Social and Political Portrait* (New York, 1960), 153-54; Forester, *The General* (London), 207.

18. SDB to Samuel Butler, 28 July 1930, Butler MSS (MCHC); Burks to SDB 7 Oct. 1930, Butler MSS (NS).

19. SDB court-martial specifications, NA, RG 80, Corresp. File 00 (1926-40), SDB; *Philadelphia Inquirer*, 30 Jan. 1931.

20. *New York Times*, 27-30 Jan. 1931.

21. Ibid.; R.L. Wilbur to Hoover, 5 Feb. 1931, HHL, Presidential Papers, box 36; brochure, *Philadelphia Inquirer*, 30 Jan. 1931.

22. Heflin quoted in *New York Times*, 31 Jan. 1931; *Congressional Record*, 71 Cong., 3 sess. (4 and 9 Feb. 1931) 74:4, 3919-20 and 4295-97.

23. *New York Times*, 3 Feb. 1931; SDB and Martha Strayer series, *Washington Daily News*, 4 Feb. 1931 and following days; doggerel, ibid., 2 Feb. 1931; Mussolini quoted, *Washington Evening Star*, 30 Jan. 1931; John P. Diggins, *Mussolini and Fascism: The View from America* (Princeton, 1972), 36.

24. *Outlook and Independent* 157 (11 and 25 Feb. 1931).

25. *New York Times*, 29 Jan., and 1, 2, and 5 Feb. 1931; *Washington Daily News*, 4 Feb. 1931.

26. Vanderbilt (New York, 1935), 163-64, and (New York, 1959), 55.

27. Lt. Gen. Pedro A. del Valle interview (1966), 45, MCOHC; Leonard reminder, Thomas R. Butler interview with author, July 1984; *Herald*, 5 Feb. 1931; offers of testimony, draft chap. 25 of SDB autobiography, Butler MSS (NS), and *Sunday Star* (Washington), 29 Apr. 1951.

28. Henry L. Stimson Diaries, 15:52-74, Yale University.

29. *New York Times*, 9, 10, and 15 Feb. 1931; *Baltimore Sun*, 15 Feb. 1931; SDB, *Old Gimlet Eye*, 309-10; SDB-Adams correspondence, 8 Feb. 1931, NA, RG 80, Corresp. File 00 (1926-40), SDB.

30. *Literary Digest*, 28 Feb. 1931; Craige to Lejeune, 11 Feb. 1931, Lejeune MSS.

31. *New York Tribune*, 26 Apr. 1931; *New York Times*, 25, 26 and 28 Apr., 2 and 8 May 1931; Stimson Diaries, 16:32.

32. *New York Times*, 19 and 22 Feb., 8 and 22 Mar., and 25 Apr. 1931.

33. His daughter remembered her husband, Brig. Gen. John Wehle, saying SDB could recite all the names: Ethel Butler Wehle interview (1950), SDB file, MCHC.

34. *Liberty*, 5 Dec. 1931; SDB to Dimitman, 27 July 1931, Butler MSS (NS); chief of naval operations quoted in *Washington Star*, 27 Nov. 1931; Hoover in *New York Times*, 22 Aug. 1931.

35. SDB to FDR, 17 July 1933, FDRL, OF, 18E; Lee to SDB, 4 Mar. 1931, Butler MSS (NS).

36. Lee to Lejeune, 31 Oct., and Lejeune to Lee, 4 Dec. 1933, Lejeune MSS; Armstead (on behalf of Lee) to SDB, 13 June 1933, SDB to Mrs. Lee, 19 Mar. 1935, Wise to SDB, n.d. (ca. Jan. 1935), and SDB to Wise, 31 Jan. 1935, Butler MSS (NS). SDB tried to enlist Lejeune, stating "my informant suggested telegraphing you"; SDB to Lejeune, 18 Feb. 1935, Lejeune MSS.

37. *Baltimore Sun*, 3 Mar 1935; *Congressional Record*, 74 Cong., 1 sess. (28 Feb.-5 Mar. 1935), 2739-40, 2925-27, 2862; *Washington Post*, 3 Mar. 1935; Brooke Russell Astor, *Footprints: An Autobiography* (Garden City, N.Y., 1980). For more extensive analysis, Donald F. Bittner, "Conflict under the Dome: Senator Hugo Black, Major General Smedley Butler, and the Challenged Promotion of Major General John H. Russell," presented at American Historical Association convention, Dec. 1984.

38. SDB quoted, *Baltimore Sun*, 3 Mar. 1935; Lejeune to Trammell, 14 Feb. 1935, *Congressional Record*, 74 Cong., 1 sess. (4 Mar. 1935), 2863.

39. SDB to Mrs. Harry Lee, 19 Mar. 1935, Butler MSS (NS).

CHAPTER 15: RENEGADE MARINE

1. Flyer for Hagerstown, Md., speech, 10 May 1931, Butler MSS (MCHC); Thomas flyer, n.d., SDB file, MCHC; *Evansville Press*, 29 Mar. 1931.

2. Charles E. Meilachowitz to author, 1 Dec. 1975; Thomas R. Butler interview with author, Sept. 1978.

3. Receipts, Butler MSS (NS); *New York Times*, 3 Mar. 1932.

4. *New York Times*, 3 and 6 Mar. 1932.

5. *Digest*, 30 Apr. 1932; *Record*, 20, 21, 24, and 28 Apr. 1932; election data in *Philadelphia Evening Bulletin*, 22 June 1940; "drubbing" and 167 speeches in SDB to Robinson, 10 May 1932, Butler MSS (NS).

6. *Philadelphia Record*, 1 May 1932; Howell to SDB, 16 Sept. 1932, and SDB to Howell, 18 Aug. 1932, Butler MSS (NS). For SDB's campaign in two Philadelphia wet wards, see John Thomas Salter, *Boss Rule: Portraits in City Politics* (New York, 1935), 93 and 200.

7. *Record*, 29 Apr. 1932; Mrs. Graham Dougherty quoted in ibid., 28 Apr.; Karl Reed Bierly to SDB, 2 May 1932, Butler MSS (NS).

8. SDB to Col. James J. Meade, USMC, 7 May, and to Robinson, 10 May 1932, Butler MSS (NS).

9. SDB to Robinson, 10 May 1932, and to Kenneth F. Kressler, chairman, Republican City Committee, Easton, Pa., 2 Sept. 1931, Butler MSS (NS).

10. SDB to Robinson, 10 May 1932, Butler MSS (NS).

11. *New York Times*, 20 July 1932.

12. Smith to Chief of Staff, 20 July 1932, NA, RG 165, Entry 63, box 3083; *New York Times*, 21 July 1932. Cf. Roger Daniels, *The Bonus March* (Westport, Conn., 1971), 139, citing police report of SDB's 19 July speech, and *B.E.F. News* 1:7 (6 Aug. 1932), copy in HI, Herbert Hoover MSS, box 283.

13. *New York Times*, 1-3 Aug. 1932; Walter W. Waters, *The Whole Story of the Bonus Army* as told to William C. White (New York, 1933), 158-59; SDB, "The Soldier Asks for Pay," *New Outlook* 161 (Nov. 1932).

14. *New York Times*, 30 June, 8 Sept., and 18 Oct. 1932; SDB to Robinson, 1 Dec. 1932, Butler MSS (NS).

15. HHL, Misrepresentations-Butler, Smedley.

16. SDB to John Wehle, 21 Nov., and "square a debt," SDB to Hawthorne, 1 Dec. 1932, Butler MSS (NS).

17. SDB to Dimitman, 29 June and 27 July 1931, and to Thomas, 25 June 1932, Butler MSS (NS); Thomas to author, 24 Mar. 1977. It sold 6,000 copies during the first two years in print; royalty statements, Butler MSS (NS).

18. *New York Times*, 30 Nov. 1931. Cf. John M. MacKenzie, *Propaganda and Empire: Manipulation of British Public Opinion, 1880-1960* (Manchester, 1984), ch. 8.

19. *Caco*, SDB to Dimitman, 29 June and 27 July 1931, Butler MSS (NS).

20. Radio, *New York Times*, 26 Apr. and 13 May 1931, and 4 Oct. 1934; Passaic, ibid., 31 May 1933.

21. "Dumbest," SDB quoted in Walter Wilson, "Where Smedley Butler Stands," *New Masses* 17 (12 Nov. 1935); SDB, "Wipe Out the Gangsters!" *Forum* 86:4 (Oct. 1931).

22. *New York Times*, 10 Dec. 1932.

23. Ibid., 11 Dec. 1933; Val O'Farrell to Howe, 11 Dec. 1933, FDRL, PPF 6728. According to Jules Archer in *Plot to Seize the White House* (New York, 1973), 151, O'Farrell was a former New York City detective.

24. *Philadelphia Record*, 21 Nov. 1934.

25. *New York Times* and *Philadelphia Record*, 21 and 22 Nov. 1934; Clark quoted in *Times*, 3 Dec. 1934; *Time*, 3 Dec. 1934; Van Zandt in ibid. and *Philadelphia Record*, 23 Nov. 1934.

26. Dickstein to McCormack, 1 Nov. 1934, American Jewish Archives, Samuel Dickstein MSS, box 2; *Philadelphia Record*, 22 Nov. 1934.

27. Dawsey, Memorandum for Director, 8 Aug. 1936, FBI hdqrs. file 62-41602-2X.

28. SDB testimony, U.S., House, Un-American Affairs Committee (HUAC), *Hearings, Investigation of Nazi Propaganda Activities and Investigation of Certain Other Propaganda Activities*, 73 Cong., 2 sess. (Washington, 1934), pts. 1 and 2. The story is told in much greater detail than herein in John L. Spivak, *A Man in His Time* (New York, 1967), and especially in Archer, *Plot to Seize the White House*. Archer's is the most thorough, complete account and construes the plot as broadly credible, but is based almost entirely on printed sources—the same as herein. Archer interviewed McCormack, Spivak, and others, but did not uncover much new information.

29. SDB to MacGuire, 19 Sept. 1933, Butler MSS (NS).

30. HUAC, *Investigation*, pt. 1, 13-14.

31. Ibid., 18.

32. Ibid., 21.

33. *Philadelphia Record*, 21 Nov. 1934; HUAC, *Investigation*, pt. 1, 142.

34. HUAC, *Investigation*, pt. 1, 142-45; Dickstein to McCormack, 24 Dec. 1934, Dickstein MSS, box 2.

35. *New York Times*, 22 Nov. 1934.

36. For exposition of suppressed testimony and HUAC rationales, including quotes used here, see John L. Spivak, "Wall Street's Fascist Conspiracy," pts. 1 and 2, *New Masses* 14:5 and 6 (29 Jan. and 5 Feb. 1935).

37. Ibid.; Spivak, *A Man in His Time*, ch. 24.

38. *Time*, 3 Dec. 1934 and 25 Feb. 1935, and extended rendition in Archer, *Plot*, 186-88, 218; Frank A. Warren, *Liberals and Communism: The 'Red Decade' Revisited* (Bloomington, 1966), 99.

39. Text, SDB speech, 17 Feb. 1935 in Agnes Law (CBS) to Dickstein, 20 Feb. 1935, and Dickstein, ABC/CBS radio speech, 8 pp., typewritten, 26 Feb. 1935, Dickstein MSS, box 2; HUAC, House Report No. 153, 74 Cong., 1 sess. (15 Feb. 1935), quoted in George Seldes, *One Thousand Americans* (New York, 1947), 290-92; *New York Times*, 16 Feb. 1935.

40. George Wolfskill, *The Revolt of the Conservatives: A History of the American Liberty League* (Boston, 1962), 98, 101. Others credited SDB with good faith, e.g., Sen. Paul H. Douglas, who commented regarding the plot that "Butler was eccentric and irascible, but was always regarded as a man of honor"; Douglas, *In the Fullness of Time* (New York, 1971), 102.

41. Long, *My First Days* (Harrisburg, Pa., 1935), 6, 25, and ch. 6; *New York Times*, 16 Sept. 1935; SDB to Bozarth, 7 Jan. 1934, and to Gottschalk, 22 Mar. 1936, Butler MSS (NS).

42. Spivak, *A Man in His Time*, 328-29; vote, Thomas R. Butler interview, Mar. 1976.

43. Identical wording to the 1935 *Common Sense* version appears as a 20 Aug. 1931 SDB speech in Archer, *Plot*, 118-19, no source cited. Archer said the speech was not accurately reported in major newspapers because it was too radical. Newspaper reports indicate different emphases altogether. Cf. *New York Times*, *Hartford Times*, and *Hartford Courant*, 21 Aug. 1931. SDB was sharing the platform with Sen. Hiram Bingham, who argued against granting independence to the Philippines.

44. SDB, "America's Armed Forces," pt. 2, *Common Sense* 4:11 (Nov.1935).

45. SDB to editor, 19 Nov. 1933, quoted in Robert Sherrill, *Why They Call It Politics*, 3d ed. (New York, 1979), 50; *Nation* 136:3524 (18 Jan. 1933).

46. SDB to wife, 9 Oct. 1912, Butler MSS (NS).

47. Harbord (Boston, 1935), 552-53; Harbord to SDB, 27 Sept. 1935, Butler MSS (NS). Cf. ibid., 20 Apr. 1932.

48. Lester to Hoover, 26 Aug. 1938, FBI, hdqrs. file 62-33617-7; ibid., file no. obliterated, cf. 94-36821-X9 and 62-33617-8; Hoover to SDB, 2 Sept. 1938, 62-33617-7, 15 Oct. 1938, 94-36821-X10, and 5 Feb. 1936, 62-39829-6; SDB to Hoover, 18 Jan. 1940, 62-33617-8; FBI agent to Hoover, 17 Apr. 1940, 66-3579-2167.

49. Lester to Hoover, n.d. (ca. 4 Mar. 1936), FBI, hdqrs. file 62-30951-29X, cf. 62-30951-34; Hoover to obliterated addressee, 30 Mar. 1961, with agent's annotation, 62-33617-9.

50. Hoover to Randolph (secretary of HUAC), 12 Dec. 1934, FBI, hdqrs. file 62-33617-4; Dawsey memorandum, 8 Aug. 1936, 62-41602-2X; agent to Hoover, 17 Apr. 1940, 66-3579-2167. SDB apparently turned over to federal authorities literature he received from some organizations, cf. William H. Houghton, Treasury Dept. Secret Service, to SDB, 18 May 1934, Butler MSS (NS). For 1932-33 appeals to SDB from strange organizations, see "Organizations" file, ibid.

51. Walker, *Critical History of Police Reform* (Lexington, Mass., 1977), 78, 139, 152-53, 159; SDB, "Wipe Out the Gangs," *Forum* (Oct. 1931).

52. SDB, "America's Armed Forces," 5-pt. serial, *Common Sense*, 4:10-5:3 (Oct. 1934-

Mar. 1935). For hostile War Dept. appraisal, see Dalton to G-2, 30 Sept. 1935, NA, RG 165, Entry 65, box 757, file 2045-1250.

53. Alfred M. Bingham, "War Mongering on the Left," *Common Sense* 6:5 (May 1937); Harvey Klehr, *The Heyday of American Communism* (New York, 1984), 110-12, 372-73. J.E. Hoover characterized the peace campaign as "the most important phase of the united front program of the Communist Party"; Hoover to Watson (secretary to the president), 6 Dec. 1940, FDRL, OF 10b, box 24.

54. Murray to SDB, 5 Aug. 1936, Butler MSS (NS); Cook to FDR, n.d., ca. 14 May 1941, FBI hdqrs. file 94-8-205-[obliterated].

55. Wilson, "Where Smedley Butler Stands," *New Masses* 17 (Nov. 1935). For SDB veterans speech, cf. *New York Times*, 16 June 1935.

56. Wilson, "Where Smedley Butler Stands."

57. *New York Times*, 16 June 1935 and 29 Sept. 1936.

58. Speech in *Labor Herald* (Rochester, N.Y., and Wilmington, Del.), 13 Apr. 1935, copy in Butler MSS (NS); Dimitman interview (1976); SDB to Dimitman, 15 Mar., and to Jesse Laventhol, 21 Jan. 1935, Butler MSS (NS).

59. SDB, *War Is a Racket* (New York: Round Table Press, 1935), repr. Torrance, Cal.: Noontide Press, 1984, and in John Whiteclay Chambers, ed., *Three Generals on War* (New York, 1973); *Reader's Digest* 26:158 (June 1935).

60. SDB, "War Is a Racket," *Forum* 92 (Sept. 1934); Dimitman interview (1976); SDB, *War Is a Racket*, 3, 9, 10.

61. SDB, *War Is a Racket*, 28-29, 32-33, 36.

62. Ibid., 38-39, 42-44.

63. *New York Times*, 29 Dec. 1935 and 4 Jan. 1936; recording of ABC speech, Butler MSS (NS); Baldwin Reminiscences (1953-54), 359, CUOHC.

64. Brecht to SDB, 9 Nov. 1936, Butler MSS (NS); David Mandel, member, to author, 1 Dec. 1975; *New York Times*, 22 Nov. 1940.

65. *New York Times*, 12 Aug. 1935 and 9 Feb. 1936.

66. SDB, "America's Armed Forces," pt. 3 *Common Sense* 4:12 (Dec. 1935); SDB to H.L. Roosevelt, 9 Feb. 1935, Butler MSS (NS).

67. SDB, "America's Armed Forces," pt. 3.

68. Ibid.

69. SDB, "How Safe Is America?" *Liberty* 13:47 (21 Nov. 1936); SDB, "Amendment for Peace," *Woman's Home Companion* 63:9 (Sept. 1936).

70. Ludlow to SDB, 15 June, 23 Oct., and 21 Nov. 1935, Butler MSS (NS); U.S., House, Subcommittee on the Judiciary, *Hearing, To Amend the Constitution with Respect to the Declaration of War*, 74 Cong., 1 sess. (Washington, 1935), 24-25; *New York Times*, 10 Nov. 1935; Ludlow to SDB, 16 Sept. 1937, Butler MSS (NS).

71. Naval Affairs Committee, *Hearings, Naval Expansion Program*, 142-43.

72. Robert A. Divine, in his Cold-War vintage *The Illusion of Neutrality* (Chicago, 1962), 41, stigmatized "the narrow provincialism that characterized the isolationists." For a less dismissive view, cf. Wayne S. Cole, *Roosevelt and the Isolationists, 1932-45* (Lincoln, Neb., 1983).

73. Millett, *Semper Fidelis*, 336. This was to identify the Corps with the big-war mission and disassociate from "obsolete" colonial small-war imagery.

74. "Reactionary," SDB, "America's Armed Forces," pt. 1, *Common Sense* 4:10 (Oct. 1935); Naval Affairs Committee, *Hearings, Naval Expansion Program*, 142-43.

75. "Japan happens," Naval Affairs Committee, *Hearings, Naval Expansion Program*, 150; abandon territories, ibid., 147-48, and *New York Times*, 10 Apr. 1938; "damned oil companies," SDB speech at Bloomsburg State College, Pa., Ben Singer to author, 12 Dec. 1975; "get the hell out," *New York Times*, 1 Sept. 1937.

76. French, ed. *Common Sense Neutrality* (New York, 1939), 75-76; *New York-Times*, 1 and 24 Sept. 1939.

77. *Time* 30:11 (13 Sept. 1937).

78. Ibid.; *New York Times*, 4 Sept. 1937.

79. *Time* 33:12 (20 Mar. 1939)—CMC Russell had arranged for James Roosevelt to be commissioned, with no prior service, as a lieutenant colonel in the USMC Reserve, Millett, *Semper Fidelis*, 335; Daniels to FDR, 16 Aug. 1937, FDRL, PPF 86. During the Pacific War, Roosevelt served as executive officer of Carlson's Raiders.

80. Thomas R. Butler and Smedley D. Butler, Jr. interview, Mar. 1976; Edith Wehle interview with author, Newtown Square, Pa., Sept. 1978; Dimitman interview, Mar. 1976. Cf. Vandegrift to SDB, 5 May 1939, Butler MSS (NS).

81. "War dogs," ABC speech, 3 Jan. 1936, "mean, cruel," CBS speech, 14 July 1937, recordings in Butler MSS (NS); radio script, 6 Oct. 1939, ibid.

82. SDB to Mrs. H.L. Cassard, 18 Apr. 1940, Butler MSS (NS).

83. Quaker Meetings, Thomas R. Butler to author, 3 June 1985; *Philadelphia Inquirer*, 23 May 1940.

84. *Philadelphia Inquirer*, 24 and 18 Apr. 1940.

85. Ibid., 22 June 1940; Thomas R. Butler interview, Mar. 1976; Mrs. SDB to Lejeune, Oct. 1940, Lejeune MSS; *New York Times*, 19 July 1940.

86. *New York Times* and *Philadelphia Inquirer*, 22 June 1940; Kendrick quoted in Alice and Carl Lindborg, et al., *Historic Newtown Township, 1681-1983* (Newtown Square, Pa., 1984), 337; *Congressional Record*, 76 Cong., 1 Sess., 86:10 (appendix, 22 June 1940), 4845, and (27 Aug. 1940), 11006-07; FDR to Mrs. SDB, 22 June 1940, FDRL, PPF 6728.

87. *New York Times*, 25 June 1940; Thomas R. Butler to author, 12 July 1979.

88. *San Francisco Call-Bulletin*, 30 Apr. 1942, clipping in SDB file, MCHC, cf. *New York Times*, 2 Sept. 1937—he said 1,200 marines were "worth 12,000 any other soldiers."

89. Plaque, *New York Times*, 25 July 1950; Thomas R. Butler interviews, 1976 and 1978.

CHAPTER 16: EPILOGUE

1. Shoup, "The New American Militarism," *Atlantic* 223:4 (Apr. 1969); see also James A. Donovan, Col., USMC, *Militarism, U.S.A.* (New York, 1970), which is an expansion of the Shoup article; Valentine, "Retired General Remembers." See also Archer, *Plot to Seize the White House*, 242-43.

2. See Marcus Cunliffe, *Soldiers and Civilians: The Martial Spirit in America, 1775-1865* (Boston, 1968), for popular politics and professionals versus amateurs.

3. Janowitz (New York, 1960), 150, 153, 165, and 172.

Selected Bibliography

UNPUBLISHED SOURCES

(Lists only sources that are cited more than once in the notes, and does not include government documents.)

Adriance, Harry C., Sgt., USMC. Recollections. State Historical Society of Wisconsin, Madison. Copy in MCHC.

Allen, Niel R. MSS. Hoover Institute, Palo Alto, Cal.

Barnett, George, Maj. Gen., USMC. MSS, including "Soldier and Sailor Too," n.d. (ca. 1920s). MCHC.

Blake, Robert, Maj. Gen., USMC. Interview, 1968. MCOHC.

Bristol, Mark L., Adm., USN. MSS. Library of Congress.

Burger, Joseph Charles, Lt. Gen., USMC. Interview, 1969. MCOHC.

Butler, Smedley D., Maj. Gen., USMC. MSS. Part of the collection is at MCHC and part at the Butler family home in Newtown Square, Pa.

Butler, Smedley D., Jr. (son of SDB). Interviews with author, Newtown Square, Pa., Mar. 1976 and Sept. 1978.

Butler, Thomas R. (son of SDB). Interviews with author, Newtown Square, Pa., Mar. 1976, Sept. 1978, and July 1984.

Campbell, Chandler, Capt., USMC. MSS and Diaries. MCHC.

Caperton, William B., Rear Adm., USN. MSS. Library of Congress.

———. "History of a Flag Career." MS, n.d. (ca. 1920). NA, RG 45, Subj File 1911-27, ZN Caperton, box 802.

Cates, Clifton B., Gen., USMC. Interview, 1967. MCOHC.

Cloud, George H., Maj. Gen., USMC. Interview, 1970. MCOHC.

Cochrane, Henry Clay, Brig. Gen., USMC. MSS and Diaries. MCHC.

Coolidge, Calvin. MSS. Library of Congress.

Daniels, Josephus. MSS. Library of Congress.

Denby, Edwin H. MSS. Burton Collection, Detroit Public Library.

Dessez, Lester A., Gen., USMC. Interview, 1970. MCOHC.

Dickstein, Samuel. MSS. American Jewish Archives, Cincinnati.

Dimitman, E.Z. Interview with author, Philadelphia, 19 Mar. 1976.

Fuller, Ben H., Maj. Gen., USMC. MSS. MCHC.

Good, George F., Jr., Lt. Gen., USMC. Interview, 1970. MCOHC.

Jones, Louis R., Maj. Gen., USMC. Interview, 1970. MCOHC.

Lejeune, John A., Maj. Gen., USMC. MSS. Library of Congress.

Megee, Vernon E., Gen., USMC. Interview, 1967. MCOHC.

Miller, Adoph B., marine officer, MSS and Dairies. MCHC.
Pendleton, Joseph H., Maj. Gen., USMC. MSS. MCHC.
Pfeiffer, Omar T., Maj. Gen., USMC. Interview, 1968. MCOHC.
Pinchot, Gifford. MSS. Library of Congress.
Robinson, Ray A., Gen., USMC. Interview, 1968. MCOHC.
Rogers, Ford O., Maj. Gen., USMC. Interview, 1966. MCOHC.
Silverthorn, Merwin H., Lt. Gen., USMC. Interview, 1969. MCOHC.
Smith, Julian C., Lt. Gen., USMC. Interview, 1968. MCOHC.
Stimson, Henry L. Diaries. Yale University.
Train, Harold C., Adm., USN. Recollections, 1965. CUOHC.
Underhill, James L., Lt. Gen., USMC. Interview, 1968. MCOHC.
Upshur, William P., Maj. Gen., USMC. MSS. Southern Historical Collection, University of North Carolina.
Vandegrift, Alexander A., Gen., USMC. Interview, 1962. MCOHC.
Wallace, William J., Lt. Gen., USMC. Interview, 1967. MCOHC.
Wehle, Ethel Butler (daughter of SDB). Interviews with author, Newtown Square, Pa., Mar. 1976.
Worton, William A., Maj. Gen., USMC. Interview, 1967. MCOHC.

BUTLERANIA

(Published writings by SDB plus selected topical works.)

Archer, Jules. *The Plot to Seize the White House.* New York, 1973.
Asprey, Robert B. "The Court-Martial of Smedley Butler." *Marine Corps Gazette* 43:12 (Dec. 1959).
Baldwin, Fred D. "Smedley D. Butler and Prohibition Enforcement in Philadelphia, 1924-25." *Pennsylania Magazine of History and Biography* 84:3 (July 1960).
Bartlett, Merrill L. "Old Gimlet Eye." *U.S. Naval Institute Proceedings* 112 (Nov. 1986).
Butler, Smedley D. "Amendment for Peace." *Woman's Home Companion* 63:9 (Sept. 1936).
———. "America—Keep Your Feet on the Ground." *Philadelphia Record*, 27 Aug. 1939.
———. "American Marines in China." *Annals, American Academy of Political and Social Sciences* 144 (July 1929).
———. "America's Armed Forces." *Common Sense*: pt. 1, "Military Boondoggling," 4:10 (Oct. 1935); pt. 2, "'In Time of Peace': The Army," 4:11 (Nov. 1935); pt. 3, "'Happy Days Are Here Again': The Navy," 4:12 (Dec. 1935); pt. 4, "The National Guard," 5:1 (Jan. 1936); pt. 5, "The Police: 250,000 Cops Can't Be Wrong," 5:3 (Mar. 1936).
———. "The Bonus or Else!" *Liberty* 13:2 (11 Jan. 1936).
———. "Can We Rule Ourselves? Or Shall We Have Fascism?" *Real America* 5:2 (Apr. 1935).
———. "Dame Rumor: The Biggest Liar in the World." *American Magazine* 111:6 (June 1931).

————. "Dog Eat Dog: Will America, Goaded by Capital, Embrace Fascism?" *Real America* 5:1 (Mar. 1935).

————. "Fight Rackets by War Edict." Newspaper clipping, n.d. (ca. 1933). U.S., Dept. of Justice, Federal Bureau of Investigation (FBI) file 62- 23190-261.

————. "The 'Fightingest' Man I Know." *American Magazine* 112:3 (Sept. 1931). (About Sgt. Maj. Daniel Daily, USMC).

————. "Forget the Communists." *Real America* 5:2 (Apr. 1935).

————. "General Butler Assails Arms Credits as Drawing U.S. Inevitably into War." *Philadelphia Inquirer*, 1 Oct. 1939.

————. "How Safe Is America?" *Liberty* 13:47 (21 Nov. 1936).

————. "How Shall We Go to War." *Liberty* 15:11 (12 Mar. 1938).

————. "It's Up to You." *Foreign Service* (Veterans of Foreign Wars) 21:7 (Mar. 1934).

————. "Ludlow Amendment Will Protect Your Boys." *Philadelphia Record*, 29 Aug. 1939.

————. "Major General Smedley D. Butler." Article, no title, in Paul Comly French, ed., *Common Sense Neutrality: Mobilizing for Peace*. New York, 1939.

————. "Making War on the Gangs: A Plan to Take the Police out of Politics." *Forum* 85:3 (Mar. 1931).

————. "The Marines Who Wouldn't Fight." Eight-pt. serial, North American Newspaper Alliance, starting Sept. 1929. Copies in SDB file, MCHC.

————. "Mothers: Must You Let Your Boy Die?" *Philadelphia Record*, 28 Aug. 1939.

————. "Notes on Staff Activities of Third Brigade, U.S. Marine Corps, Serving in China." *Marine Corps Gazette* 14:1 (Mar. 1929).

————. *Old Gimlet Eye: The Adventures of Smedley D. Butler as Told to Lowell Thomas*. New York, 1933. Reprint, Quantico: Marine Corps Association, 1981.

————. "Opera-Bouffe Revolts: What Usually Happens When the Marines Have Landed." *Liberty* 8 (10 Oct. 1931).

————. "Politics Versus Disabled Vets." *Real America* 4:5 (Jan. 1935).

————. "Should the World War Veterans' Service Certificates be Paid in Cash?" *Congressional Digest* 11:11 (Nov. 1932).

————. "Smashing Crime and Vice." 30-pt. serial, Bell Syndicate and North American Newspaper Alliance, Apr.-May 1926. Copies in SDB file, MCHC.

————. "The Soldier Asks for Pay." *New Outlook* 161 (Nov. 1932).

————. "There Is No Other Horse." *Christian Herald* (Oct. 1931).

————. "To Hell with the Admirals! Why I Retired at Fifty." *Liberty* (5 Dec. 1931).

————. "The Toughest Five Minutes of My Life." *Liberty* 8:27 (4 July 1931).

————. "The Umbrella of Honor." *The Illustrated Blue Book of Fiction* 65:2 (June 1937).

————. "U.S. Rapidly Entering upon New Era of Nationalism, Gen. Butler Finds." *Washington Herald*, 19 Nov. 1933.

————. *War Is a Racket*. New York: Round Table Press, 1935. Condensed version in *Reader's Digest* 26:158 (June 1935). Reprints, Torrance, Cal.: Noontide Press, 1984; and in John Whiteclay Chambers, ed., *Three Generals on War* (New York, 1973).

————. "War Is a Racket." *Forum* 92 (Sept. 1934).

————. "Wipe Out the Gangs!" *Forum* (Oct. 1931).

————. "You've Got to Get Mad: Too Many Veterans Believe in Santa Claus." *Foreign Service* 21:4 (Dec. 1933).

Butler, Smedley D., and Arthur J. Burks. *Walter Garvin in Mexico*. Philadelphia, 1927.

Butler, Smedley D., and Martha Strayer. "Smedley Butler was 'Scared to Death' and Homesick on His First Marine Assignment," and sequent articles. *Washington Daily News*, 4 Feb. 1931 and following days.

Butler Family Association. *Noble Butler: Ancestors and Descendants*. Kennett Square, Pa., 1982.

Cochran, Robert T. "Smedley Butler: A Pint-size Marine for All Seasons." *Smithsonian* (June 1984).

Conway, Martha E., and Riley Aikman. "Butler House." *Leatherneck* 67:2 (Feb. 1984).

McCaleb, Kenneth. "Life Story of Butler . . . Fighting Quaker." Series in *Philadelphia Record*, Feb. 1931. Copies in SDB file, MCHC.

Neufield, Gabrielle M., and James S. Santelli. "Smedley Butler's Air Corps: The First Marine Aviators in China." *U.S. Naval Institute Proceedings* 103 (Apr. 1977).

Valentine, Tom. "Retired General Remembers Military Hero Smedley Butler." *The Spotlight for America First* (Washington, D.C.), 10:12 (19 Mar. 1984). An interview with Brig. Gen. William C. Lemly, USMC, ret.

Venzon, Anne C. "The Papers of General Smedley Darlington Butler, U.S.M.C., 1915-18." Ph.D. diss., Princeton University, 1982.

Wilson, Walter. "Where Smedley Butler Stands." *New Masses* 17 (12 Nov. 1935).

Index

Abend, Hallett, 190
Adams, Charles Francis, 205-7, 211
Adriance, Harry C.: quoted, 19
advanced-base force, 27-28, 33, 35, 44, 61, 71, 74, 112, 125. *See also* expeditionary forces
Alber, Joseph, 203, 208
alcohol: drinking and abuse of, 11, 17, 24-26, 33-34, 58-59, 71, 107, 136, 162, 166, 172, 178-79, 189, 190. *See also* prohibition
Alert, 31
Alexis, Stephen, 87
American Expeditionary Forces (A.E.F., France), 101, 104, 108
American Federation of Labor, 235
American Legion, 203, 220-29, 233-34, 242; Royal Family, 222-23, 227
Andrews, Lincoln C., 150
Annapolis, 43, 45
anti-imperialism, 173, 175, 182, 189, 205, 231-32, 236-43, 245, 247. *See also* imperialism
Arai, K., 194
Archer, Jules, 231-32
Arévalo, Juan José, 247
automobile industry (Detroit), 140-41
aviation: experimental development, 135-37; Butler bill, 165; in China, 188-89, 196

Baldwin, Roger, 238
Barnett, George, 60-61, 75, 89-90, 96-101, 107, 111-12, 124, 131, 138, 165, 167, 207-8; on Haitian killings, 93, 117-18; 1918 Barnett amendment, 98-99, 115; Barnett putsch, 110, 114-23
Barnett, Lelia Montague (Mrs. George Barnett), 99, 107, 115, 117, 119, 122
Bartlett, Merrill L., 124

Bauer, Max, 185
Beard, Charles A., 242
Bellegarde, Dantès, 211-12
Benson, Elmer A., 235
Benson, William S., 109
Bevan, James, 19, 23-24, 26
Biddle, William P., 36-37
Bingham, Hiram, 174, 184-85
Black, Hugo, 214
Blake, Robert: quoted, 101, 120
Bonilla, Manuel, 30-32
bonus, veterans', 216, 218-19, 222, 225-26
Bonus Expeditionary Force (B.E.F., Bonus March), 218-19, 222
Boone, Joel T., 212
Borodin, Mikhail, 184
Boxer expedition (China, 1900), 14-26, 225; Boxer Protocol, 25, 186, 188, 194; use of Boxer analogy, 44, 47-48, 63-65, 67, 180-81, 198
Brickner, Barnett R., 238
Bristol, Mark L., 183-86, 191, 194-95, 197-99, 206, 275n15
Brodsky, Joseph, 235
Brooklyn, 25, 27
Broun, Haywood, 238
Browder, Earl, 233, 235
Brown Brothers, New York banking house (Brown Seligman Co.), 45, 54, 231
Bryan, William Jennings: Mexican policy, 63-64, 69; Haitian policy, 82
Buffalo, 38-39, 56
bulldog symbol: origins, 139
Burger, Joseph Charles: quoted, 178
Burks, Arthur J., 65, 203, 208, 274n4
Butler, Ethel Conway Peters ("Bunny," wife of SDB), 32, 89, 94, 141, 156, 161, 163-64, 191, 245-46
Butler, Ethel Peters ("Snooks," daughter of SDB, Mrs. John Wehle), 33, 46, 94, 159, 161, 163, 215

Butler, Horace (brother of SDB), 7, 22, 96, 202
Butler, Samuel (brother of SDB), 7, 202
Butler, Smedley D.: family background, 6; illnesses and wounds, 6, 19-20, 23, 28, 33-34, 48-50, 131, 134, 160, 164-66, 190, 236, 245; education, 6-7, 60, 120, 243n1; Quaker influence and imagery, 6, 97, 112, 162, 178, 245; and father's political influence, 8-9, 11, 13, 20-21, 28, 31, 35-37, 60-61, 72, 96-97, 98-99, 110, 112, 118-22, 124, 130, 134-35, 156, 171, 219, 248; and warrior ethos, 8, 10, 15-16, 26, 45-47, 58-60, 65, 72-75, 96, 103, 105, 109-10, 121, 123, 131, 197, 213-14, 220, 232, 234; views on education, 9-10, 59-60, 74-75, 98, 111-14, 153, 191; author of military-adventure stories, 15, 28-29, 65-66, 94, 167, 203, 219-20; leadership style, 26, 84, 98, 102-4, 106-7, 109, 113, 131-34, 137, 189-90, 192, 217, 222, 233, 274n70; attitude toward navy, 28, 36, 45-46, 60, 125-26, 177, 186, 199, 212, 237, 239; celebrated as pulp adventure-story hero, 32, 54, 71-72, 174, 209; marriage, 32-33, 65; as coal mine manager, 34-35; commercial civilian job offers, 35, 140-41, 202, 236; anti-imperialism of, 54, 182, 189, 200, 204-5, 232, 236-43, 247, 249; opposes Wall Street and capitalists, 54, 216, 218-19, 222-32, 235-36, 240, 243; civilian police contacts and expertise, 55, 60, 90, 92, 129, 141-62, 203-4, 212, 222, 232-34, 248; opposes highbrow professionalism, 59-60, 74-75, 98, 110-13, 121, 149, 152-53, 206, 212-14, 220, 241-42, 248; medals awarded to, 20, 72-73, 81, 90, 109, 165, 212-14, 221; populist tendencies of, 98, 109, 112-14, 131, 155, 169-70, 172, 218, 221-22, 230-31, 235-36, 238, 247-49; public-speaking career, 141, 203, 208, 215, 235; prospects for elected public office, 151, 154, 201, 203-4, 208, 212, 215; becomes teetotaler, 160, 162; on Northwest "frontiersmen," 170-72; and firefighting, 191-92; retirement from Marine Corps, 212-13; 1932 Senate primary candidacy, 215-17; and veterans' bonus, 216, 218-19, 223, 231; and FDR, 219, 223, 233, 235, 238-39, 244; and Herbert Hoover, 219, 239; antiwar advocacy by, 220, 223, 232-33, 236-45, 249; and hero archetype, 220-21, 224; as partisan in veterans' politics, 221-23, 233, 238, 242-43; and FBI, 224, 233-34; cooperates with Secret Service, 224, 278n50; leftist political tendencies of, 231-33, 235-36, 249; and imperialism-gangsterism analogy, 232, 236; on communists, 235; on labor unions, 235-36; on 1930s Japanese threat, 237, 242; on Spanish Civil War, 238; criticizes Theodore Roosevelt, 239; supports Ludlow amendment, 240; as "military isolationist," 240-41; on 1937 *Panay* incident, 242; on 1930s European politics, 242, 245; death, 245-46
Butler, Smedley D., Jr. (son of SDB), 39, 45, 72, 94, 202, 218
Butler, Thomas R. (son of SDB), 59, 72, 202, 243
Butler, Thomas S. (father of SDB), 6, 21, 35-37, 59, 68, 74, 92, 97-99, 112, 114-16, 121, 130, 134, 137, 155-56, 158, 165, 167, 202, 204, 219, 239; career sketch, 124-25, 171; death, 201
Butler Field (Quantico), 133-34
Butt, Archie, 35-37

cacos: literal meaning, 79
California, 44, 47
Campbell, Chandler, 79-80
Caperton, William B., 77, 83, 85-86, 88, 97
Capone, Al, 231-32
Carlson, Evans F., 132
Carney, Edward P., 156
Castner, Joseph C., 190-91, 194, 277n44
Cates, Clifton B., 116-17, 165-67
Cavendish-Venables, H., 48, 57
Cavité naval base, 10-12, 27, 33-34
Cayotepe, battle of, 48-49, 52-54
Chaffee, Adna R., 25
Challener, Richard D., 52
Chang Tso-lin, 180-84, 193-95
Chaumont, 178
Chester, 68
Chevy Chase Club, 132
Chiang Kai-shek, 179-80, 183-85, 193
China: 1900 U.S. intervention in, 14-26, 200; 1927-29 intervention in, 173-200, 209, 231; U.S. military adviser scheme for, 184-85; Thousand Blessings Umbrellas, 199-200, 202, 246; 1937 *Panay* incident, 242. *See also* Boxer expedition; Peking; Shanghai; Tientsin; Tsinan Incident

Christie amphibious tank, 128, 142
Christmas, Albert Grant, 227
Civilian Conservation Corps, 223
Civil War (U.S.) battle reenactments, 134-36, 168
Clark, Bennett Champ, 242, 244
Clark, Robert Sterling, 223-29
Cochrane, Henry Clay, 7-9, 17, 25
cocktail trial, 164-68
Cole, Eli K., 74-76, 80, 111-12, 202
colonial relief expeditions. *See* relief expeditions
Common Sense (magazine), 231-34, 239
Communist Party, 235
Congressional Medals of Honor, 15, 20, 72-73, 79, 81, 90, 212, 214, 221
constabularies: colonial, 55, 62, 78, 83-85, 90-94, 96-97, 145, 148, 150-51, 154, 172; national and state, paramilitary, 144-45, 161, 170-72, 233. *See also* police
Coolidge, Calvin, 126, 136-37, 143; on SDB's civilian police work, 142, 154-55, 157-58; on prohibition, 150; on China, 173, 175, 183-85
corvée (Haiti), 92-93, 96, 117-18, 126
Coughlin, Charles, 221, 234-35
courts-martial: cocktail trial, 164-68; of SDB, 150, 207, 209-12
Craige, John H., 119, 122, 211
Cuba, 126, 157; 1898 U.S. intervention in, 7-9, 231; U.S. military occupation of, 56, 62, 91
Cukela, Louis, 123, 214
Culebra, 28, 61, 142
Cumberland, William W., 95

Daggett, A. S., 20
Daly, Dan, 79
Danache, B., 95
Daniels, Addie (Mrs. Josephus Daniels), 100, 119, 131
Daniels, Josephus: education schemes, 59-60, 112-14, 131, 138; and Marine Corps politics, 61, 99-100, 108, 114-19, 121-23, 213; on 1914 Mexican intervention, 69, 73; on SDB's CMH, 72-73; and 1915 Haitian intervention, 76-77, 81, 86, 91, 93, 97; supports SDB, 93, 109, 151, 206, 211, 243; and World War I, 99-100, 103, 108; on prohibition, 113, 151; on crime in Philadelphia, 142
Daniels, Josephus, Jr., 99-100, 103, 107-8
Darlington, Isabel (aunt of SDB), 203-4

Darrow, Clarence, 235
Dartiguenave, Philippe Sudre, 83, 85-87, 89, 91-92, 94-95
Davis, Henry C., 177, 183-84, 186-87, 193
Davis, James J., 206, 215-17
Davis, John W., 228
Davis, Richard Harding, 28-29, 71
De Boo, Katherine ("Mother"), 131
del Valle, Pedro A.: quoted, 210
Denby, Edwin H., 118-19, 122, 127, 130, 133, 135, 137, 140-41
Dessez, Lester A., 98-100
"devil dog" nickname: origin of, 139
Dewey, John, 35, 72
Díaz, Adolpho, 42-43, 48, 53, 56, 63, 172
Dickstein, Samuel, 224, 227, 229
diehards (China): defined, 174
Dies, Martin, 245
Dimitman, E. Z. ("Dimmy"), 148-49, 161, 202-3, 212, 236
Dominican Republic (San Domingo), 126; 1916 U.S. intervention in, 84, 92, 231
Doyle, William H., 225-26
duckboard saga, 103-6, 233
Duncan, C. J., 184

Egypt: colonial analogy to, 87, 92
elections, marine controlled, 56, 86-87, 91, 93, 117, 204-5
Elliott, George F., 12, 32
Elliott, George W., 155, 157-58
Estrada, Juan J., 39-40, 42
expeditionary forces, 9-10, 12, 35, 38, 43-45, 55-56, 61-62, 70, 74, 85, 98, 125-26, 129, 134, 142, 152, 168, 172-73, 178, 198, 200, 241; marines preferred over army for, 9, 44-45, 126, 173-74, 177. *See also* advanced-base force

Farnham, Roger L., 82, 90-91, 93, 96, 112, 129
Federal Bureau of Investigation (FBI), 224, 233-34
Feland, Logan F., 206-7
Felton, Samuel M., 32
Feng, Yu-hsiang, 196
Fifteenth Infantry, 45, 178, 182, 186, 190, 192, 194
Fletcher, Frank Friday, 63-66, 68
Fogelson, Robert M., 144-45
football, 7, 136-41, 169, 267n38
Ford, James, 235
Forester, C. S., 207
Fort Rivière: battle of, 80-81, 211-12, 220

Fourth Brigade (USMC, France), 123
Fourth Regiment (USMC, San Diego, Shanghai), 163, 168, 170, 178, 182, 190
France: comments on U.S. imperialism, 66, 86-87; 1918-19 American Expeditionary Forces in, 96-109
Frank, Benis M., 119-20
French, Paul Comly, 225-27, 242
French Foreign Legion, 132
Frey, H., 17, 22
Fu, Sun, 183
Fuller, Ben H., 24, 206-7
Funston, Frederick, 69-71

Garrison, Lindley M., 59, 68-69
Gendarmerie d'Haiti, 78, 83-85, 89, 90-94, 96-97, 148, 172
Georgetown University, 137, 141
Germany: influence in Mexico, 63, 70; driven out of Haiti, 82, 90-91, 261n49; comments on U.S. imperialism, 82
Gettysburg: battle reenactment, 135-36
Goethals, George W., 59-60
Good, George F., 132, 137
Goodrell, Mancil C., 8, 26
Grayson, Cary T., 115
Great Britain: comments on U.S. imperialism, 31, 56-58, 62; 1927-29 diplomacy in China, 184, 195, 200
Green, Ned M., 169
Greene, Francis V., 159
Guam, 12
gung ho spirit, 132

Haggard, Godfrey, 56
Haiti: 1915-34 U.S. intervention in, 74-97, 118, 126, 204, 212, 231, 260n40; lifestyle of American colony in, 94; U.S. high commissionership of, 95, 126-27, 207; issue in 1920 U.S. election, 117-18; 1929 uprising in, 205. See also corvée; Fort Rivière; Gendarmerie d'Haiti
Harbord, James G., 103, 140; supports SDB, 211, 233
Harding, Warren G., 129-30, 143; 1920 election of, 117-18; Haitian policy, 126-27; at Civil War reenactments, 135-36
Hart, John N., quoted, 182
Haverford School, 6-7, 141
Haynes, R. A., 150
Heflin, James T., 209
Helmick, Eli A., 103, 107-8, 112, 137
Henderson, 182

hero archetype, 15-16, 220-21, 224. See also Butler, Smedley D.
Hill, Charles S. ("Jumbo"), 178, 190, 273n56
Hintze, Paul von, 63
Honduras: 1903 U.S. intervention in, 28-32, 203, 220
Hoover, Herbert, 16, 18, 143, 213, 242; alleged 1900 cowardice of, 18, 210, 219; and SDB court-martial, 150, 209-11; Haitian policy of, 205; on Marine Corps politics, 206-8; 1932 election of, 216, 219; and Bonus March, 218; lauded as anti-imperialist, 239
Hoover, J. Edgar, 224, 233-34, 279n53
Howe, Louis, 223
HUAC. See Un-American Activities Committee
Huerta, Victoriano, 62-63, 66-68, 71, 73
Hughes, Charles Evans, 126-27
Hughes, Langston, 238
Huntington, Robert W., 7
Hunton, Eppa, 133, 141
Hurley, Patrick J., 211

imperialism, U.S.: in military-adventure genre literature, 28-29, 65, 71, 167, 220; British comments on, 31, 56-58, 62; Nicaraguan comments on, 49, 53; French comments on, 66, 86-87; Mexican reaction to, 73; Haitian reaction to, 76, 81, 89, 91, 93, 95, 205; German comments on, 82; U.S. naval intelligence comments on, 82; comments on, in U.S. Congress, 205, 245; gangsterism analogy, 232. See also anti-imperialism
influenza epidemic of 1918, 100-102

Janowitz, Morris, 207, 249
Japan: 1927-29 intervention in China by, 180, 184-86, 191, 193-200; as threat during 1930s, 237, 242
Johnson, Hugh S., 224, 229
Jones, Louis R., quoted, 134, 136, 173, 179
Justin, 43-44

Keck, Morris M., 107
Kellogg, Frank B., 173
Kendrick, W. Freeland, 142, 147, 149, 151, 153-58, 245
Khaki Shirts, 218, 230
Knox, Philander, 38, 40, 43
Kung, H. H., 183

Kuomintang (KMT, Chinese Nationalists), 174, 176, 179-80, 182, 184-86, 193-96, 199, 203

La Guardia, Fiorello, 242
Lamont, Thomas, 224, 229
Lampson, Miles, 184, 195
Langer, William L., 106
Lauchheimer, Charles H., 99, 123
League Against War and Fascism, 234, 238
Lee, Harry, 123, 213-14
Lee, Josh, 242
Lejeune, John A., 61, 68-70, 72, 75-77, 84-86, 94, 97-99, 108, 111-26, 130, 137, 153-54, 162, 164, 171-72, 174, 177, 185-86, 198, 200, 202, 204, 206, 211, 213-14, 243, 245
Lemly, William C., 247; quoted, 131, 138, 189
Leonard, Henry L., 17-19, 210-11
Lewis, Sinclair, 230
Liberty League, 228, 230
Lind, John, 62-67
Long, Huey, 221, 223, 230-31, 235
Longest Day (film), 247
Lovett, Robert Morss, 235
Ludlow, Louis: and Ludlow amendment, 240
Lundeen, Ernest, 235, 245

MacArthur, Douglas, 72, 138, 207, 223-24, 229
McClure, John, 203-4
McCormack, John W., 224, 227
MacGuire, Gerald C., 224-29
McIlhenny, John H., 90-91, 93, 96
Mackey, Harry A., 158, 212
McKinley, William, 89
MacMurray, John V. A., 177, 180-84, 186, 195-97; career of, 180
MacNider, Hanford, 224
Madriz, José, 40-42
Mahan, Alfred Thayer, 239
Mahoney, John P. S., 189, 192
mail guard, 130, 167-72
Marcantonio, Vito, 235
Marine Corps: small-war expeditionary mission, 9-10, 35, 44-45, 74, 110-11, 125, 134, 200; marines preferred over army, 9, 44-45, 126, 173-74, 177, 197; 1908 removal from warships, 35-36; 1910-30s warrior versus technocrat conflict, 74-77, 80, 123-24, 127-28, 207, 213-14, 248; small-war versus big-war expeditionary mission, 74, 111, 123, 125-26, 128, 143, 198, 279n73; staff versus line controversy, 98-99, 111-12, 114-15, 121, 124; World War I policy, 101, 114; explanation of Corps politics, 110-28; deference and formality in, 117, 131; publicity and public relations, 124, 129-32, 134-36, 139-40, 142-43, 169-71, 174, 192, 198-99, 248; origins of bulldog and devil dog imagery, 139, 220-21; survival in 1920s, 143; Hollywood movies on, 169-70, 202. See also aviation; elections; football; mail guard; Quantico Marine Base
Marine Corps Institute, 114, 131-32
Marine Corps League, 234-35
Marine Officers School, 125
Martin, Joe, 124
Marvin, George, 89, 91
Maverick, Maury, 233-35
Mayflower, 130
Meade, Robert L., 17-20
Megee, Vernon E., quoted, 136
Mena, Louis, 43, 48-52, 255n13
Metro Goldwyn Mayer (MGM), 168-69
Mexico: 1914 U.S. intervention in, 61-73, 167-68, 214, 231; SDB's invasion plan for, 64-70, 187. See also Veracruz
military analogy (policy reform), 144-45, 148, 153-54, 157, 170-72, 248
Miller, Adolph B., 78-79, 189
Miller, Ellis B., 189, 246
Millett, Alan R., 111, 120, 125
Mills, Chester P., 150
Mitchell, William ("Billy"), 135, 164, 209
Monocacy, 15
Morgan, John Pierpont, 222, 224, 226, 229, 231
Munro, Dana G., 127
Murphy, Grayson M.-P., 223-25, 228-29
Mussolini, Benito, 168, 226, 230; 1931 car incident, 208-11

Nanking Incident, 174-77
National City Bank of New York, 82, 112, 231
National Guard, 236
Naval Affairs Committee, U.S. House of Representatives, 36, 83, 97, 110, 114, 118-19, 124-25, 239; TSB dominance of, 125

Naval Affairs Committee, U.S. Senate, 108, 130, 214, 240-42
nègre masqué, Le, 87, 105
Neville, Wendell C., 68-69, 72, 121, 200, 202, 205-6; 1919 Neville Board, 123; death, 206
Newark, 8
New Market: battle reenactment, 136
New Masses (magazine), 229, 231, 235
New York, 9
Nicaragua, 126; 1910 U.S. interventions in, 38-42; 1912 intervention in, 43-57, 71, 77, 204-5, 231-32, 238; 1927 intervention in, 172, 200
Ninth Infantry, 17
Norris, George W., 219
Noveleta: battle of, 11
Nye, Gerald P., 235

"Old Gimlet Eye" (SDB nickname): origin of, 50
Old Gimlet Eye, 219-20
Olongapo, 33-34
Open Door policy, 180, 200
"Opera-Bouffe Revolts" (Honduras), 28-29, 31, 220
Oregon: state police, 212
O'Shaughnessy, Edith, 64, 71

Panama: 1903 U.S. intervention in, 32; 1910-14 Panama battalion, 38-50, 53, 56, 58-61, 67-68; Canal Zone garrison duty, 58-60
Panther, 29, 30-31
Peking: 1900 occupation of, 21-25; 1927 relief preparations for, 187-88, 198-99
Pendleton, Joseph H., 33, 47-48, 51-56, 92, 117, 164
Penrose, Boies, 36-37
Pepper, George Wharton, 155, 167-68
Pershing, John J., 70, 101, 107, 135, 149
Pfeiffer, Omar T.: quoted, 178
Philadelphia: Navy Yard, 27, 32, 125, 245; crime and law enforcement in, 142, 144-61, 169; magistrates courts, 151, 156; political mores in, contrasted with Latin America, 161, and with Pacific Northwest, 171; SDB and 1931 unemployment relief in, 212, 215
Philippines: U.S. 1899 intervention in, 10-12; U.S. base at Olongapo, 33-34
Pinchot, Gifford, 142; and prohibition, 147, 150, 155, 158; as SDB political ally, 151,

157, 161, 167-68, 206, 212; and 1932 SDB election campaign, 216-17
Pittsburgh, 176, 184
police: paramilitary reform of, 144-51, 154, 161-62, 170-72, 212, 233-34, 236; technocratic professionalism in, 149, 152-53, 234. See also Philadelphia
Pontanezen Barracks and Camp, 100-109, 113, 146
Prairie, 27
prohibition (18th amendment), 136, 142, 145-70 passim, 204, 216-17; federal enforcement of, 150-51, 169. See also alcohol
Prohibition Bureau, 150
Puller, Lewis B. ("Chesty"), 120
punitive campaigns, 19, 23, 25, 29, 49, 52-53, 70, 77, 79-82, 175, 179

Quantico Marine Base, 97-98, 110, 112, 117, 120, 125, 129-43, 146, 171, 202, 204, 206-7, 212, 248; founded, 97-98; as military university, 112-14, 122, 131-32, 138. See also aviation; football

racism, 10, 29, 49, 54, 65, 71, 75-76, 81, 83-89, 94-95, 167, 174-75, 191, 261n46
Radford, Cyrus, 126-27, 141
Rameau, Pierre Benoit, 76
Reader's Digest (magazine), 236
Reed, David A., 206
Reid, George, 9
relief expeditions, colonial, 16, 22-24, 44, 63-70, 175, 178, 183, 186-88, 198
Rinehart, Mary Roberts, 104, 147
Robinson, Ray A. ("Torchy"), 102, 107, 116, 120, 162, 164, 167, 182, 189, 191, 199, 217-18, 243
Rogers, Ford O.: quoted, 135, 137
Rogers, Will, 174
Roosevelt, Eleanor (Mrs. Franklin D. Roosevelt), 107, 242
Roosevelt, Franklin D. (FDR), 73, 221, 243; and 1915-17 Haitian intervention, 81, 89-93, 96, 117; and Marine Corps politics, 99, 117-18, 213; and World War I, 100, 108; supports SDB, 211-12; object of 1934 Wall Street plot, 223-24, 226, 228; on SDB's death, 246
Roosevelt, Henry Latrobe ("Harry"), 90, 141, 239
Roosevelt, James (son of FDR), 243

Roosevelt, Theodore: "big stick" policy of, 27-28; and 1904 Corollary, 30; and 1908 shipboard marines controversy, 35-36; on police, 144; on SDB, 210, 245; as imperialist, 239
Royal Family. See American Legion
Russell, John H., 72, 90, 93, 117, 200, 206-7, 275n15; and 1919 Russell Board, 123, 213; as U.S. High Commissioner to Haiti, 127-28; and 1935 Senate confirmation fight, 213-24, "Battle of Russell's Run," 214

San Diego: marine football in, 140, 169; marine base in, 154, 162-69
San Pasqual: battle reenactment, 168-69
Second Division (USA-USMC), 114, 130
Services of Supply (S.O.S.), 101, 103, 106-7, 109
Shanghai: 1927 U.S. intervention in, 176-79, 247; 1930s marine garrison in, 242
Shark and the Sardines, 247
Shek. See Chiang Kai-shek
Shenandoah (New Market) expedition, 136
Sherer, Louis ("Dutch"), 107
Shoup, David M., 247
Shriners, 142
Silverthorn, Merwin H., 130, 133
"Smashing Crime and Vice" (SDB newspaper serial), 161, 163-64
Smith, Al, 228, 230
Smith, Julian C., 59-60, 120
smoking (cigarettes), 105, 131
Sokolsky, George, 178
Solace, 13
Soong, Mei-ling, 183-84
Soong, T. V., 183
Southerland, William H. H., 46-56
Spivak, John L., 229, 231, 235
sports, 133, 138, 140. See also Butler Field; football
Spring-Rice, Cecil, 62
Sproul, William C., 136
Standard Oil Co. of New York (SOCONY), 174, 176, 188-89, 191-92, 231, 240, 242
Stern, J. David, 225
Stimson, Henry L., 44, 206; on SDB court-martial, 209-12
"stormy petrel" (SDB nickname), 72
Suffolk, 64

Taft, William Howard: and 1910 commandancy fight, 36-37; and Nicaragua policy,

40, 44, 52-53; visits Panama, 59; and Haitian policy, 82
Teapot Dome naval oil scandal, 141
Tell It to the Marines (film), 169
tenderloin: origin of term, 163
Tennessee, 74
Terhune, Warren, 45-46
Third Brigade (USMC, China), 182
Thirteenth Regiment (USMC), 99-100, 102, 109
Thomas, Lowell, 215, 219-20, 236
Thomas, Norman, 231, 242
369th Infantry, 105-6
Tientsin: 1900 Battle of, 14-20, 25, 219; 1927-29 U.S. intervention in, 180-200; attractions of garrison life in, 191
Train, Harold C., 47, 50
Treasury Department, Secret Service, 150, 224, 278n50
Tsinan Incident, 194-96
Turkey, 20, 183-84

Un-American Activities Committee, U.S. House of Representatives (HUAC), 223-30, 245
Underhill, James L.: quoted, 267
Upshur, William P. ("Deacon"), 81, 89, 98, 131, 136

Vandegrift, Alexander A., 46, 72, 84, 91, 116, 134, 136, 164, 167-68, 176, 182, 188-89, 196, 243, 246
Vandenberg, Arthur H., 242-43
Vanderbilt, Cornelius, Jr., 210
Van Zandt, James E., 223-24
Vare, William S., 151, 158, 167-68, 216
Veracruz, 78, 154; 1914 U.S. intervention in, 8, 64, 67-73
veterans' movements, 221-22. See also American Legion; bonus, veterans'; Marine Corps League; Veterans of Foreign Wars
Veterans of Foreign Wars (VFW), 221, 223-24, 226, 231, 238, 243
Vietnam War, 247
Vinson, Carl, 125, 240
Virginia Military Institute (V.M.I.), 133, 136-38, 141
Vollmer, August, 149, 152, 159

Walker, Samuel, 152-53, 234
Waller, Littleton W. T., 12, 17, 21, 24, 33, 36-37, 60-61, 72, 75-81, 83-89, 94-95, 97, 110-11, 114, 126

Wall Street plot (1934), 223-31, 234; filmed as *The November Plan*, 247
"Wall Street's Fascist Conspiracy," 229, 235
Walter Garvin in Mexico, 65, 167, 220
War Is a Racket, 236-37, 240
warrior ideal, 8, 10, 15-16, 26, 59-60, 65, 105, 143, 149, 197, 207, 213-14, 220-21, 247. *See also* Butler, Smedley D.
Washington, George, 53, 231, 236
Washington, 74
Weeks, John M., 122
Wehle, John (son-in-law of SDB), 215, 219
Weitzel, George T., 43-45, 47, 49, 51, 54
Wheeler, Burton K., 182
Wickersham Commission on Law Enforcement, 204
Wilbur, Curtis D., 126, 164-65
Wilderness campaign, 134-35
Williams, Alexander S. (USMC), 93, 96, 163-68, 205
Williams, Alexander S. ("Clubber"), 163
Williams, Clarence S., 176-77, 181, 183-84, 197-98
Williams, Dion, 213

Williams, Robert H., 120, 123
Wilson, F. M. Huntington, 39-40, 43-44, 51-52, 62
Wilson, Walter, 235
Wilson, Woodrow, 56, 107; Mexican policy of, 61-62, 66-69, 73; Haitian policy of, 77, 81-83; naval policy of, 97; and Marine Corps politics, 115-17, 123; on police, 144; internationalist rhetoric of, 237, 241
Wise, Frederick M. ("Fritz"), 20, 24, 33, 69, 91, 132, 213-14
Wolfskill, George, 230
Woman's Home Companion (magazine), 240
Wood, Leonard, 35, 62, 70, 97, 149
Woods, Louis E.: quoted, 137
World War I, 70, 90-91, 94, 96-109, 236-37, 240
Wornham, Thomas A.: quoted, 131
Worton, William A., 116, 120, 190-91
Wu, C. C., 183

Zelaya, José Santos, 39-40, 55-56
Zeledón, Benjamin F., 48, 51-53